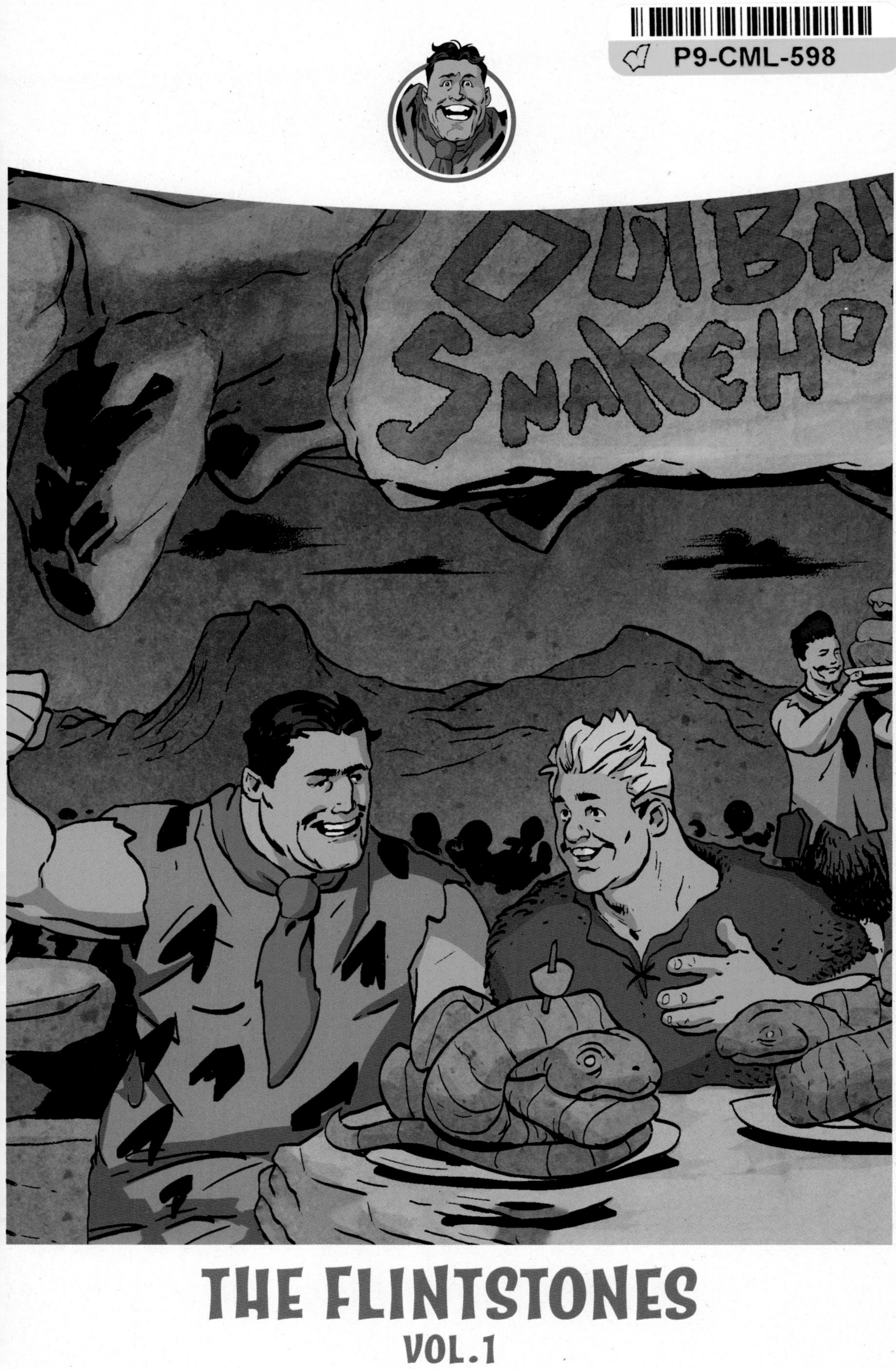

THE FLINTSTONES
VOL.1

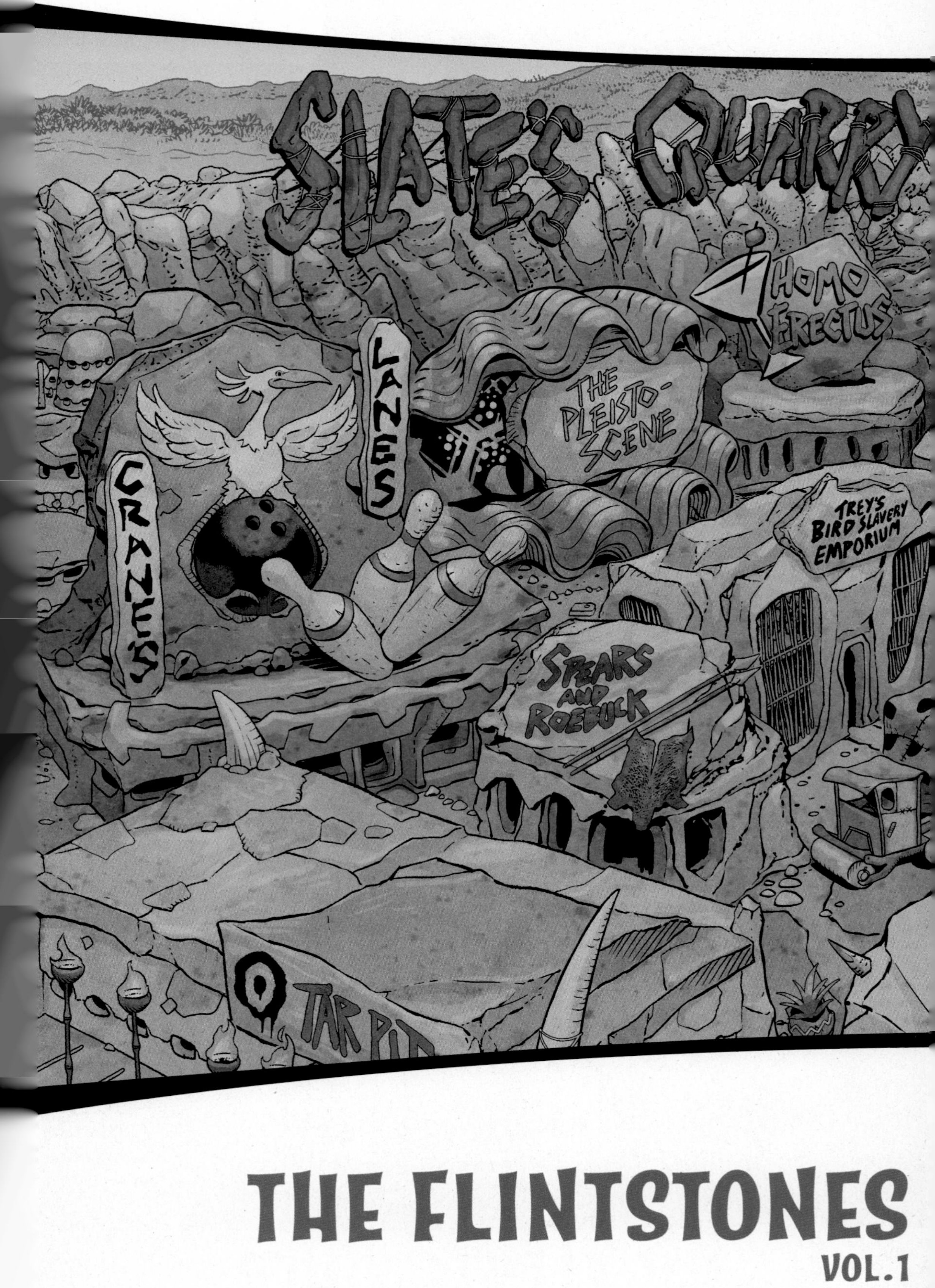
SLATE'S QUARRY
HOMO ERECTUS
LANES
CRANES
THE PLEISTO-SCENE
TREY'S BIRD SLAVERY EMPORIUM
SPEARS AND ROEBUCK
TAR PIT

THE FLINTSTONES
VOL.1

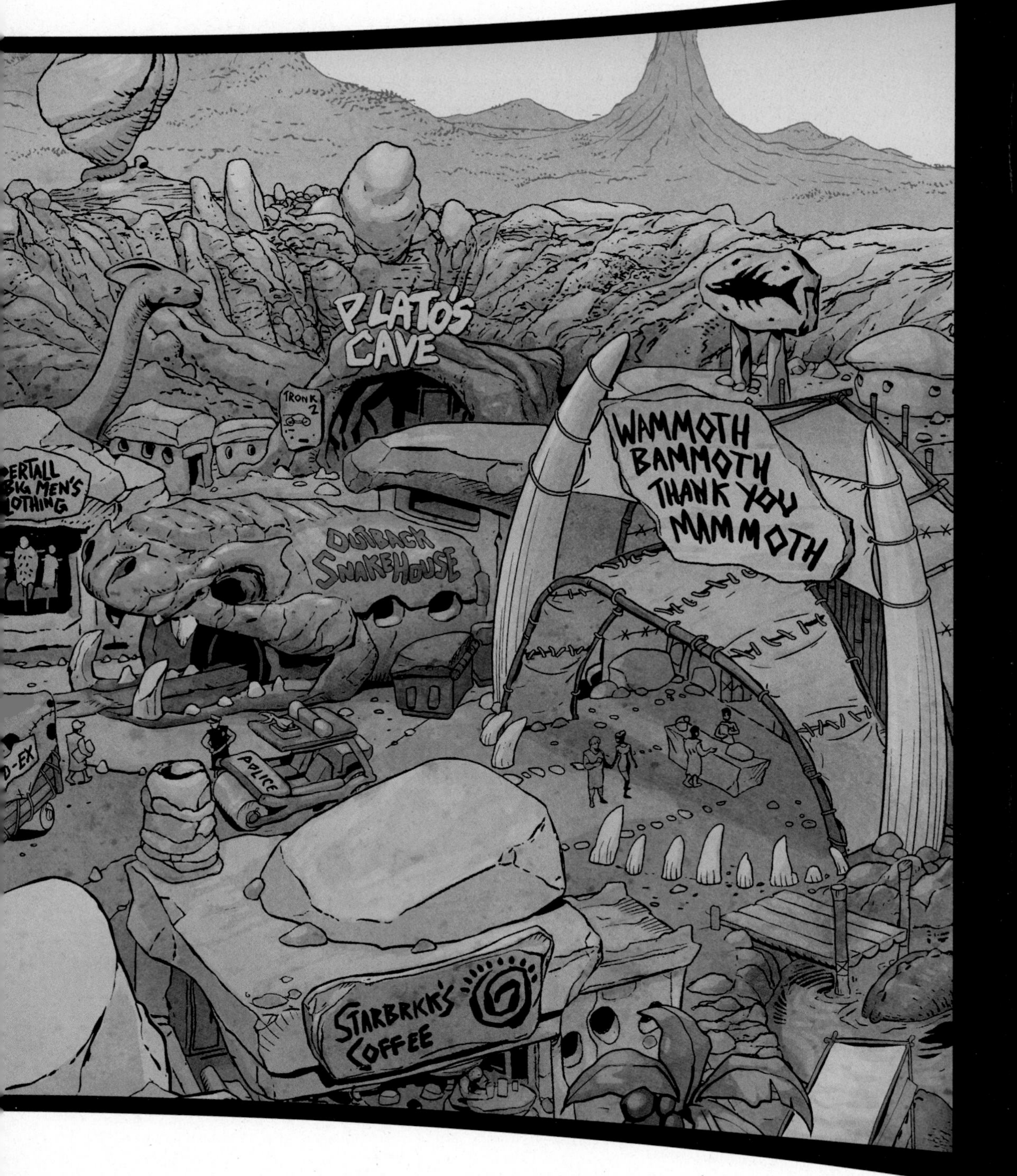
PLATO'S CAVE
WAMMOTH BAMMOTH THANK YOU MAMMOTH
BIG MEN'S
OUTBACK SNAKEHOUSE
POLICE
STARBRKK'S COFFEE

MARK RUSSELL writer
STEVE PUGH artist
CHRIS CHUCKRY colorist
DAVE SHARPE letterer
STEVE PUGH collection cover artist

MARIE JAVINS Editor - Original Series BRITTANY HOLZHERR Assistant Editor - Original Series
JEB WOODARD Group Editor - Collected Editions ERIKA ROTHBERG Editor - Collected Edition
STEVE COOK Design Director - Books CURTIS KING JR. Publication Design

BOB HARRAS Senior VP - Editor-in-Chief, DC Comics

DIANE NELSON President DAN DIDIO Publisher JIM LEE Publisher GEOFF JOHNS President & Chief Creative Officer
AMIT DESAI Executive VP - Business & Marketing Strategy, Direct to Consumer & Global Franchise Management
SAM ADES Senior VP - Direct to Consumer BOBBIE CHASE VP - Talent Development MARK CHIARELLO Senior VP - Art, Design & Collected Editions
JOHN CUNNINGHAM Senior VP - Sales & Trade Marketing ANNE DePIES Senior VP - Business Strategy, Finance & Administration
DON FALLETTI VP - Manufacturing Operations LAWRENCE GANEM VP - Editorial Administration & Talent Relations
ALISON GILL Senior VP - Manufacturing & Operations HANK KANALZ Senior VP - Editorial Strategy & Administration
JAY KOGAN VP - Legal Affairs THOMAS LOFTUS VP - Business Affairs JACK MAHAN VP - Business Affairs
NICK J. NAPOLITANO VP - Manufacturing Administration EDDIE SCANNELL VP - Consumer Marketing
COURTNEY SIMMONS Senior VP - Publicity & Communications JIM (SKI) SOKOLOWSKI VP - Comic Book Specialty Sales & Trade Marketing
NANCY SPEARS VP - Mass, Book, Digital Sales & Trade Marketing

THE FLINTSTONES VOL. 1

Published by DC Comics. Compilation and all new material Copyright © 2017 Hanna-Barbera. All Rights Reserved. Originally published in single magazine form
in THE FLINTSTONES 1-6. Copyright © 2016 Hanna-Barbera. All Rights Reserved. All characters, their distinctive likenesses and related elements featured in
this publication are trademarks of Hanna-Barbera. DC Logo: ™ and © DC Comics. The stories, characters and incidents featured in this publication are entirely
fictional. DC Comics does not read or accept unsolicited submissions of ideas, stories or artwork.

DC Comics, 2900 West Alameda Ave., Burbank, CA 91505
Printed by Solisco Printers, Scott, QC, Canada. 2/17/17. First Printing.
ISBN: 978-1-4012-6837-4

Library of Congress Cataloging-in-Publication Data is available.

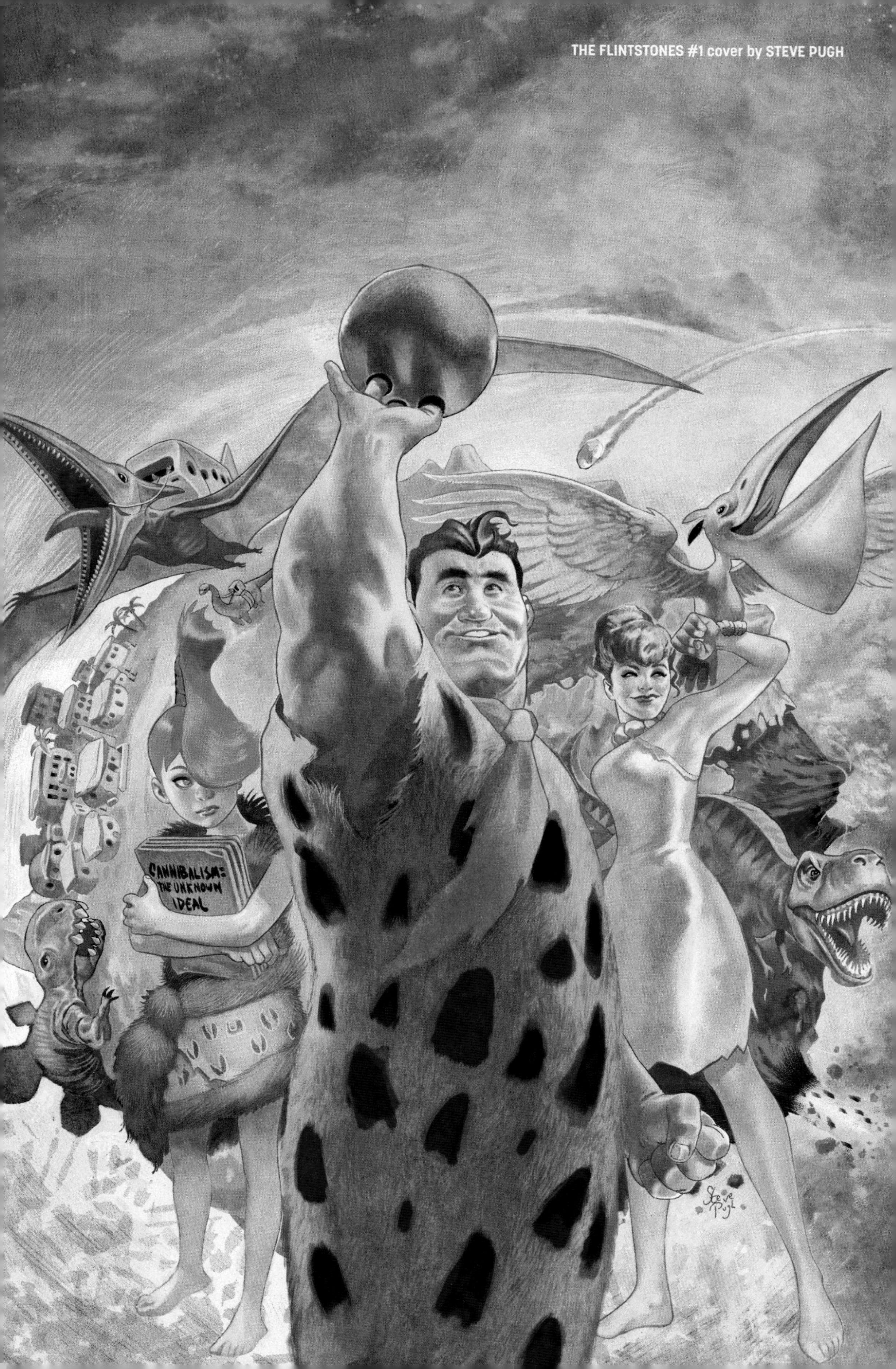

THE FLINTSTONES #1 cover by STEVE PUGH

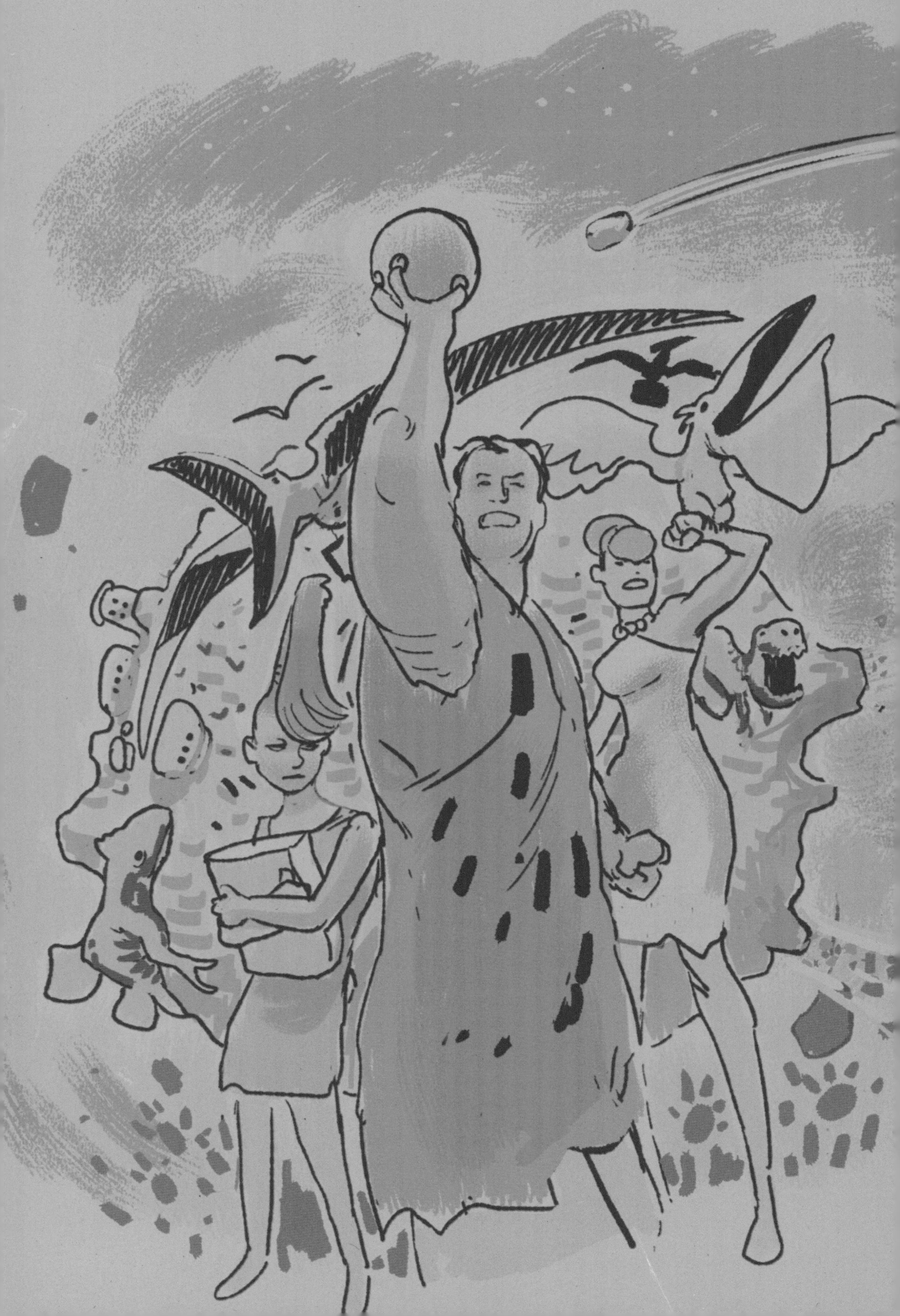

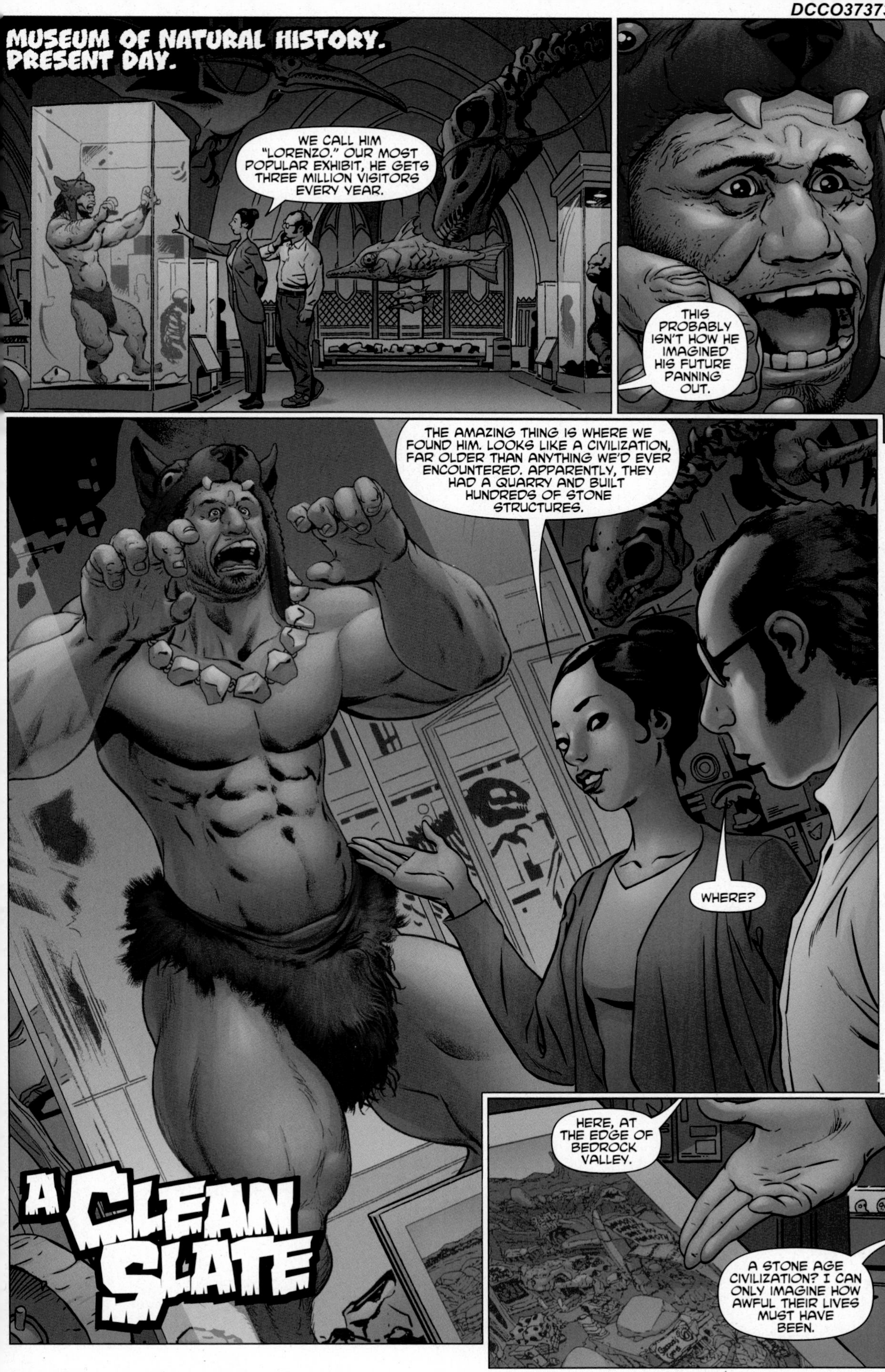
MUSEUM OF NATURAL HISTORY. PRESENT DAY.
WE CALL HIM "LORENZO." OUR MOST POPULAR EXHIBIT, HE GETS THREE MILLION VISITORS EVERY YEAR.
THIS PROBABLY ISN'T HOW HE IMAGINED HIS FUTURE PANNING OUT.
THE AMAZING THING IS WHERE WE FOUND HIM. LOOKS LIKE A CIVILIZATION, FAR OLDER THAN ANYTHING WE'D EVER ENCOUNTERED. APPARENTLY, THEY HAD A QUARRY AND BUILT HUNDREDS OF STONE STRUCTURES.
WHERE?
A CLEAN SLATE
HERE, AT THE EDGE OF BEDROCK VALLEY.
A STONE AGE CIVILIZATION? I CAN ONLY IMAGINE HOW AWFUL THEIR LIVES MUST HAVE BEEN.

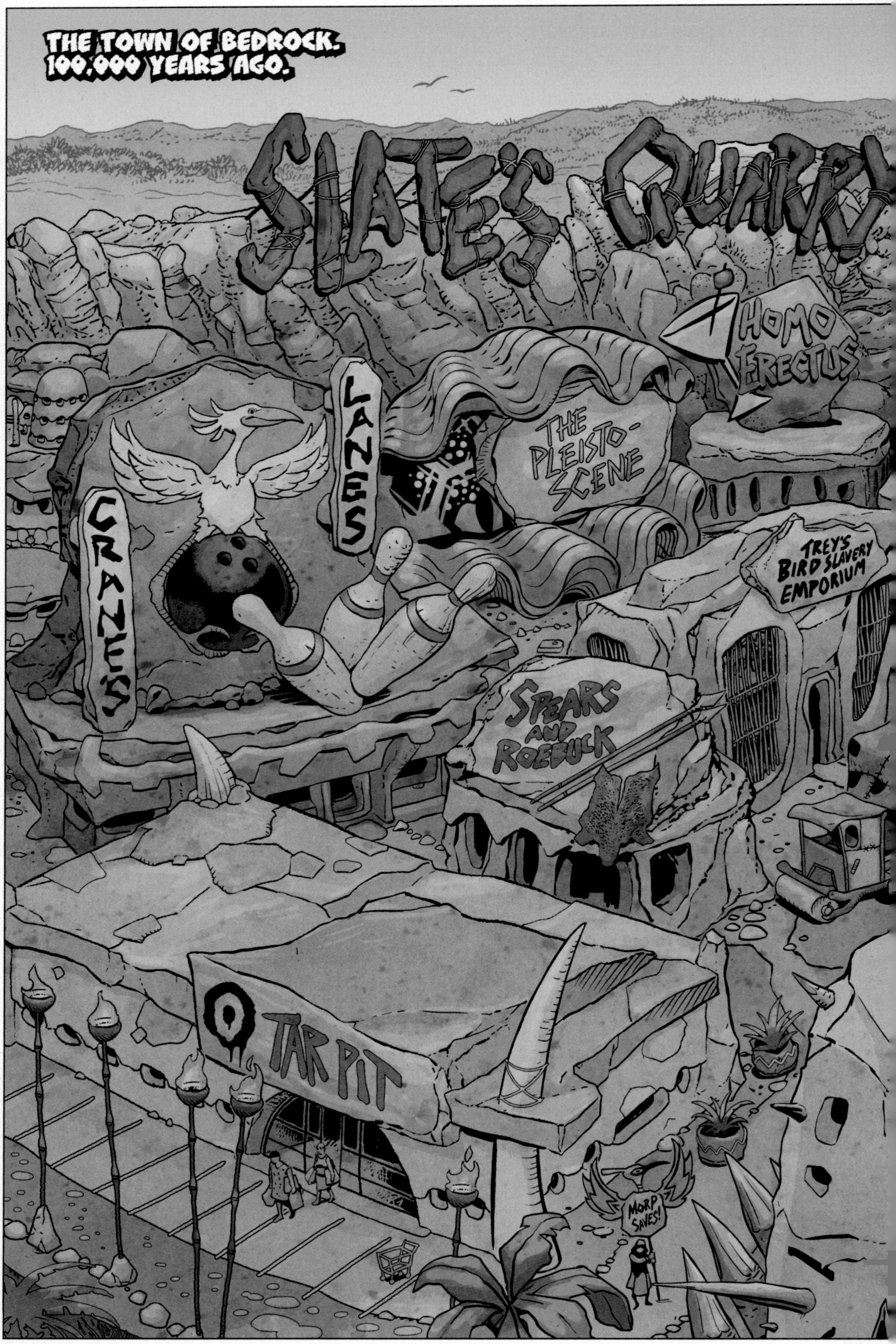
THE TOWN OF BEDROCK. 100,000 YEARS AGO.
SLATE'S QUARRY
HOMO ERECTUS
LANES
THE PLEISTO-SCENE
CRANES
TREY'S BIRD SLAVERY EMPORIUM
SPEARS AND ROEBUCK
TAR PIT
MORP SAVES!

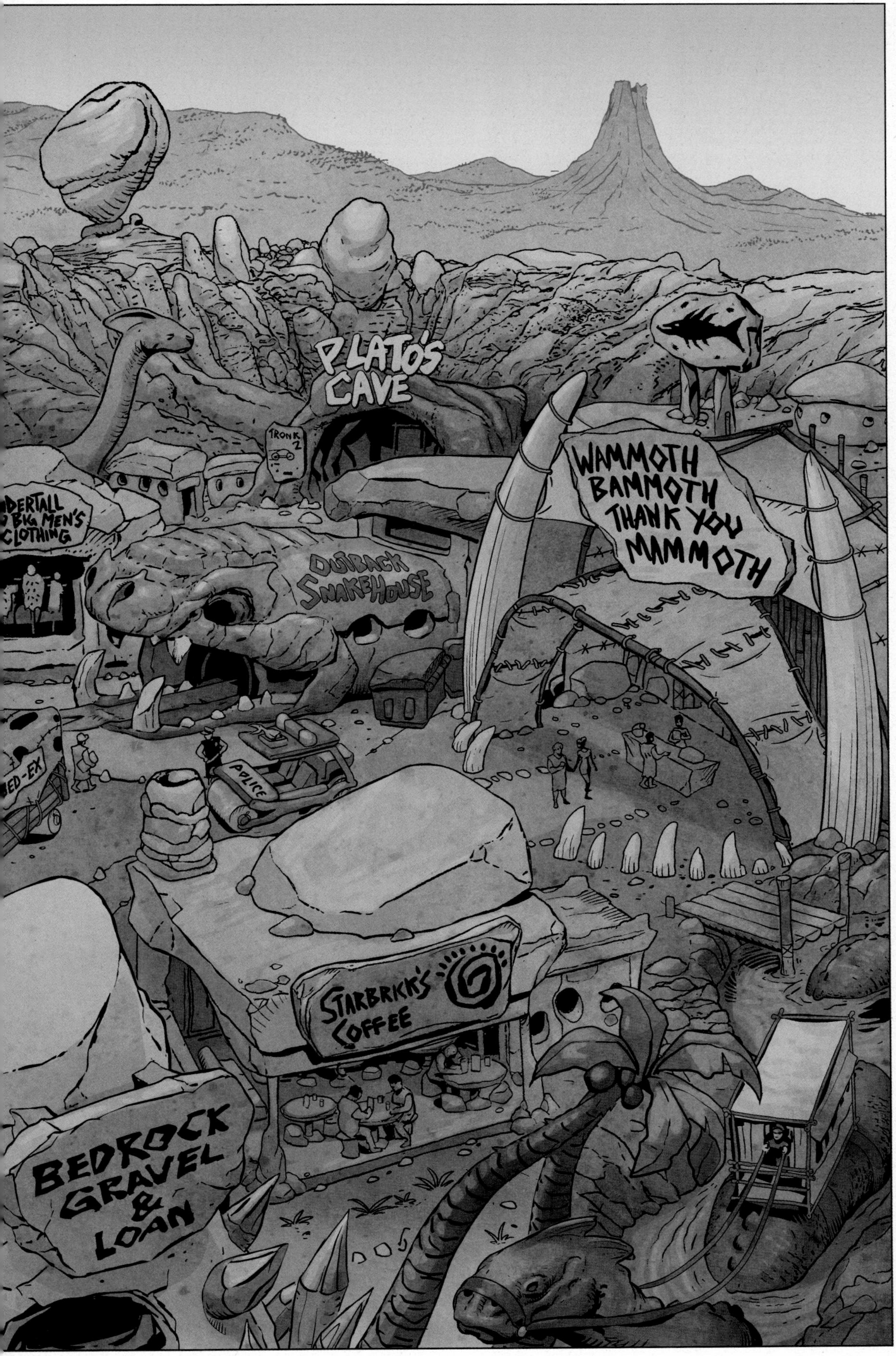
PLATO'S CAVE
TRONK 2
WAMMOTH BAMMOTH THANK YOU MAMMOTH
BIG MEN'S CLOTHING
OUTBACK SNAKEHOUSE
POLICE
STARBRICK'S COFFEE
BEDROCK GRAVEL & LOAN

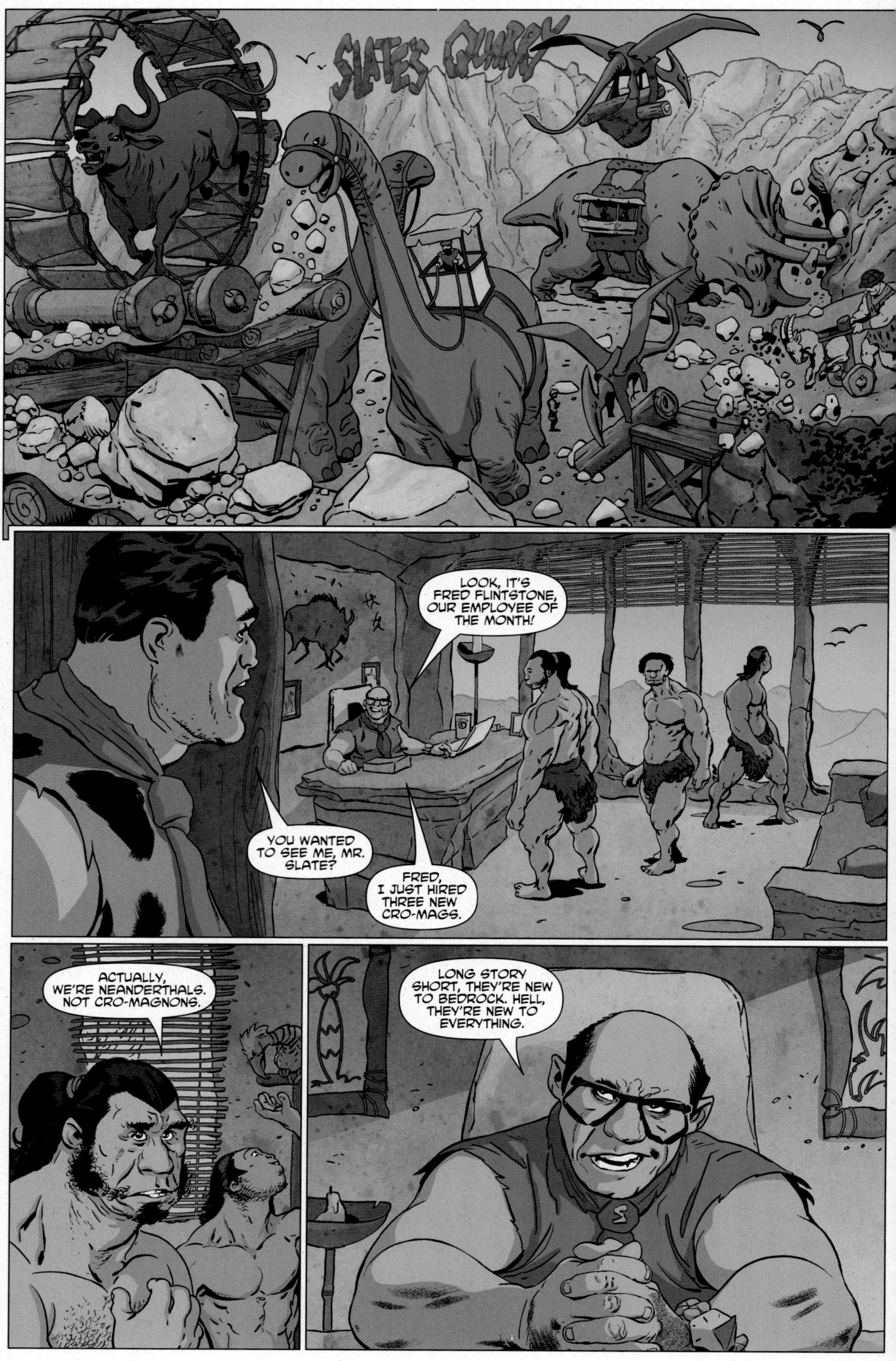
SLATE'S QUARRY
LOOK, IT'S FRED FLINTSTONE, OUR EMPLOYEE OF THE MONTH!
YOU WANTED TO SEE ME, MR. SLATE?
FRED, I JUST HIRED THREE NEW CRO-MAGS.
ACTUALLY, WE'RE NEANDERTHALS. NOT CRO-MAGNONS.
LONG STORY SHORT, THEY'RE NEW TO BEDROCK. HELL, THEY'RE NEW TO EVERYTHING.

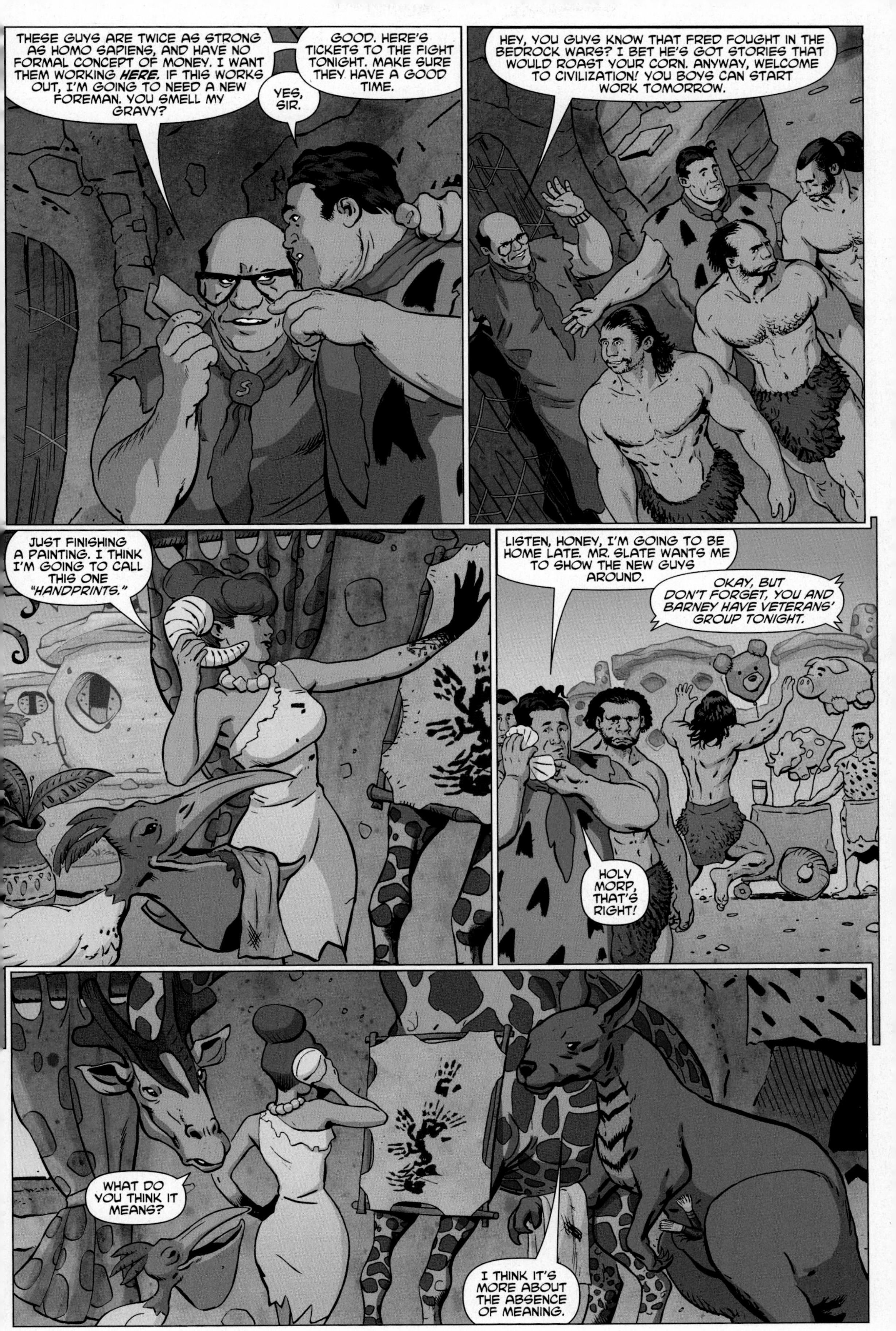
THESE GUYS ARE TWICE AS STRONG AS HOMO SAPIENS, AND HAVE NO FORMAL CONCEPT OF MONEY. I WANT THEM WORKING *HERE.* IF THIS WORKS OUT, I'M GOING TO NEED A NEW FOREMAN. YOU SMELL MY GRAVY?
YES, SIR.
GOOD. HERE'S TICKETS TO THE FIGHT TONIGHT. MAKE SURE THEY HAVE A GOOD TIME.
HEY, YOU GUYS KNOW THAT FRED FOUGHT IN THE BEDROCK WARS? I BET HE'S GOT STORIES THAT WOULD ROAST YOUR CORN. ANYWAY, WELCOME TO CIVILIZATION! YOU BOYS CAN START WORK TOMORROW.
JUST FINISHING A PAINTING. I THINK I'M GOING TO CALL THIS ONE *"HANDPRINTS."*
LISTEN, HONEY, I'M GOING TO BE HOME LATE. MR. SLATE WANTS ME TO SHOW THE NEW GUYS AROUND.
OKAY, BUT DON'T FORGET, YOU AND BARNEY HAVE VETERANS' GROUP TONIGHT.
HOLY MORP, THAT'S RIGHT!
WHAT DO YOU THINK IT MEANS?
I THINK IT'S MORE ABOUT THE ABSENCE OF MEANING.

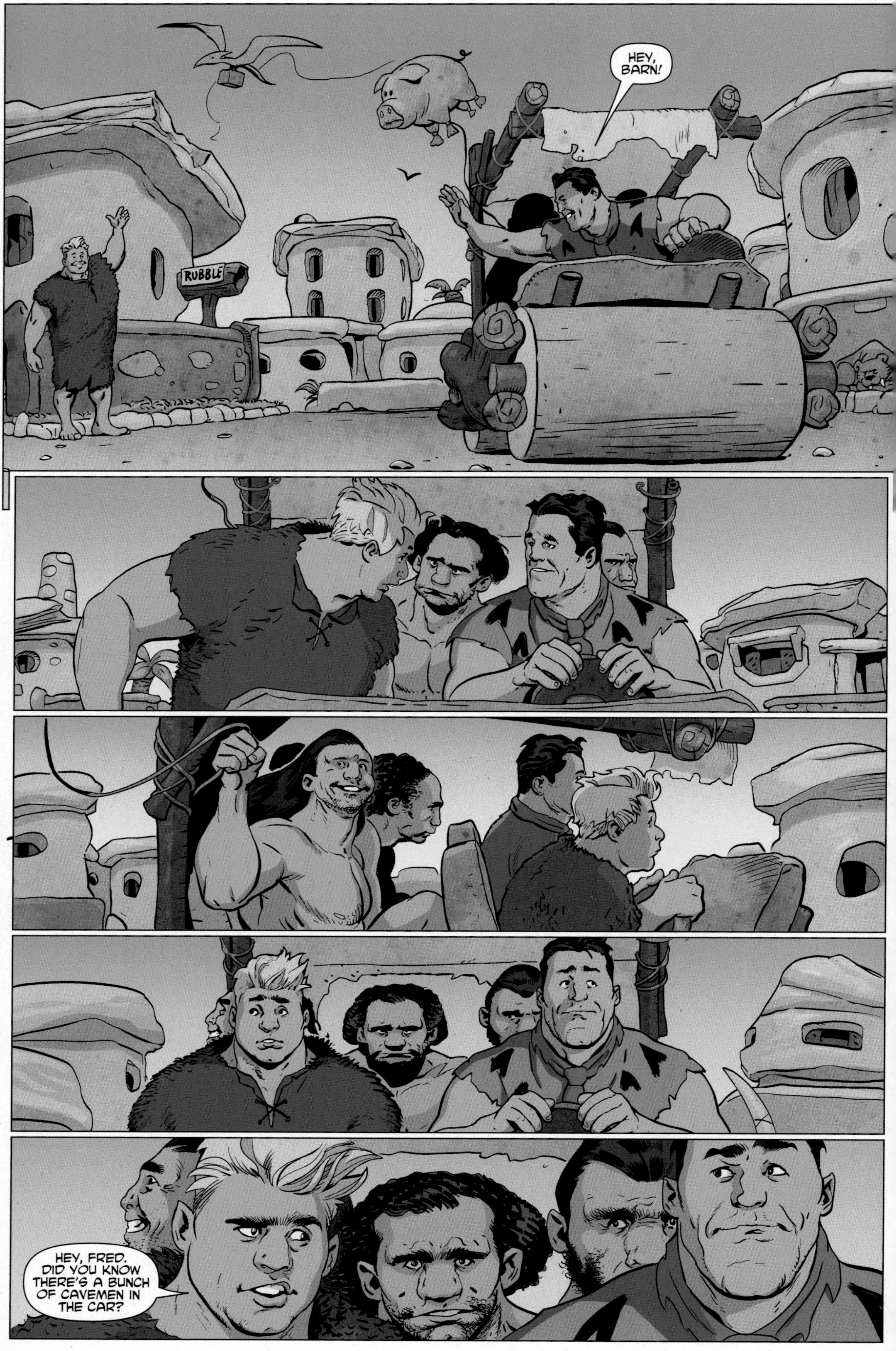
HEY, BARN!
RUBBLE
HEY, FRED. DID YOU KNOW THERE'S A BUNCH OF CAVEMEN IN THE CAR?

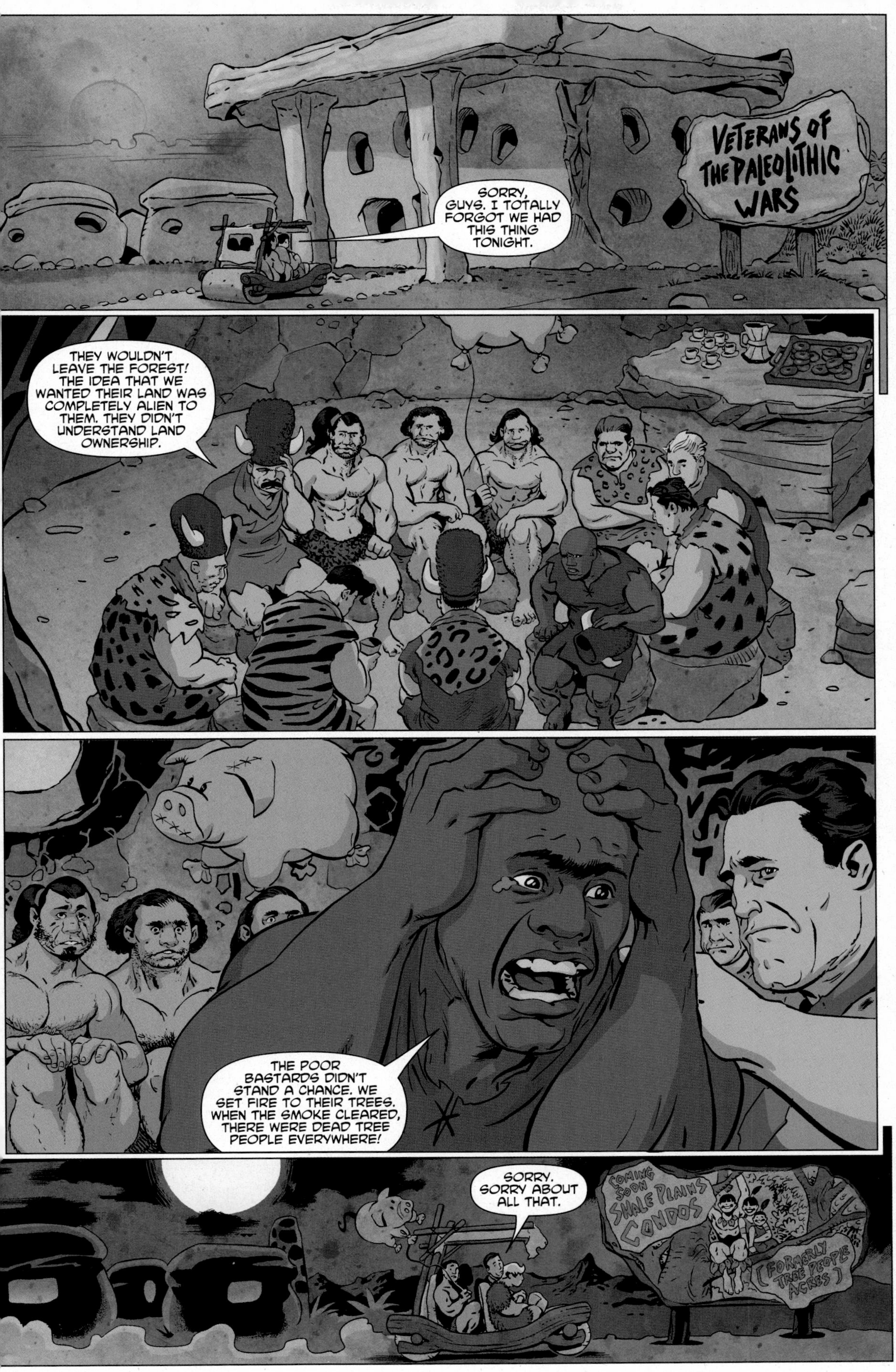
VETERANS OF THE PALEOLITHIC WARS
SORRY, GUYS. I TOTALLY FORGOT WE HAD THIS THING TONIGHT.
THEY WOULDN'T LEAVE THE FOREST! THE IDEA THAT WE WANTED THEIR LAND WAS COMPLETELY ALIEN TO THEM. THEY DIDN'T UNDERSTAND LAND OWNERSHIP.
THE POOR BASTARDS DIDN'T STAND A CHANCE. WE SET FIRE TO THEIR TREES. WHEN THE SMOKE CLEARED, THERE WERE DEAD TREE PEOPLE EVERYWHERE!
SORRY. SORRY ABOUT ALL THAT.
COMING SOON SHALE PLAINS CONDOS
(FORMERLY TREE PEOPLE ACRES)

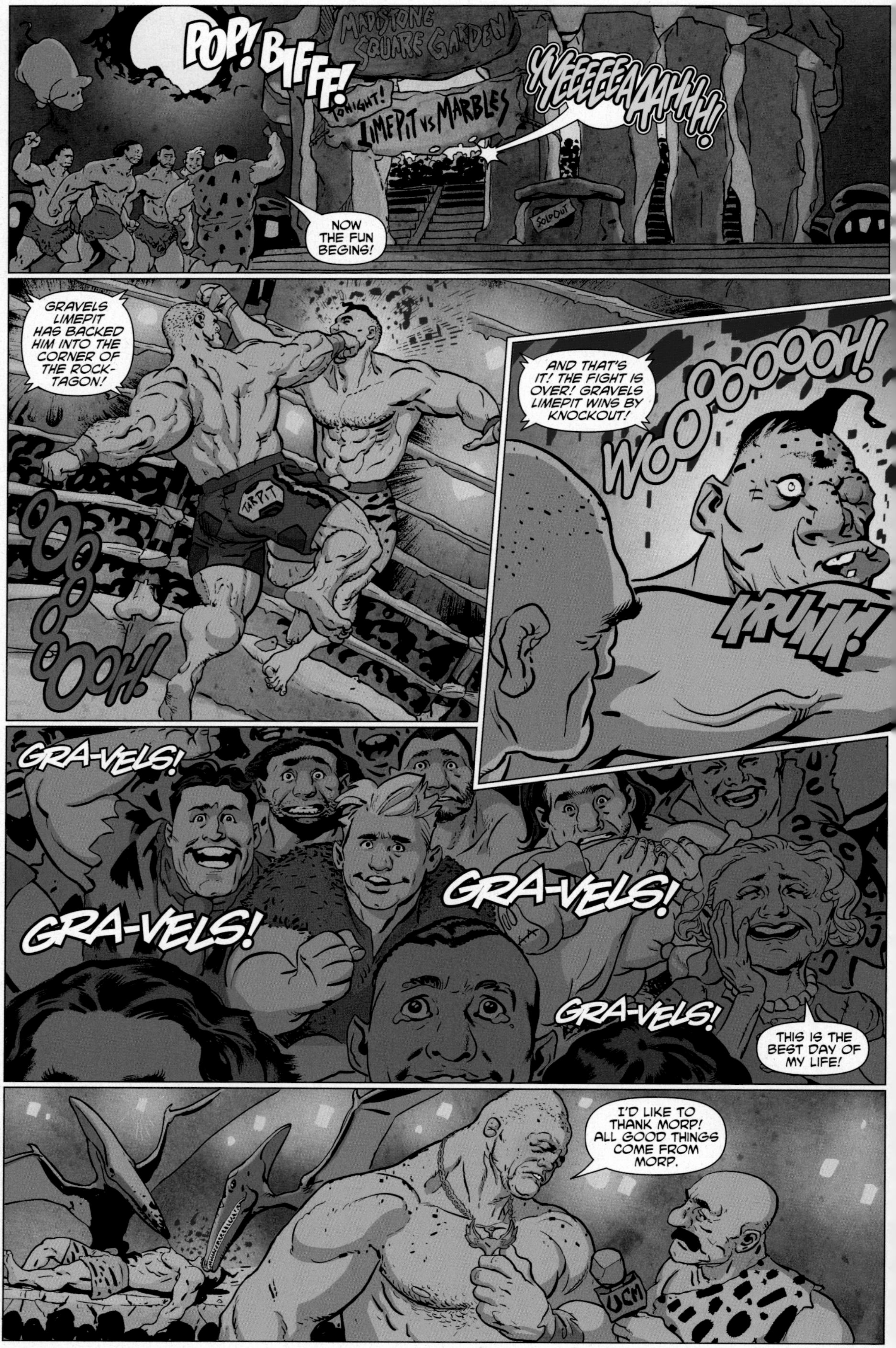
POP! BIFFF!
MADSTONE SQUARE GARDEN
TONIGHT! LIMEPIT vs MARBLES
YYEEEEEAAAHHH!!
NOW THE FUN BEGINS!
SOLD OUT
GRAVELS LIMEPIT HAS BACKED HIM INTO THE CORNER OF THE ROCK-TAGON!
OOOOOOOOOH!
AND THAT'S IT! THE FIGHT IS OVER! GRAVELS LIMEPIT WINS BY KNOCKOUT!
WOOOOOOOOH!
KRUNK!
GRA-VELS!
GRA-VELS!
GRA-VELS!
GRA-VELS!
THIS IS THE BEST DAY OF MY LIFE!
I'D LIKE TO THANK MORP! ALL GOOD THINGS COME FROM MORP.
UCM

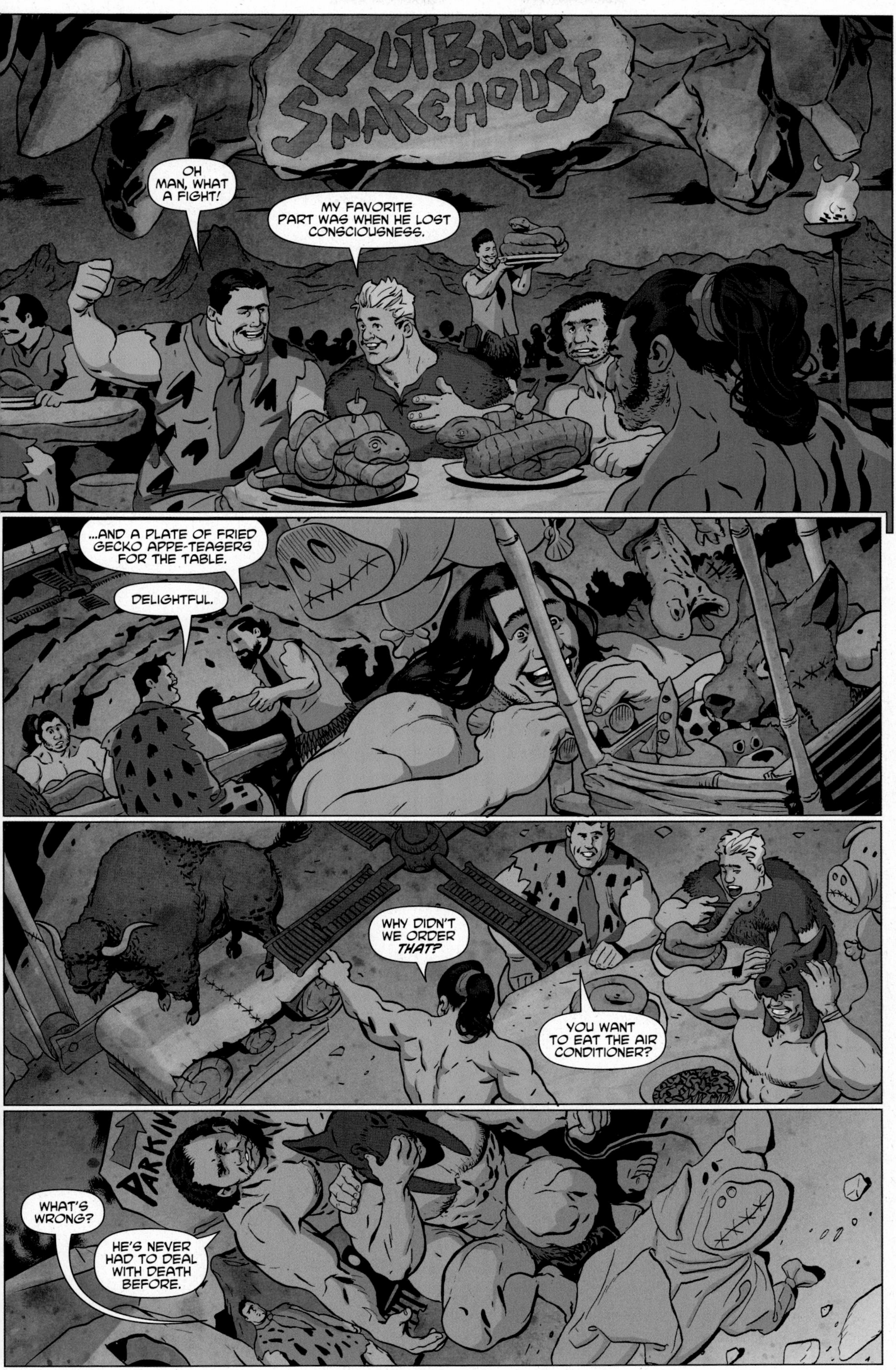

OUTBACK SNAKEHOUSE
OH MAN, WHAT A FIGHT!
MY FAVORITE PART WAS WHEN HE LOST CONSCIOUSNESS.
...AND A PLATE OF FRIED GECKO APPE-TEASERS FOR THE TABLE.
DELIGHTFUL.
WHY DIDN'T WE ORDER *THAT?*
YOU WANT TO EAT THE AIR CONDITIONER?
WHAT'S WRONG?
HE'S NEVER HAD TO DEAL WITH DEATH BEFORE.

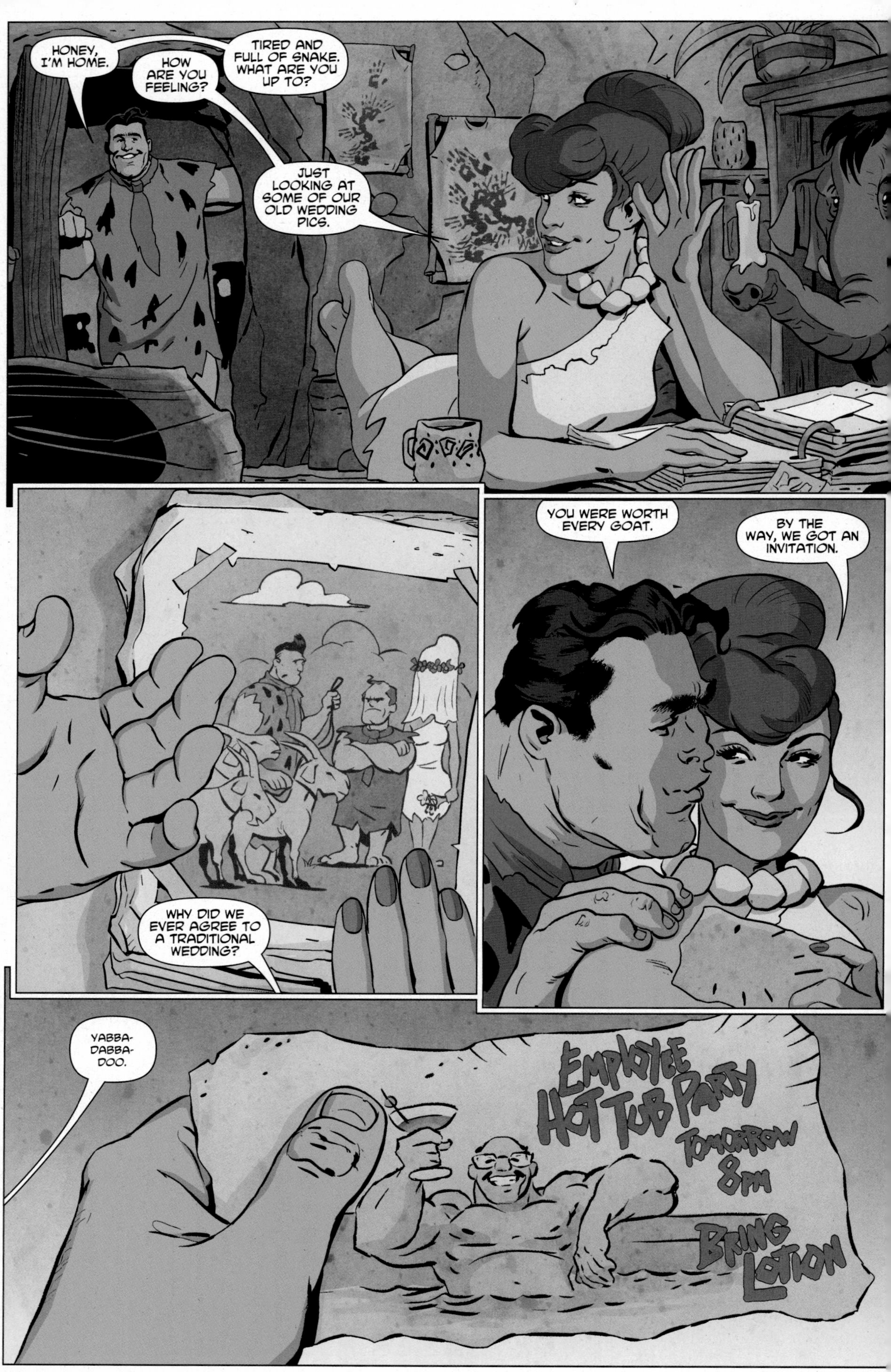

HONEY, I'M HOME.
HOW ARE YOU FEELING?
TIRED AND FULL OF SNAKE. WHAT ARE YOU UP TO?
JUST LOOKING AT SOME OF OUR OLD WEDDING PICS.
WHY DID WE EVER AGREE TO A TRADITIONAL WEDDING?
YOU WERE WORTH EVERY GOAT.
BY THE WAY, WE GOT AN INVITATION.
YABBA-DABBA-DOO.
EMPLOYEE HOT TUB PARTY
TOMORROW 8PM
BRING LOTION

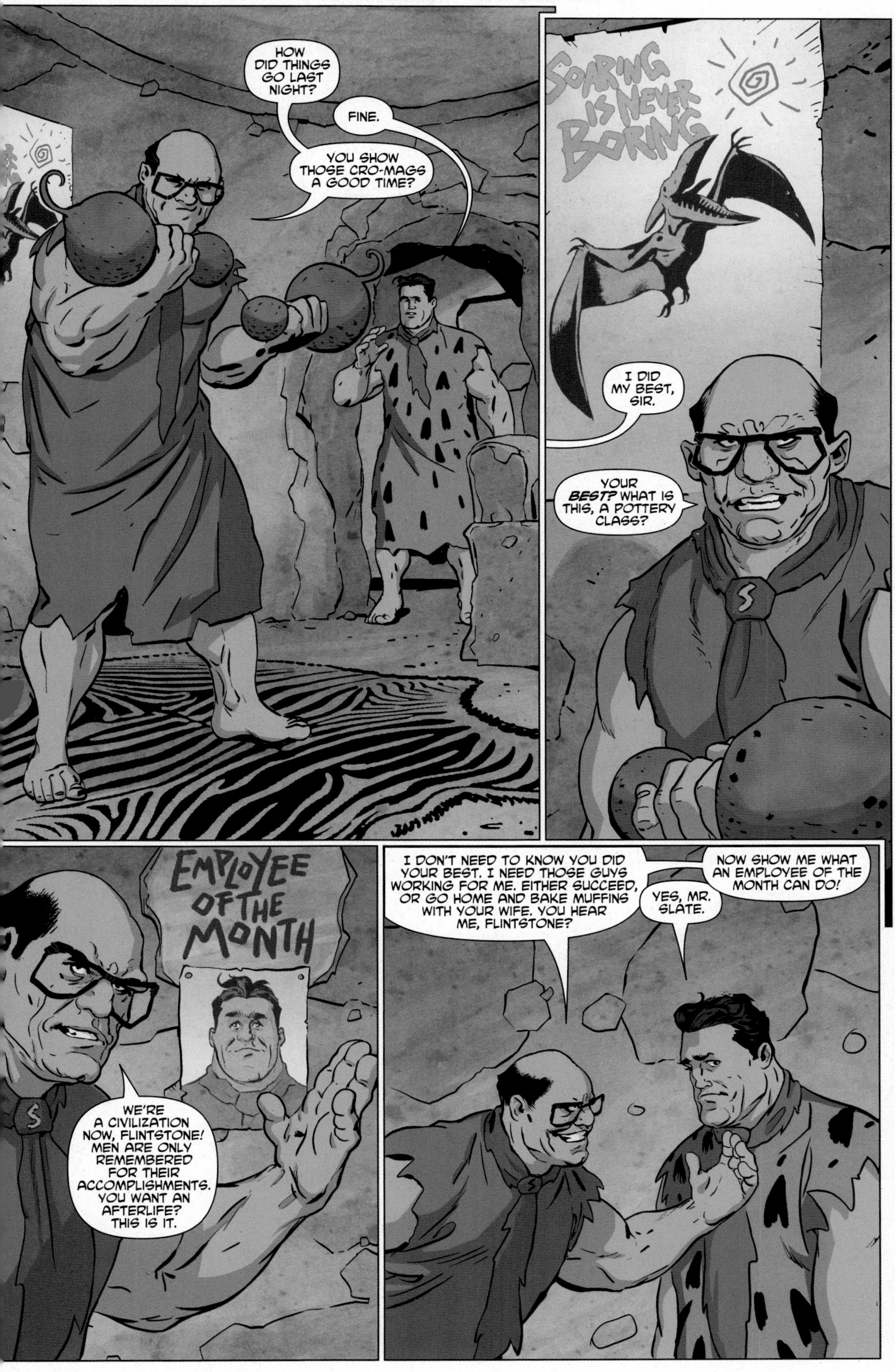
HOW DID THINGS GO LAST NIGHT?
FINE.
YOU SHOW THOSE CRO-MAGS A GOOD TIME?
SOARING IS NEVER BORING
I DID MY BEST, SIR.
YOUR *BEST?* WHAT IS THIS, A POTTERY CLASS?
EMPLOYEE OF THE MONTH
WE'RE A CIVILIZATION NOW, FLINTSTONE! MEN ARE ONLY REMEMBERED FOR THEIR ACCOMPLISHMENTS. YOU WANT AN AFTERLIFE? THIS IS IT.
I DON'T NEED TO KNOW YOU DID YOUR BEST. I NEED THOSE GUYS WORKING FOR ME. EITHER SUCCEED, OR GO HOME AND BAKE MUFFINS WITH YOUR WIFE. YOU HEAR ME, FLINTSTONE?
YES, MR. SLATE.
NOW SHOW ME WHAT AN EMPLOYEE OF THE MONTH CAN DO!

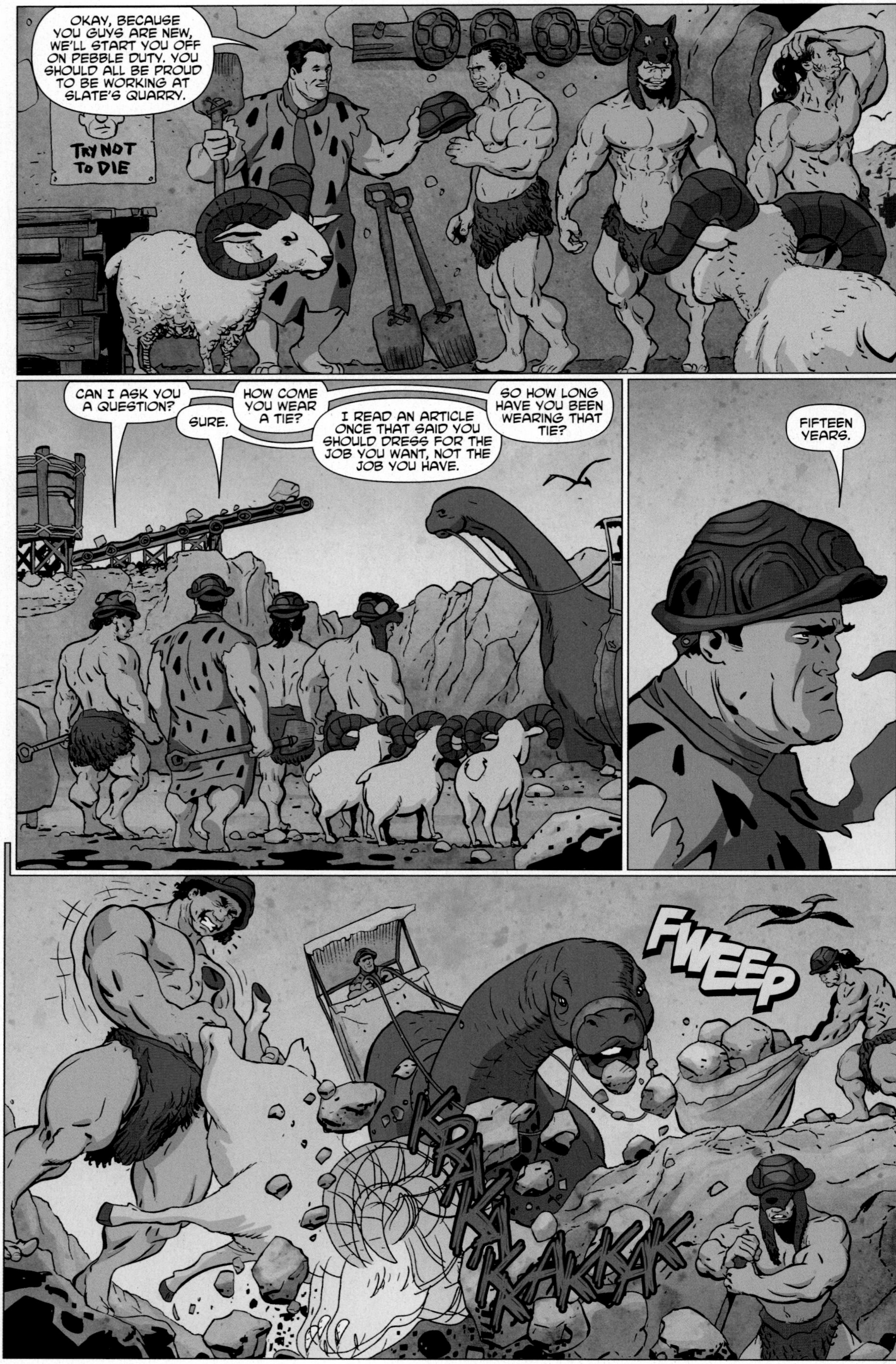
OKAY, BECAUSE YOU GUYS ARE NEW, WE'LL START YOU OFF ON PEBBLE DUTY. YOU SHOULD ALL BE PROUD TO BE WORKING AT SLATE'S QUARRY.
TRY NOT TO DIE
CAN I ASK YOU A QUESTION?
SURE.
HOW COME YOU WEAR A TIE?
I READ AN ARTICLE ONCE THAT SAID YOU SHOULD DRESS FOR THE JOB YOU WANT, NOT THE JOB YOU HAVE.
SO HOW LONG HAVE YOU BEEN WEARING THAT TIE?
FIFTEEN YEARS.
FWEEP
KRAKAKAKAK

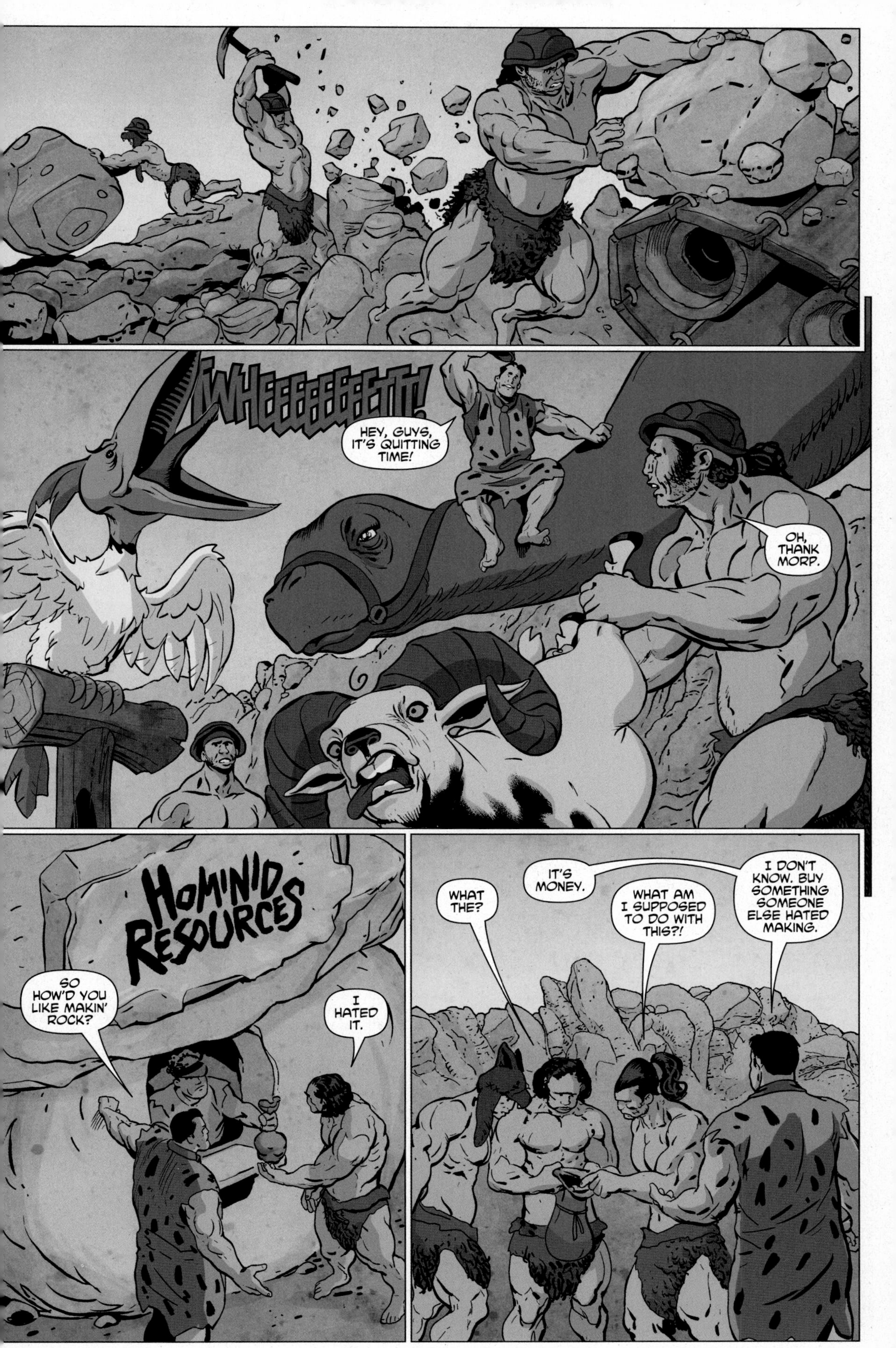
IWHEEEEEEEETT!
HEY, GUYS, IT'S QUITTING TIME!
OH, THANK MORP.
HOMINID RESOURCES
SO HOW'D YOU LIKE MAKIN' ROCK?
I HATED IT.
WHAT THE?
IT'S MONEY.
WHAT AM I SUPPOSED TO DO WITH THIS?!
I DON'T KNOW. BUY SOMETHING SOMEONE ELSE HATED MAKING.

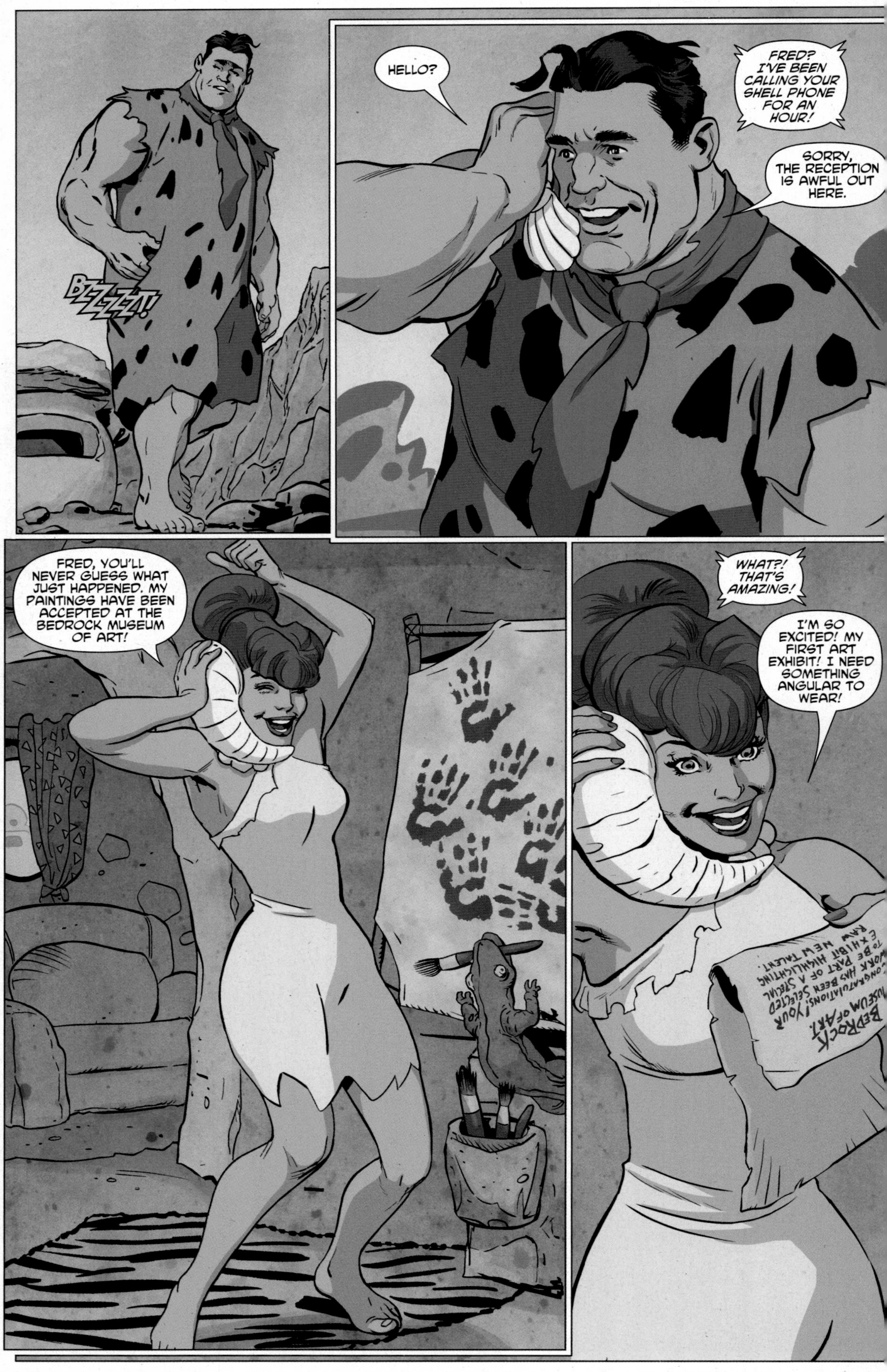
BZZZZZT!
HELLO?
FRED? I'VE BEEN CALLING YOUR SHELL PHONE FOR AN HOUR!
SORRY, THE RECEPTION IS AWFUL OUT HERE.
FRED, YOU'LL NEVER GUESS WHAT JUST HAPPENED. MY PAINTINGS HAVE BEEN ACCEPTED AT THE BEDROCK MUSEUM OF ART!
WHAT?! THAT'S AMAZING!
I'M SO EXCITED! MY FIRST ART EXHIBIT! I NEED SOMETHING ANGULAR TO WEAR!
BEDROCK MUSEUM OF ART.
CONGRATULATIONS! YOUR WORK HAS BEEN SELECTED TO BE PART OF A SPECIAL EXHIBIT HIGHLIGHTING RAW NEW TALENT.

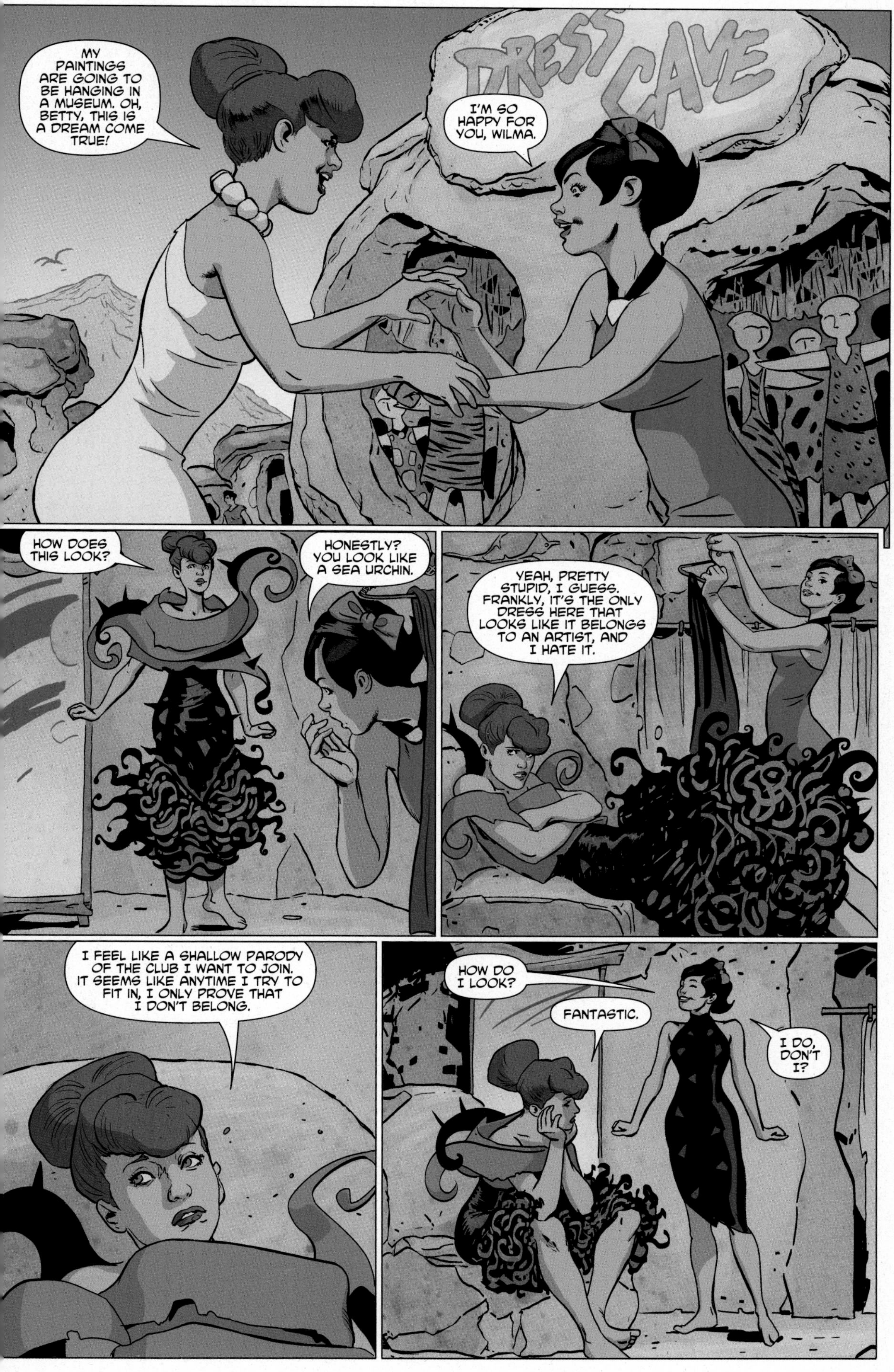
MY PAINTINGS ARE GOING TO BE HANGING IN A MUSEUM. OH, BETTY, THIS IS A DREAM COME TRUE!
DRESS CAVE
I'M SO HAPPY FOR YOU, WILMA.
HOW DOES THIS LOOK?
HONESTLY? YOU LOOK LIKE A SEA URCHIN.
YEAH, PRETTY STUPID, I GUESS. FRANKLY, IT'S THE ONLY DRESS HERE THAT LOOKS LIKE IT BELONGS TO AN ARTIST, AND I HATE IT.
I FEEL LIKE A SHALLOW PARODY OF THE CLUB I WANT TO JOIN. IT SEEMS LIKE ANYTIME I TRY TO FIT IN, I ONLY PROVE THAT I DON'T BELONG.
HOW DO I LOOK?
FANTASTIC.
I DO, DON'T I?

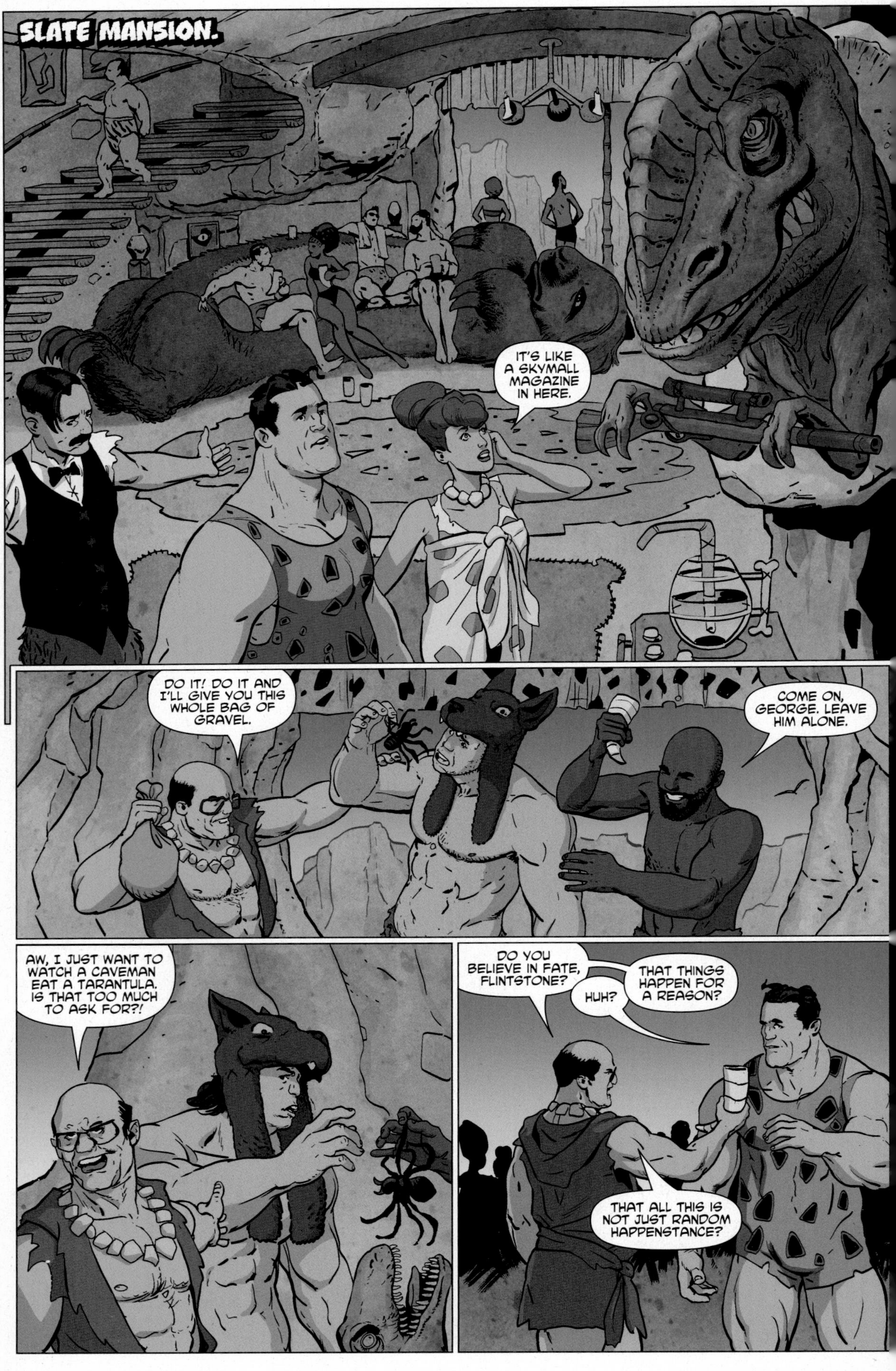
SLATE MANSION.
IT'S LIKE A SKYMALL MAGAZINE IN HERE.
DO IT! DO IT AND I'LL GIVE YOU THIS WHOLE BAG OF GRAVEL.
COME ON, GEORGE. LEAVE HIM ALONE.
AW, I JUST WANT TO WATCH A CAVEMAN EAT A TARANTULA. IS THAT TOO MUCH TO ASK FOR?!
DO YOU BELIEVE IN FATE, FLINTSTONE?
HUH?
THAT THINGS HAPPEN FOR A REASON?
THAT ALL THIS IS NOT JUST RANDOM HAPPENSTANCE?

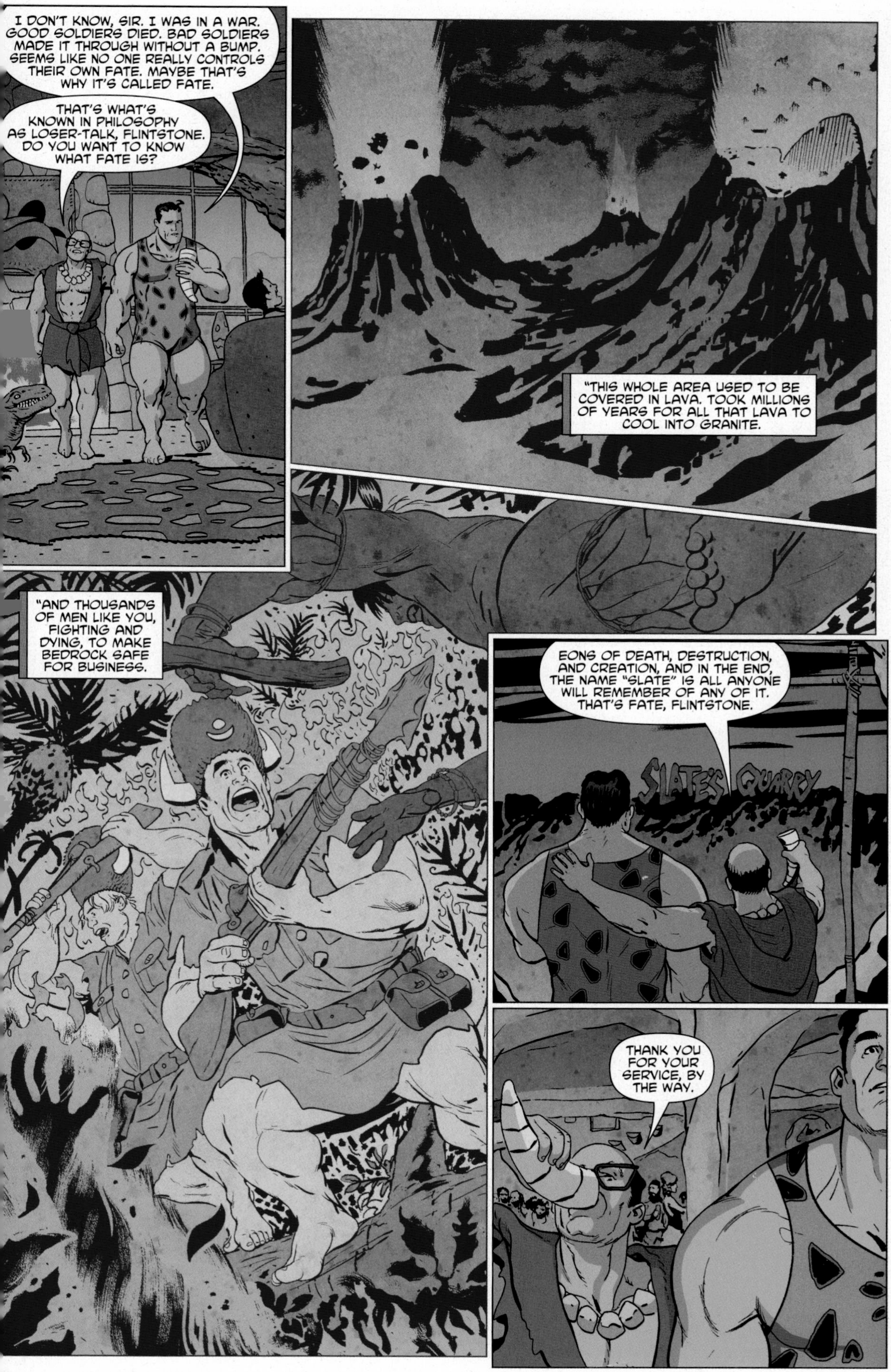
I DON'T KNOW, SIR. I WAS IN A WAR. GOOD SOLDIERS DIED. BAD SOLDIERS MADE IT THROUGH WITHOUT A BUMP. SEEMS LIKE NO ONE REALLY CONTROLS THEIR OWN FATE. MAYBE THAT'S WHY IT'S CALLED FATE.
THAT'S WHAT'S KNOWN IN PHILOSOPHY AS LOSER-TALK, FLINTSTONE. DO YOU WANT TO KNOW WHAT FATE IS?
"THIS WHOLE AREA USED TO BE COVERED IN LAVA. TOOK MILLIONS OF YEARS FOR ALL THAT LAVA TO COOL INTO GRANITE.
"AND THOUSANDS OF MEN LIKE YOU, FIGHTING AND DYING, TO MAKE BEDROCK SAFE FOR BUSINESS.
EONS OF DEATH, DESTRUCTION, AND CREATION, AND IN THE END, THE NAME "SLATE" IS ALL ANYONE WILL REMEMBER OF ANY OF IT. THAT'S FATE, FLINTSTONE.
SLATE'S QUARRY
THANK YOU FOR YOUR SERVICE, BY THE WAY.

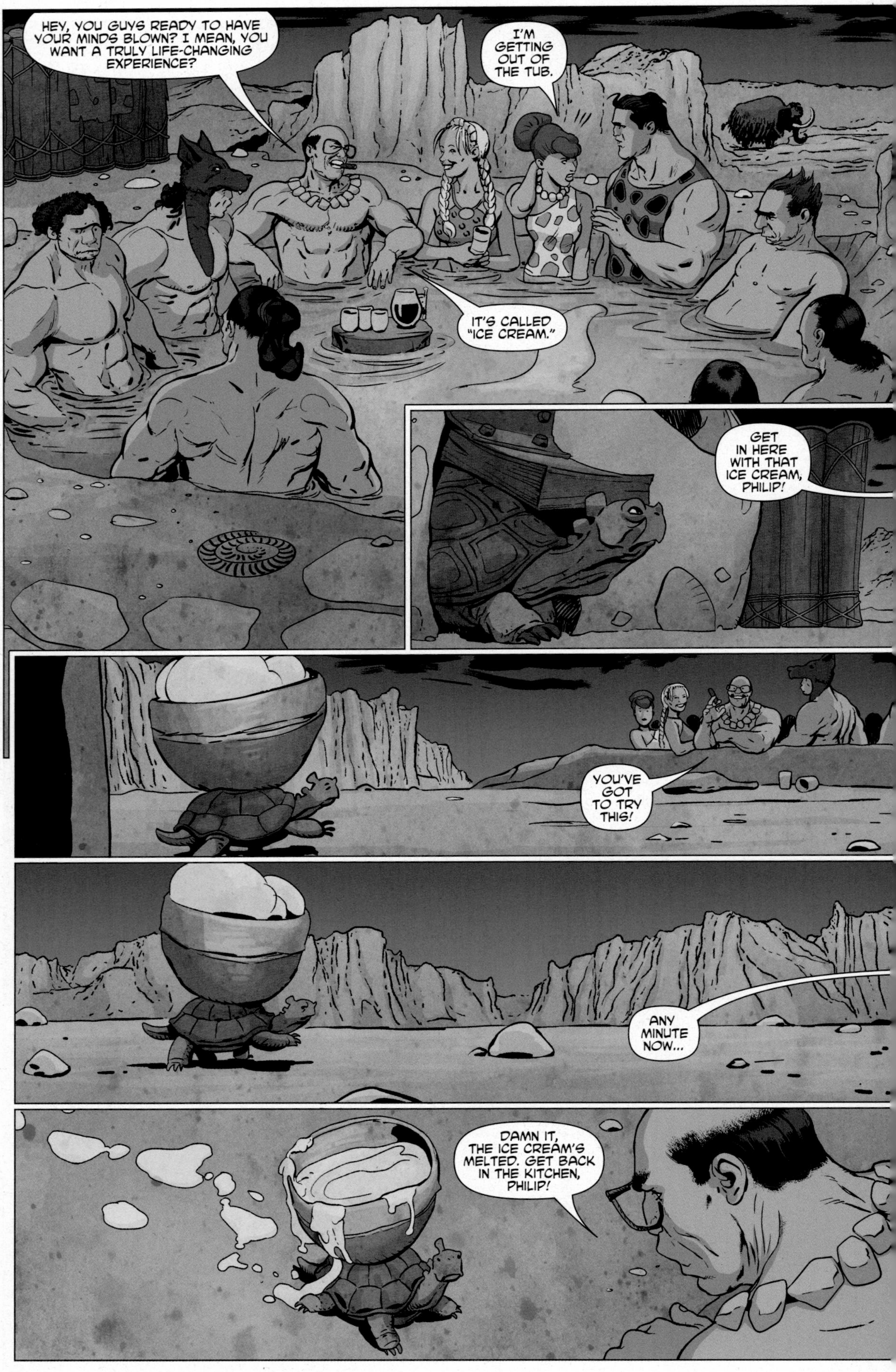
HEY, YOU GUYS READY TO HAVE YOUR MINDS BLOWN? I MEAN, YOU WANT A TRULY LIFE-CHANGING EXPERIENCE?
I'M GETTING OUT OF THE TUB.
IT'S CALLED "ICE CREAM."
GET IN HERE WITH THAT ICE CREAM, PHILIP!
YOU'VE GOT TO TRY THIS!
ANY MINUTE NOW...
DAMN IT, THE ICE CREAM'S MELTED. GET BACK IN THE KITCHEN, PHILIP!

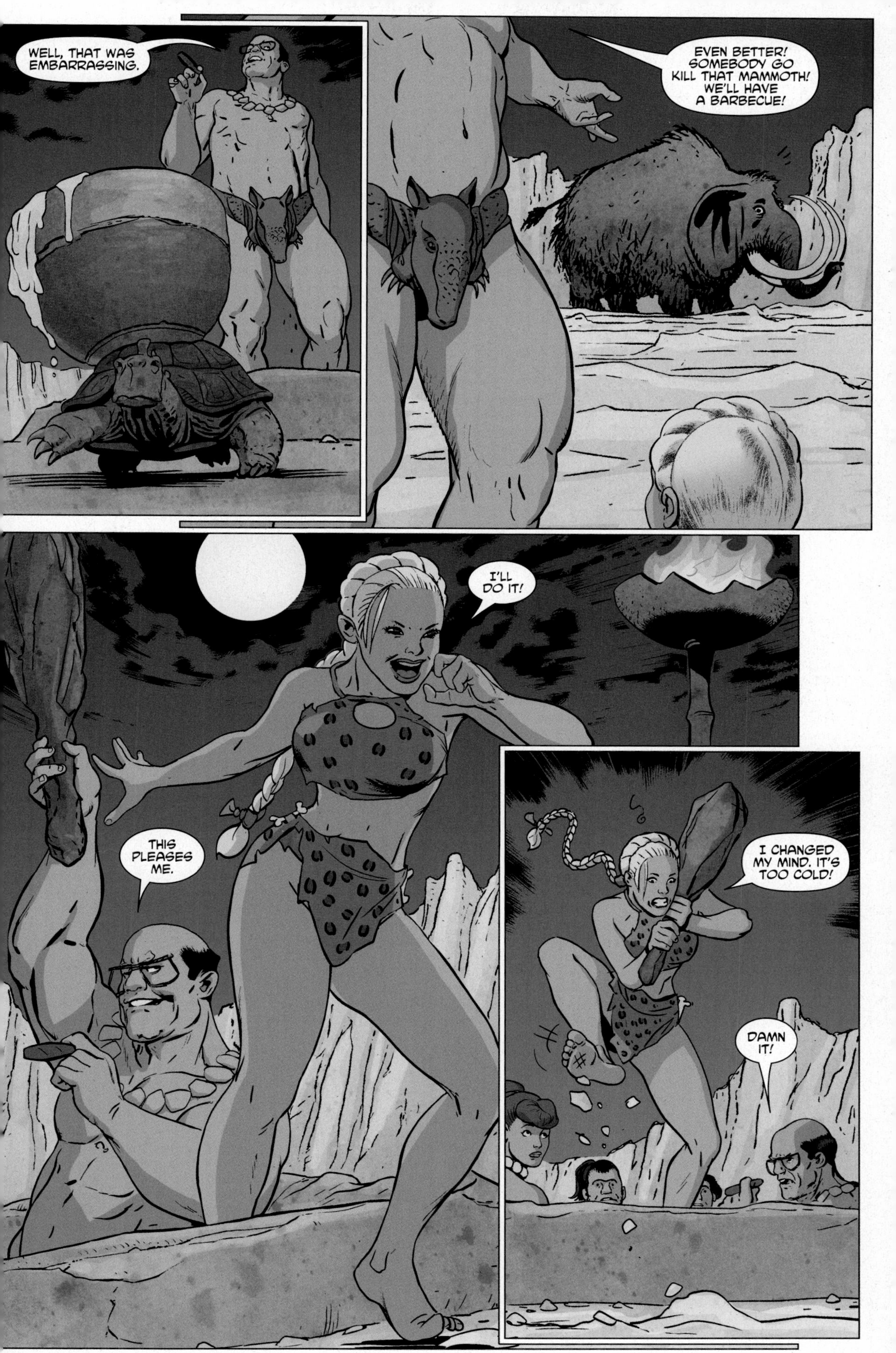
WELL, THAT WAS EMBARRASSING.
EVEN BETTER! SOMEBODY GO KILL THAT MAMMOTH! WE'LL HAVE A BARBECUE!
I'LL DO IT!
THIS PLEASES ME.
I CHANGED MY MIND. IT'S TOO COLD!
DAMN IT!

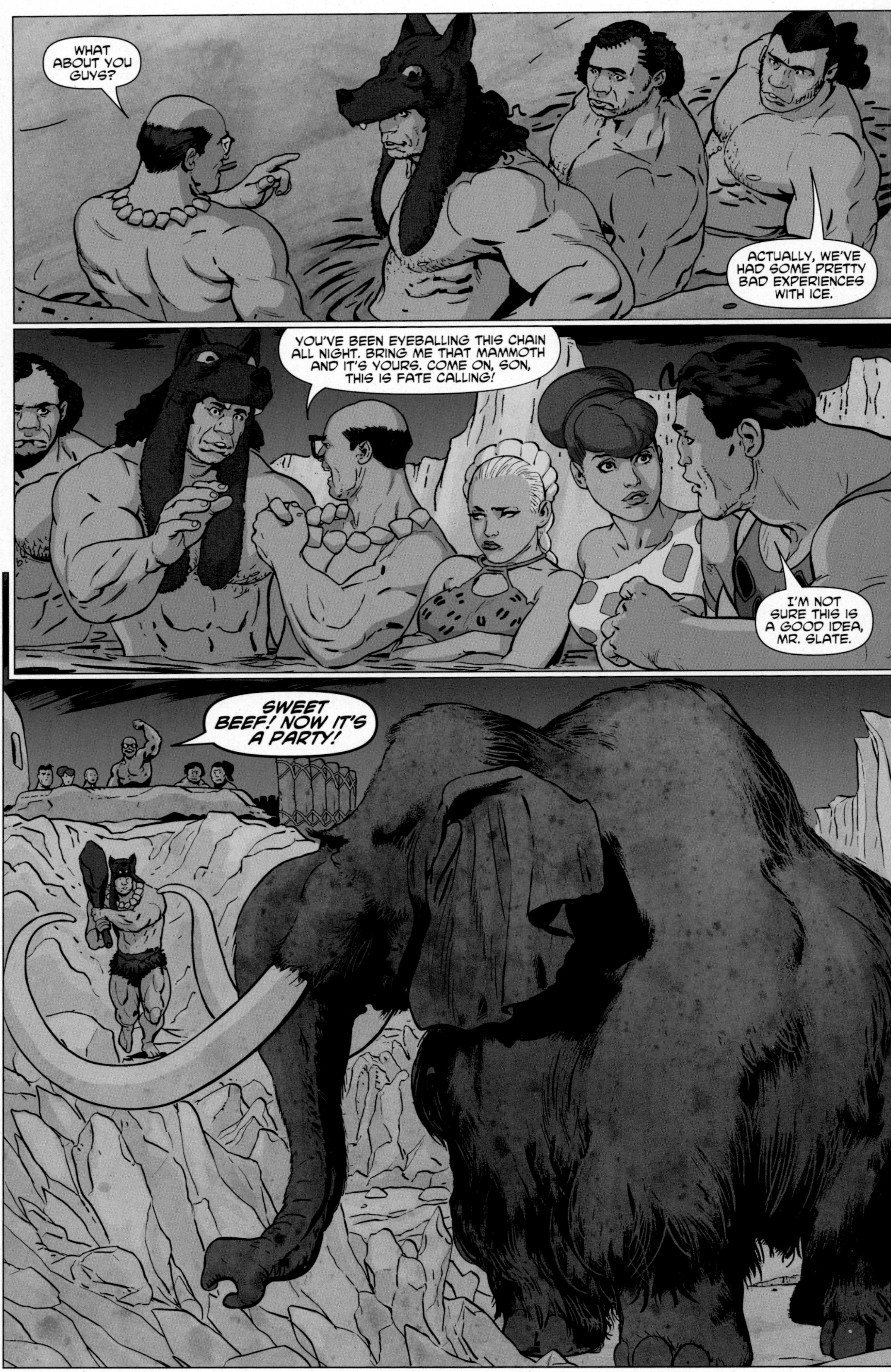
WHAT ABOUT YOU GUYS?
ACTUALLY, WE'VE HAD SOME PRETTY BAD EXPERIENCES WITH ICE.
YOU'VE BEEN EYEBALLING THIS CHAIN ALL NIGHT. BRING ME THAT MAMMOTH AND IT'S YOURS. COME ON, SON, THIS IS FATE CALLING!
I'M NOT SURE THIS IS A GOOD IDEA, MR. SLATE.
SWEET BEEF! NOW IT'S A PARTY!

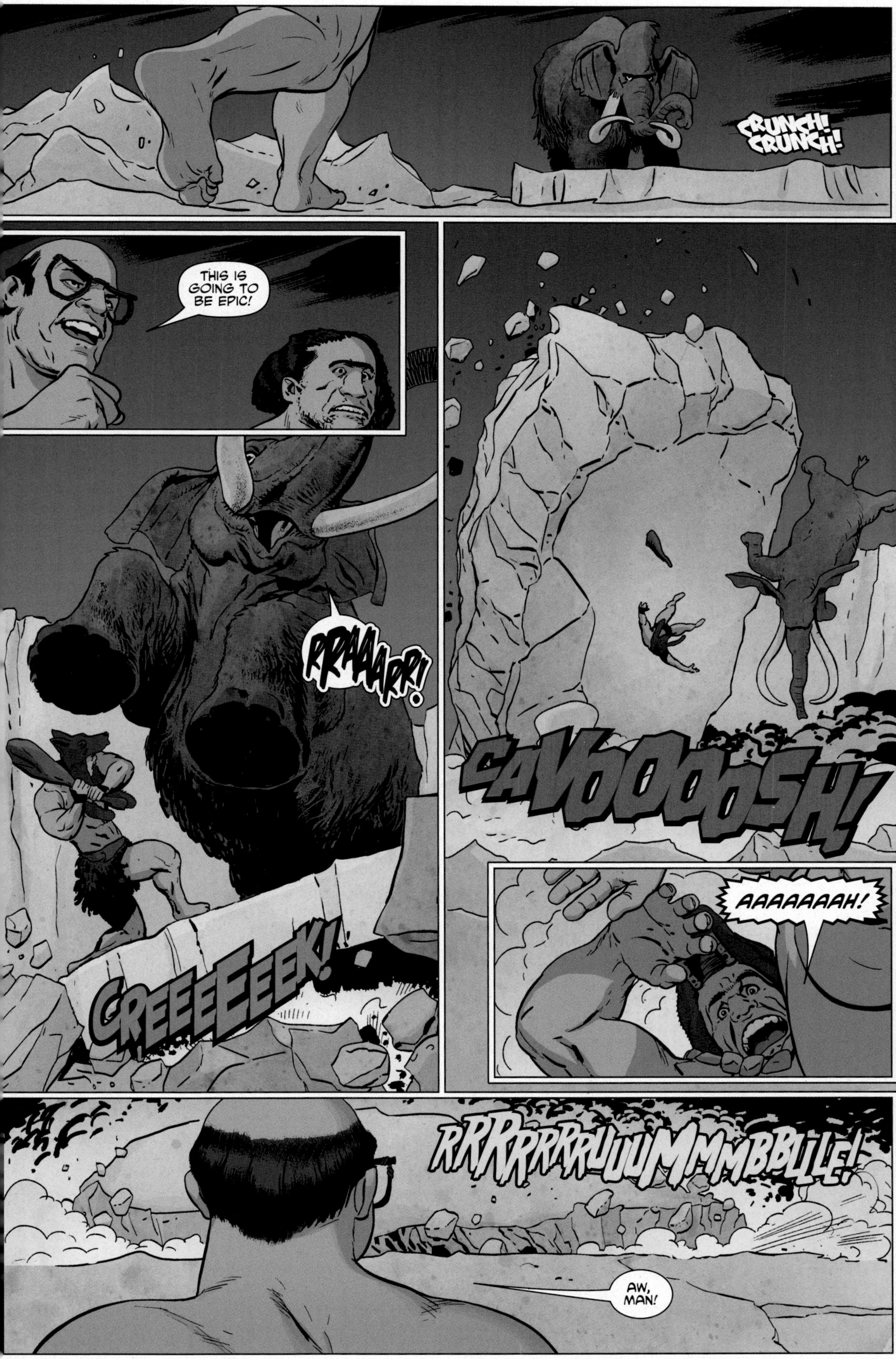
CRUNCH! CRUNCH!
THIS IS GOING TO BE EPIC!
RRAAAARR!
GREEEEEEK!
CAVOOOOOSH!
AAAAAAAH!
RRRRRRRRUUUMMMBBLLE!
AW, MAN!

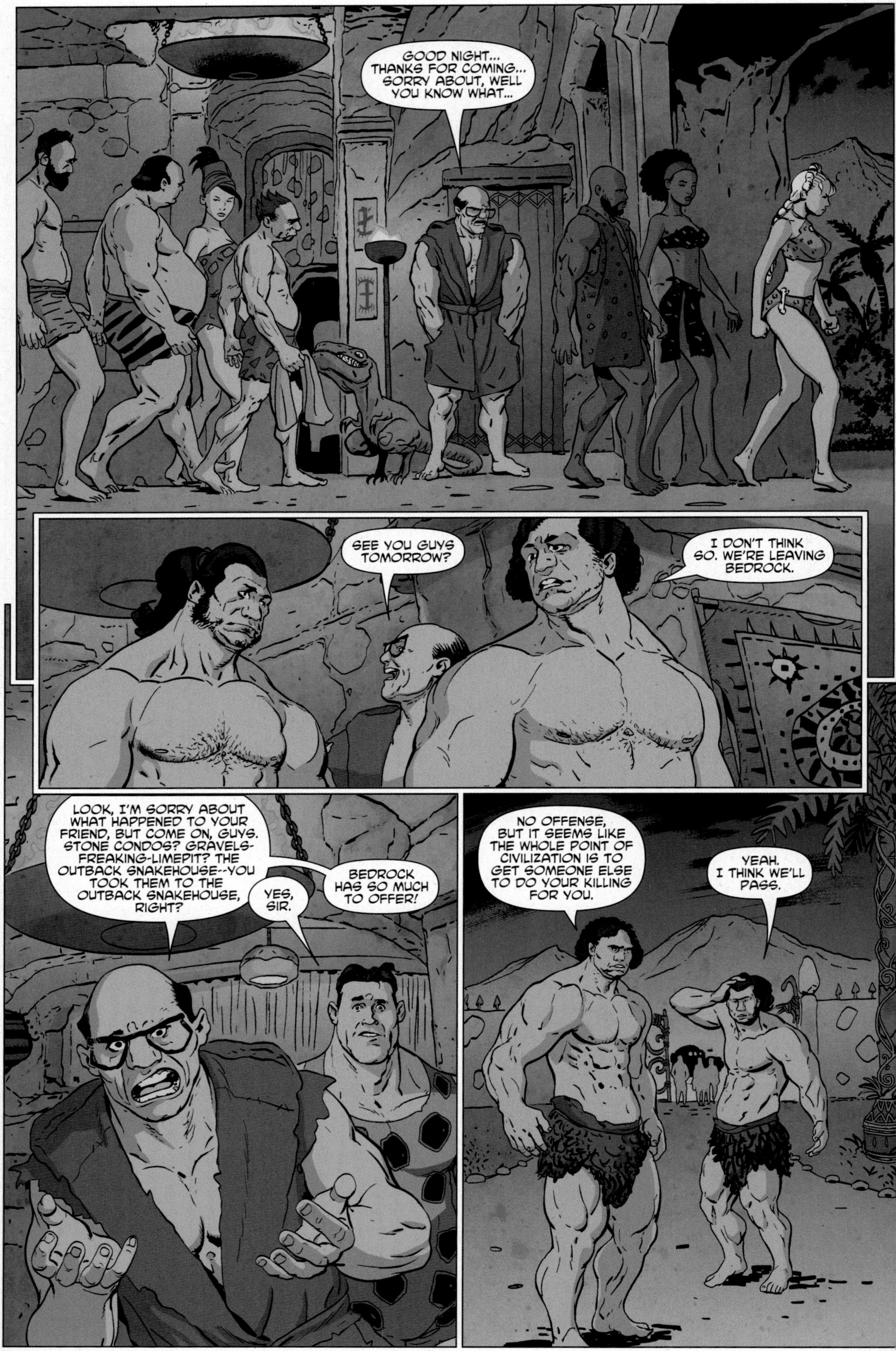
GOOD NIGHT... THANKS FOR COMING... SORRY ABOUT, WELL YOU KNOW WHAT...
SEE YOU GUYS TOMORROW?
I DON'T THINK SO. WE'RE LEAVING BEDROCK.
LOOK, I'M SORRY ABOUT WHAT HAPPENED TO YOUR FRIEND, BUT COME ON, GUYS. STONE CONDOS? GRAVELS-FREAKING-LIMEPIT? THE OUTBACK SNAKEHOUSE--YOU TOOK THEM TO THE OUTBACK SNAKEHOUSE, RIGHT?
YES, SIR.
BEDROCK HAS SO MUCH TO OFFER!
NO OFFENSE, BUT IT SEEMS LIKE THE WHOLE POINT OF CIVILIZATION IS TO GET SOMEONE ELSE TO DO YOUR KILLING FOR YOU.
YEAH. I THINK WE'LL PASS.

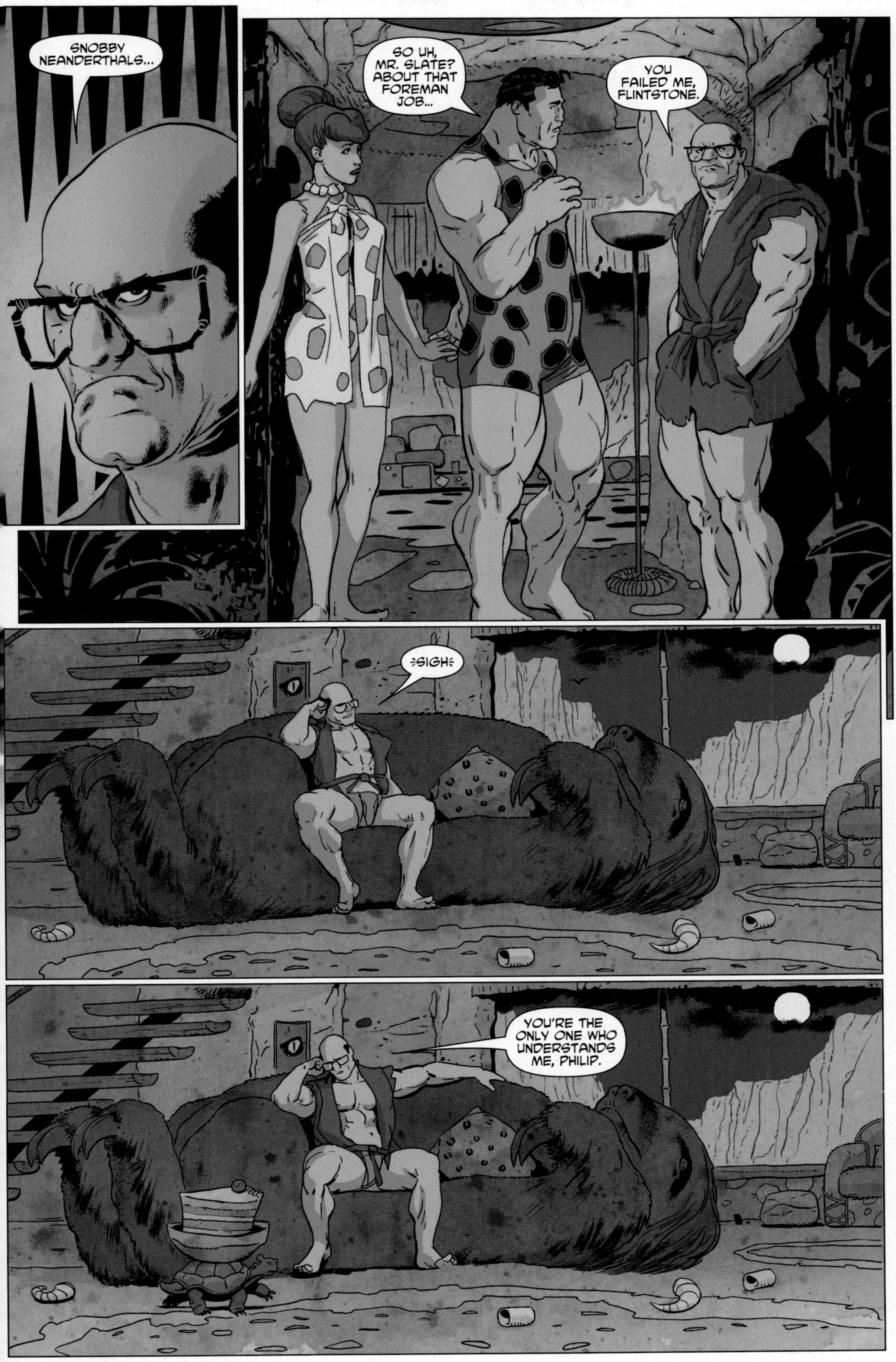
SNOBBY NEANDERTHALS...
SO UH, MR. SLATE? ABOUT THAT FOREMAN JOB...
YOU FAILED ME, FLINTSTONE.
SIGH
YOU'RE THE ONLY ONE WHO UNDERSTANDS ME, PHILIP.

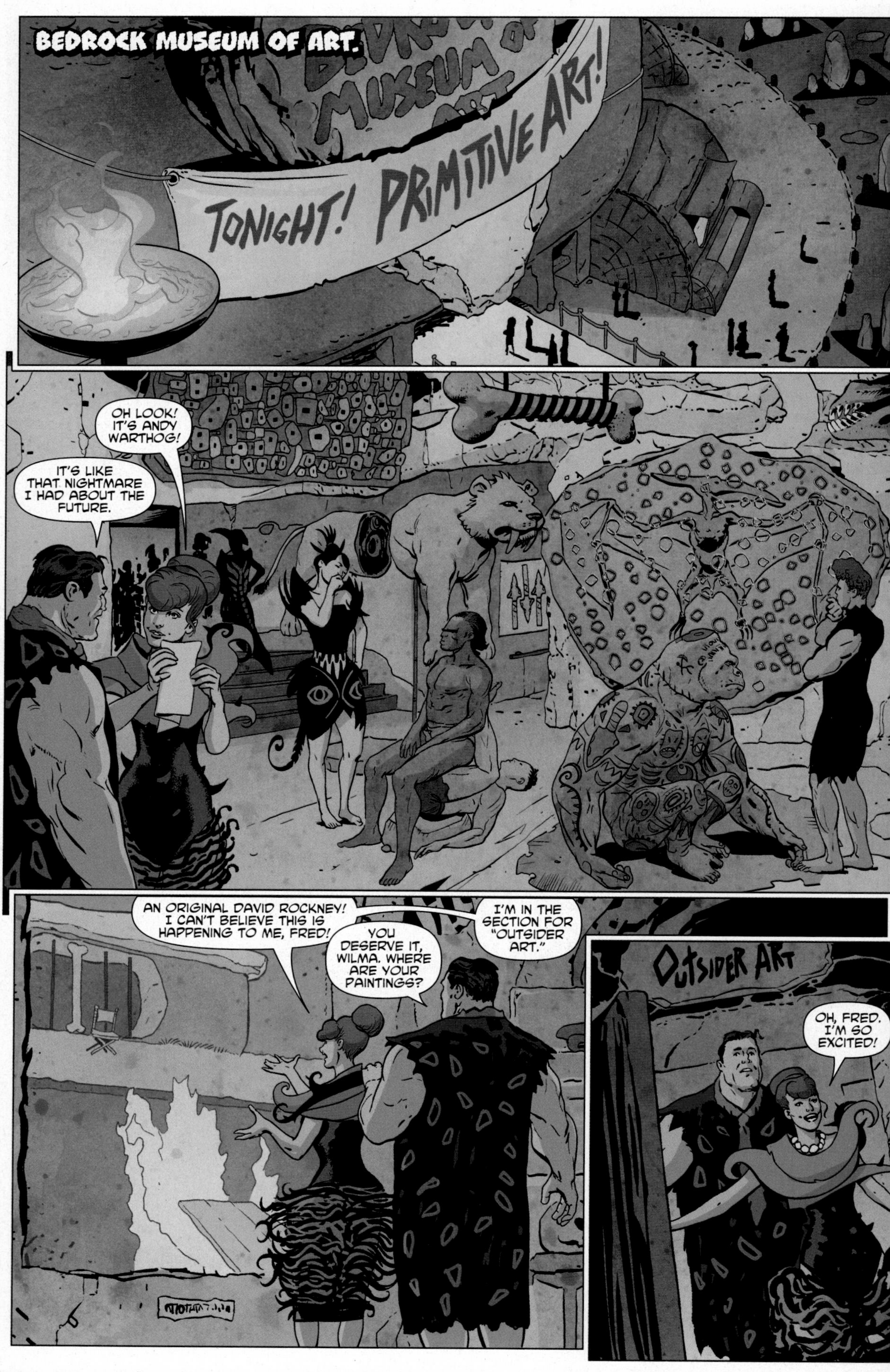
BEDROCK MUSEUM OF ART.
MUSEUM
TONIGHT! PRIMITIVE ART!
OH LOOK! IT'S ANDY WARTHOG!
IT'S LIKE THAT NIGHTMARE I HAD ABOUT THE FUTURE.
AN ORIGINAL DAVID ROCKNEY! I CAN'T BELIEVE THIS IS HAPPENING TO ME, FRED!
YOU DESERVE IT, WILMA. WHERE ARE YOUR PAINTINGS?
I'M IN THE SECTION FOR "OUTSIDER ART."
OUTSIDER ART
OH, FRED. I'M SO EXCITED!

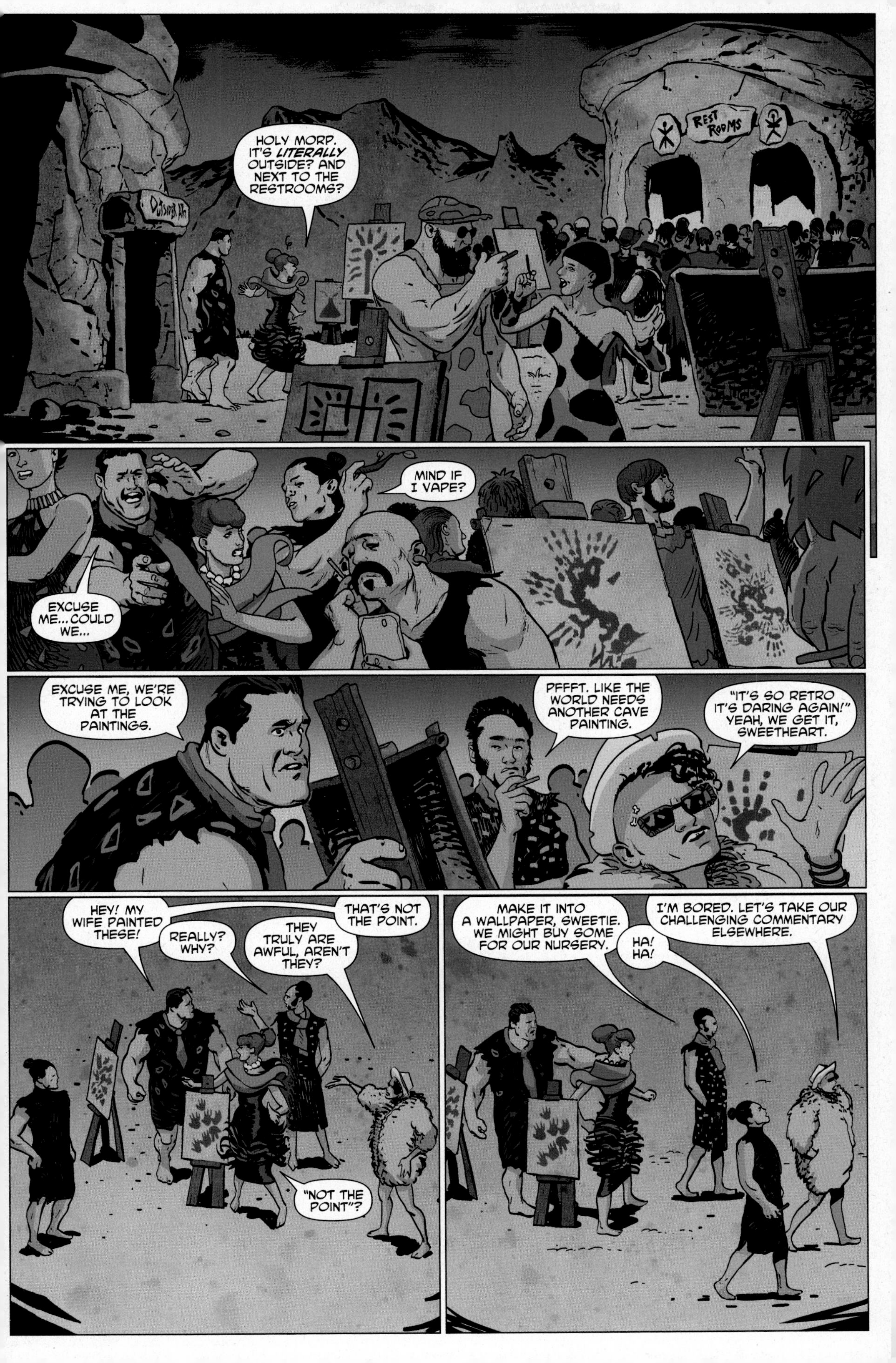
OUTSIDER ART
HOLY MORP. IT'S *LITERALLY* OUTSIDE? AND NEXT TO THE RESTROOMS?
REST ROOMS
MIND IF I VAPE?
EXCUSE ME...COULD WE...
EXCUSE ME, WE'RE TRYING TO LOOK AT THE PAINTINGS.
PFFFT. LIKE THE WORLD NEEDS ANOTHER CAVE PAINTING.
"IT'S SO RETRO IT'S DARING AGAIN!" YEAH, WE GET IT, SWEETHEART.
HEY! MY WIFE PAINTED THESE!
REALLY? WHY?
THEY TRULY ARE AWFUL, AREN'T THEY?
THAT'S NOT THE POINT.
"NOT THE POINT"?
MAKE IT INTO A WALLPAPER, SWEETIE. WE MIGHT BUY SOME FOR OUR NURSERY.
HA! HA!
I'M BORED. LET'S TAKE OUR CHALLENGING COMMENTARY ELSEWHERE.

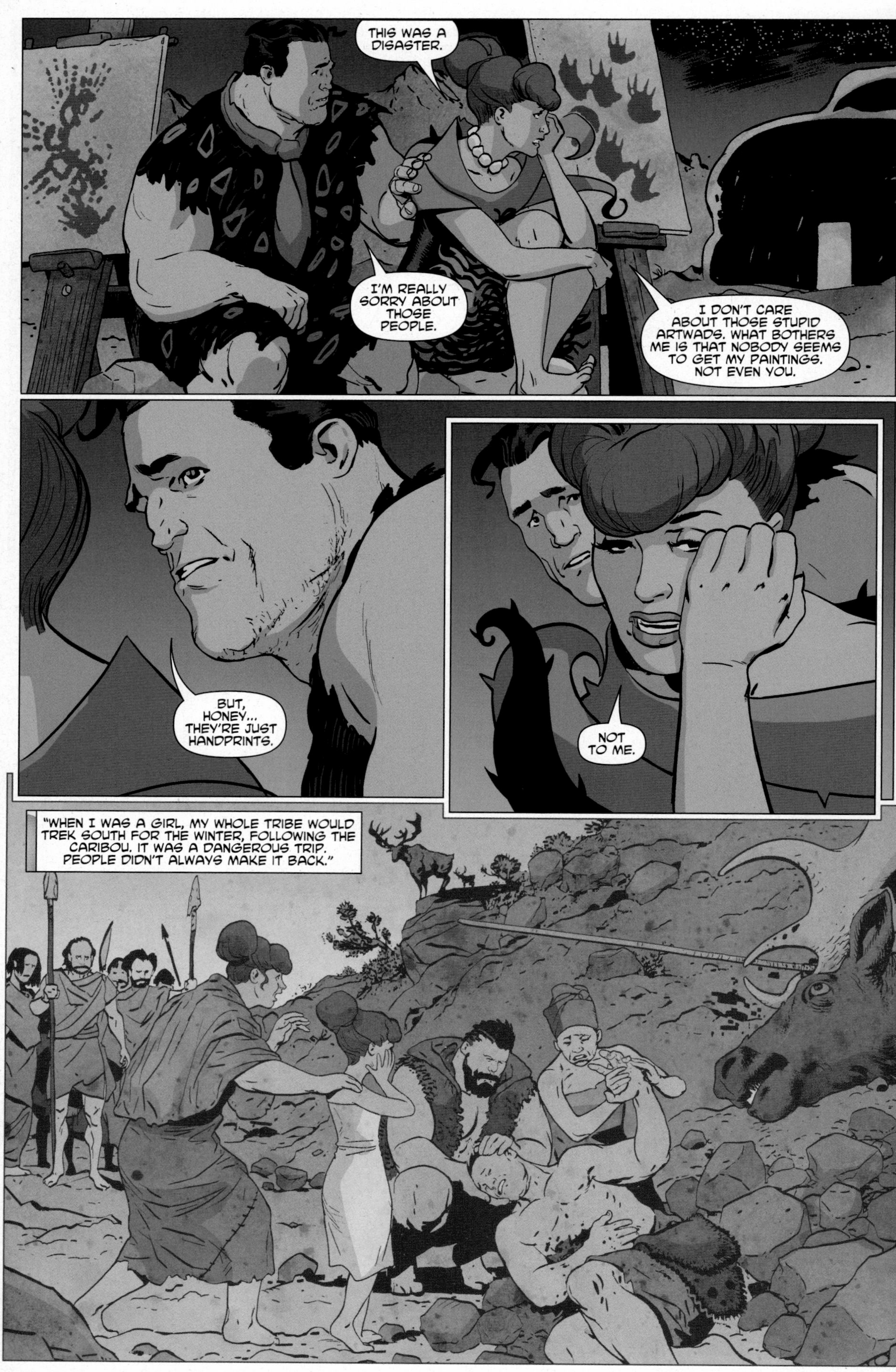
THIS WAS A DISASTER.
I'M REALLY SORRY ABOUT THOSE PEOPLE.
I DON'T CARE ABOUT THOSE STUPID ARTWADS. WHAT BOTHERS ME IS THAT NOBODY SEEMS TO GET MY PAINTINGS. NOT EVEN YOU.
BUT, HONEY... THEY'RE JUST HANDPRINTS.
NOT TO ME.
"WHEN I WAS A GIRL, MY WHOLE TRIBE WOULD TREK SOUTH FOR THE WINTER, FOLLOWING THE CARIBOU. IT WAS A DANGEROUS TRIP. PEOPLE DIDN'T ALWAYS MAKE IT BACK."

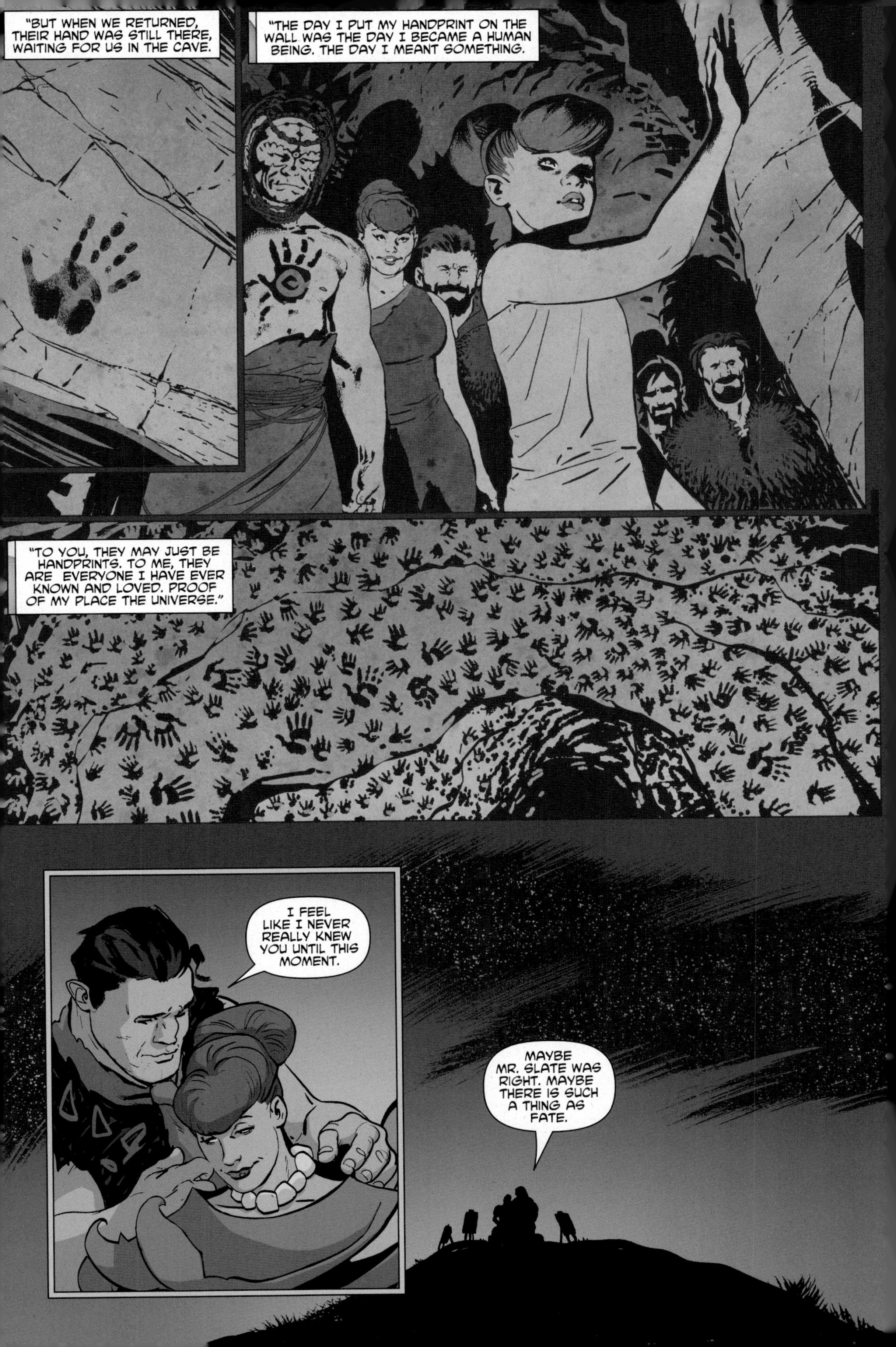
"BUT WHEN WE RETURNED, THEIR HAND WAS STILL THERE, WAITING FOR US IN THE CAVE.
"THE DAY I PUT MY HANDPRINT ON THE WALL WAS THE DAY I BECAME A HUMAN BEING. THE DAY I MEANT SOMETHING.
"TO YOU, THEY MAY JUST BE HANDPRINTS. TO ME, THEY ARE EVERYONE I HAVE EVER KNOWN AND LOVED. PROOF OF MY PLACE THE UNIVERSE."
I FEEL LIKE I NEVER REALLY KNEW YOU UNTIL THIS MOMENT.
MAYBE MR. SLATE WAS RIGHT. MAYBE THERE IS SUCH A THING AS FATE.

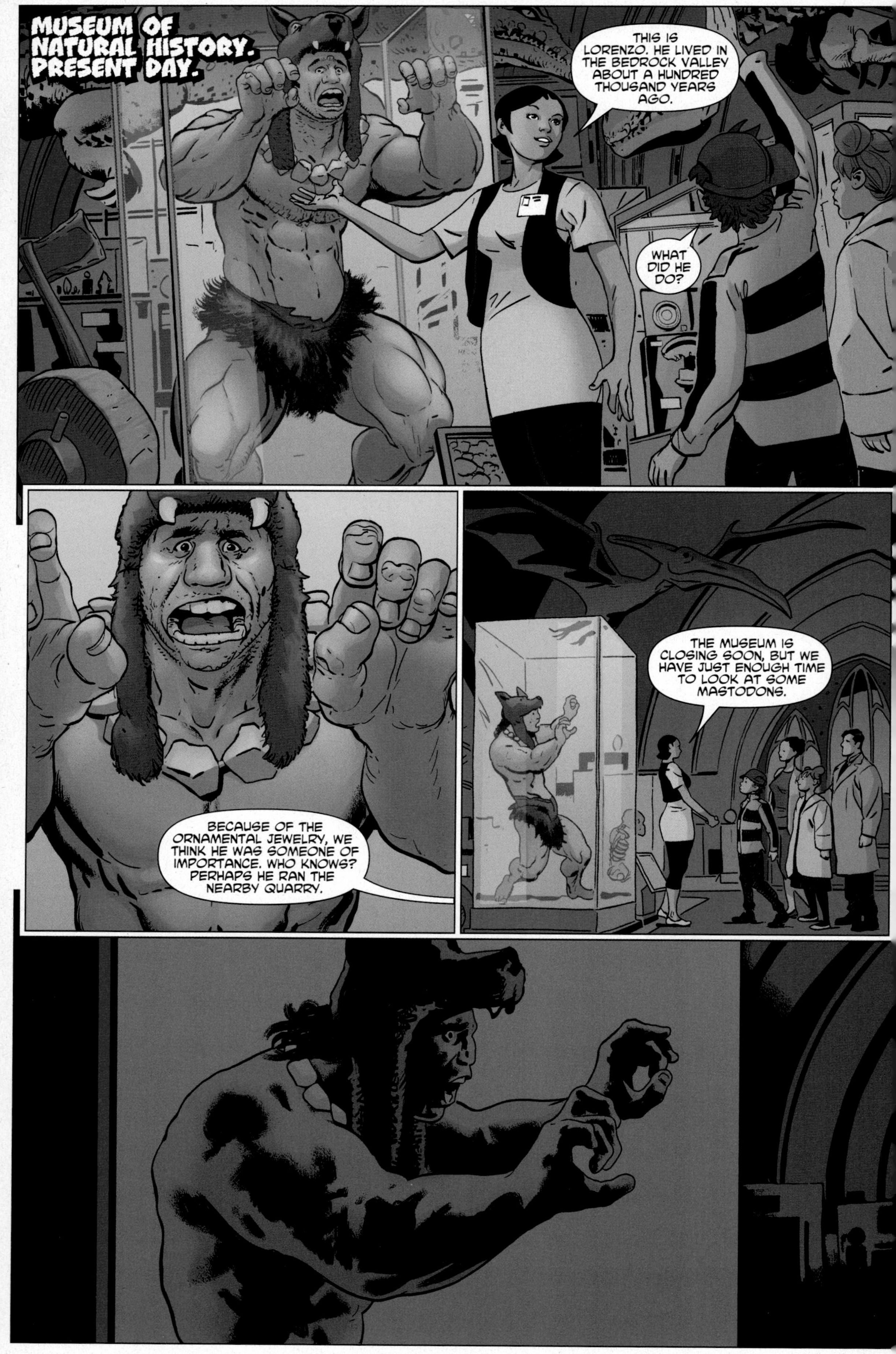
MUSEUM OF NATURAL HISTORY. PRESENT DAY.
THIS IS LORENZO. HE LIVED IN THE BEDROCK VALLEY ABOUT A HUNDRED THOUSAND YEARS AGO.
WHAT DID HE DO?
BECAUSE OF THE ORNAMENTAL JEWELRY, WE THINK HE WAS SOMEONE OF IMPORTANCE. WHO KNOWS? PERHAPS HE RAN THE NEARBY QUARRY.
THE MUSEUM IS CLOSING SOON, BUT WE HAVE JUST ENOUGH TIME TO LOOK AT SOME MASTODONS.

THE FLINTSTONES #2 cover by AMANDA CONNER and PAUL MOUNTS

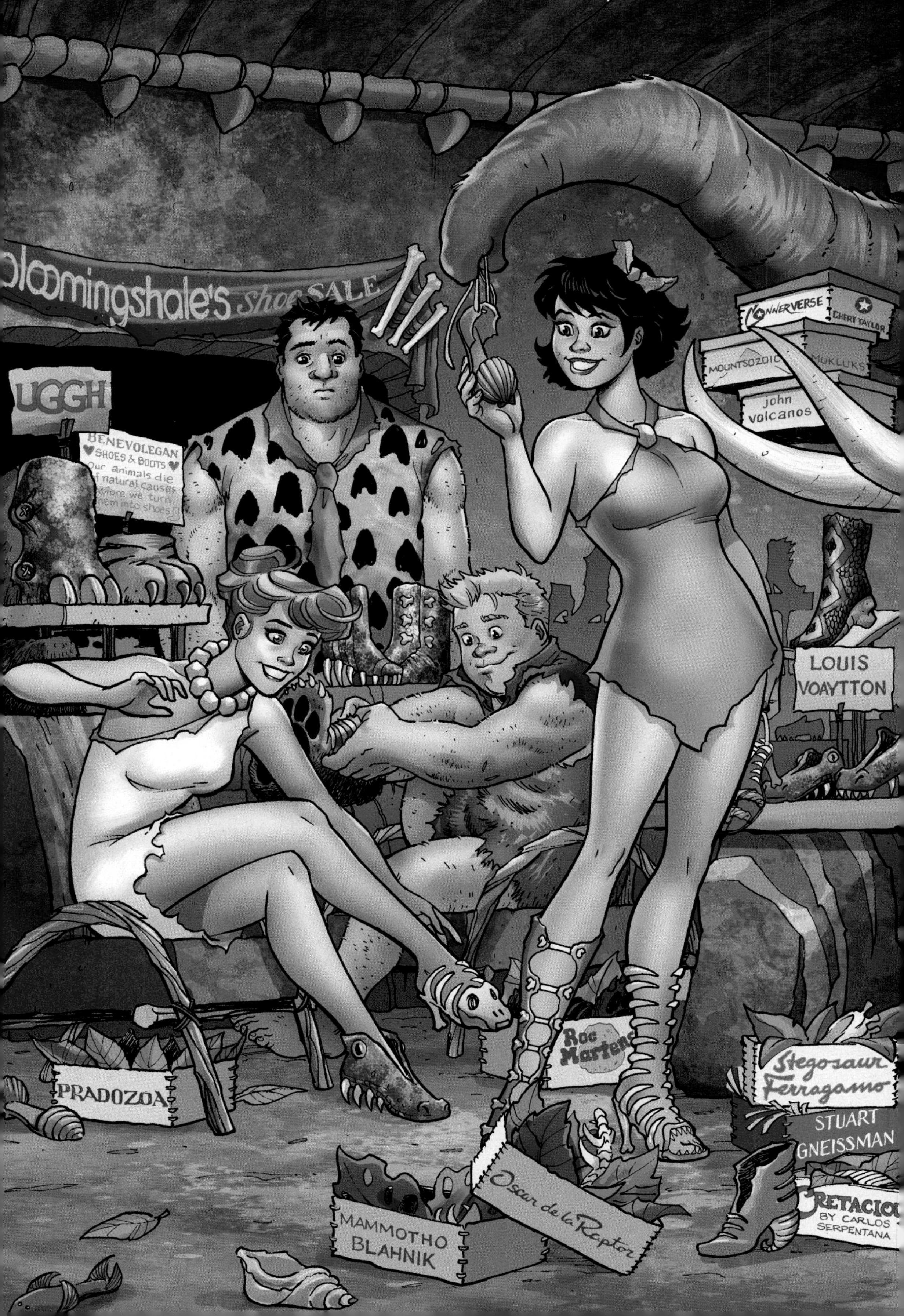
loomingshale's Shoe SALE
UGGH
BENEVOLEGAN
♥SHOES & BOOTS♥
Our animals die
f natural causes
efore we turn
HEM into shoes
CONNERVERSE
CHERT TAYLOR
MOUNTSOZOIC
MUKLUKS
john
volcanos
LOUIS
VOAYTTON
Roc
Martens
PRADOZOA
Stegosaur
Ferragamo
STUART
GNEISSMAN
Oscar de la Raptor
MAMMOTHO
BLAHNIK
CRETACIO
BY CARLOS
SERPENTANA

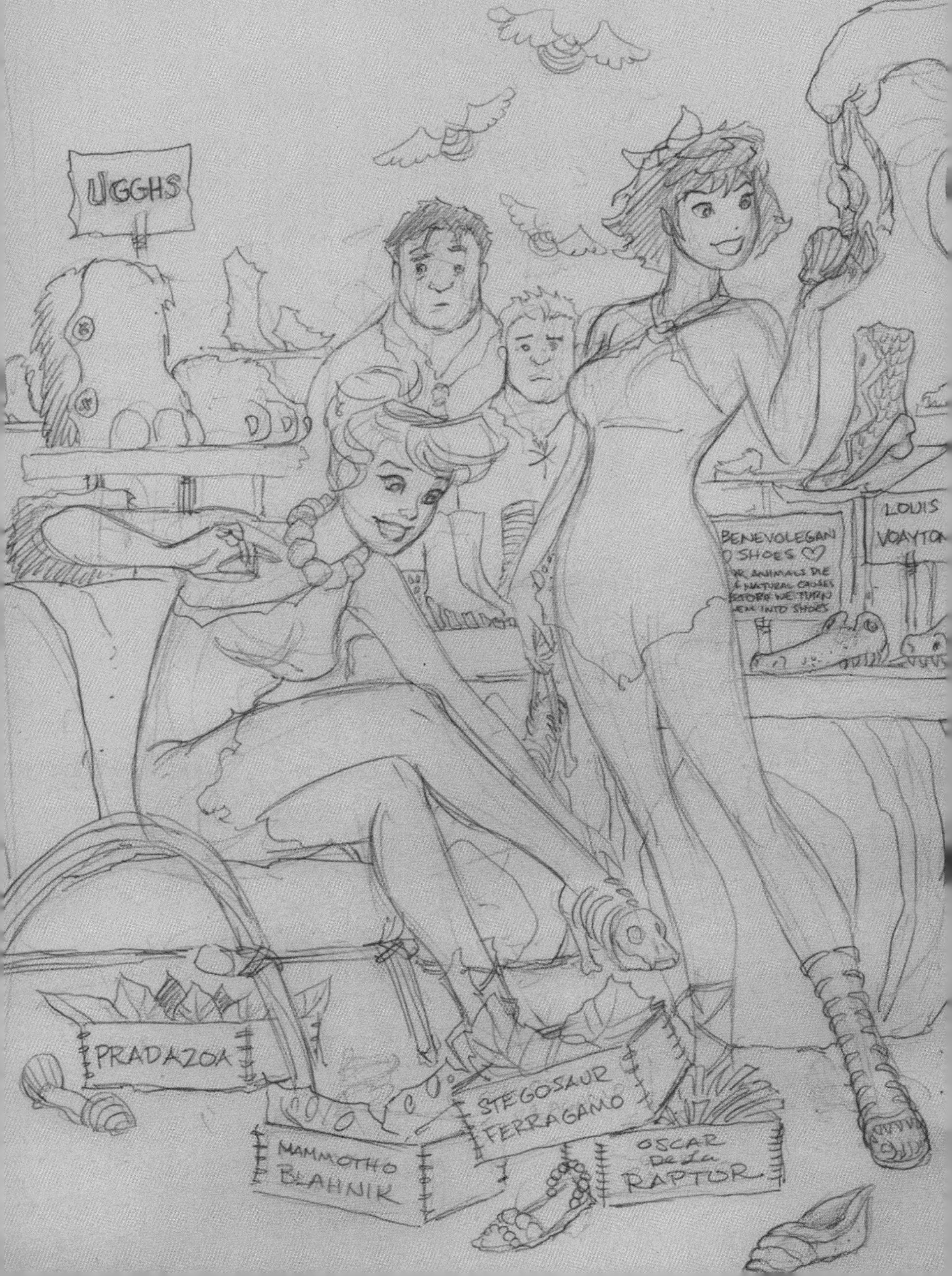
UGGHS
BENEVOLEGANI SHOES ♡
LOUIS VOAYTON
PRADAZOA
STEGOSAUR FERRAGAMO
MAMMOTHO BLAHNIK
OSCAR De La RAPTOR

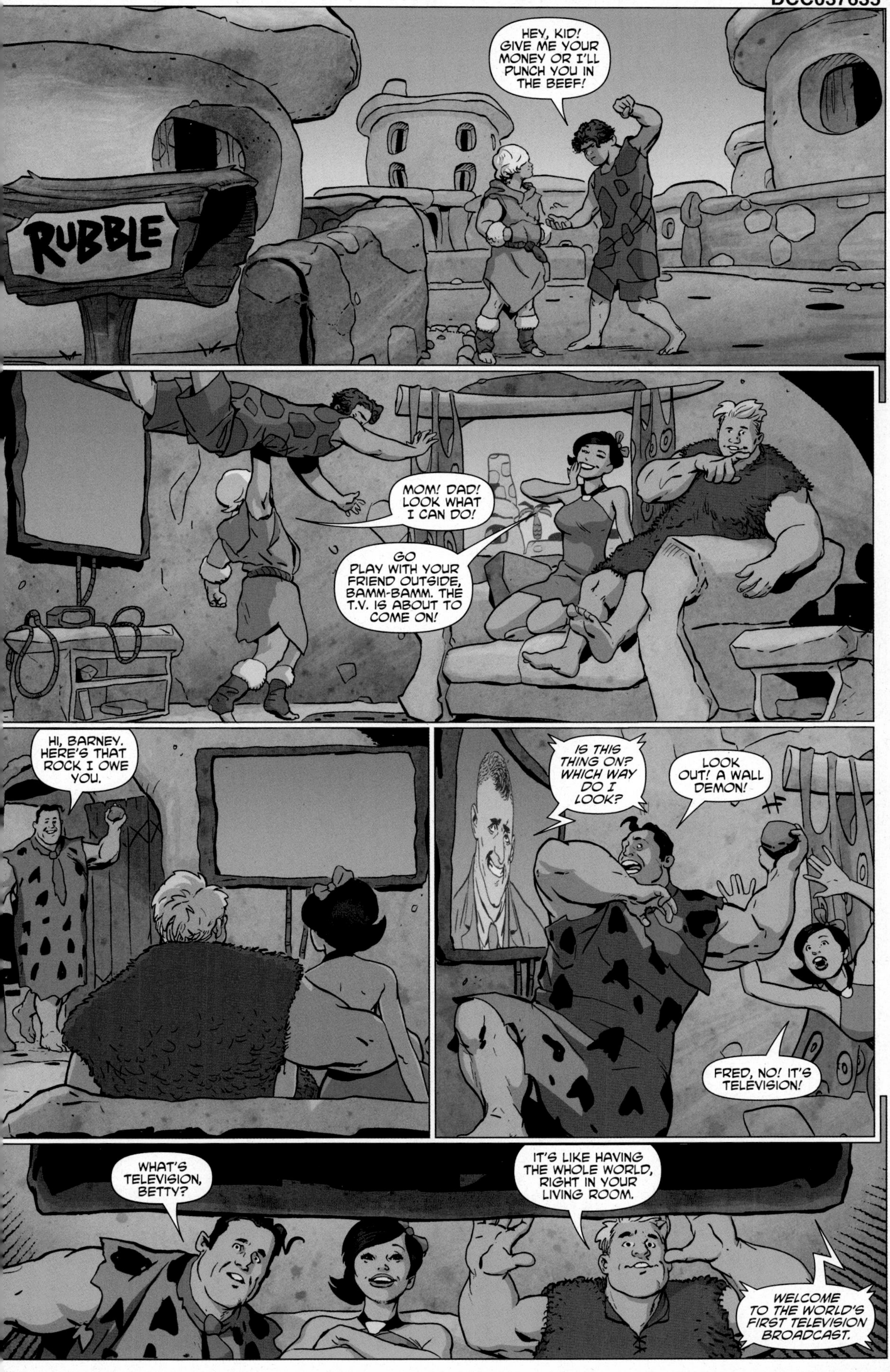

RUBBLE
HEY, KID! GIVE ME YOUR MONEY OR I'LL PUNCH YOU IN THE BEEF!
MOM! DAD! LOOK WHAT I CAN DO!
GO PLAY WITH YOUR FRIEND OUTSIDE, BAMM-BAMM. THE T.V. IS ABOUT TO COME ON!
HI, BARNEY. HERE'S THAT ROCK I OWE YOU.
IS THIS THING ON? WHICH WAY DO I LOOK?
LOOK OUT! A WALL DEMON!
FRED, NO! IT'S TELEVISION!
WHAT'S TELEVISION, BETTY?
IT'S LIKE HAVING THE WHOLE WORLD, RIGHT IN YOUR LIVING ROOM.
WELCOME TO THE WORLD'S FIRST TELEVISION BROADCAST.

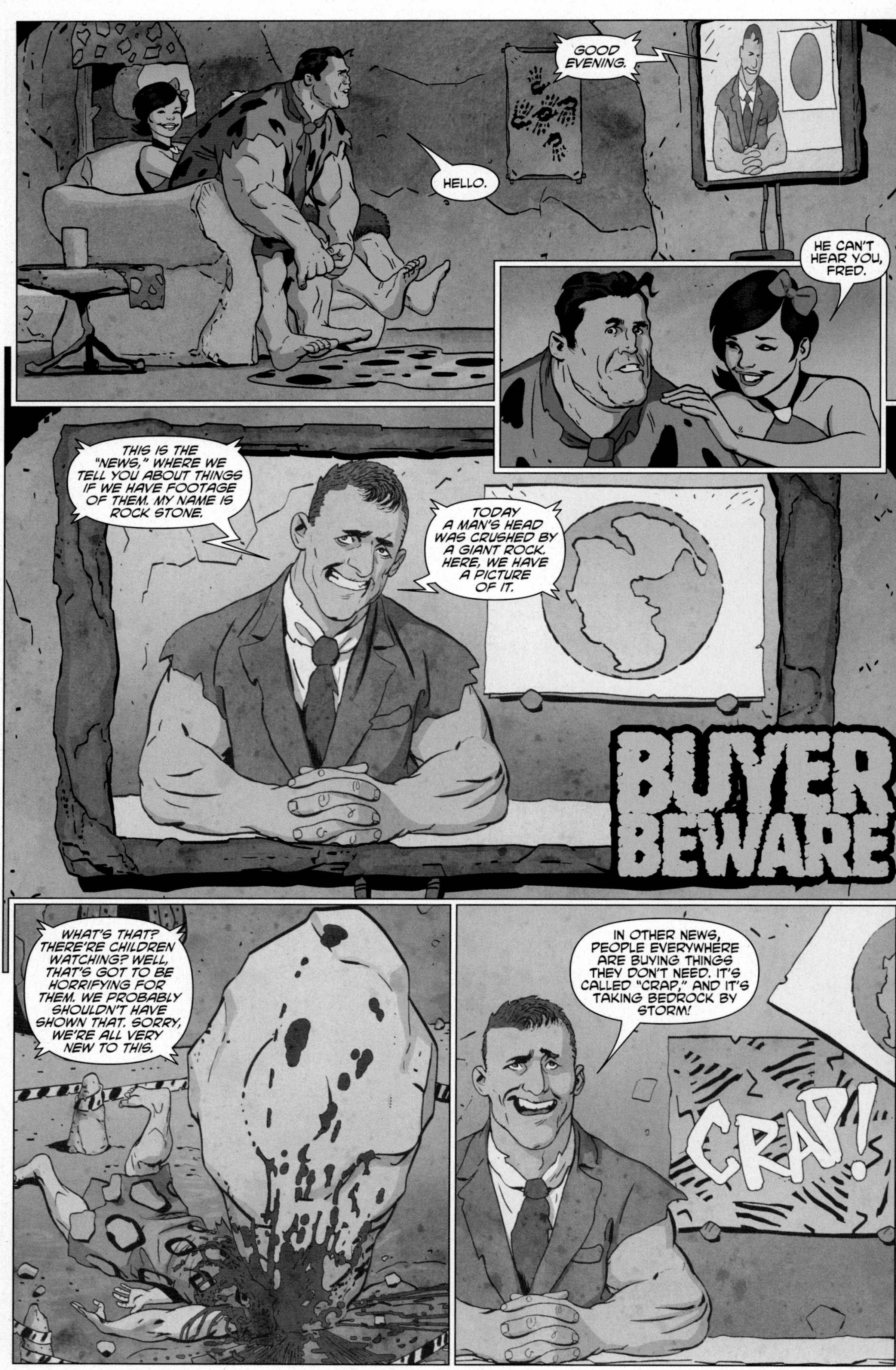

GOOD EVENING.
HELLO.
HE CAN'T HEAR YOU, FRED.
THIS IS THE "NEWS," WHERE WE TELL YOU ABOUT THINGS IF WE HAVE FOOTAGE OF THEM. MY NAME IS ROCK STONE.
TODAY A MAN'S HEAD WAS CRUSHED BY A GIANT ROCK. HERE, WE HAVE A PICTURE OF IT.
BUYER BEWARE
WHAT'S THAT? THERE'RE CHILDREN WATCHING? WELL, THAT'S GOT TO BE HORRIFYING FOR THEM. WE PROBABLY SHOULDN'T HAVE SHOWN THAT. SORRY, WE'RE ALL VERY NEW TO THIS.
IN OTHER NEWS, PEOPLE EVERYWHERE ARE BUYING THINGS THEY DON'T NEED. IT'S CALLED "CRAP," AND IT'S TAKING BEDROCK BY STORM!
CRAP!

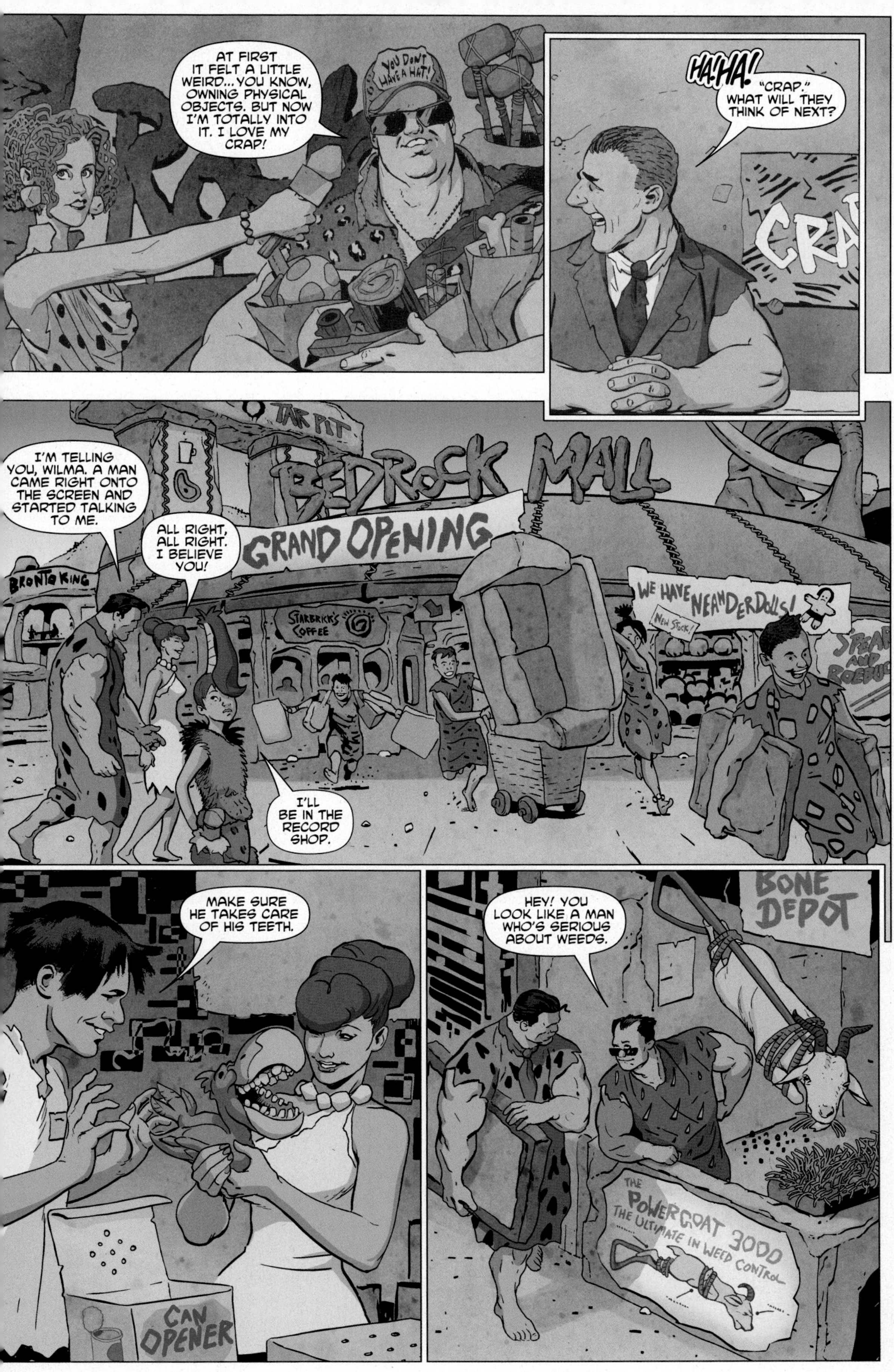
YOU DON'T HAVE A HAT!
AT FIRST IT FELT A LITTLE WEIRD...YOU KNOW, OWNING PHYSICAL OBJECTS. BUT NOW I'M TOTALLY INTO IT. I LOVE MY CRAP!
HA HA!
"CRAP." WHAT WILL THEY THINK OF NEXT?
TAR PIT
BEDROCK MALL
GRAND OPENING
I'M TELLING YOU, WILMA. A MAN CAME RIGHT ONTO THE SCREEN AND STARTED TALKING TO ME.
ALL RIGHT, ALL RIGHT. I BELIEVE YOU!
BRONTO KING
STARBRICK'S COFFEE
WE HAVE NEANDERDOLLS!
NEW STOCK!
I'LL BE IN THE RECORD SHOP.
MAKE SURE HE TAKES CARE OF HIS TEETH.
CAN OPENER
BONE DEPOT
HEY! YOU LOOK LIKE A MAN WHO'S SERIOUS ABOUT WEEDS.
THE POWERGOAT 3000
THE ULTIMATE IN WEED CONTROL

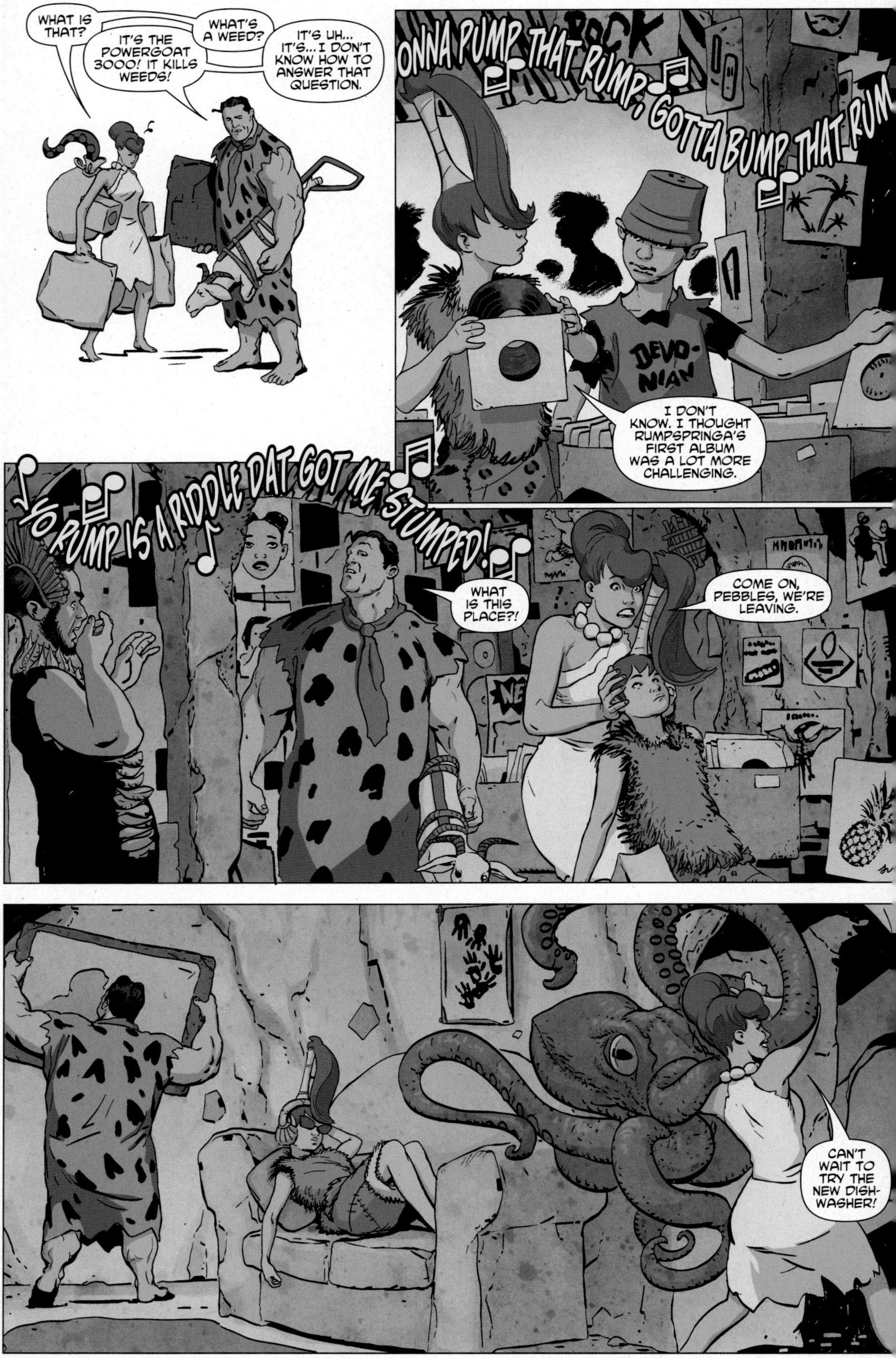
WHAT IS THAT?
IT'S THE POWERGOAT 3000! IT KILLS WEEDS!
WHAT'S A WEED?
IT'S UH... IT'S... I DON'T KNOW HOW TO ANSWER THAT QUESTION.
ONNA PUMP THAT RUMP, GOTTA BUMP THAT RUM
I DON'T KNOW. I THOUGHT RUMPSPRINGA'S FIRST ALBUM WAS A LOT MORE CHALLENGING.
DEVO-NIAN
YO RUMP IS A RIDDLE DAT GOT ME STUMPED!
WHAT IS THIS PLACE?!
COME ON, PEBBLES, WE'RE LEAVING.
CAN'T WAIT TO TRY THE NEW DISH-WASHER!

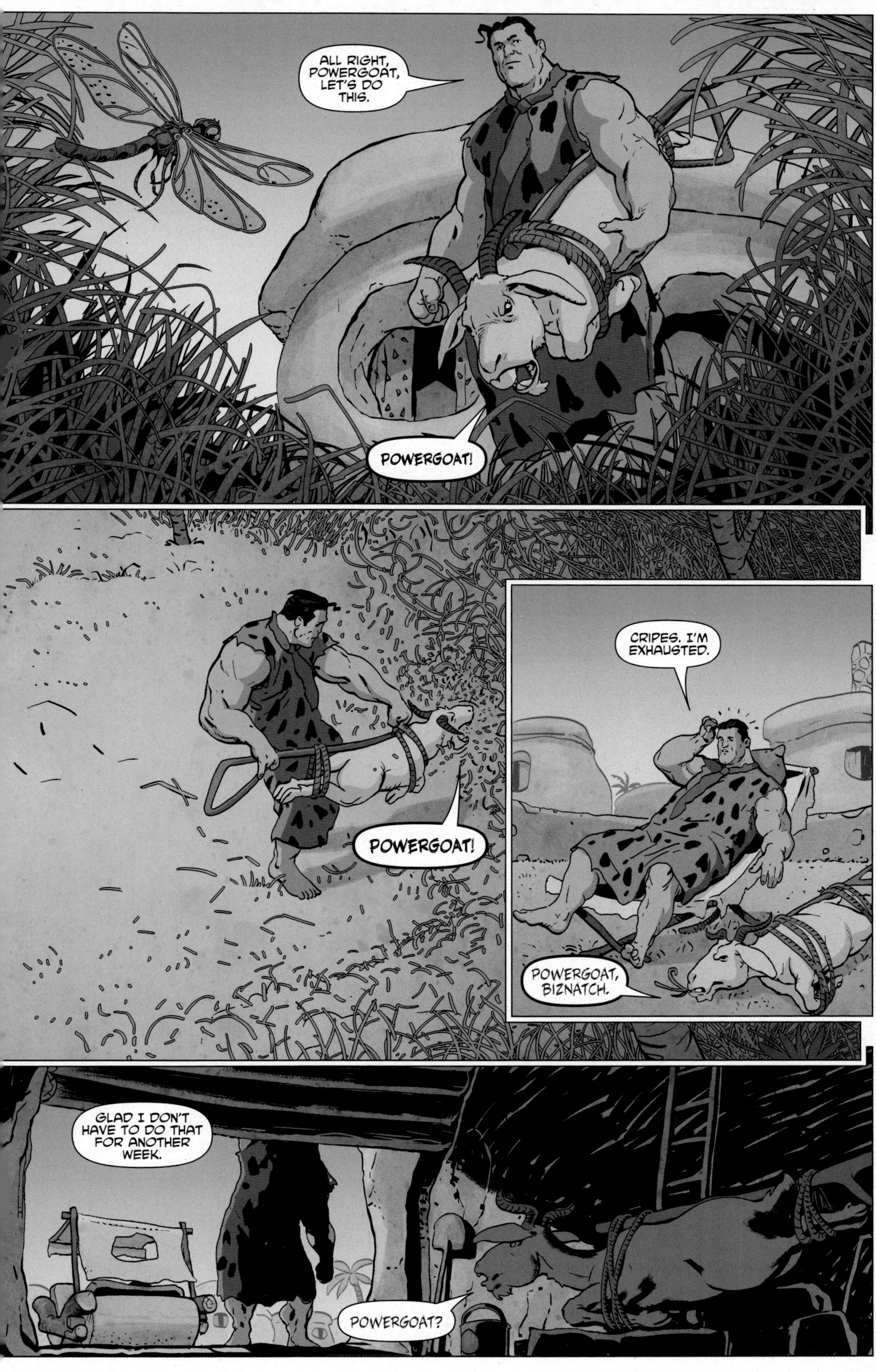
ALL RIGHT, POWERGOAT, LET'S DO THIS.
POWERGOAT!
POWERGOAT!
CRIPES. I'M EXHAUSTED.
POWERGOAT, BIZNATCH.
GLAD I DON'T HAVE TO DO THAT FOR ANOTHER WEEK.
POWERGOAT?

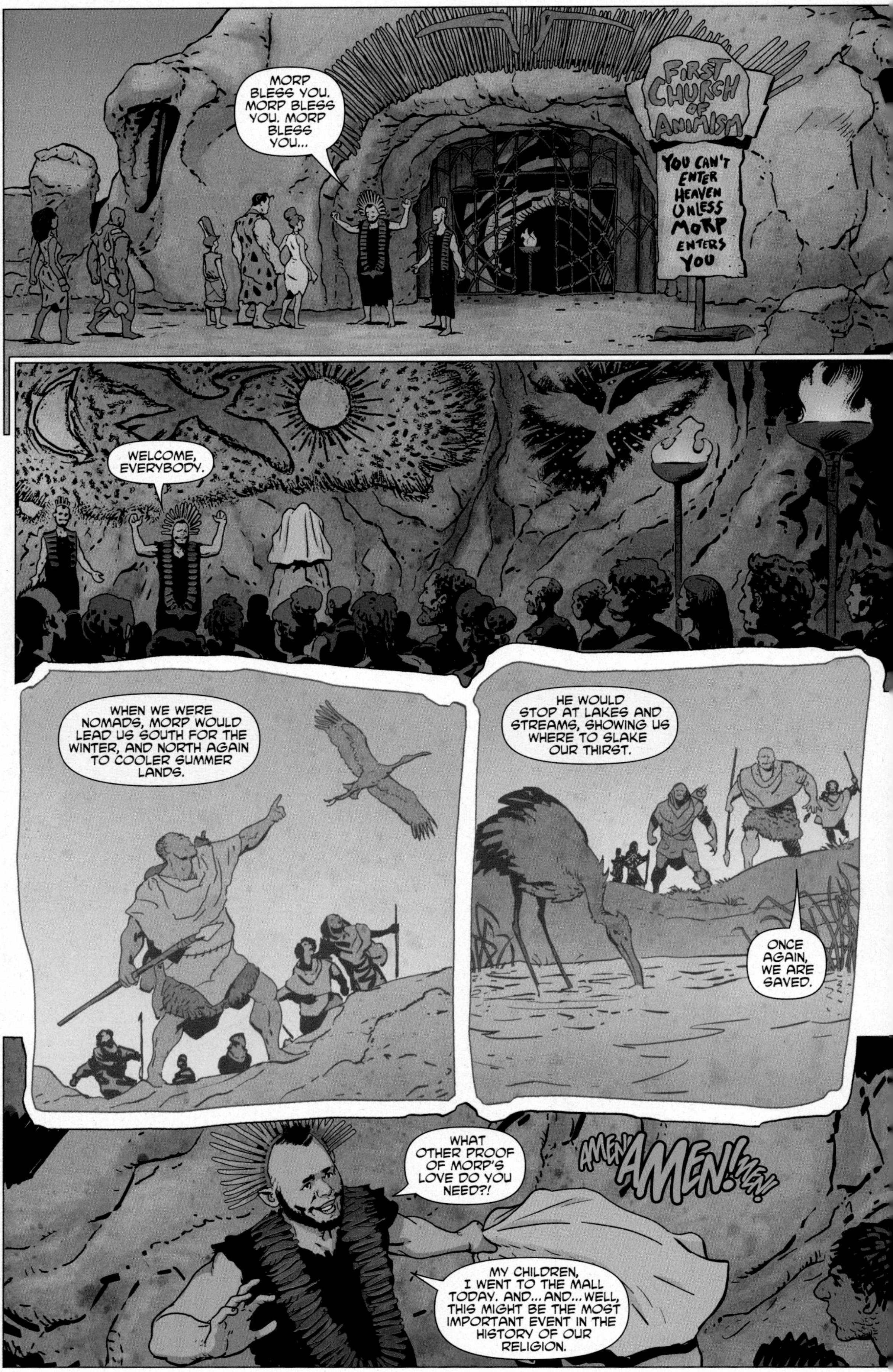

MORP BLESS YOU. MORP BLESS YOU. MORP BLESS YOU...
FIRST CHURCH OF ANIMISM
YOU CAN'T ENTER HEAVEN UNLESS MORP ENTERS YOU
WELCOME, EVERYBODY.
WHEN WE WERE NOMADS, MORP WOULD LEAD US SOUTH FOR THE WINTER, AND NORTH AGAIN TO COOLER SUMMER LANDS.
HE WOULD STOP AT LAKES AND STREAMS, SHOWING US WHERE TO SLAKE OUR THIRST.
ONCE AGAIN, WE ARE SAVED.
WHAT OTHER PROOF OF MORP'S LOVE DO YOU NEED?!
AMEN! AMEN! MEN!
MY CHILDREN, I WENT TO THE MALL TODAY. AND...AND...WELL, THIS MIGHT BE THE MOST IMPORTANT EVENT IN THE HISTORY OF OUR RELIGION.

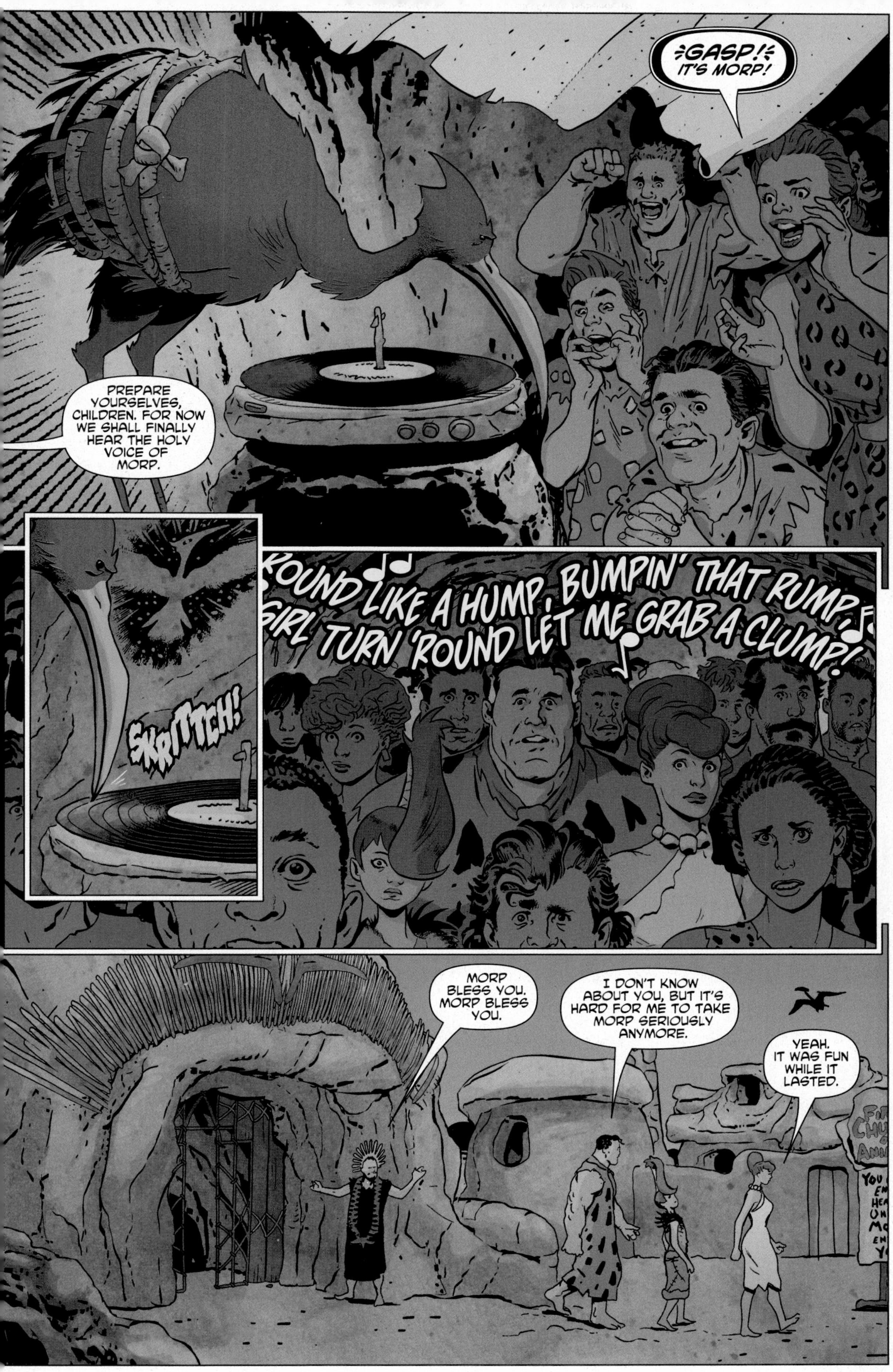
GASP! IT'S MORP!
PREPARE YOURSELVES, CHILDREN. FOR NOW WE SHALL FINALLY HEAR THE HOLY VOICE OF MORP.
SKRITTCH!
'ROUND LIKE A HUMP, BUMPIN' THAT RUMP, GIRL TURN 'ROUND LET ME GRAB A CLUMP!
MORP BLESS YOU. MORP BLESS YOU.
I DON'T KNOW ABOUT YOU, BUT IT'S HARD FOR ME TO TAKE MORP SERIOUSLY ANYMORE.
YEAH. IT WAS FUN WHILE IT LASTED.

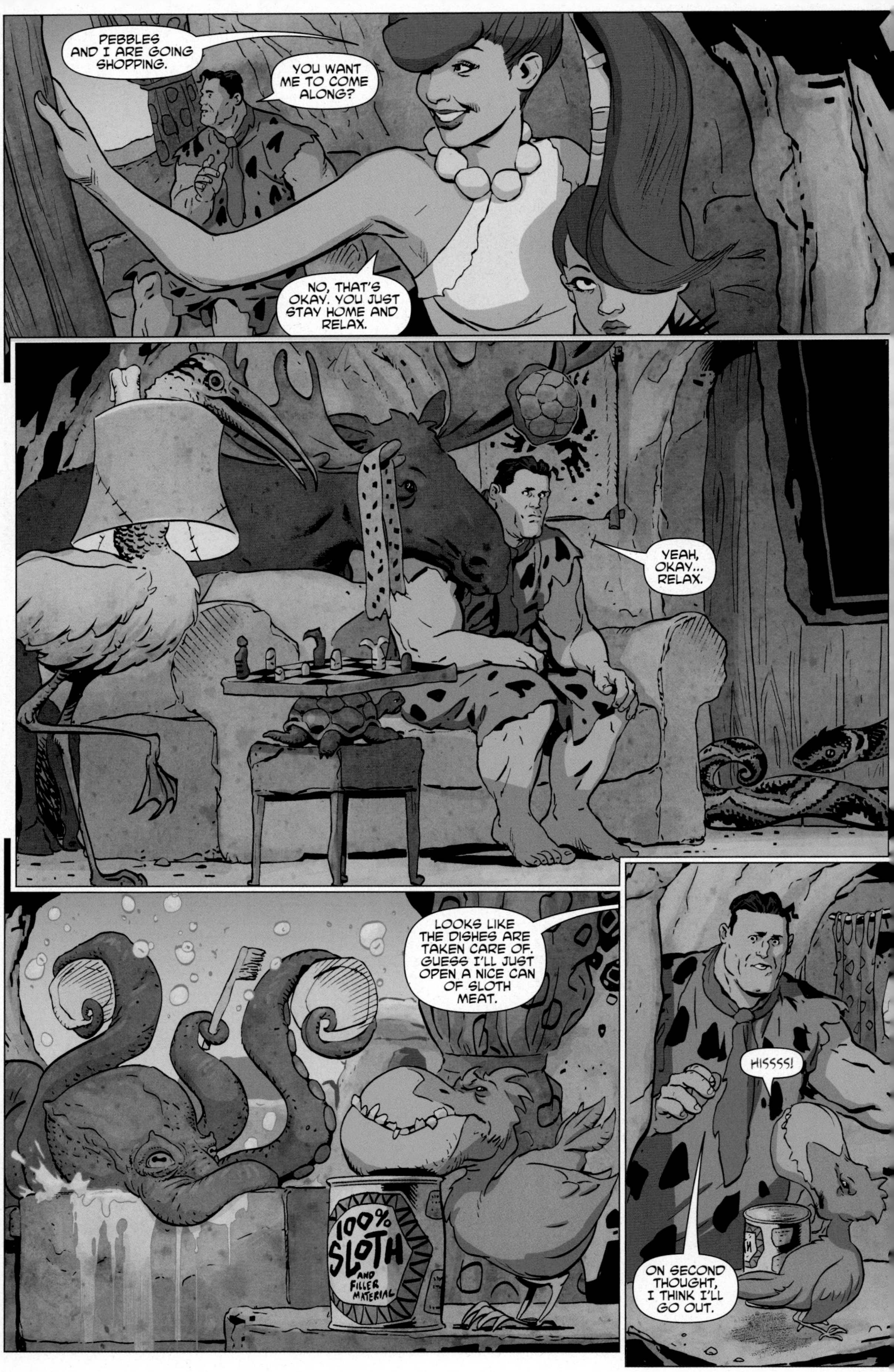
PEBBLES AND I ARE GOING SHOPPING.
YOU WANT ME TO COME ALONG?
NO, THAT'S OKAY. YOU JUST STAY HOME AND RELAX.
YEAH, OKAY... RELAX.
LOOKS LIKE THE DISHES ARE TAKEN CARE OF. GUESS I'LL JUST OPEN A NICE CAN OF SLOTH MEAT.
100% SLOTH AND FILLER MATERIAL
HISSSS!
ON SECOND THOUGHT, I THINK I'LL GO OUT.

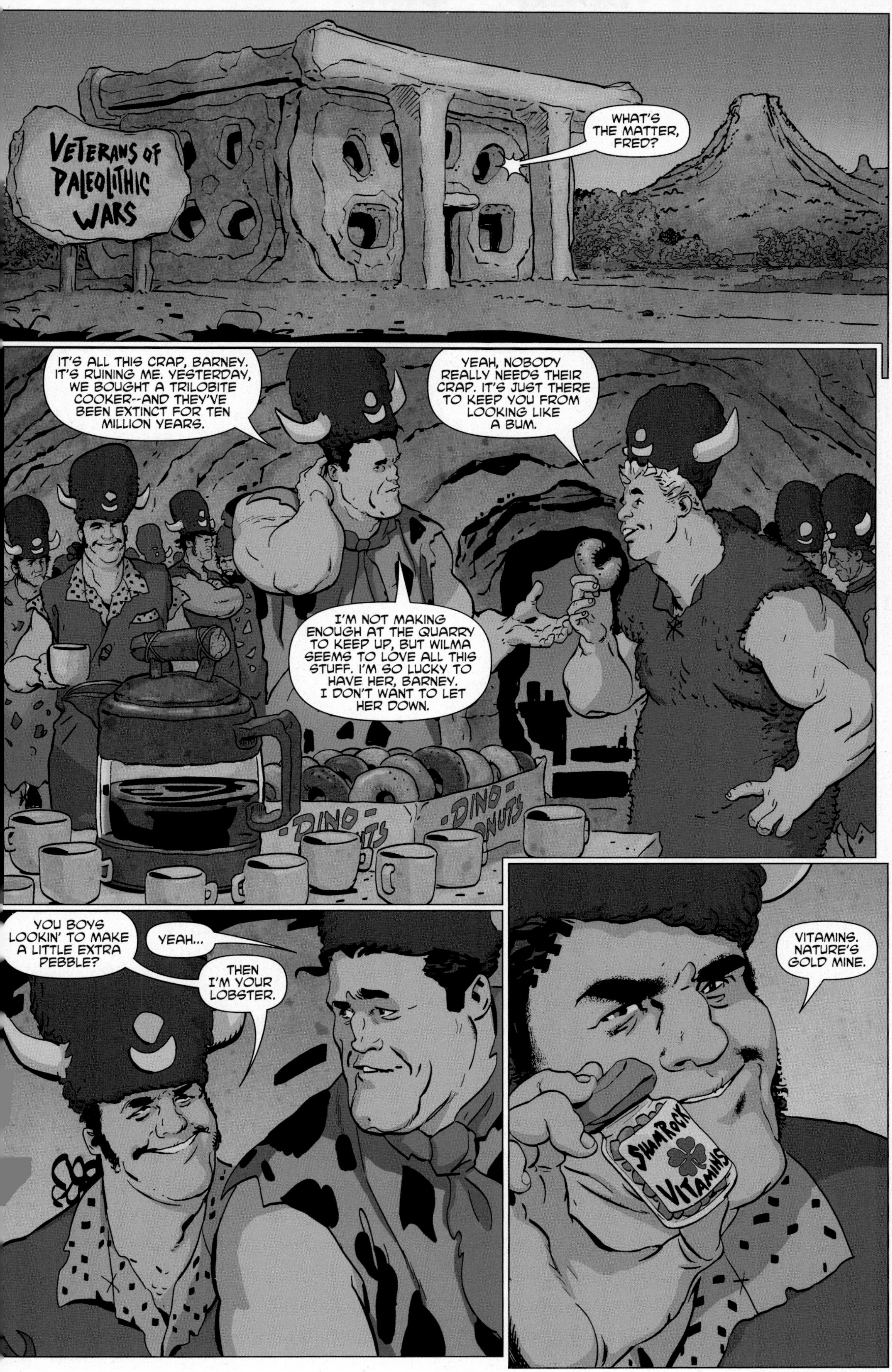
VETERANS OF PALEOLITHIC WARS
WHAT'S THE MATTER, FRED?
IT'S ALL THIS CRAP, BARNEY. IT'S RUINING ME. YESTERDAY, WE BOUGHT A TRILOBITE COOKER--AND THEY'VE BEEN EXTINCT FOR TEN MILLION YEARS.
YEAH, NOBODY REALLY NEEDS THEIR CRAP. IT'S JUST THERE TO KEEP YOU FROM LOOKING LIKE A BUM.
I'M NOT MAKING ENOUGH AT THE QUARRY TO KEEP UP, BUT WILMA SEEMS TO LOVE ALL THIS STUFF. I'M SO LUCKY TO HAVE HER, BARNEY. I DON'T WANT TO LET HER DOWN.
DINO DONUTS
YOU BOYS LOOKIN' TO MAKE A LITTLE EXTRA PEBBLE?
YEAH...
THEN I'M YOUR LOBSTER.
VITAMINS. NATURE'S GOLD MINE.
SHAMROCK VITAMINS

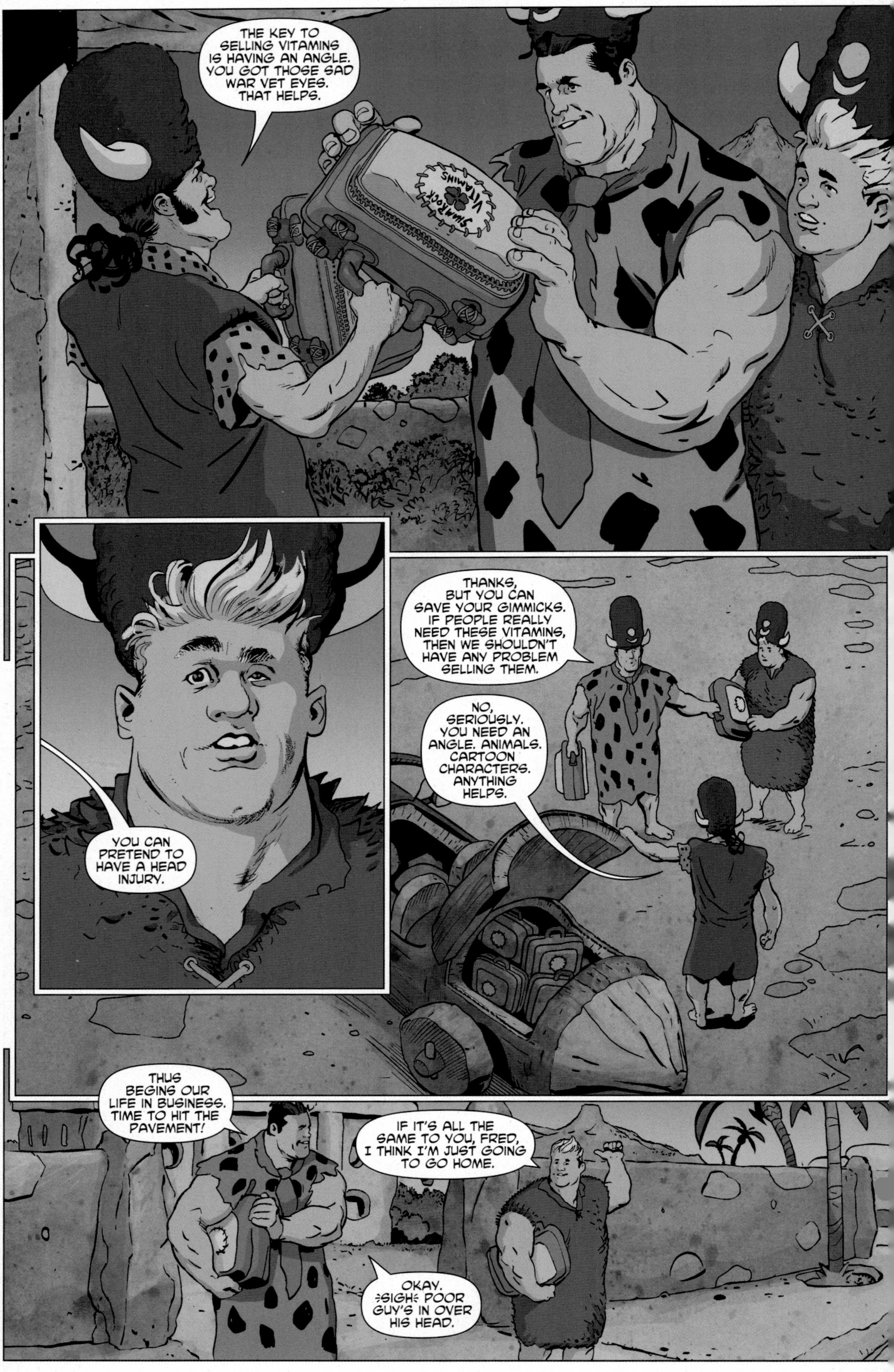
THE KEY TO SELLING VITAMINS IS HAVING AN ANGLE. YOU GOT THOSE SAD WAR VET EYES. THAT HELPS.
SHAMROCK VITAMINS
YOU CAN PRETEND TO HAVE A HEAD INJURY.
THANKS, BUT YOU CAN SAVE YOUR GIMMICKS. IF PEOPLE REALLY NEED THESE VITAMINS, THEN WE SHOULDN'T HAVE ANY PROBLEM SELLING THEM.
NO, SERIOUSLY. YOU NEED AN ANGLE. ANIMALS. CARTOON CHARACTERS. ANYTHING HELPS.
THUS BEGINS OUR LIFE IN BUSINESS. TIME TO HIT THE PAVEMENT!
IF IT'S ALL THE SAME TO YOU, FRED, I THINK I'M JUST GOING TO GO HOME.
OKAY. ⸗SIGH⸗ POOR GUY'S IN OVER HIS HEAD.

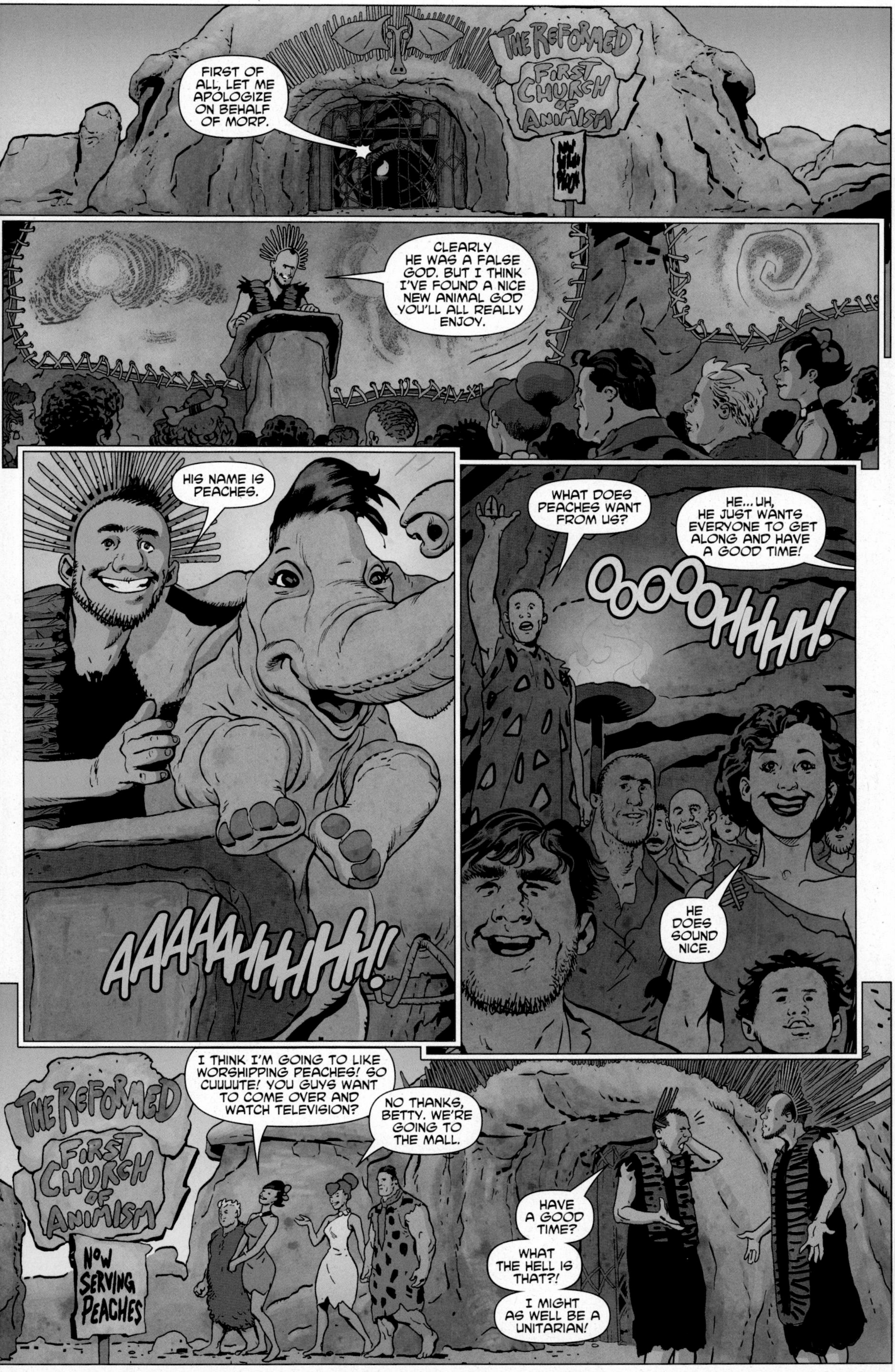
THE REFORMED FIRST CHURCH OF ANIMISM
FIRST OF ALL, LET ME APOLOGIZE ON BEHALF OF MORP.
CLEARLY HE WAS A FALSE GOD. BUT I THINK I'VE FOUND A NICE NEW ANIMAL GOD YOU'LL ALL REALLY ENJOY.
HIS NAME IS PEACHES.
AAAAHHHHH!
WHAT DOES PEACHES WANT FROM US?
HE... UH, HE JUST WANTS EVERYONE TO GET ALONG AND HAVE A GOOD TIME!
OOOOOHHHHH!
HE DOES SOUND NICE.
THE REFORMED FIRST CHURCH OF ANIMISM
NOW SERVING PEACHES
I THINK I'M GOING TO LIKE WORSHIPPING PEACHES! SO CUUUUTE! YOU GUYS WANT TO COME OVER AND WATCH TELEVISION?
NO THANKS, BETTY. WE'RE GOING TO THE MALL.
HAVE A GOOD TIME?
WHAT THE HELL IS THAT?!
I MIGHT AS WELL BE A UNITARIAN!

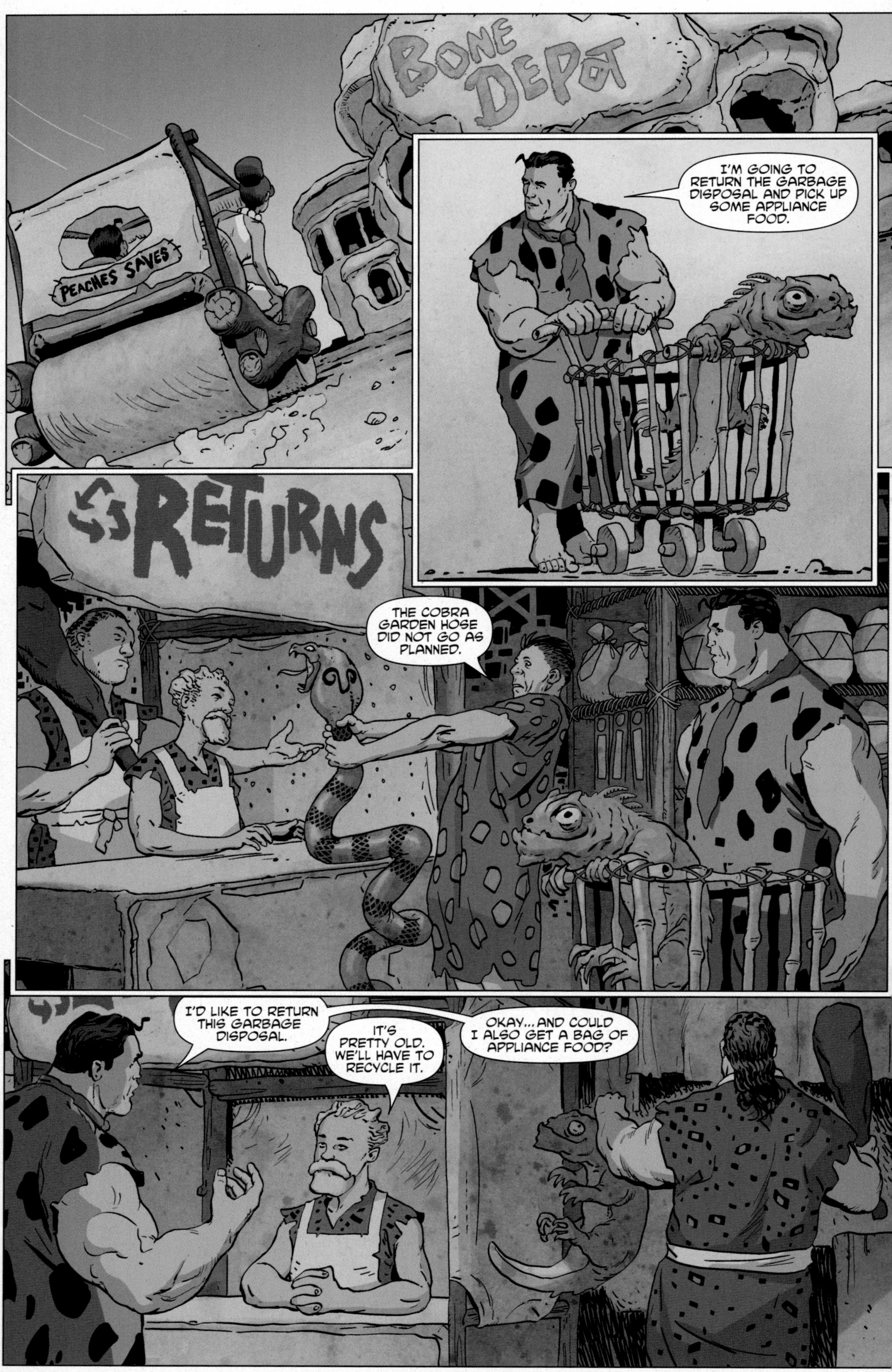
BONE DEPOT
PEACHES SAVES
I'M GOING TO RETURN THE GARBAGE DISPOSAL AND PICK UP SOME APPLIANCE FOOD.
RETURNS
THE COBRA GARDEN HOSE DID NOT GO AS PLANNED.
I'D LIKE TO RETURN THIS GARBAGE DISPOSAL.
IT'S PRETTY OLD. WE'LL HAVE TO RECYCLE IT.
OKAY... AND COULD I ALSO GET A BAG OF APPLIANCE FOOD?

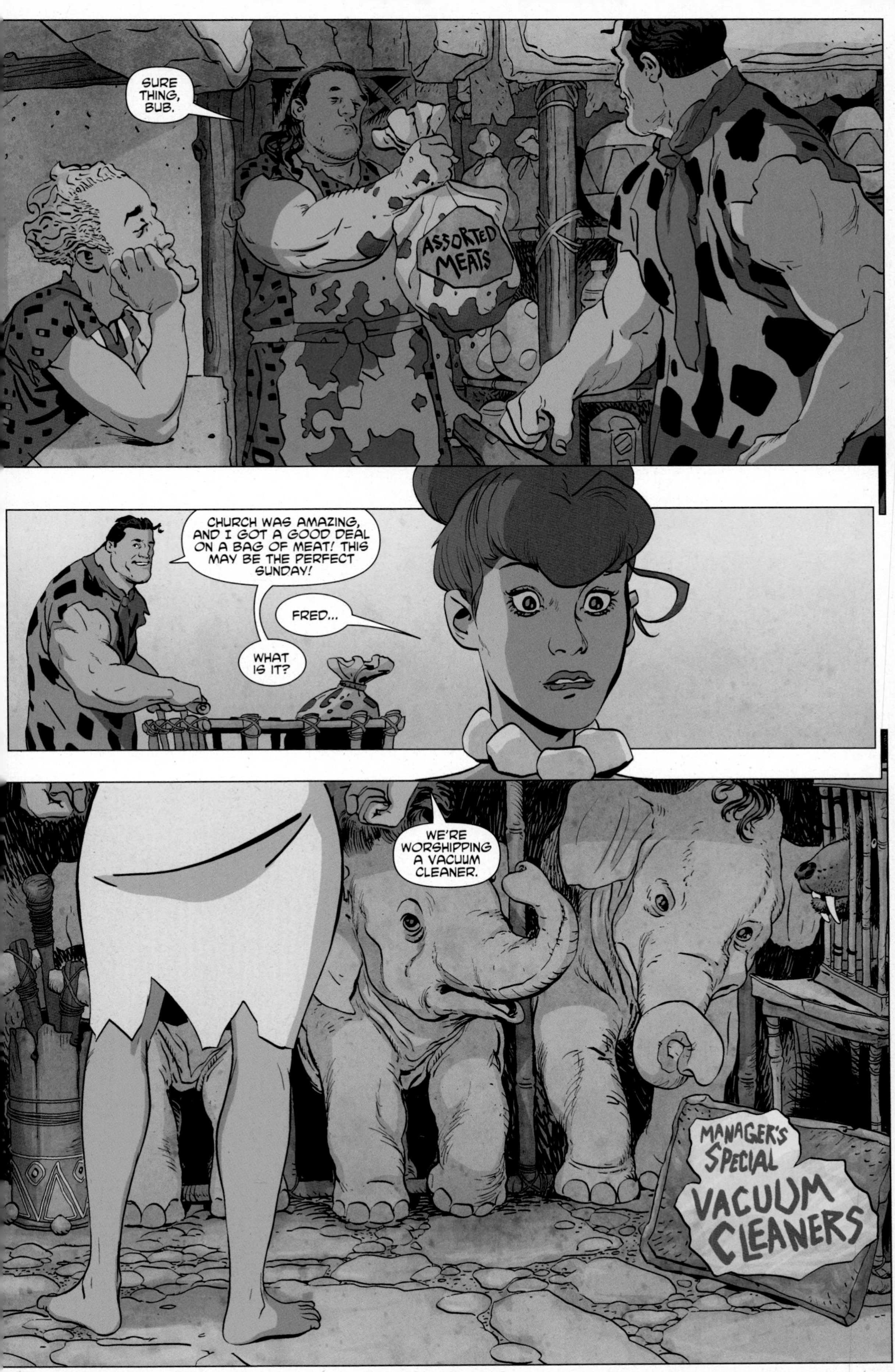
SURE THING, BUB.
ASSORTED MEATS
CHURCH WAS AMAZING, AND I GOT A GOOD DEAL ON A BAG OF MEAT! THIS MAY BE THE PERFECT SUNDAY!
FRED...
WHAT IS IT?
WE'RE WORSHIPPING A VACUUM CLEANER.
MANAGER'S SPECIAL VACUUM CLEANERS

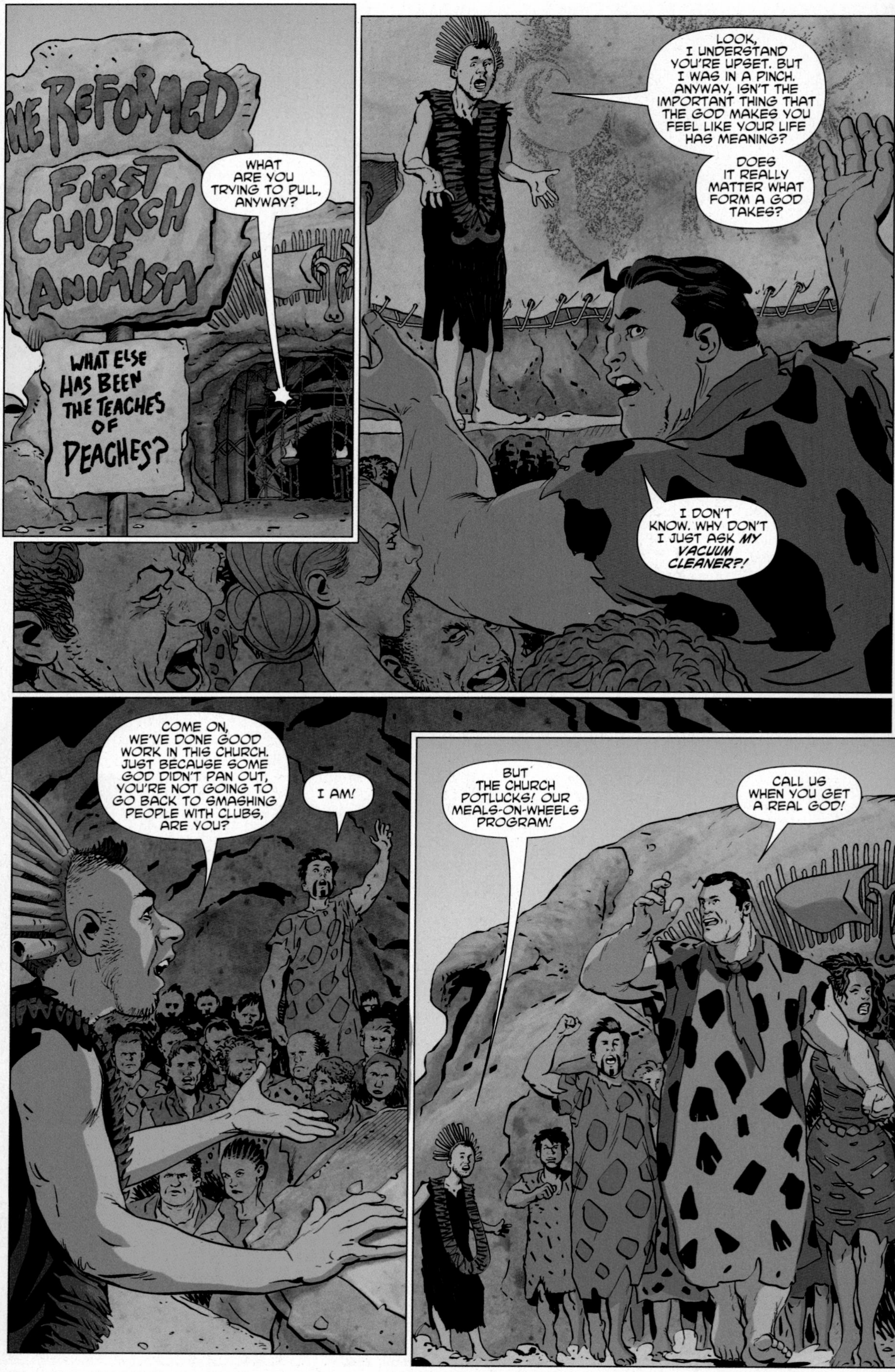

THE REFORMED FIRST CHURCH OF ANIMISM
WHAT ELSE HAS BEEN THE TEACHES OF PEACHES?
WHAT ARE YOU TRYING TO PULL, ANYWAY?
LOOK, I UNDERSTAND YOU'RE UPSET. BUT I WAS IN A PINCH. ANYWAY, ISN'T THE IMPORTANT THING THAT THE GOD MAKES YOU FEEL LIKE YOUR LIFE HAS MEANING?
DOES IT REALLY MATTER WHAT FORM A GOD TAKES?
I DON'T KNOW. WHY DON'T I JUST ASK MY VACUUM CLEANER?!
COME ON, WE'VE DONE GOOD WORK IN THIS CHURCH. JUST BECAUSE SOME GOD DIDN'T PAN OUT, YOU'RE NOT GOING TO GO BACK TO SMASHING PEOPLE WITH CLUBS, ARE YOU?
I AM!
BUT THE CHURCH POTLUCKS! OUR MEALS-ON-WHEELS PROGRAM!
CALL US WHEN YOU GET A REAL GOD!

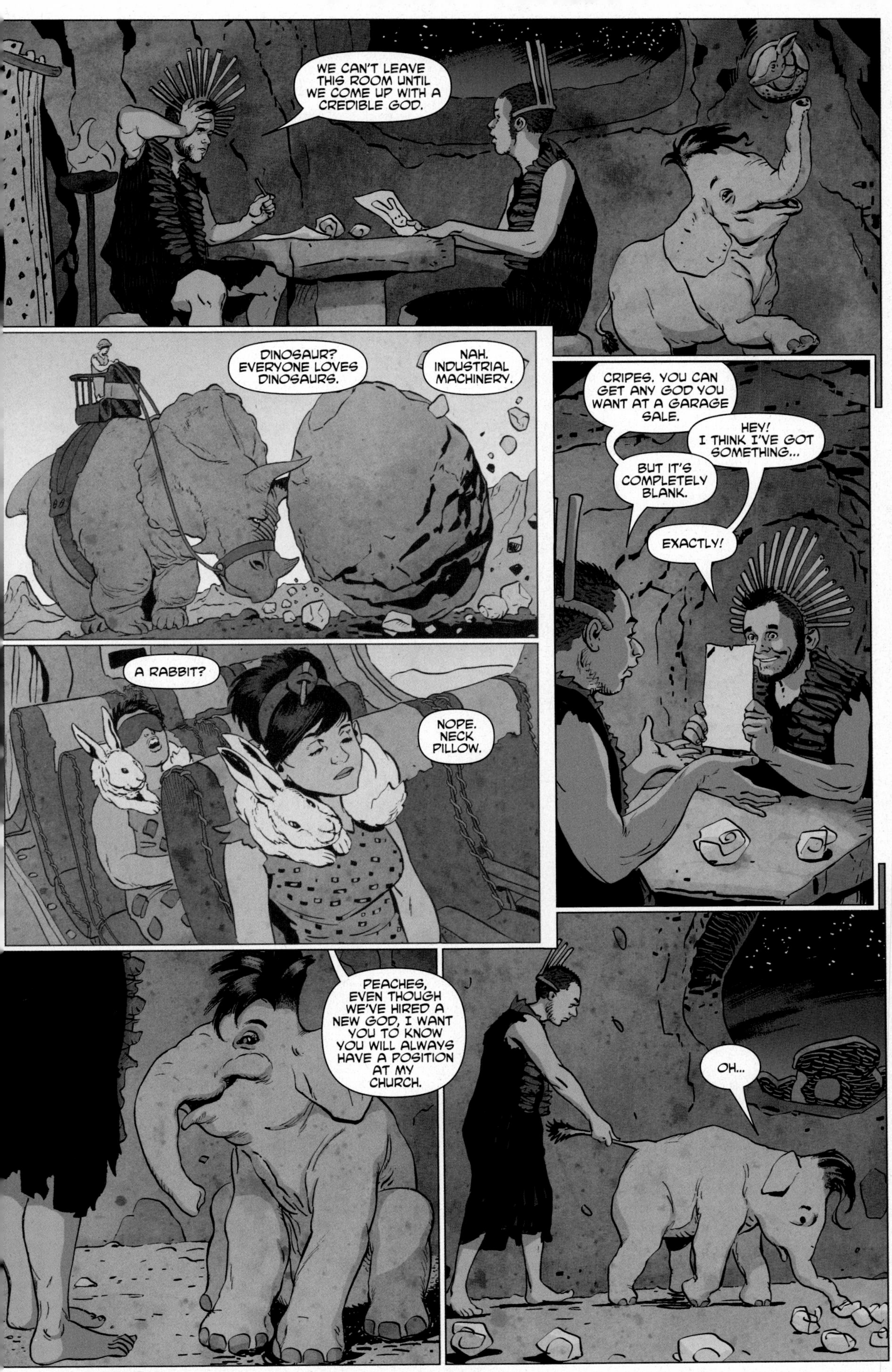
WE CAN'T LEAVE THIS ROOM UNTIL WE COME UP WITH A CREDIBLE GOD.
DINOSAUR? EVERYONE LOVES DINOSAURS.
NAH. INDUSTRIAL MACHINERY.
A RABBIT?
NOPE. NECK PILLOW.
CRIPES. YOU CAN GET ANY GOD YOU WANT AT A GARAGE SALE.
HEY! I THINK I'VE GOT SOMETHING...
BUT IT'S COMPLETELY BLANK.
EXACTLY!
PEACHES, EVEN THOUGH WE'VE HIRED A NEW GOD, I WANT YOU TO KNOW YOU WILL ALWAYS HAVE A POSITION AT MY CHURCH.
OH...

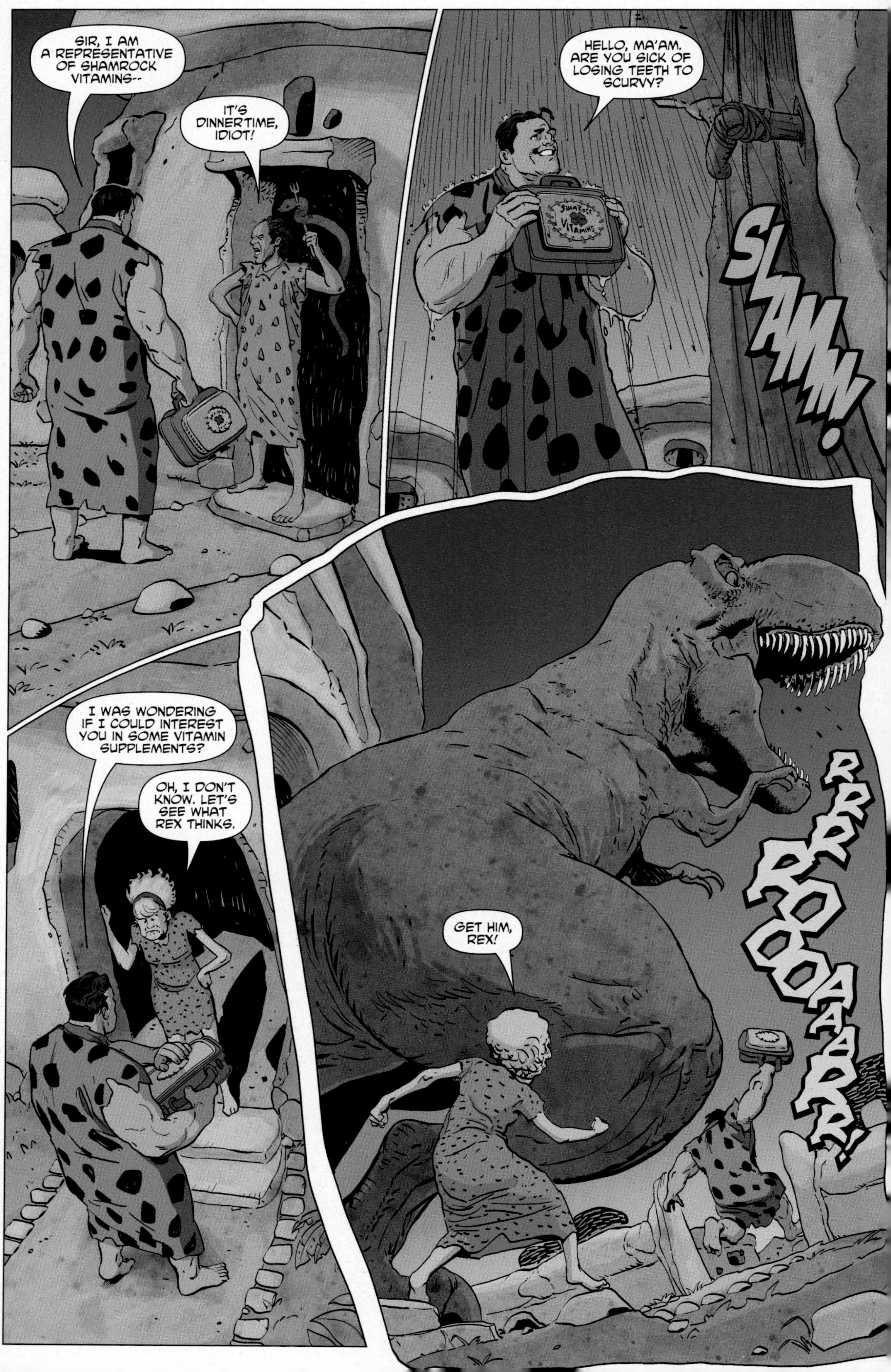

SIR, I AM A REPRESENTATIVE OF SHAMROCK VITAMINS--
IT'S DINNERTIME, IDIOT!
SHAMROCK VITAMINS
HELLO, MA'AM. ARE YOU SICK OF LOSING TEETH TO SCURVY?
SLAMM!
I WAS WONDERING IF I COULD INTEREST YOU IN SOME VITAMIN SUPPLEMENTS?
OH, I DON'T KNOW. LET'S SEE WHAT REX THINKS.
GET HIM, REX!
RRROOOOAAARR!

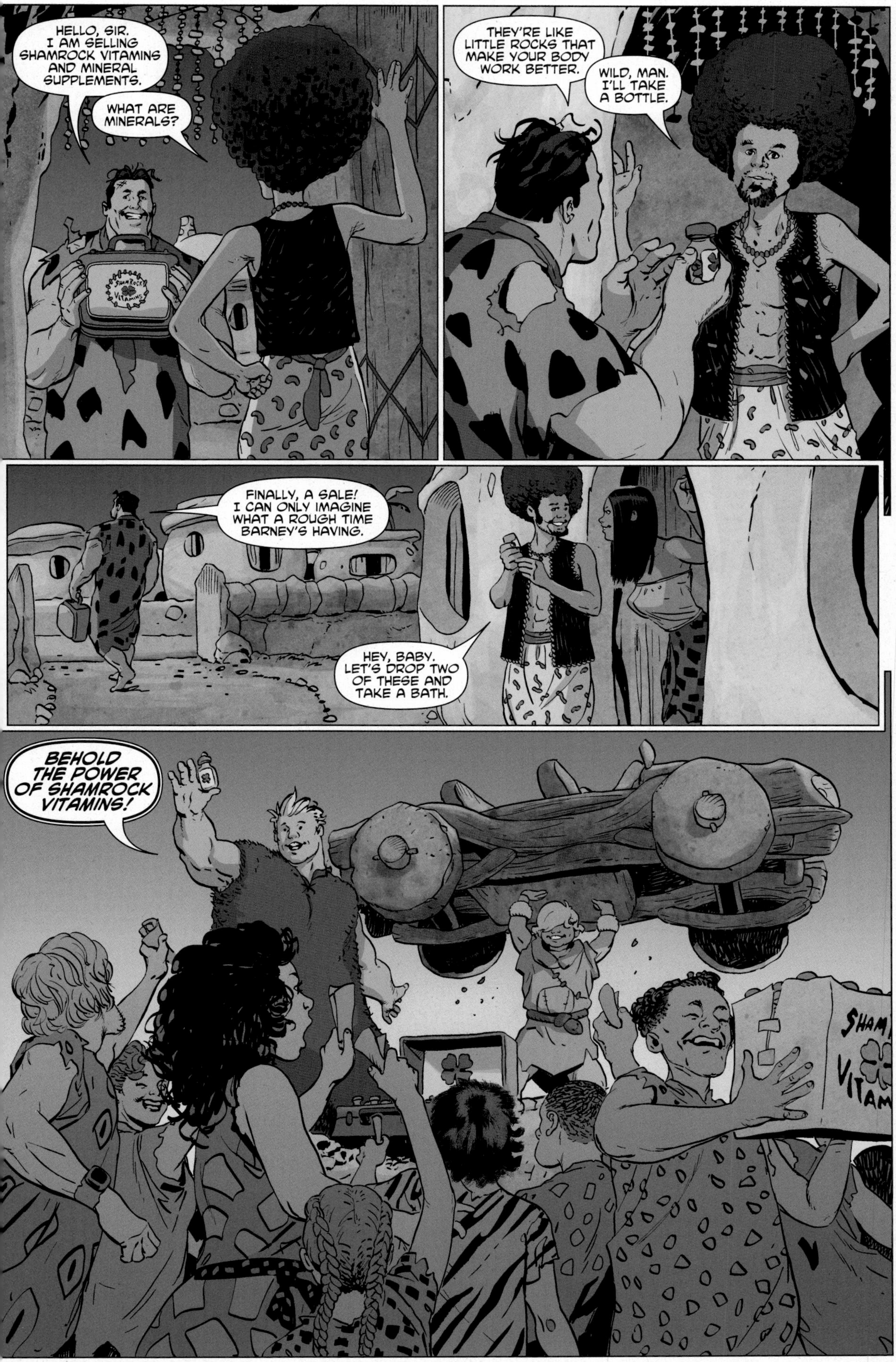
HELLO, SIR. I AM SELLING SHAMROCK VITAMINS AND MINERAL SUPPLEMENTS.
WHAT ARE MINERALS?
SHAMROCK VITAMINS
THEY'RE LIKE LITTLE ROCKS THAT MAKE YOUR BODY WORK BETTER.
WILD, MAN. I'LL TAKE A BOTTLE.
FINALLY, A SALE! I CAN ONLY IMAGINE WHAT A ROUGH TIME BARNEY'S HAVING.
HEY, BABY. LET'S DROP TWO OF THESE AND TAKE A BATH.
BEHOLD THE POWER OF SHAMROCK VITAMINS!

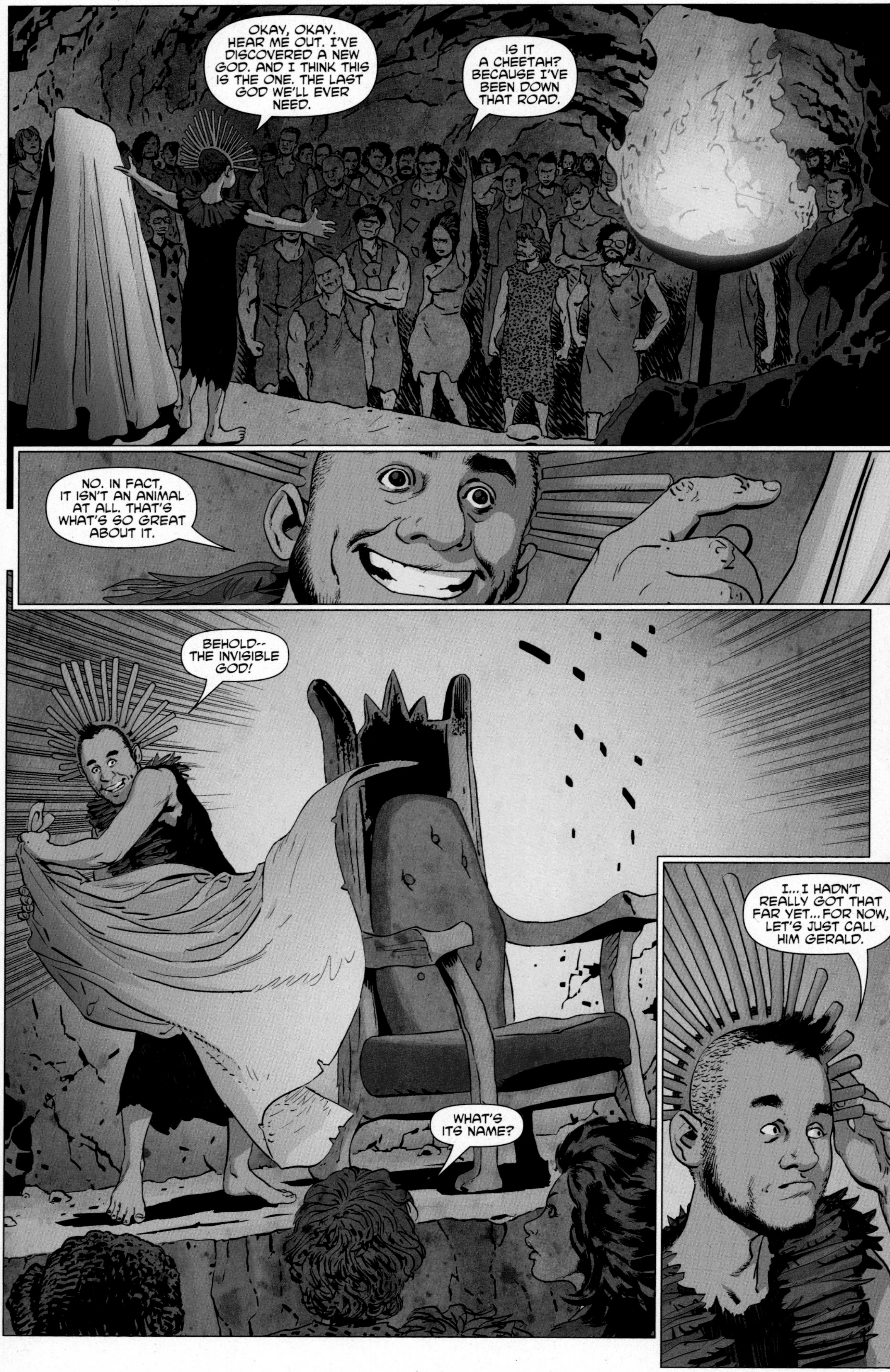

OKAY, OKAY. HEAR ME OUT. I'VE DISCOVERED A NEW GOD. AND I THINK THIS IS THE ONE. THE LAST GOD WE'LL EVER NEED.
IS IT A CHEETAH? BECAUSE I'VE BEEN DOWN THAT ROAD.
NO. IN FACT, IT ISN'T AN ANIMAL AT ALL. THAT'S WHAT'S SO GREAT ABOUT IT.
BEHOLD-- THE INVISIBLE GOD!
WHAT'S ITS NAME?
I...I HADN'T REALLY GOT THAT FAR YET...FOR NOW, LET'S JUST CALL HIM GERALD.

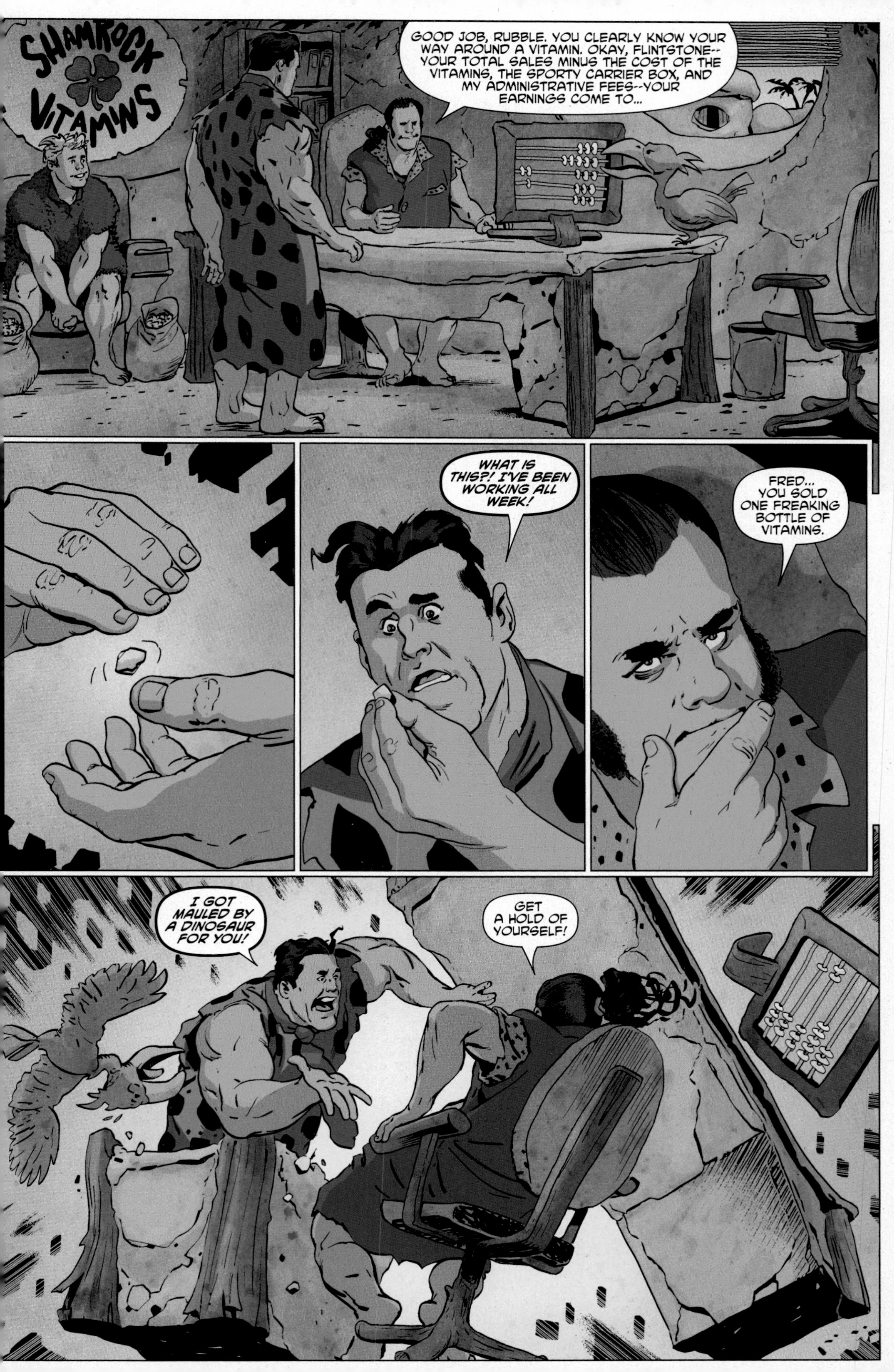
SHAMROCK VITAMINS
GOOD JOB, RUBBLE. YOU CLEARLY KNOW YOUR WAY AROUND A VITAMIN. OKAY, FLINTSTONE--YOUR TOTAL SALES MINUS THE COST OF THE VITAMINS, THE SPORTY CARRIER BOX, AND MY ADMINISTRATIVE FEES--YOUR EARNINGS COME TO...
WHAT IS THIS?! I'VE BEEN WORKING ALL WEEK!
FRED... YOU SOLD ONE FREAKING BOTTLE OF VITAMINS.
I GOT MAULED BY A DINOSAUR FOR YOU!
GET A HOLD OF YOURSELF!

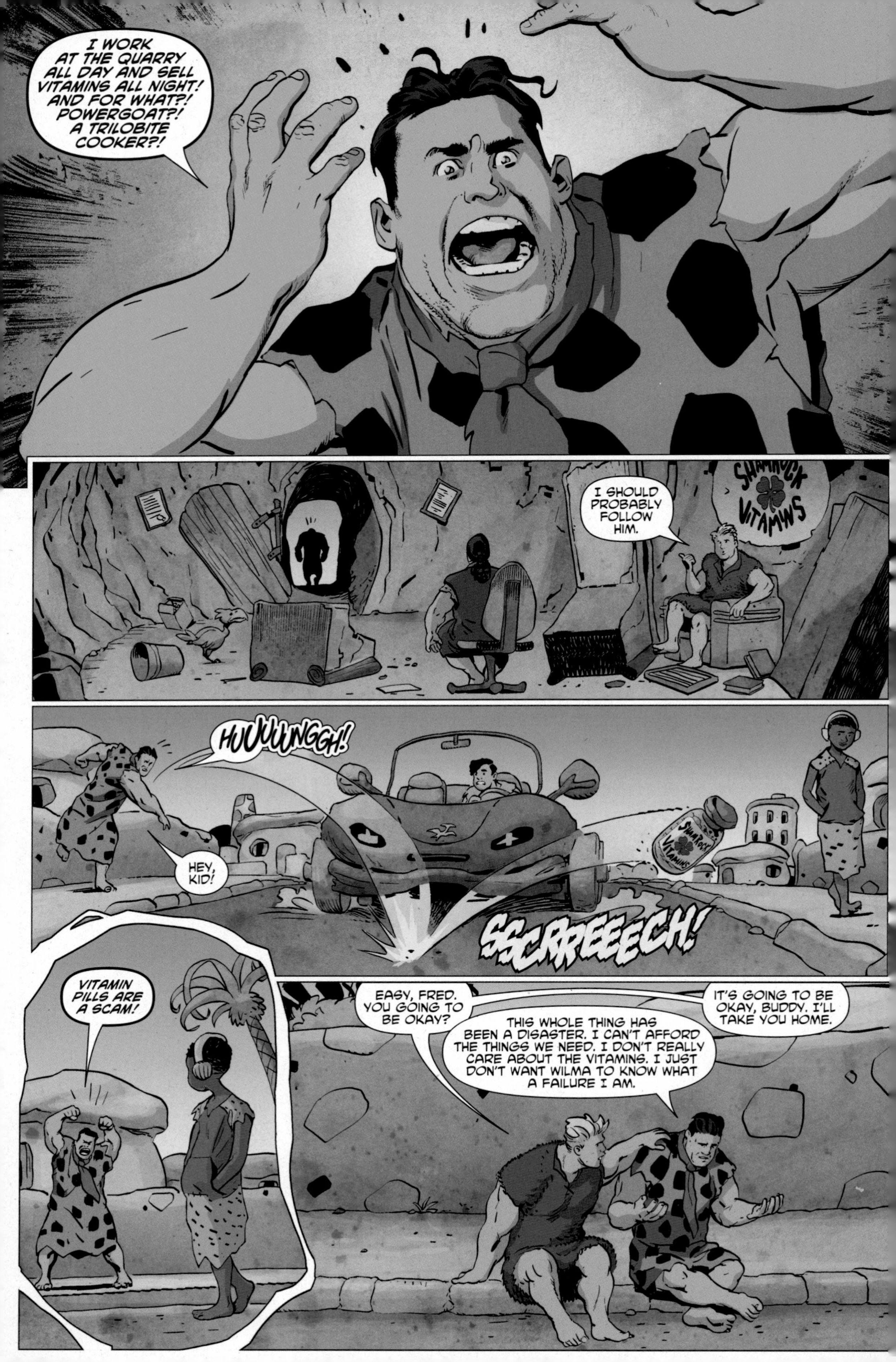
I WORK AT THE QUARRY ALL DAY AND SELL VITAMINS ALL NIGHT! AND FOR WHAT?! POWERGOAT?! A TRILOBITE COOKER?!
SHAMROCK VITAMINS
I SHOULD PROBABLY FOLLOW HIM.
HUUUUUNGGH!
HEY, KID!
SHAMROCK VITAMINS
SSCRREEEECH!
VITAMIN PILLS ARE A SCAM!
EASY, FRED. YOU GOING TO BE OKAY?
IT'S GOING TO BE OKAY, BUDDY. I'LL TAKE YOU HOME.
THIS WHOLE THING HAS BEEN A DISASTER. I CAN'T AFFORD THE THINGS WE NEED. I DON'T REALLY CARE ABOUT THE VITAMINS. I JUST DON'T WANT WILMA TO KNOW WHAT A FAILURE I AM.

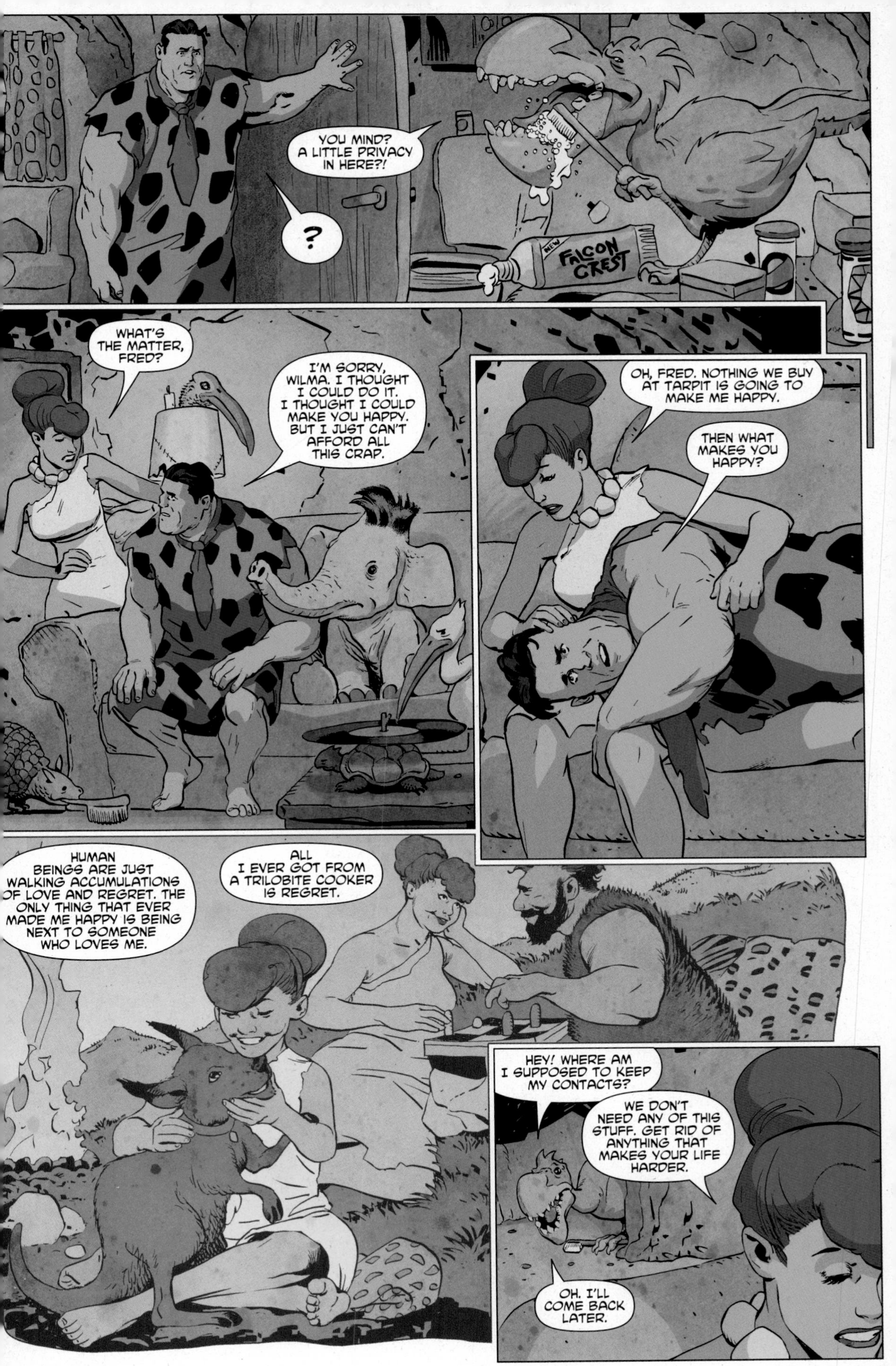
YOU MIND? A LITTLE PRIVACY IN HERE?!
?
FALCON CREST
NEW
WHAT'S THE MATTER, FRED?
I'M SORRY, WILMA. I THOUGHT I COULD DO IT. I THOUGHT I COULD MAKE YOU HAPPY. BUT I JUST CAN'T AFFORD ALL THIS CRAP.
OH, FRED. NOTHING WE BUY AT TARPIT IS GOING TO MAKE ME HAPPY.
THEN WHAT MAKES YOU HAPPY?
HUMAN BEINGS ARE JUST WALKING ACCUMULATIONS OF LOVE AND REGRET. THE ONLY THING THAT EVER MADE ME HAPPY IS BEING NEXT TO SOMEONE WHO LOVES ME.
ALL I EVER GOT FROM A TRILOBITE COOKER IS REGRET.
HEY! WHERE AM I SUPPOSED TO KEEP MY CONTACTS?
WE DON'T NEED ANY OF THIS STUFF. GET RID OF ANYTHING THAT MAKES YOUR LIFE HARDER.
OH. I'LL COME BACK LATER.

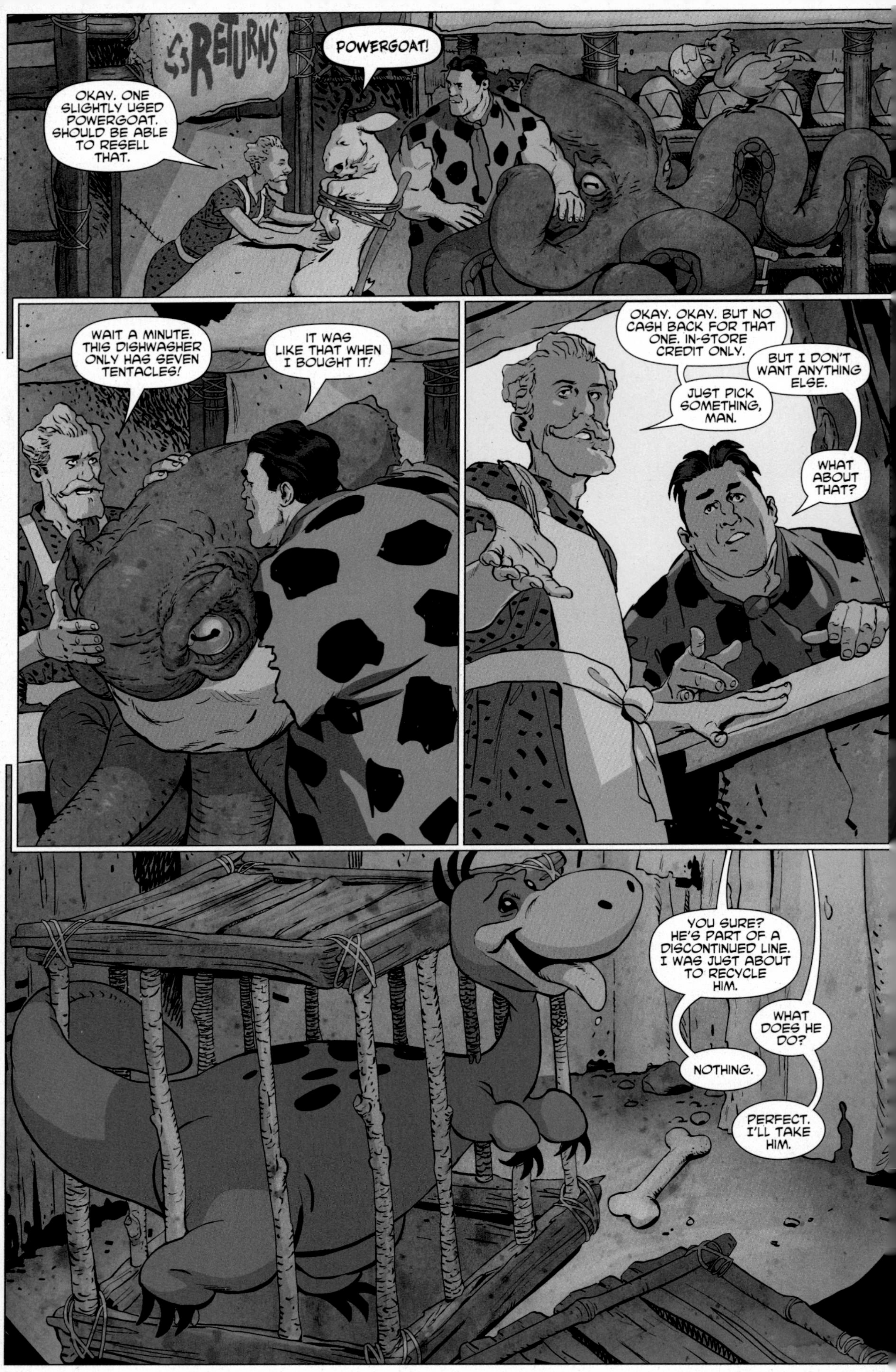

RETURNS
POWERGOAT!
OKAY. ONE SLIGHTLY USED POWERGOAT. SHOULD BE ABLE TO RESELL THAT.
WAIT A MINUTE. THIS DISHWASHER ONLY HAS SEVEN TENTACLES!
IT WAS LIKE THAT WHEN I BOUGHT IT!
OKAY. OKAY. BUT NO CASH BACK FOR THAT ONE. IN-STORE CREDIT ONLY.
BUT I DON'T WANT ANYTHING ELSE.
JUST PICK SOMETHING, MAN.
WHAT ABOUT THAT?
YOU SURE? HE'S PART OF A DISCONTINUED LINE. I WAS JUST ABOUT TO RECYCLE HIM.
WHAT DOES HE DO?
NOTHING.
PERFECT. I'LL TAKE HIM.

THE FLINTSTONES #3 cover by BEN CALDWELL

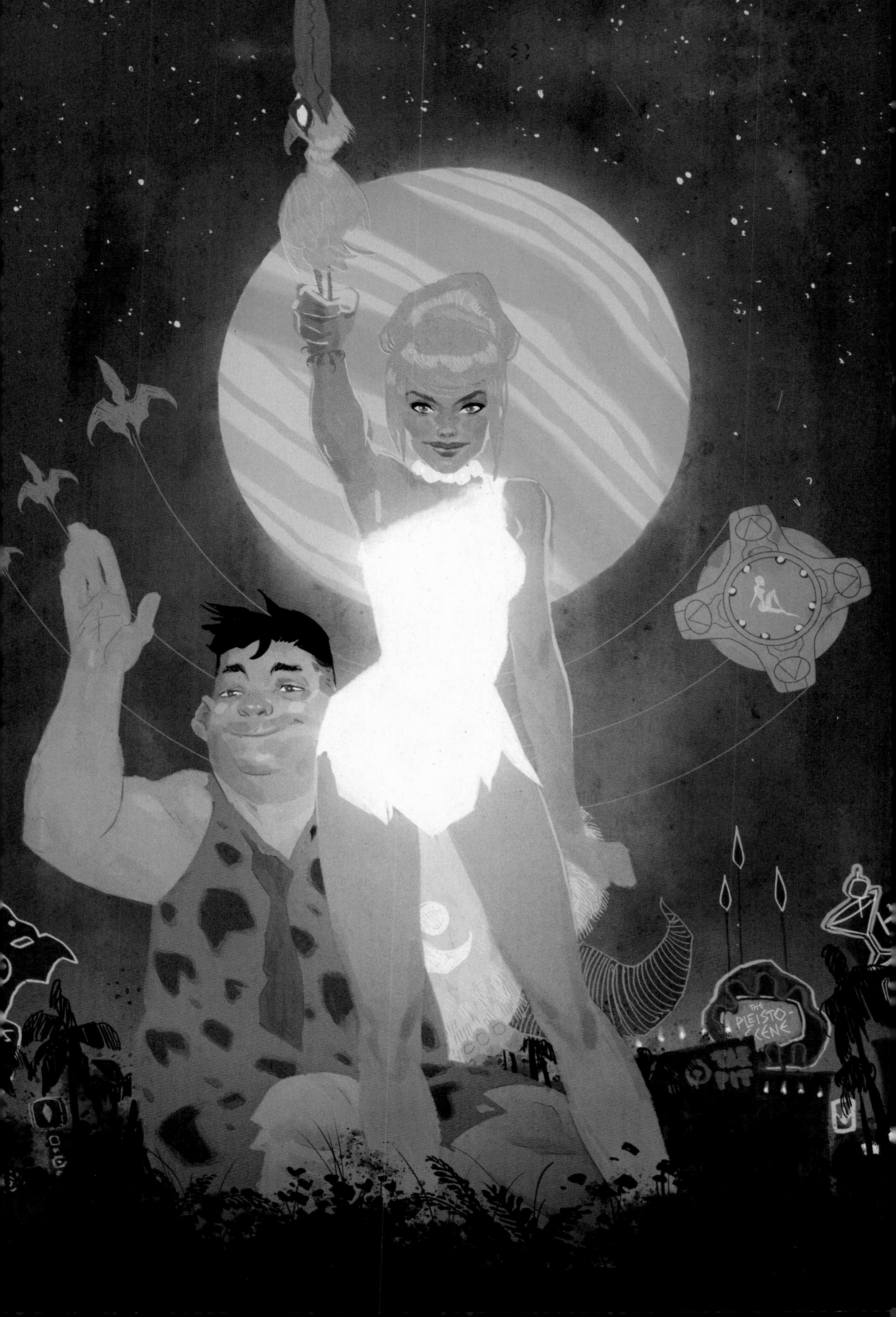

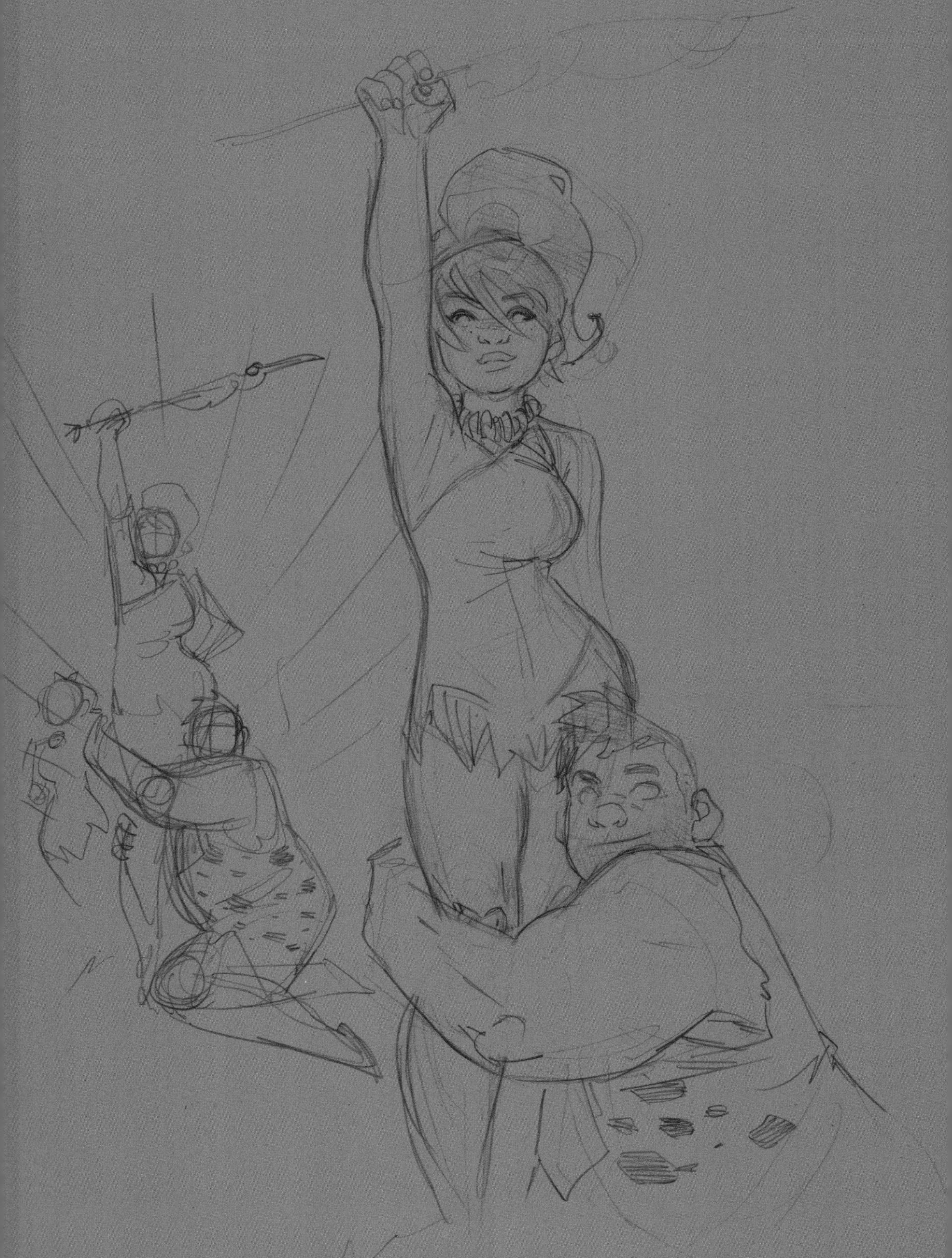

DCCO37858

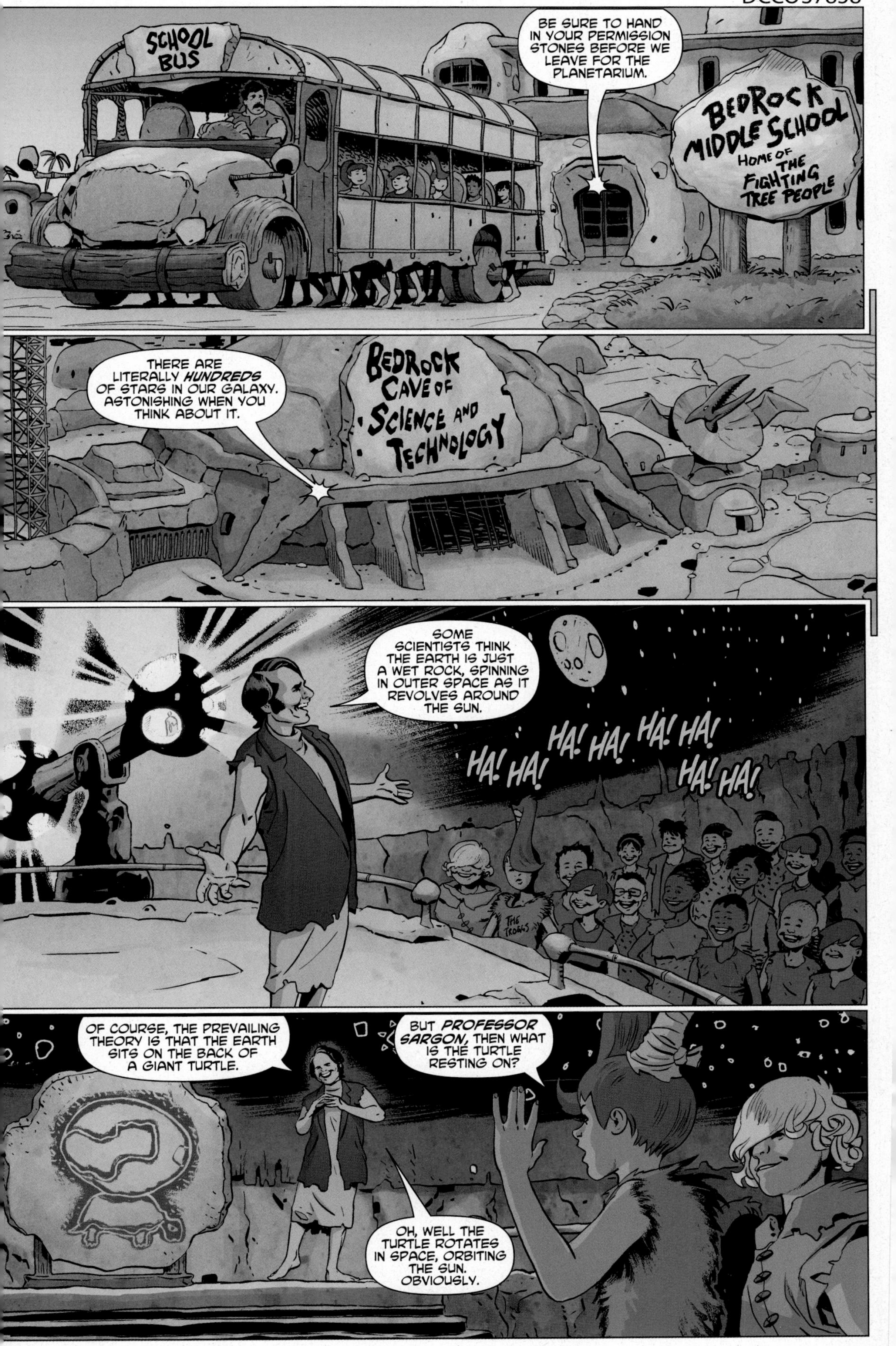
SCHOOL BUS
BE SURE TO HAND IN YOUR PERMISSION STONES BEFORE WE LEAVE FOR THE PLANETARIUM.
BEDROCK MIDDLE SCHOOL HOME OF THE FIGHTING TREE PEOPLE
BEDROCK CAVE OF SCIENCE AND TECHNOLOGY
THERE ARE LITERALLY HUNDREDS OF STARS IN OUR GALAXY. ASTONISHING WHEN YOU THINK ABOUT IT.
SOME SCIENTISTS THINK THE EARTH IS JUST A WET ROCK, SPINNING IN OUTER SPACE AS IT REVOLVES AROUND THE SUN.
HA! HA! HA! HA! HA! HA! HA! HA!
THE TROGGS
OF COURSE, THE PREVAILING THEORY IS THAT THE EARTH SITS ON THE BACK OF A GIANT TURTLE.
BUT PROFESSOR SARGON, THEN WHAT IS THE TURTLE RESTING ON?
OH, WELL THE TURTLE ROTATES IN SPACE, ORBITING THE SUN. OBVIOUSLY.

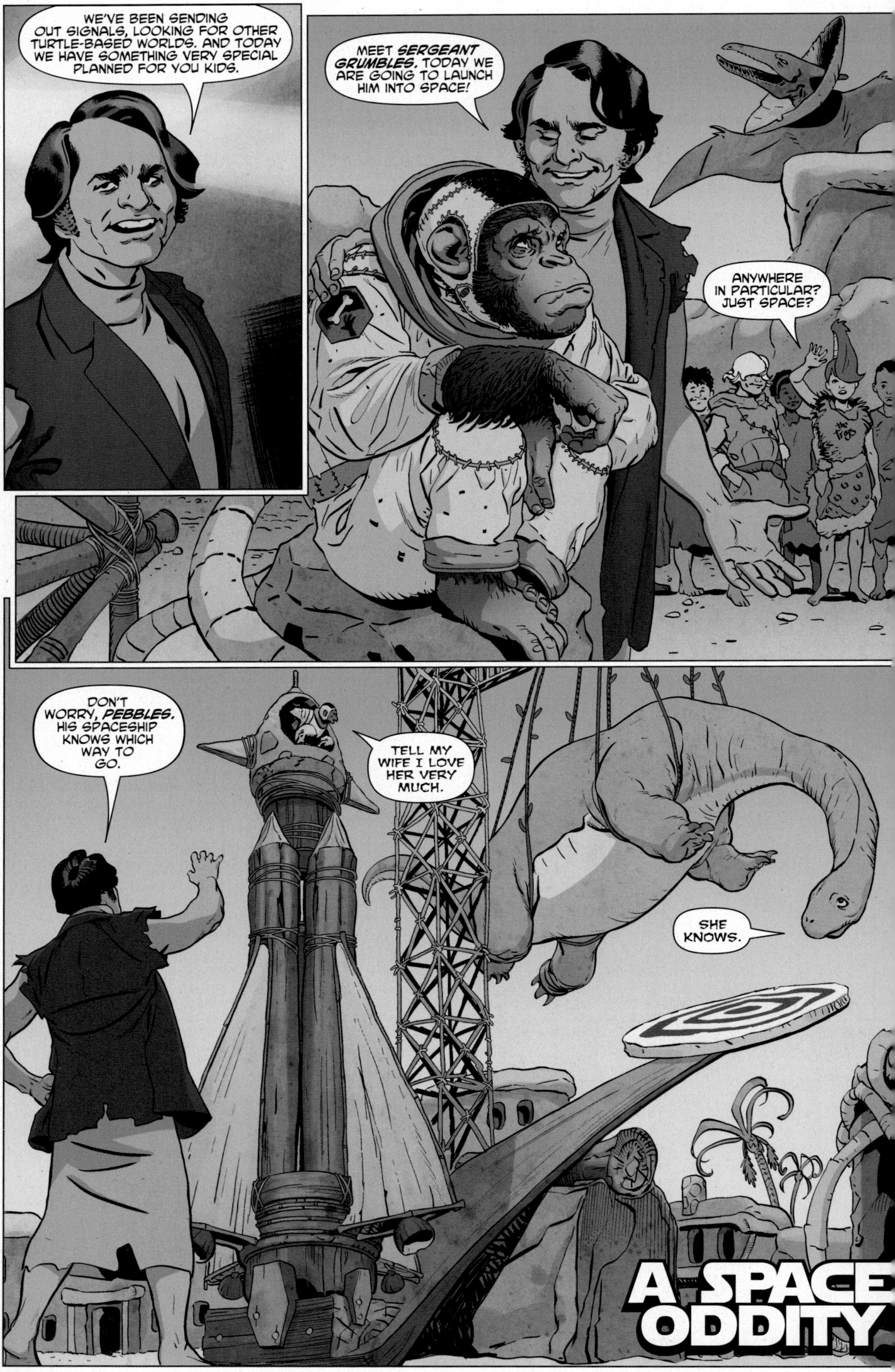
WE'VE BEEN SENDING OUT SIGNALS, LOOKING FOR OTHER TURTLE-BASED WORLDS. AND TODAY WE HAVE SOMETHING VERY SPECIAL PLANNED FOR YOU KIDS.
MEET SERGEANT GRUMBLES. TODAY WE ARE GOING TO LAUNCH HIM INTO SPACE!
ANYWHERE IN PARTICULAR? JUST SPACE?
DON'T WORRY, PEBBLES. HIS SPACESHIP KNOWS WHICH WAY TO GO.
TELL MY WIFE I LOVE HER VERY MUCH.
SHE KNOWS.
A SPACE ODDITY

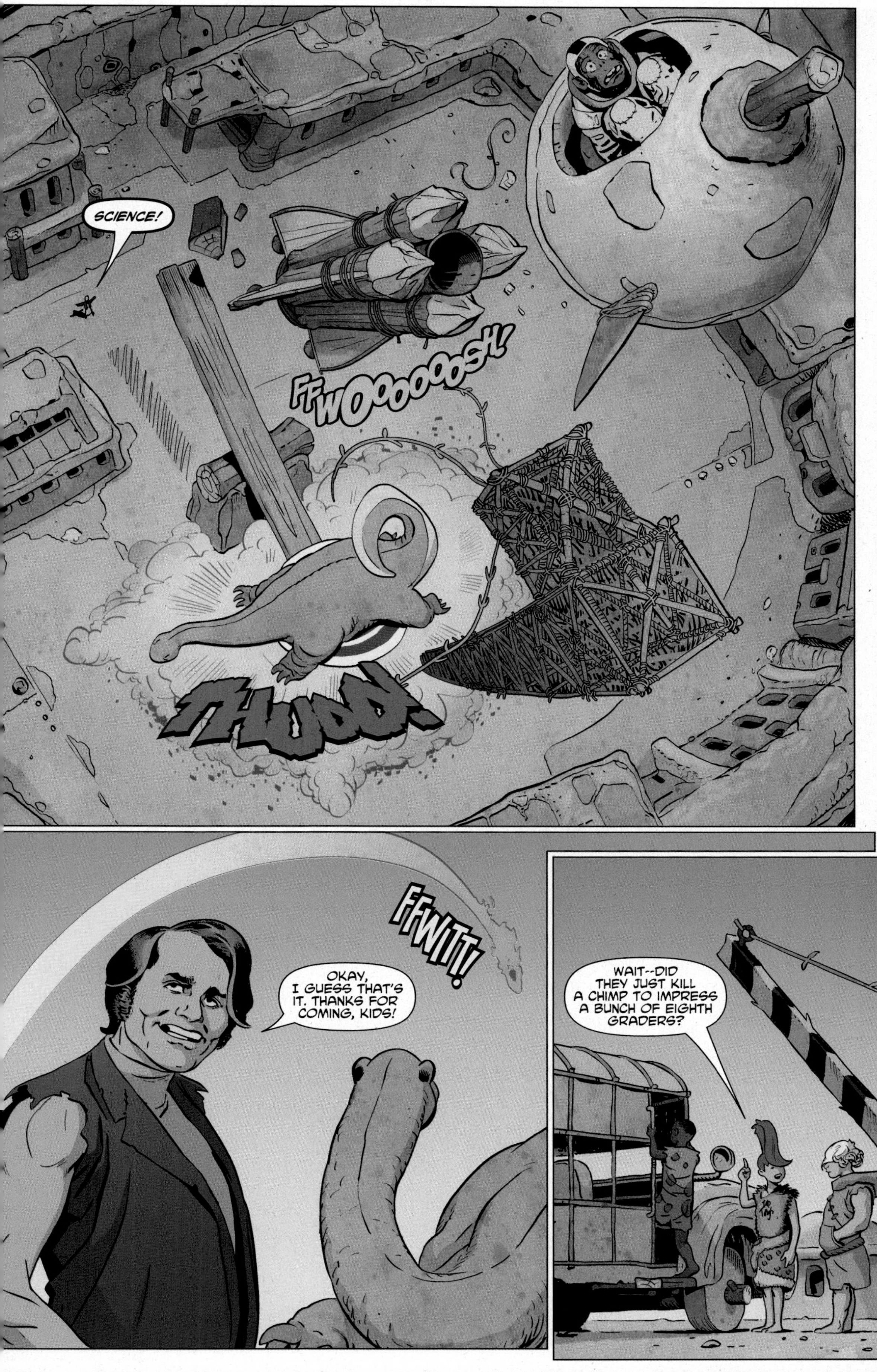
SCIENCE!
FFWOOOOOOSH!
THUDD!
FFWITT!
OKAY, I GUESS THAT'S IT. THANKS FOR COMING, KIDS!
WAIT--DID THEY JUST KILL A CHIMP TO IMPRESS A BUNCH OF EIGHTH GRADERS?

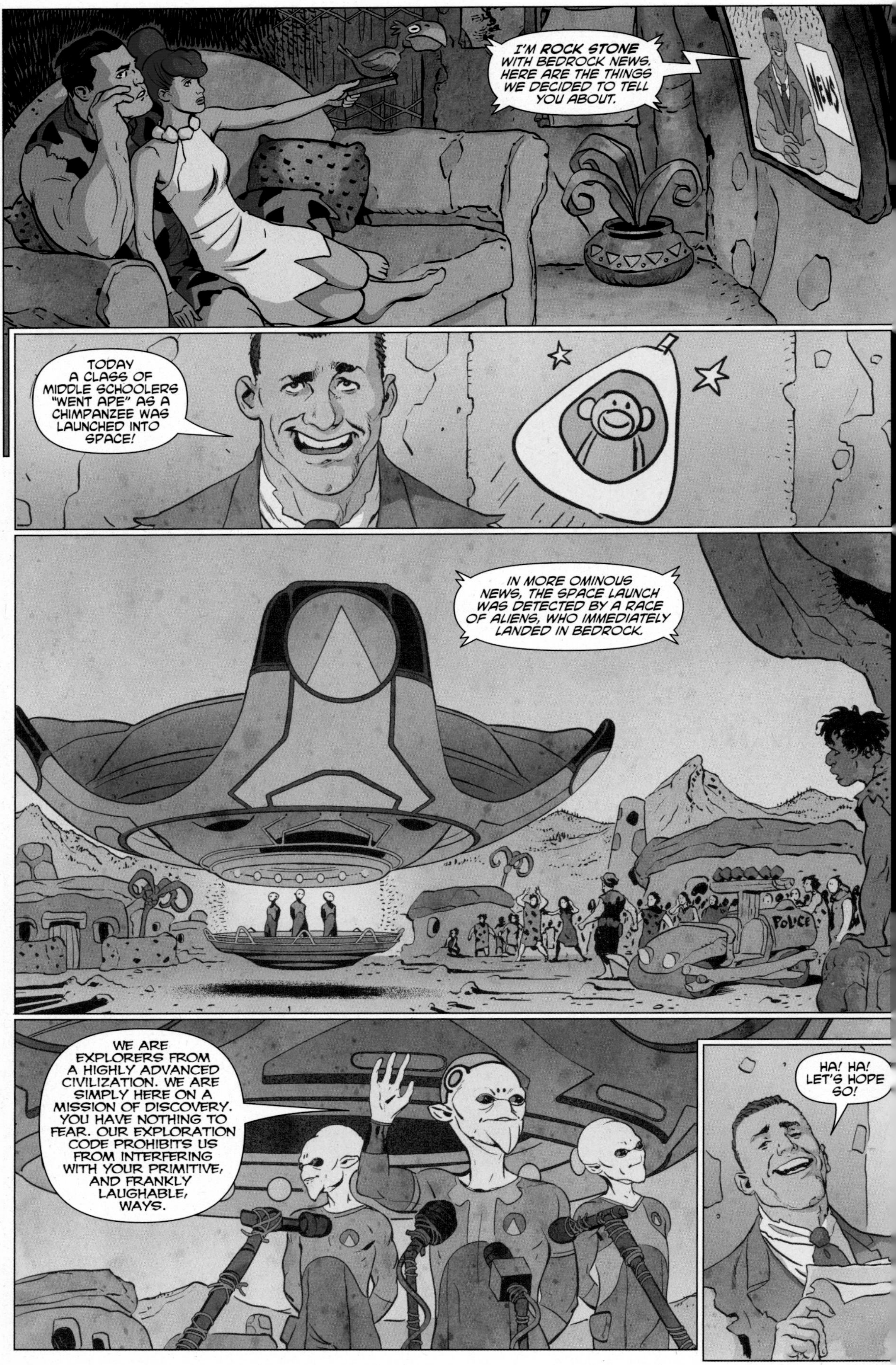
I'M ROCK STONE WITH BEDROCK NEWS. HERE ARE THE THINGS WE DECIDED TO TELL YOU ABOUT.
NEWS
TODAY A CLASS OF MIDDLE SCHOOLERS "WENT APE" AS A CHIMPANZEE WAS LAUNCHED INTO SPACE!
IN MORE OMINOUS NEWS, THE SPACE LAUNCH WAS DETECTED BY A RACE OF ALIENS, WHO IMMEDIATELY LANDED IN BEDROCK.
POLICE
WE ARE EXPLORERS FROM A HIGHLY ADVANCED CIVILIZATION. WE ARE SIMPLY HERE ON A MISSION OF DISCOVERY. YOU HAVE NOTHING TO FEAR. OUR EXPLORATION CODE PROHIBITS US FROM INTERFERING WITH YOUR PRIMITIVE, AND FRANKLY LAUGHABLE, WAYS.
HA! HA! LET'S HOPE SO!

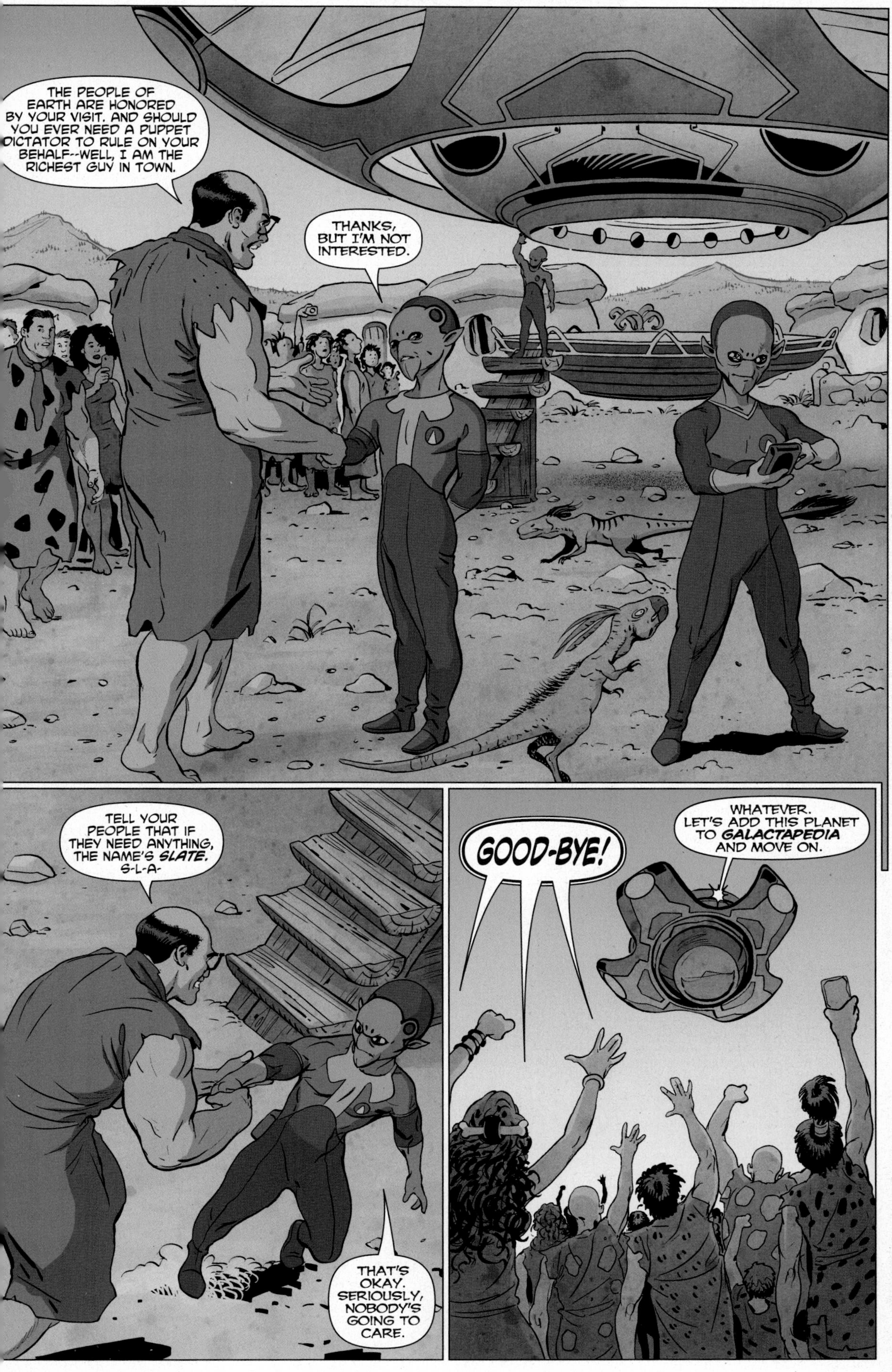
THE PEOPLE OF EARTH ARE HONORED BY YOUR VISIT. AND SHOULD YOU EVER NEED A PUPPET DICTATOR TO RULE ON YOUR BEHALF--WELL, I AM THE RICHEST GUY IN TOWN.
THANKS, BUT I'M NOT INTERESTED.
TELL YOUR PEOPLE THAT IF THEY NEED ANYTHING, THE NAME'S SLATE. S-L-A-
THAT'S OKAY. SERIOUSLY, NOBODY'S GOING TO CARE.
GOOD-BYE!
WHATEVER. LET'S ADD THIS PLANET TO GALACTAPEDIA AND MOVE ON.

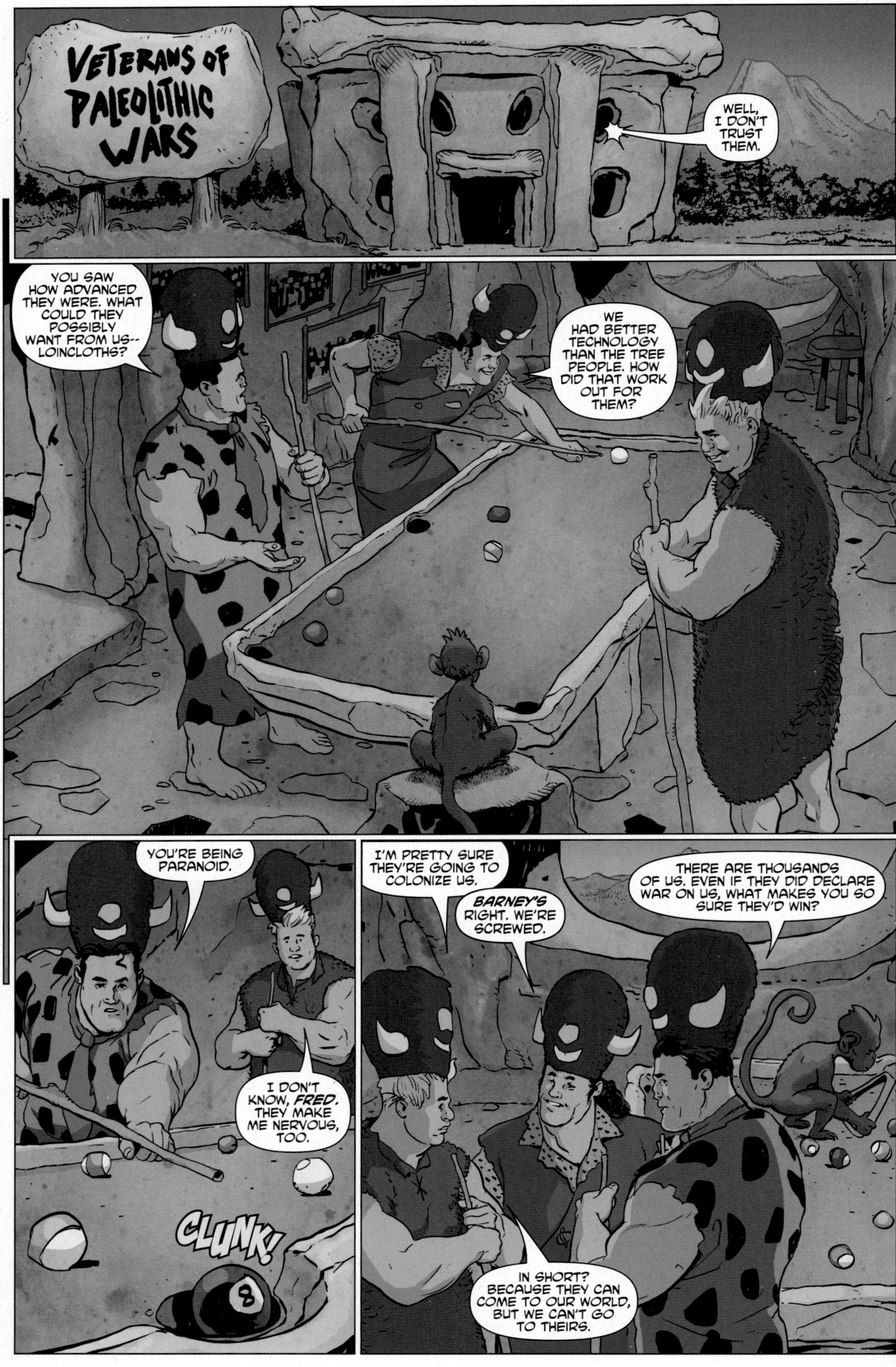
VETERANS OF PALEOLITHIC WARS
WELL, I DON'T TRUST THEM.
YOU SAW HOW ADVANCED THEY WERE. WHAT COULD THEY POSSIBLY WANT FROM US-- LOINCLOTHS?
WE HAD BETTER TECHNOLOGY THAN THE TREE PEOPLE. HOW DID THAT WORK OUT FOR THEM?
YOU'RE BEING PARANOID.
I DON'T KNOW, *FRED*. THEY MAKE ME NERVOUS, TOO.
CLUNK!
8
I'M PRETTY SURE THEY'RE GOING TO COLONIZE US.
BARNEY'S RIGHT. WE'RE SCREWED.
THERE ARE THOUSANDS OF US. EVEN IF THEY DID DECLARE WAR ON US, WHAT MAKES YOU SO SURE THEY'D WIN?
IN SHORT? BECAUSE THEY CAN COME TO OUR WORLD, BUT WE CAN'T GO TO THEIRS.

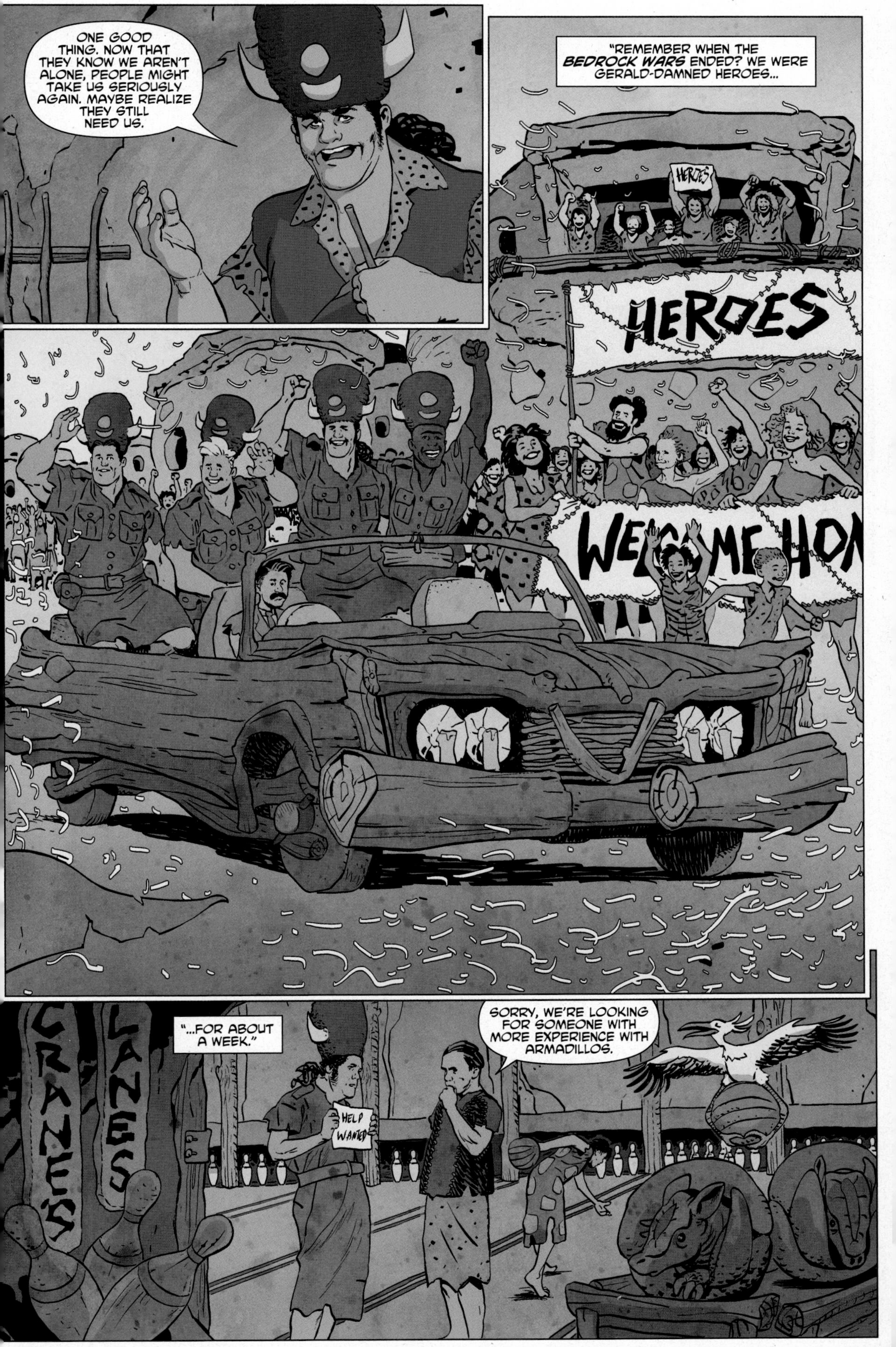

ONE GOOD THING. NOW THAT THEY KNOW WE AREN'T ALONE, PEOPLE MIGHT TAKE US SERIOUSLY AGAIN. MAYBE REALIZE THEY STILL NEED US.
"REMEMBER WHEN THE *BEDROCK WARS* ENDED? WE WERE GERALD-DAMNED HEROES...
HEROES
HEROES
WELCOME HOM
"...FOR ABOUT A WEEK."
SORRY, WE'RE LOOKING FOR SOMEONE WITH MORE EXPERIENCE WITH ARMADILLOS.
CRANES
LANES
HELP WANTED

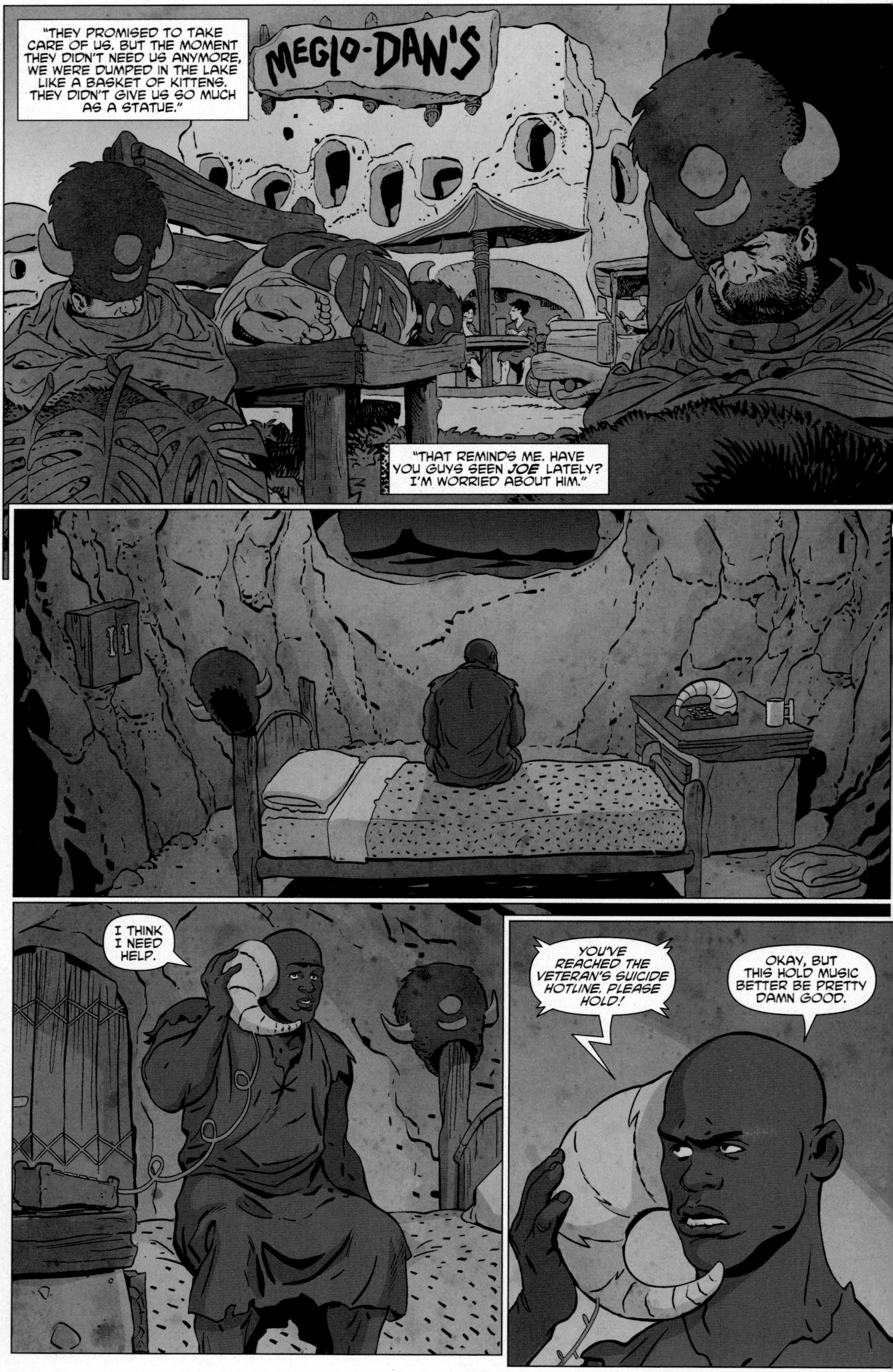
"THEY PROMISED TO TAKE CARE OF US. BUT THE MOMENT THEY DIDN'T NEED US ANYMORE, WE WERE DUMPED IN THE LAKE LIKE A BASKET OF KITTENS. THEY DIDN'T GIVE US SO MUCH AS A STATUE."
MEGLO-DAN'S
"THAT REMINDS ME. HAVE YOU GUYS SEEN JOE LATELY? I'M WORRIED ABOUT HIM."
I THINK I NEED HELP.
YOU'VE REACHED THE VETERAN'S SUICIDE HOTLINE. PLEASE HOLD!
OKAY, BUT THIS HOLD MUSIC BETTER BE PRETTY DAMN GOOD.

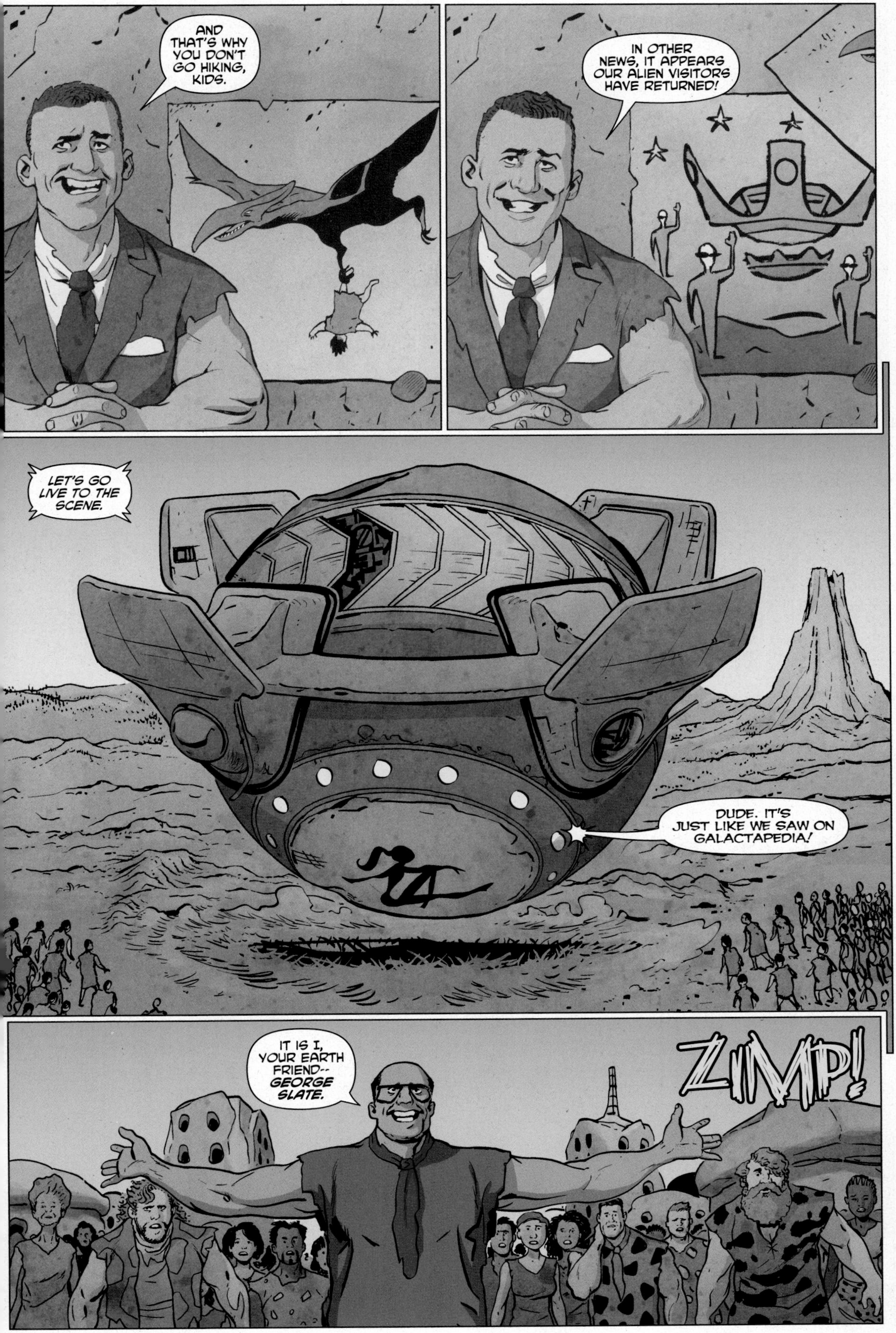
AND THAT'S WHY YOU DON'T GO HIKING, KIDS.
IN OTHER NEWS, IT APPEARS OUR ALIEN VISITORS HAVE RETURNED!
LET'S GO LIVE TO THE SCENE.
DUDE. IT'S JUST LIKE WE SAW ON GALACTAPEDIA!
ZIMP!
IT IS I, YOUR EARTH FRIEND-- GEORGE SLATE.

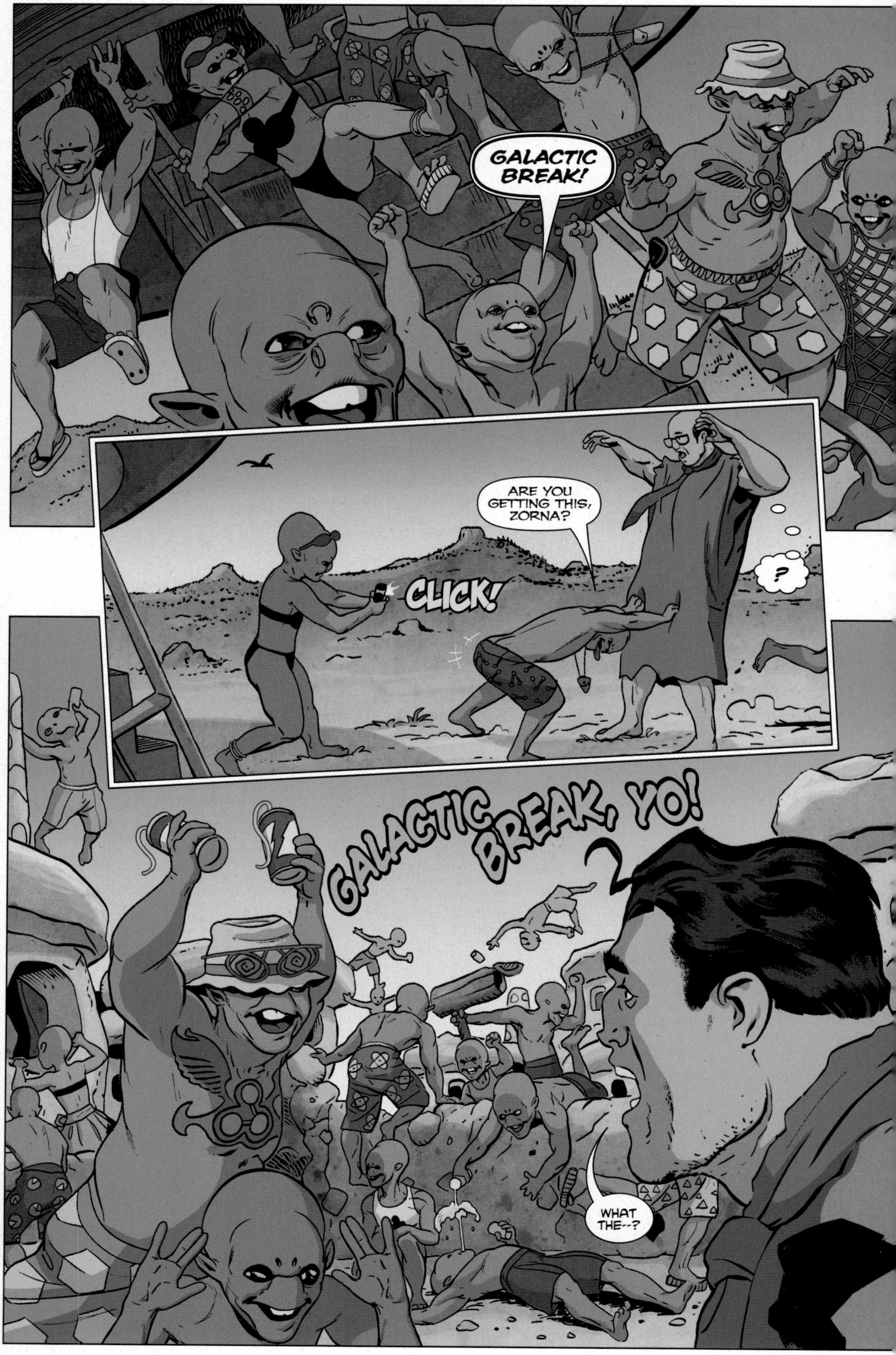
GALACTIC BREAK!
ARE YOU GETTING THIS, ZORNA?
CLICK!
?
GALACTIC BREAK, YO!
WHAT THE--?

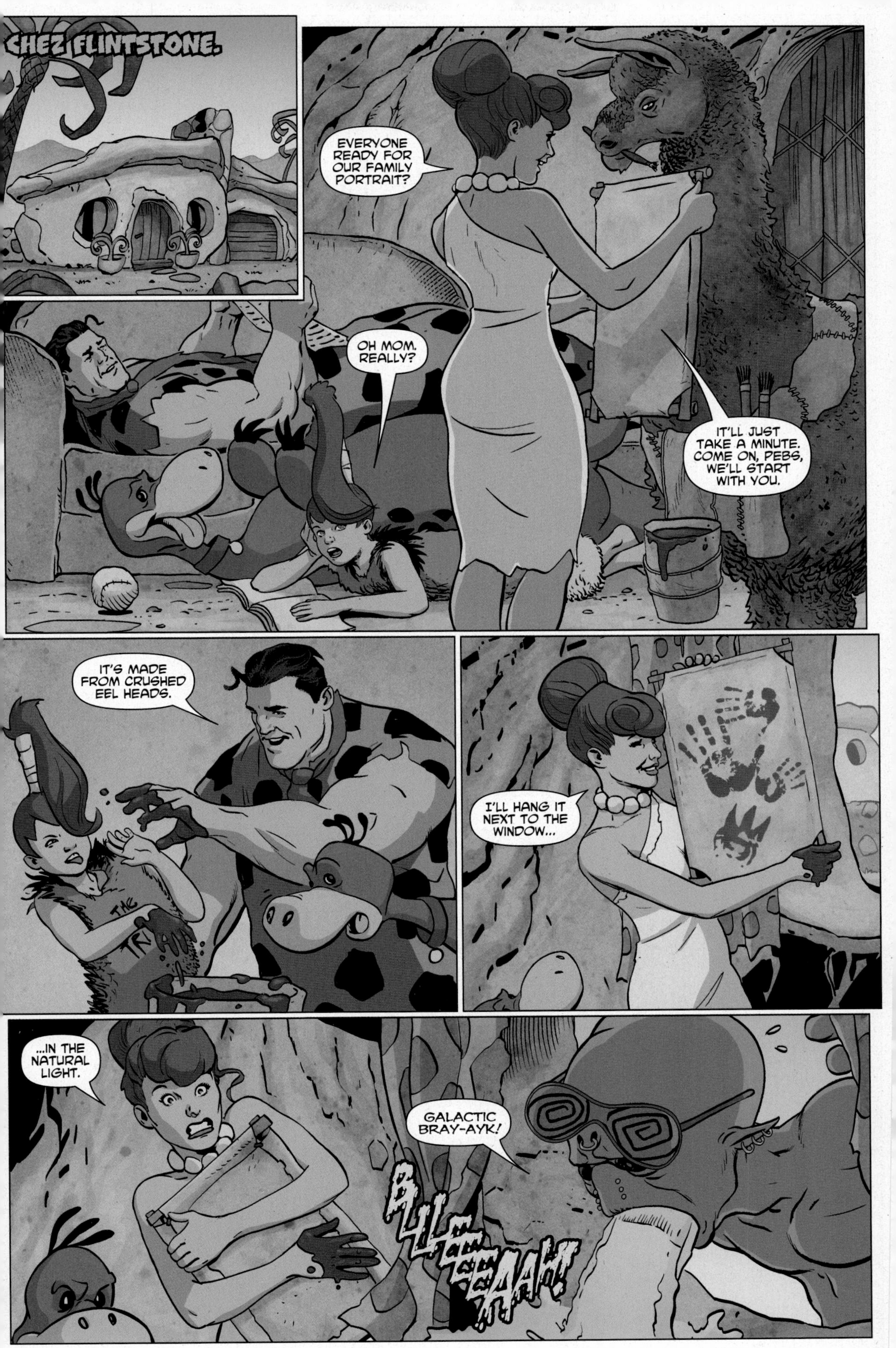
CHEZ FLINTSTONE.
EVERYONE READY FOR OUR FAMILY PORTRAIT?
OH MOM. REALLY?
IT'LL JUST TAKE A MINUTE. COME ON, PEBS, WE'LL START WITH YOU.
IT'S MADE FROM CRUSHED EEL HEADS.
I'LL HANG IT NEXT TO THE WINDOW...
...IN THE NATURAL LIGHT.
GALACTIC BRAY-AYK!
BLLEEEAAH!

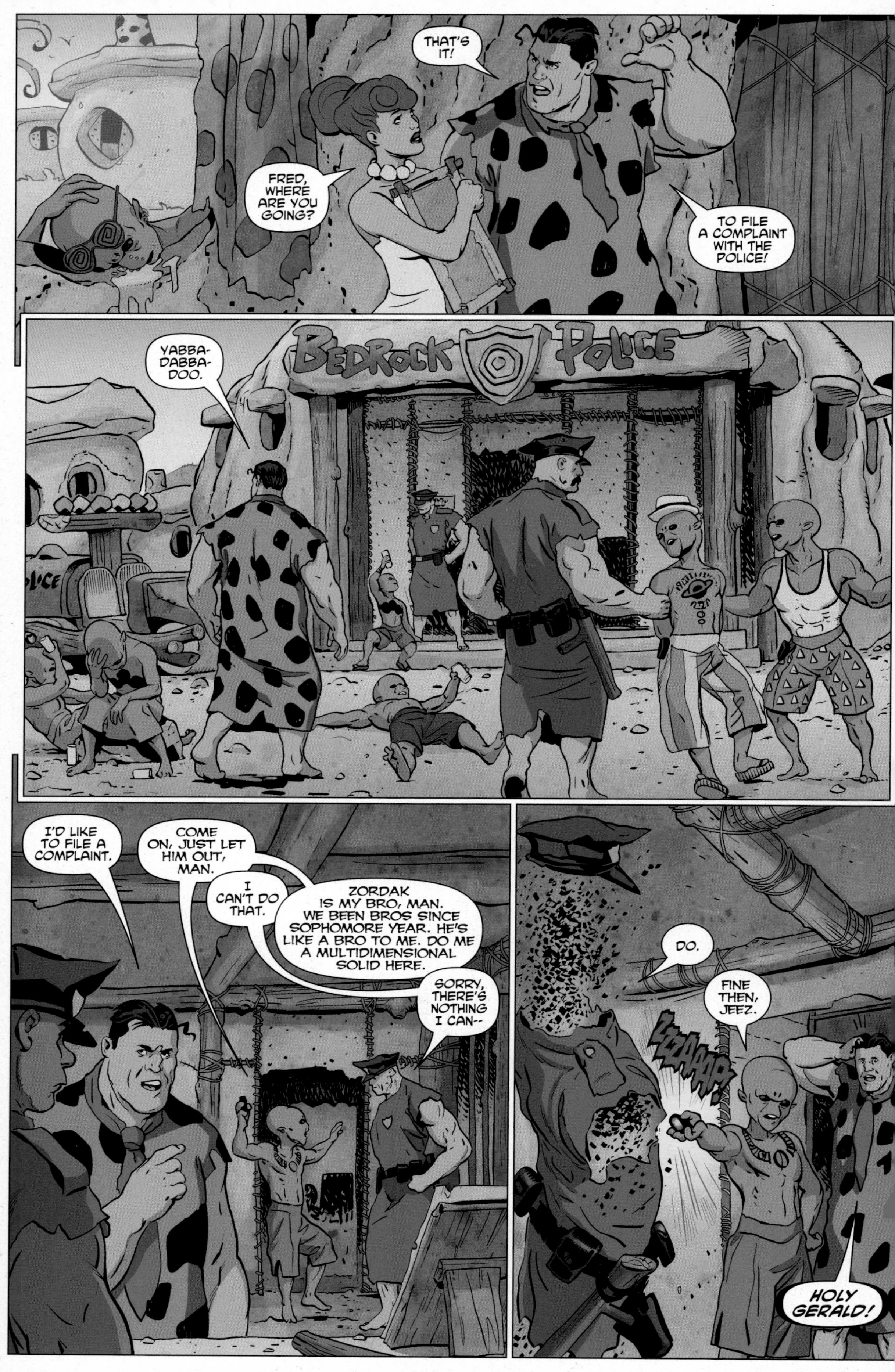
THAT'S IT!
FRED, WHERE ARE YOU GOING?
TO FILE A COMPLAINT WITH THE POLICE!
BEDROCK POLICE
YABBA-DABBA-DOO.
POLICE
I'D LIKE TO FILE A COMPLAINT.
COME ON, JUST LET HIM OUT, MAN.
I CAN'T DO THAT.
ZORDAK IS MY BRO, MAN. WE BEEN BROS SINCE SOPHOMORE YEAR. HE'S LIKE A BRO TO ME. DO ME A MULTIDIMENSIONAL SOLID HERE.
SORRY, THERE'S NOTHING I CAN--
DO.
FINE THEN, JEEZ.
HOLY GERALD!

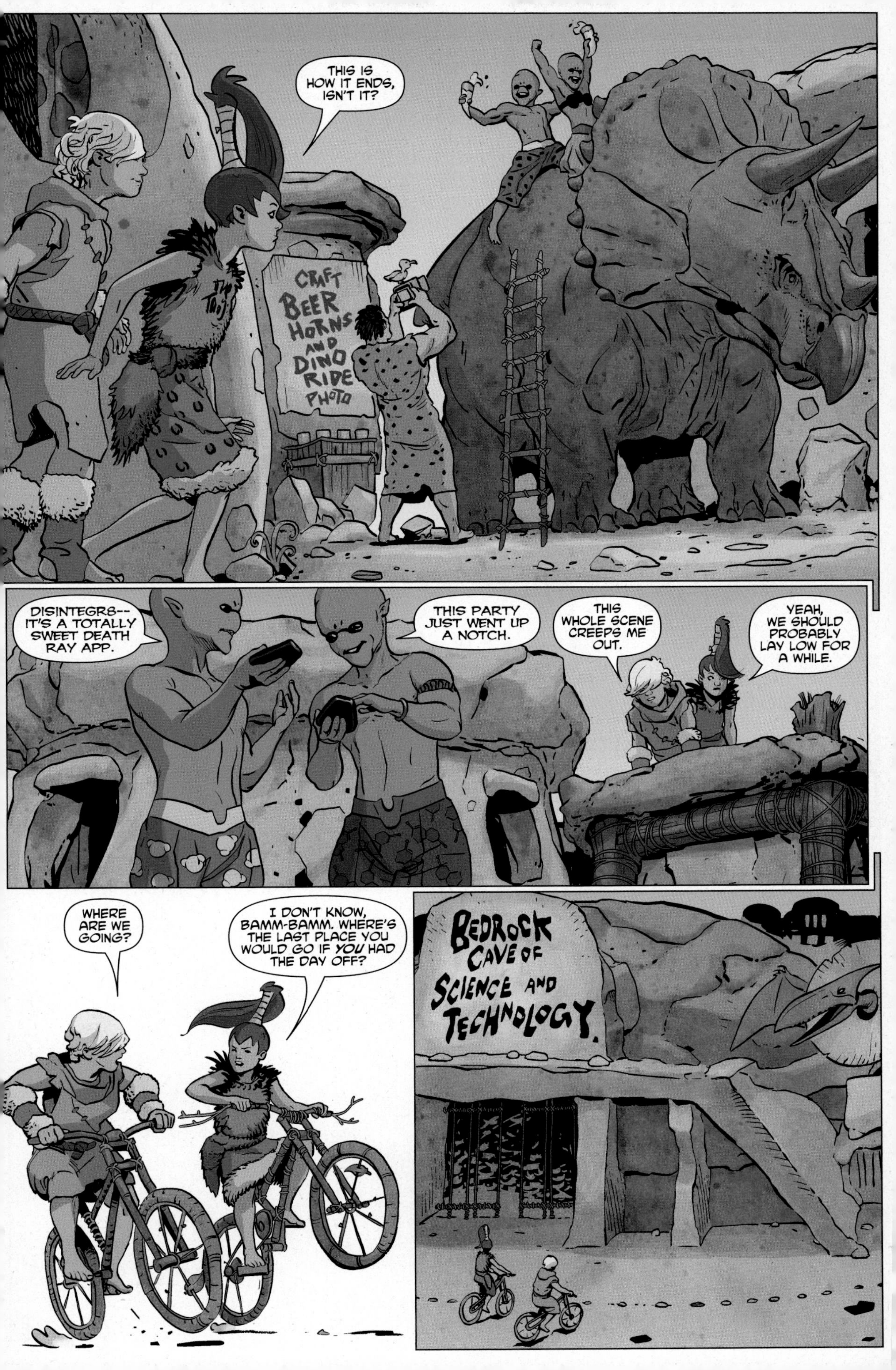
THIS IS HOW IT ENDS, ISN'T IT?
CRAFT BEER HORNS AND DINO RIDE PHOTO
DISINTEGR8-- IT'S A TOTALLY SWEET DEATH RAY APP.
THIS PARTY JUST WENT UP A NOTCH.
THIS WHOLE SCENE CREEPS ME OUT.
YEAH, WE SHOULD PROBABLY LAY LOW FOR A WHILE.
WHERE ARE WE GOING?
I DON'T KNOW, BAMM-BAMM. WHERE'S THE LAST PLACE YOU WOULD GO IF *YOU* HAD THE DAY OFF?
BEDROCK CAVE OF SCIENCE AND TECHNOLOGY.

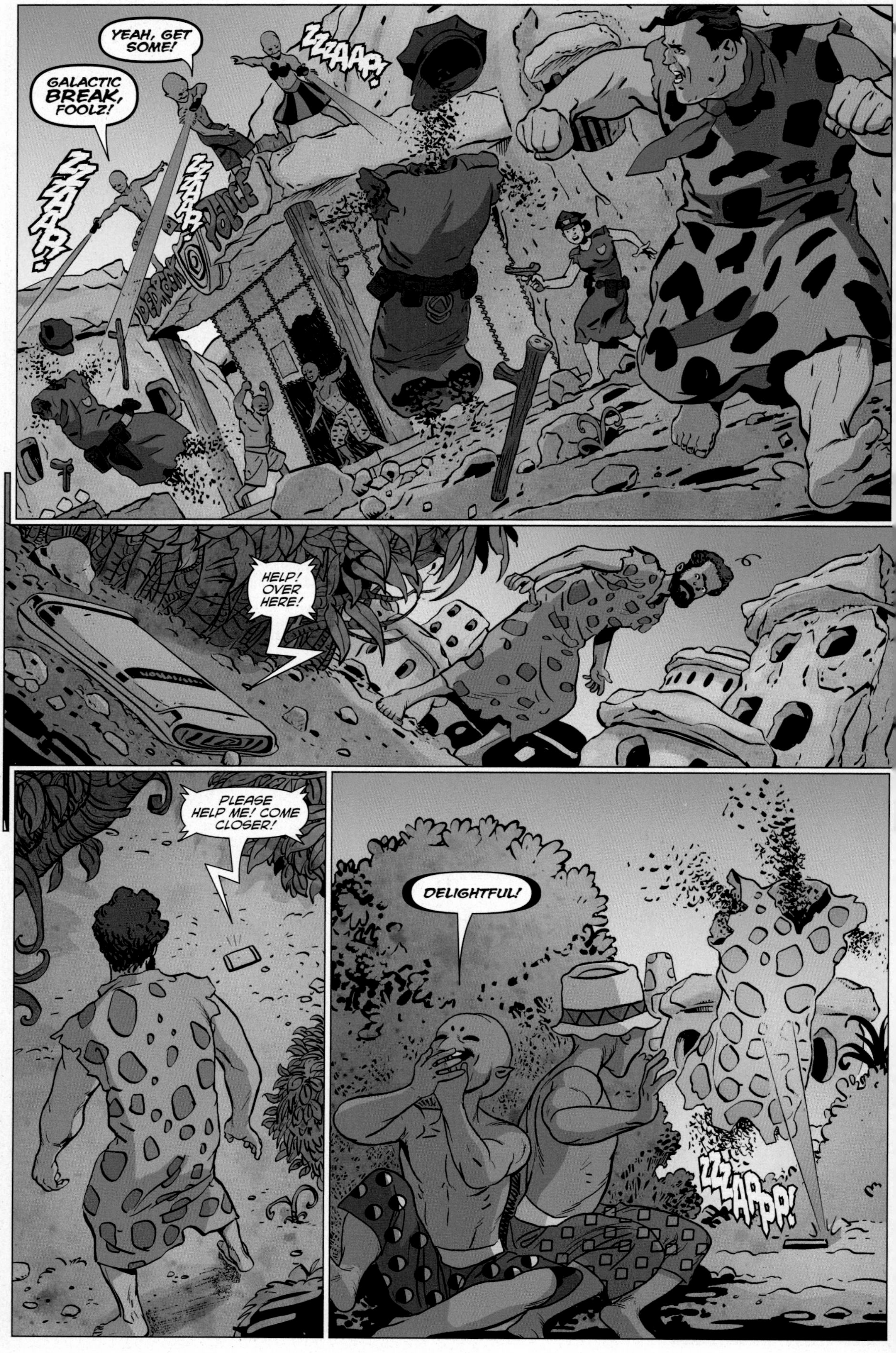

YEAH, GET SOME!
GALACTIC BREAK, FOOLZ!
ZZZAAP!
ZZZAAP!
ZZZAAP!
HELP! OVER HERE!
PLEASE HELP ME! COME CLOSER!
DELIGHTFUL!
ZZZAPP!

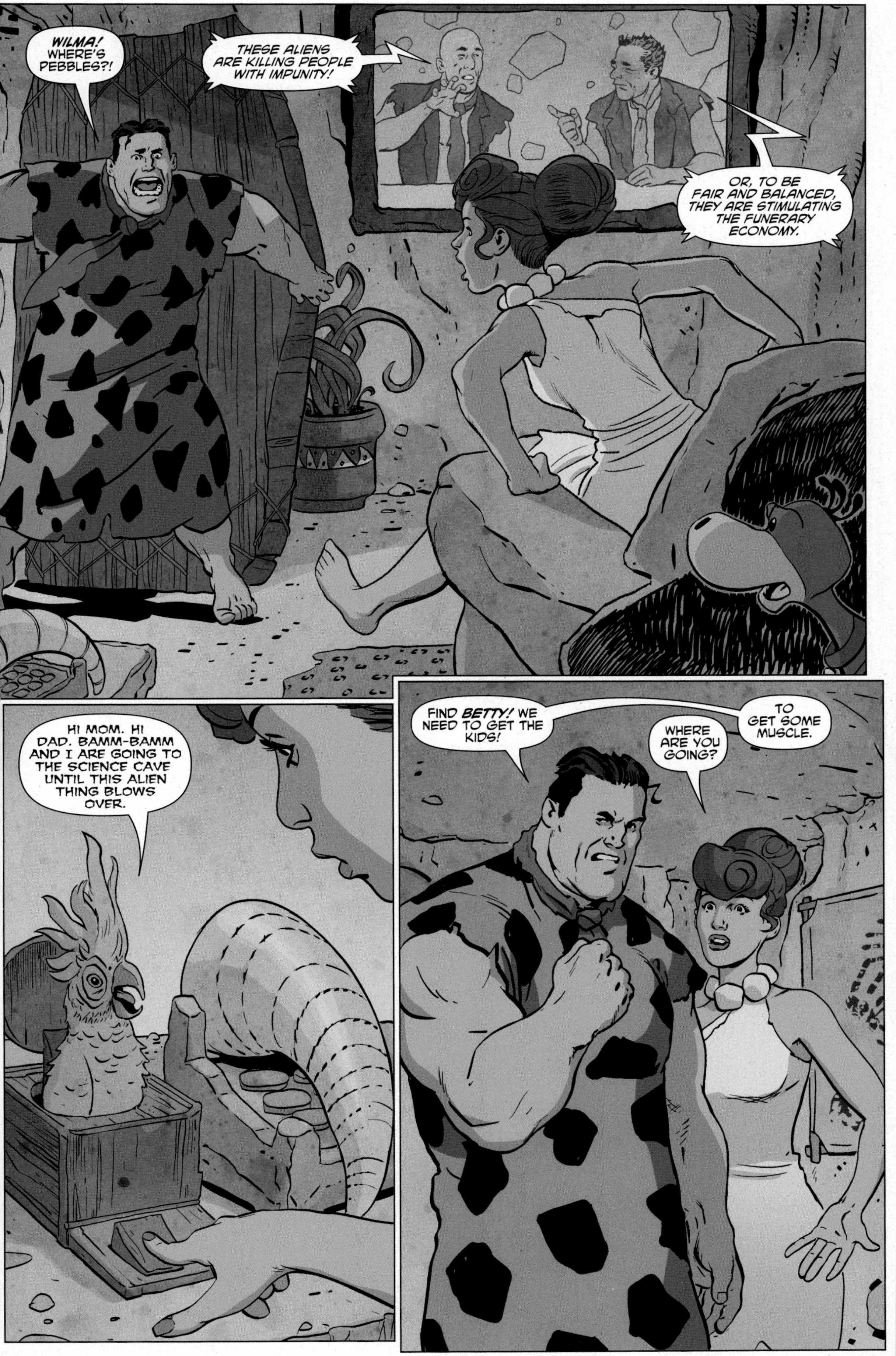
WILMA! WHERE'S PEBBLES?!
THESE ALIENS ARE KILLING PEOPLE WITH IMPUNITY!
OR, TO BE FAIR AND BALANCED, THEY ARE STIMULATING THE FUNERARY ECONOMY.
HI MOM. HI DAD. BAMM-BAMM AND I ARE GOING TO THE SCIENCE CAVE UNTIL THIS ALIEN THING BLOWS OVER.
FIND BETTY! WE NEED TO GET THE KIDS!
WHERE ARE YOU GOING?
TO GET SOME MUSCLE.

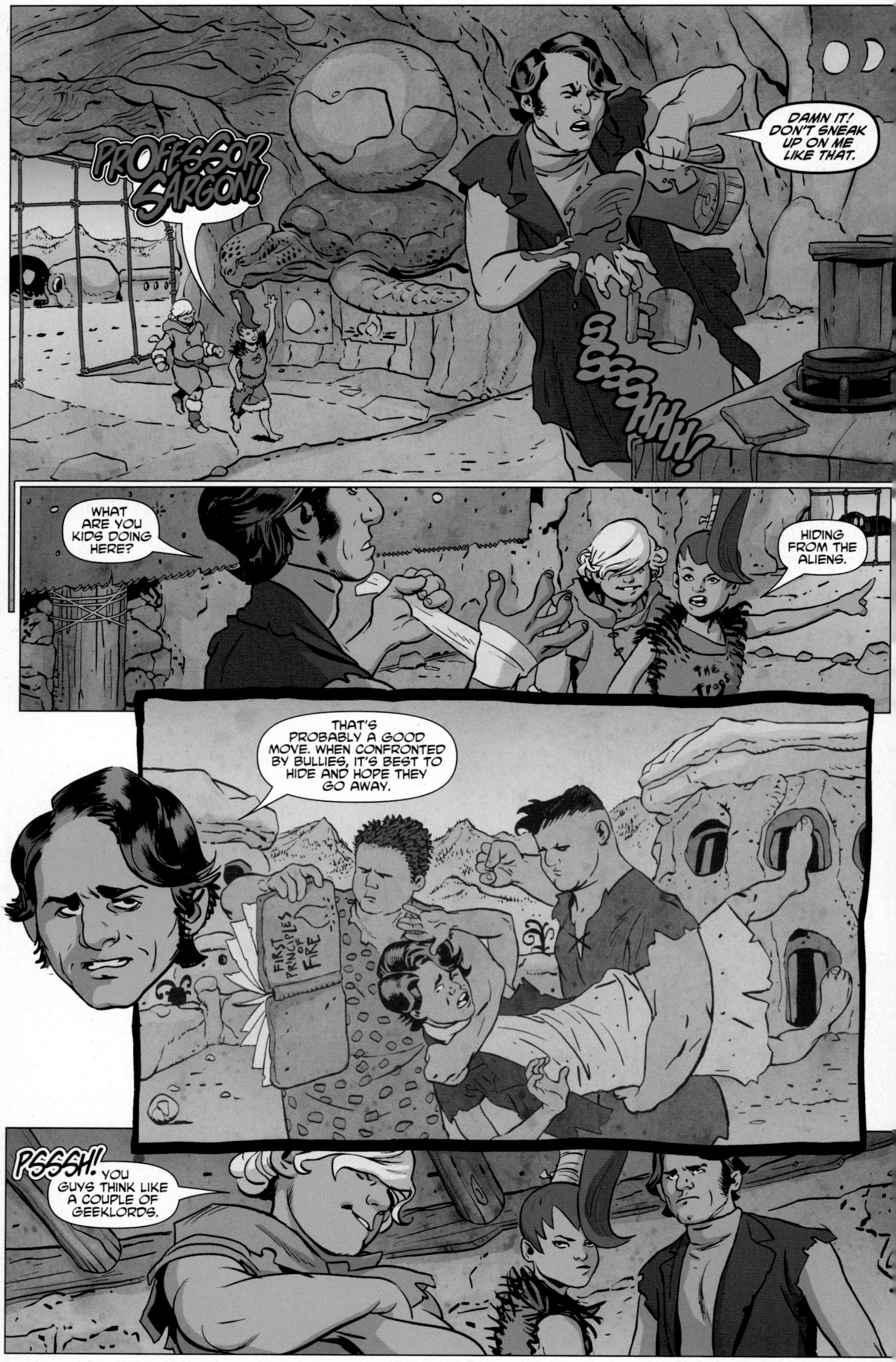
PROFESSOR SARGON!
DAMN IT! DON'T SNEAK UP ON ME LIKE THAT.
SSSSHHHH!
WHAT ARE YOU KIDS DOING HERE?
HIDING FROM THE ALIENS.
THE FROGS
THAT'S PROBABLY A GOOD MOVE. WHEN CONFRONTED BY BULLIES, IT'S BEST TO HIDE AND HOPE THEY GO AWAY.
FIRST PRINCIPLES OF FIRE
PSSSH! YOU GUYS THINK LIKE A COUPLE OF GEEKLORDS.

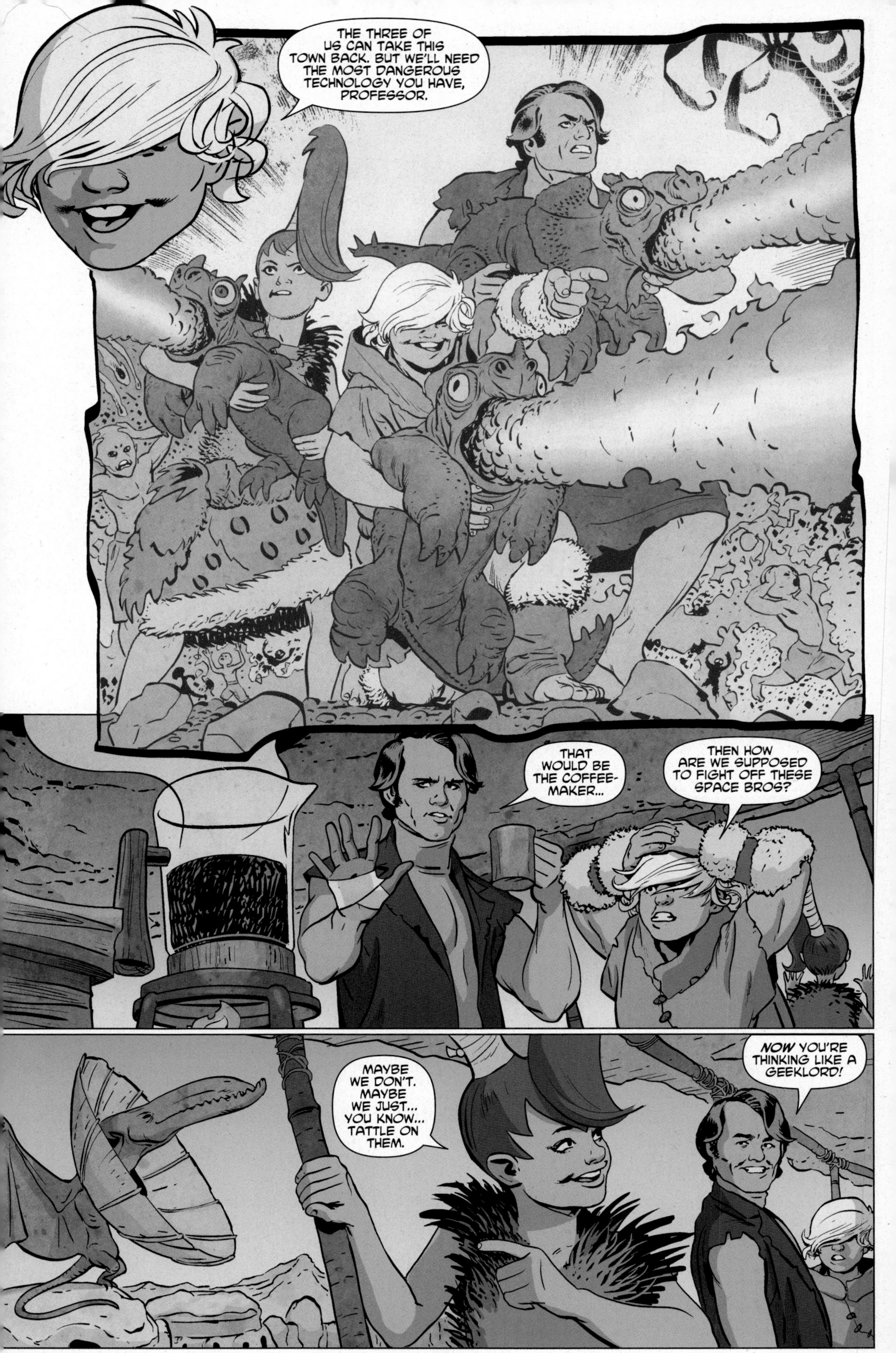
THE THREE OF US CAN TAKE THIS TOWN BACK. BUT WE'LL NEED THE MOST DANGEROUS TECHNOLOGY YOU HAVE, PROFESSOR.
THAT WOULD BE THE COFFEE-MAKER...
THEN HOW ARE WE SUPPOSED TO FIGHT OFF THESE SPACE BROS?
MAYBE WE DON'T. MAYBE WE JUST... YOU KNOW... TATTLE ON THEM.
NOW YOU'RE THINKING LIKE A GEEKLORD!

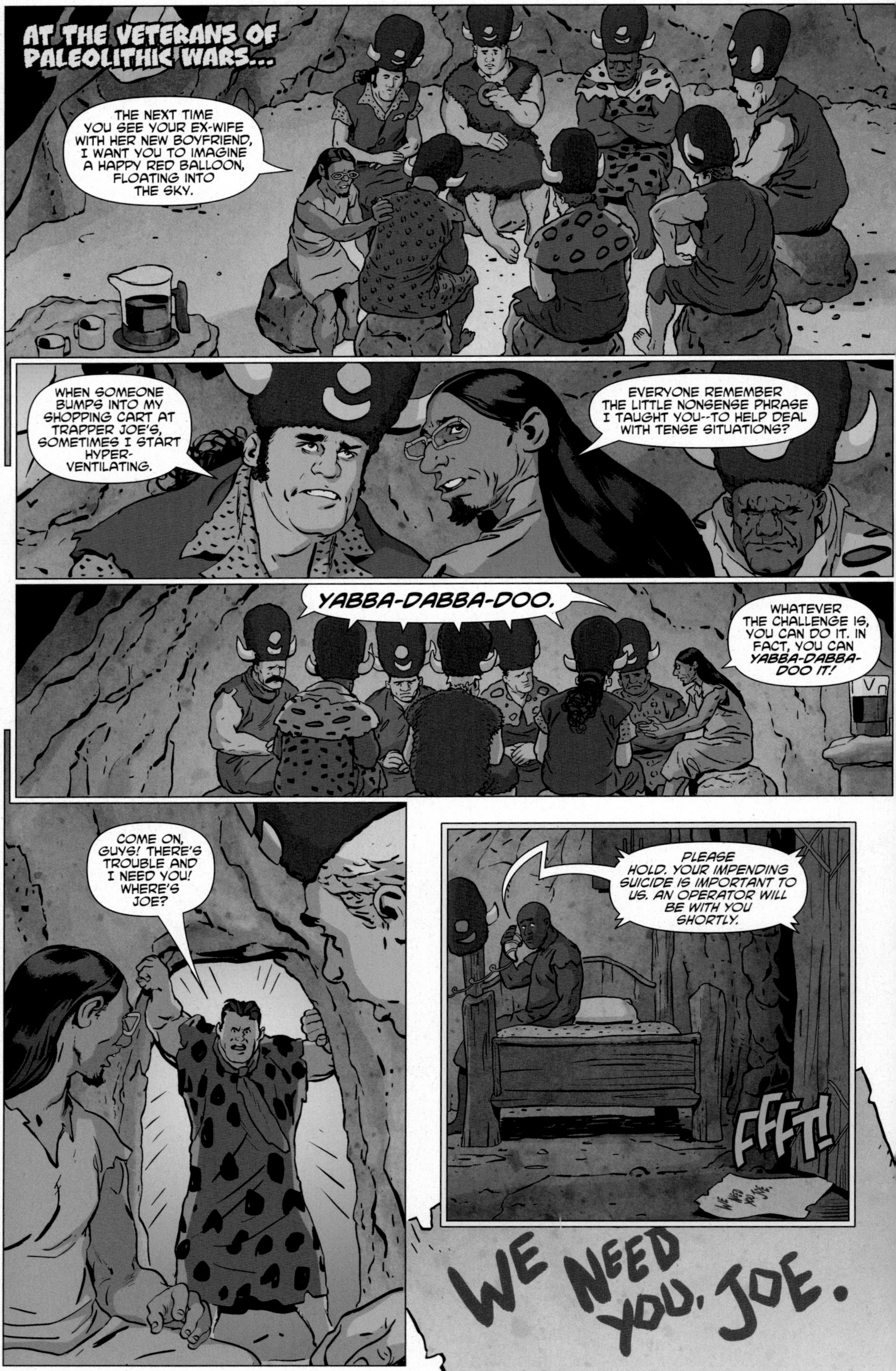
AT THE VETERANS OF PALEOLITHIC WARS...
THE NEXT TIME YOU SEE YOUR EX-WIFE WITH HER NEW BOYFRIEND, I WANT YOU TO IMAGINE A HAPPY RED BALLOON, FLOATING INTO THE SKY.
WHEN SOMEONE BUMPS INTO MY SHOPPING CART AT TRAPPER JOE'S, SOMETIMES I START HYPER-VENTILATING.
EVERYONE REMEMBER THE LITTLE NONSENSE PHRASE I TAUGHT YOU--TO HELP DEAL WITH TENSE SITUATIONS?
YABBA-DABBA-DOO.
WHATEVER THE CHALLENGE IS, YOU CAN DO IT. IN FACT, YOU CAN YABBA-DABBA-DOO IT!
COME ON, GUYS! THERE'S TROUBLE AND I NEED YOU! WHERE'S JOE?
PLEASE HOLD. YOUR IMPENDING SUICIDE IS IMPORTANT TO US. AN OPERATOR WILL BE WITH YOU SHORTLY.
FFFT!
WE NEED YOU, JOE.

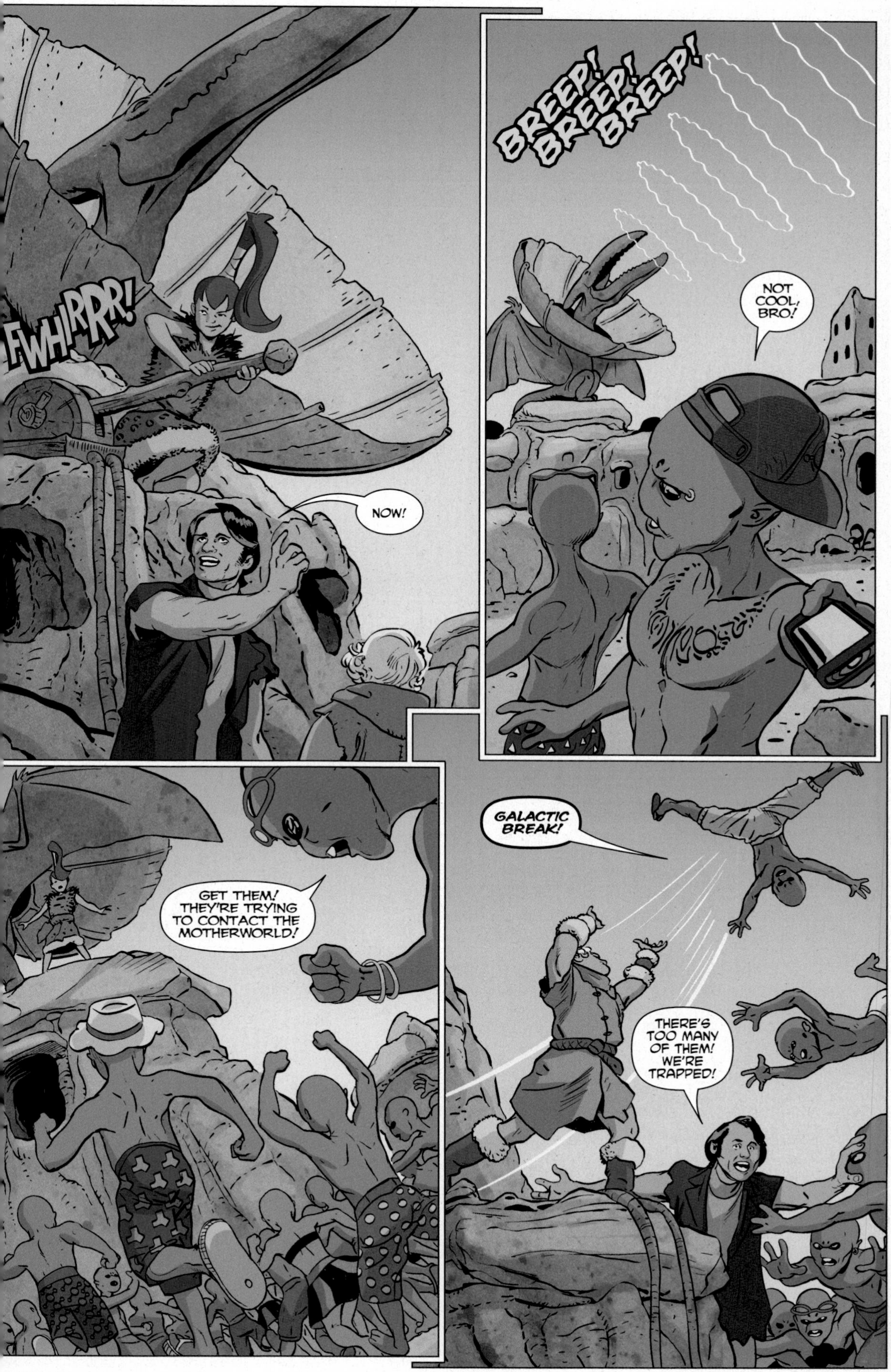
FWHIRRR!
NOW!
BREEP! BREEP! BREEP!
NOT COOL, BRO!
GET THEM! THEY'RE TRYING TO CONTACT THE MOTHERWORLD!
GALACTIC BREAK!
THERE'S TOO MANY OF THEM! WE'RE TRAPPED!

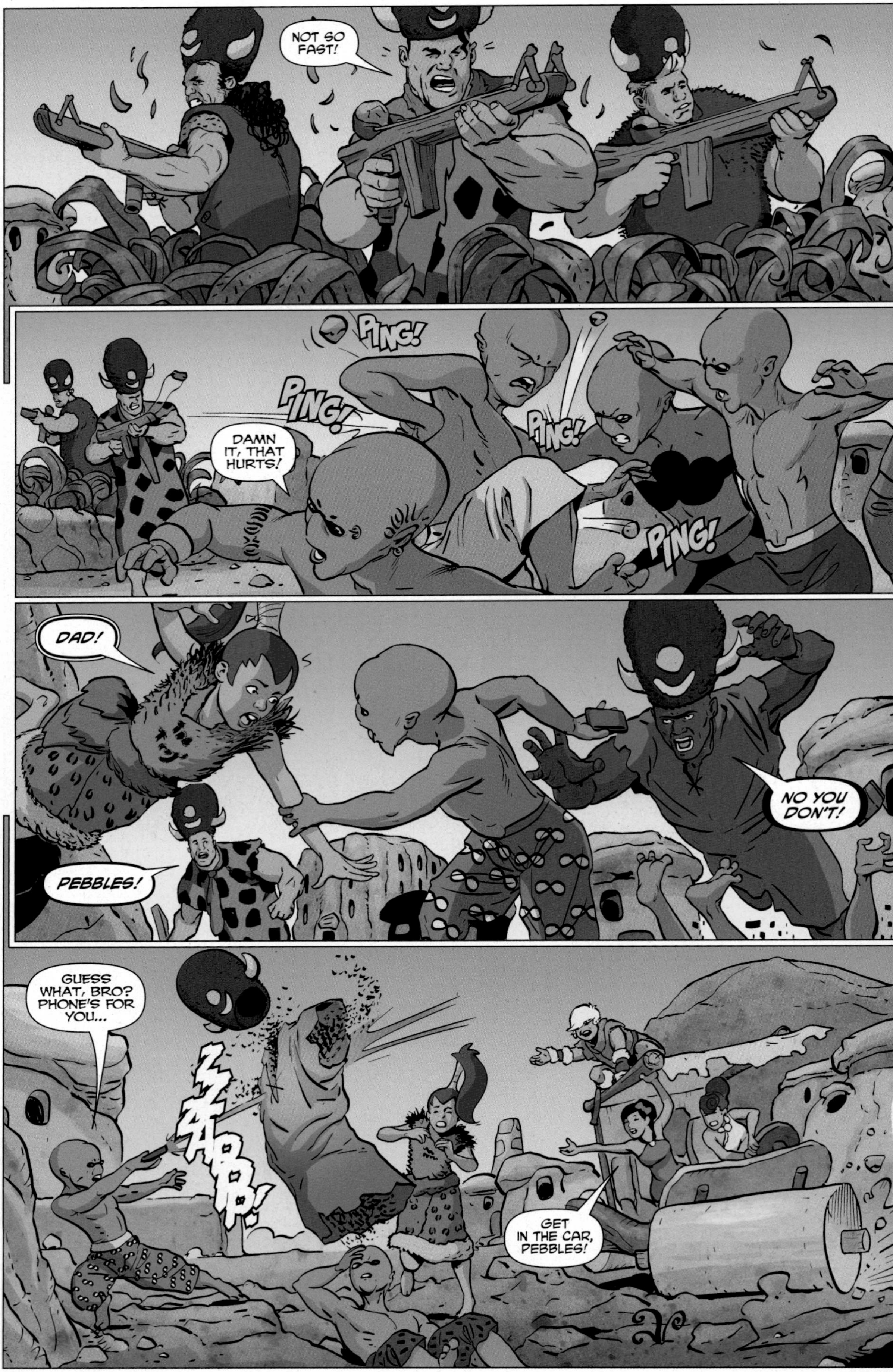
NOT SO FAST!
PING!
PING!
DAMN IT, THAT HURTS!
PING!
PING!
DAD!
NO YOU DON'T!
PEBBLES!
GUESS WHAT, BRO? PHONE'S FOR YOU...
ZZAAPP!
GET IN THE CAR, PEBBLES!

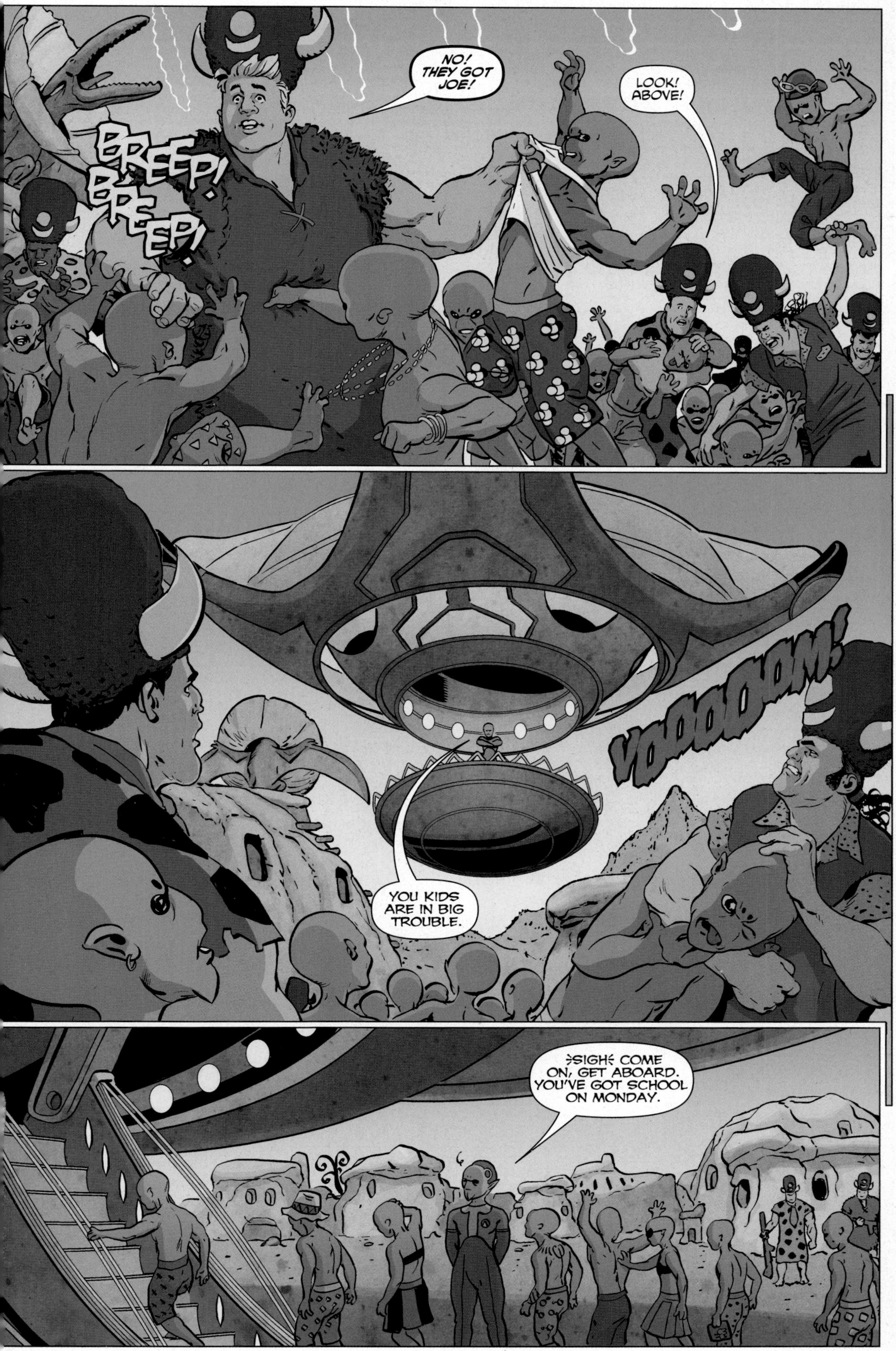
NO! THEY GOT JOE!
LOOK! ABOVE!
BREEP! BREEP!
VOOOOOM!
YOU KIDS ARE IN BIG TROUBLE.
SIGH COME ON, GET ABOARD. YOU'VE GOT SCHOOL ON MONDAY.

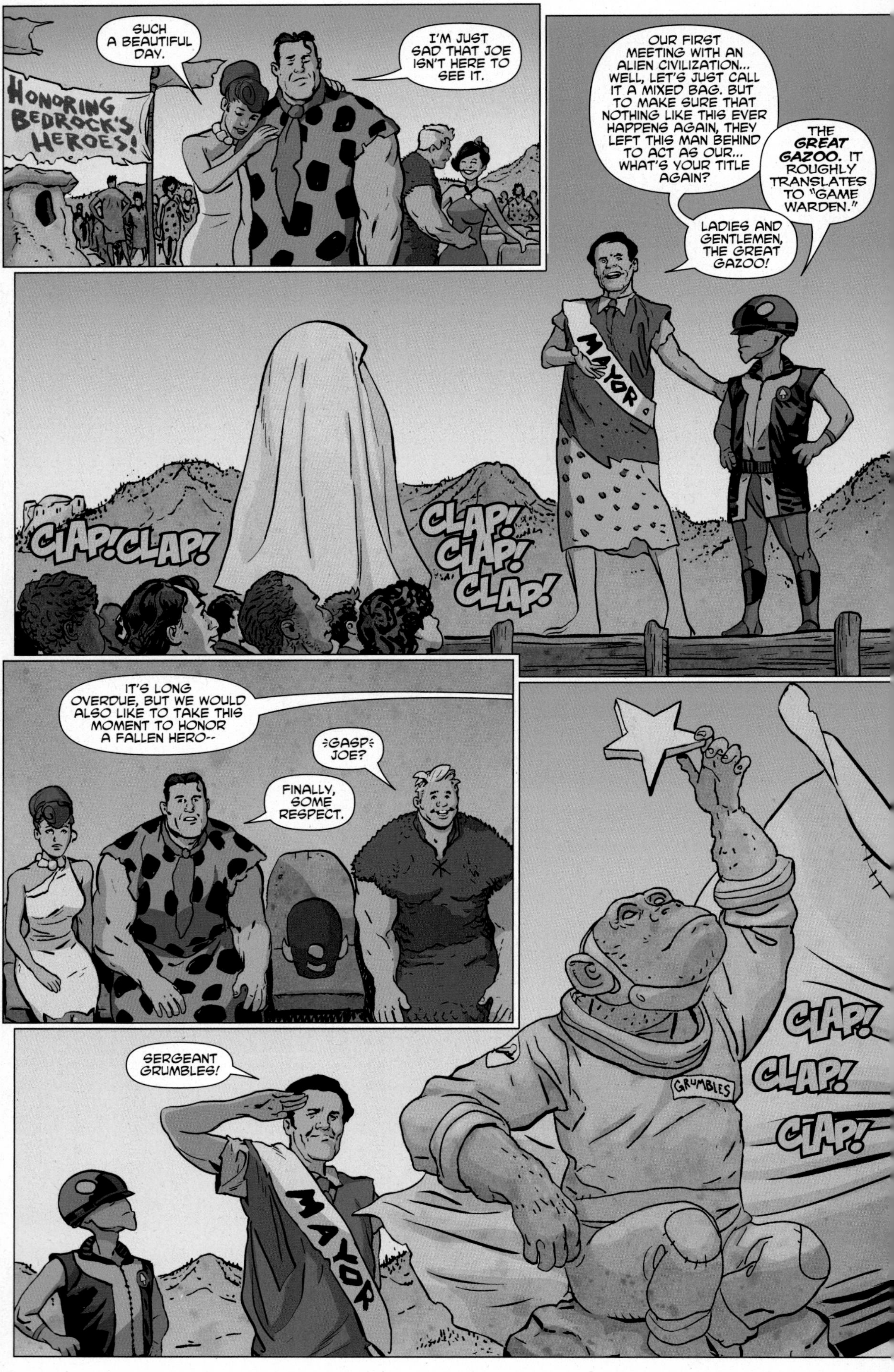
HONORING BEDROCK'S HEROES!
SUCH A BEAUTIFUL DAY.
I'M JUST SAD THAT JOE ISN'T HERE TO SEE IT.
OUR FIRST MEETING WITH AN ALIEN CIVILIZATION... WELL, LET'S JUST CALL IT A MIXED BAG. BUT TO MAKE SURE THAT NOTHING LIKE THIS EVER HAPPENS AGAIN, THEY LEFT THIS MAN BEHIND TO ACT AS OUR... WHAT'S YOUR TITLE AGAIN?
THE GREAT GAZOO. IT ROUGHLY TRANSLATES TO "GAME WARDEN."
LADIES AND GENTLEMEN, THE GREAT GAZOO!
MAYOR
CLAP! CLAP!
CLAP! CLAP! CLAP!
IT'S LONG OVERDUE, BUT WE WOULD ALSO LIKE TO TAKE THIS MOMENT TO HONOR A FALLEN HERO--
GASP JOE?
FINALLY, SOME RESPECT.
CLAP! CLAP! CLAP!
SERGEANT GRUMBLES!
GRUMBLES
MAYOR

THE FLINTSTONES #4 cover by DAN PANOSIAN

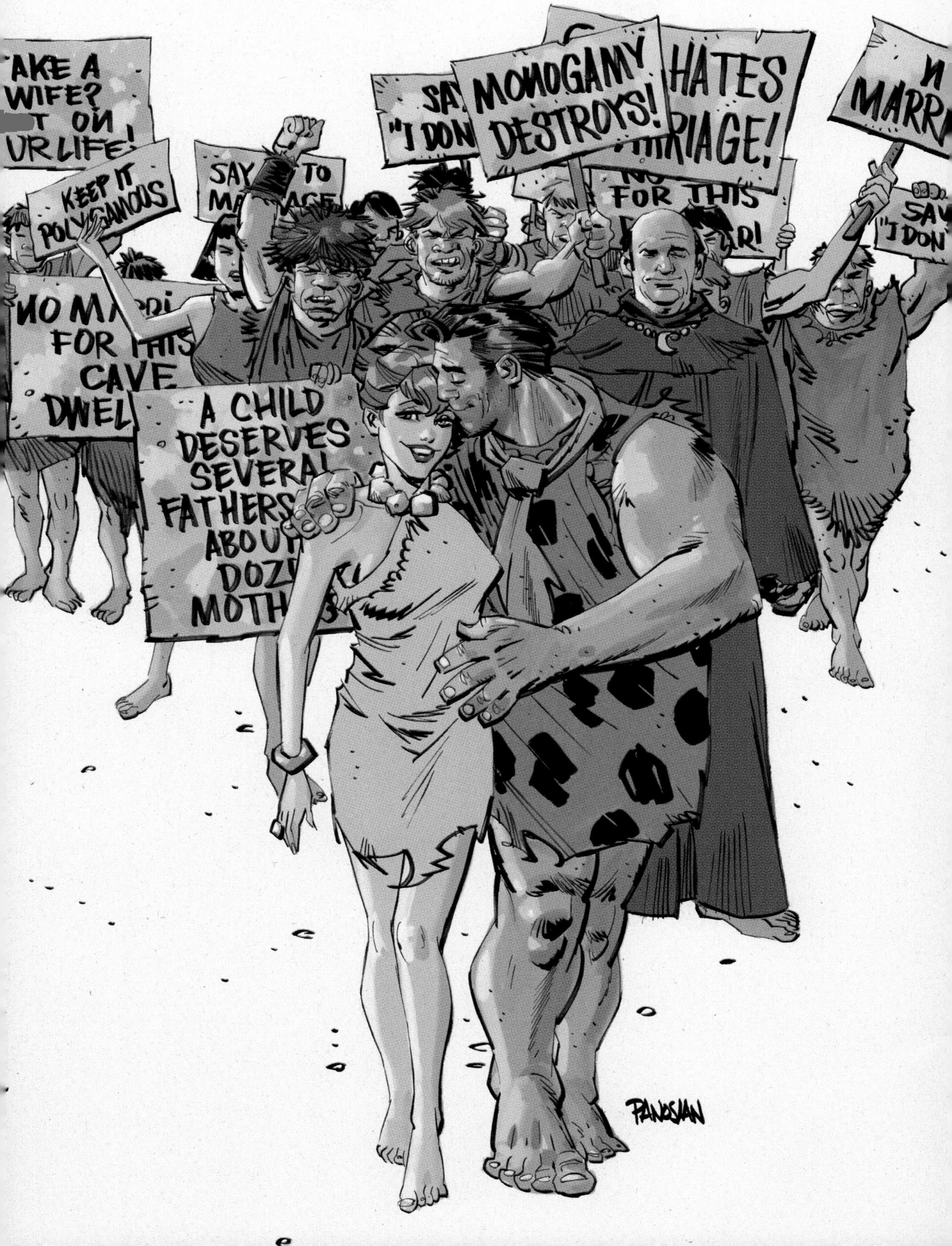

AKE A WIFE? T ON UR LIFE!
KEEP IT POLYGAMOUS
SAY TO
SAY "I DON
MONOGAMY DESTROYS!
HATES RIAGE!
FOR THIS
MARR
SAY "I DON
NO MA FOR THIS CAVE DWEL
A CHILD DESERVES SEVERAL FATHERS ABOU DOZ MOTH
PANOSIAN

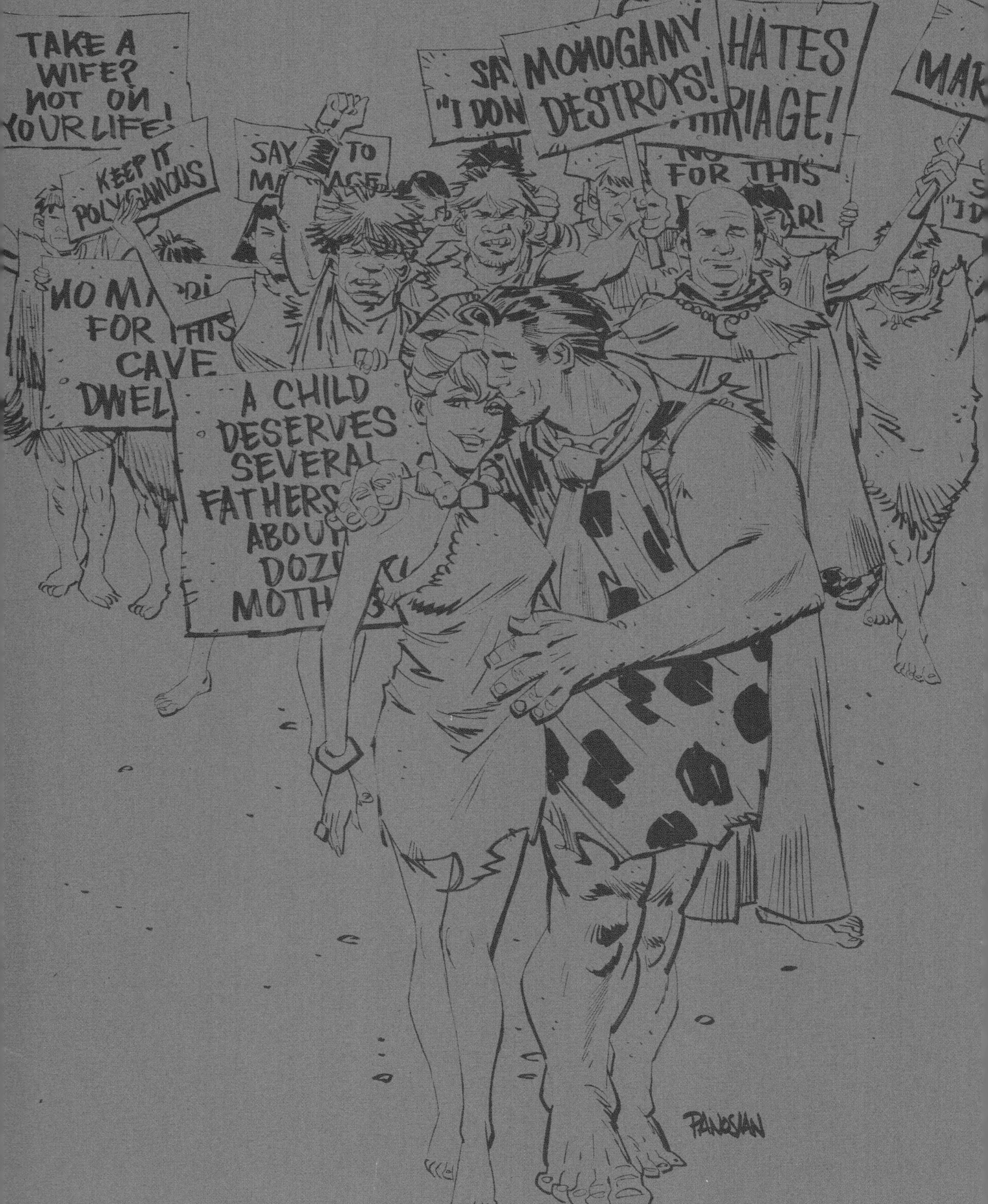
TAKE A WIFE? NOT ON YOUR LIFE!
KEEP IT POLYGAMOUS
MONOGAMY DESTROYS!
HATES
RIAGE!
FOR THIS
FOR THIS CAVE
A CHILD DESERVES SEVERAL
PANOSIAN

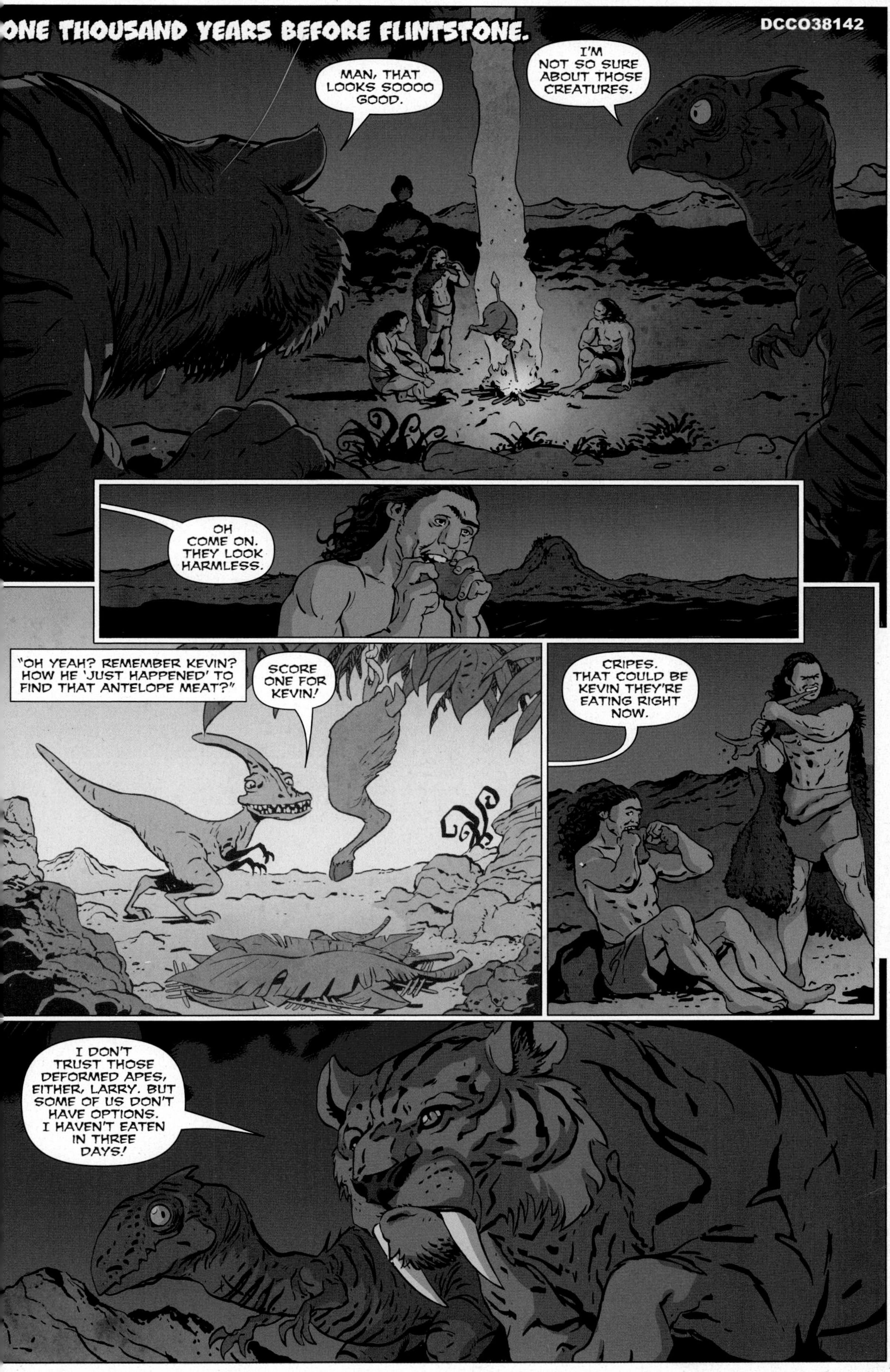
ONE THOUSAND YEARS BEFORE FLINTSTONE.
DCCO38142
MAN, THAT LOOKS SOOOO GOOD.
I'M NOT SO SURE ABOUT THOSE CREATURES.
OH COME ON. THEY LOOK HARMLESS.
"OH YEAH? REMEMBER KEVIN? HOW HE 'JUST HAPPENED' TO FIND THAT ANTELOPE MEAT?"
SCORE ONE FOR KEVIN!
CRIPES. THAT COULD BE KEVIN THEY'RE EATING RIGHT NOW.
I DON'T TRUST THOSE DEFORMED APES, EITHER, LARRY. BUT SOME OF US DON'T HAVE OPTIONS. I HAVEN'T EATEN IN THREE DAYS!

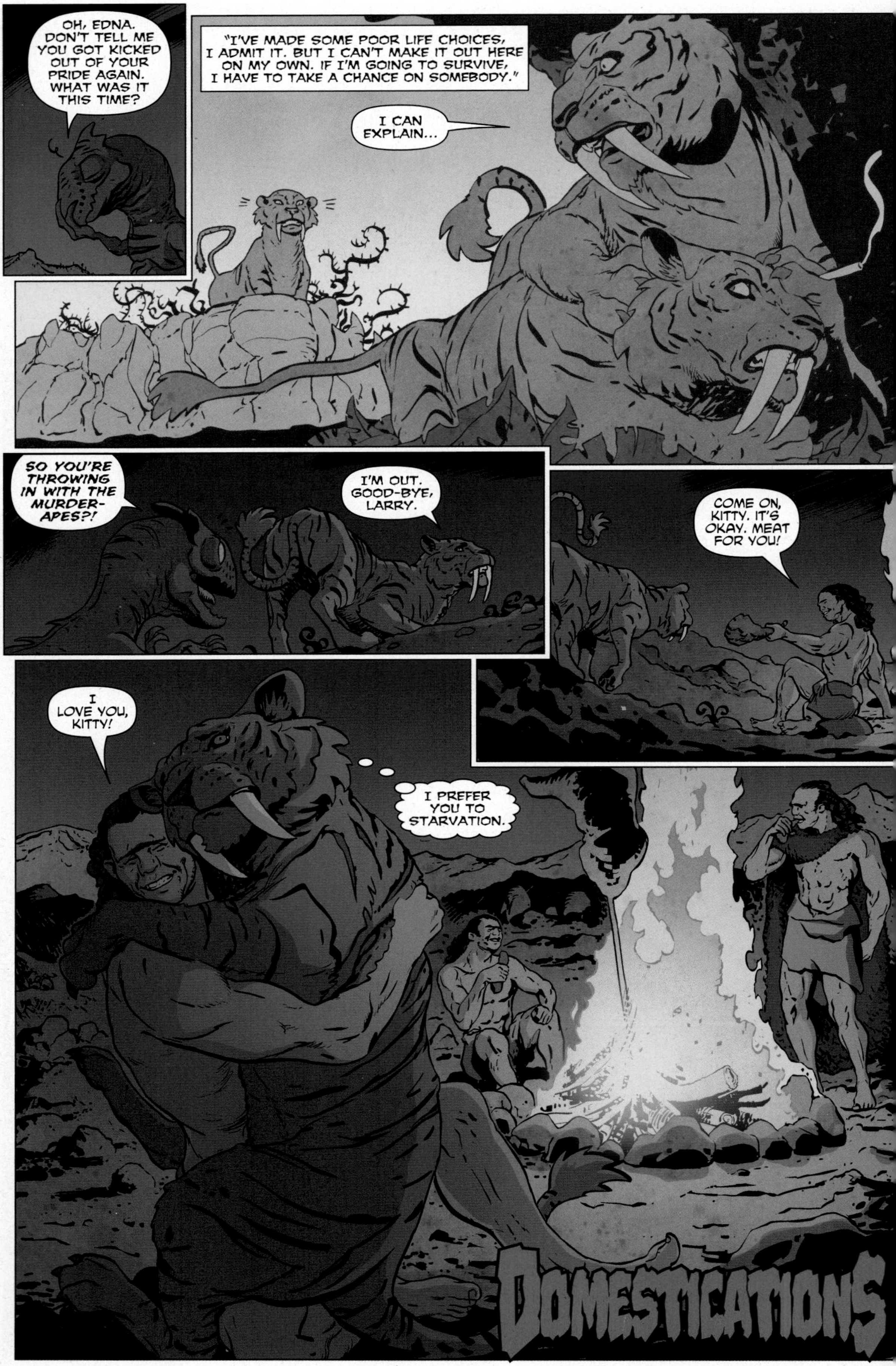
OH, EDNA. DON'T TELL ME YOU GOT KICKED OUT OF YOUR PRIDE AGAIN. WHAT WAS IT THIS TIME?
"I'VE MADE SOME POOR LIFE CHOICES, I ADMIT IT. BUT I CAN'T MAKE IT OUT HERE ON MY OWN. IF I'M GOING TO SURVIVE, I HAVE TO TAKE A CHANCE ON SOMEBODY."
I CAN EXPLAIN...
SO YOU'RE THROWING IN WITH THE MURDER-APES?!
I'M OUT. GOOD-BYE, LARRY.
COME ON, KITTY. IT'S OKAY. MEAT FOR YOU!
I LOVE YOU, KITTY!
I PREFER YOU TO STARVATION.
DOMESTICATIONS

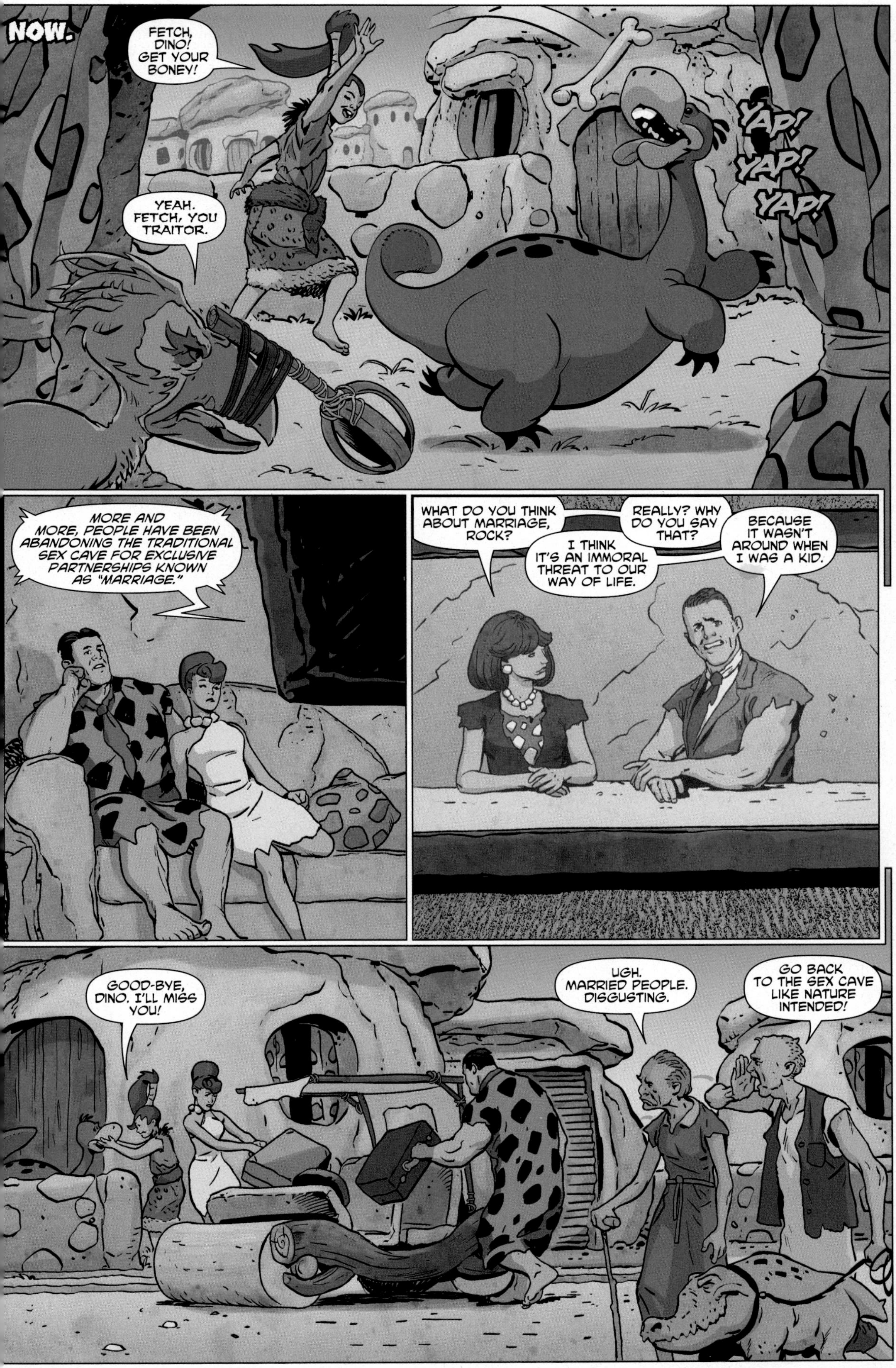
NOW.
FETCH, DINO! GET YOUR BONEY!
YEAH. FETCH, YOU TRAITOR.
YAP! YAP! YAP!
MORE AND MORE, PEOPLE HAVE BEEN ABANDONING THE TRADITIONAL SEX CAVE FOR EXCLUSIVE PARTNERSHIPS KNOWN AS "MARRIAGE."
WHAT DO YOU THINK ABOUT MARRIAGE, ROCK?
I THINK IT'S AN IMMORAL THREAT TO OUR WAY OF LIFE.
REALLY? WHY DO YOU SAY THAT?
BECAUSE IT WASN'T AROUND WHEN I WAS A KID.
GOOD-BYE, DINO. I'LL MISS YOU!
UGH. MARRIED PEOPLE. DISGUSTING.
GO BACK TO THE SEX CAVE LIKE NATURE INTENDED!

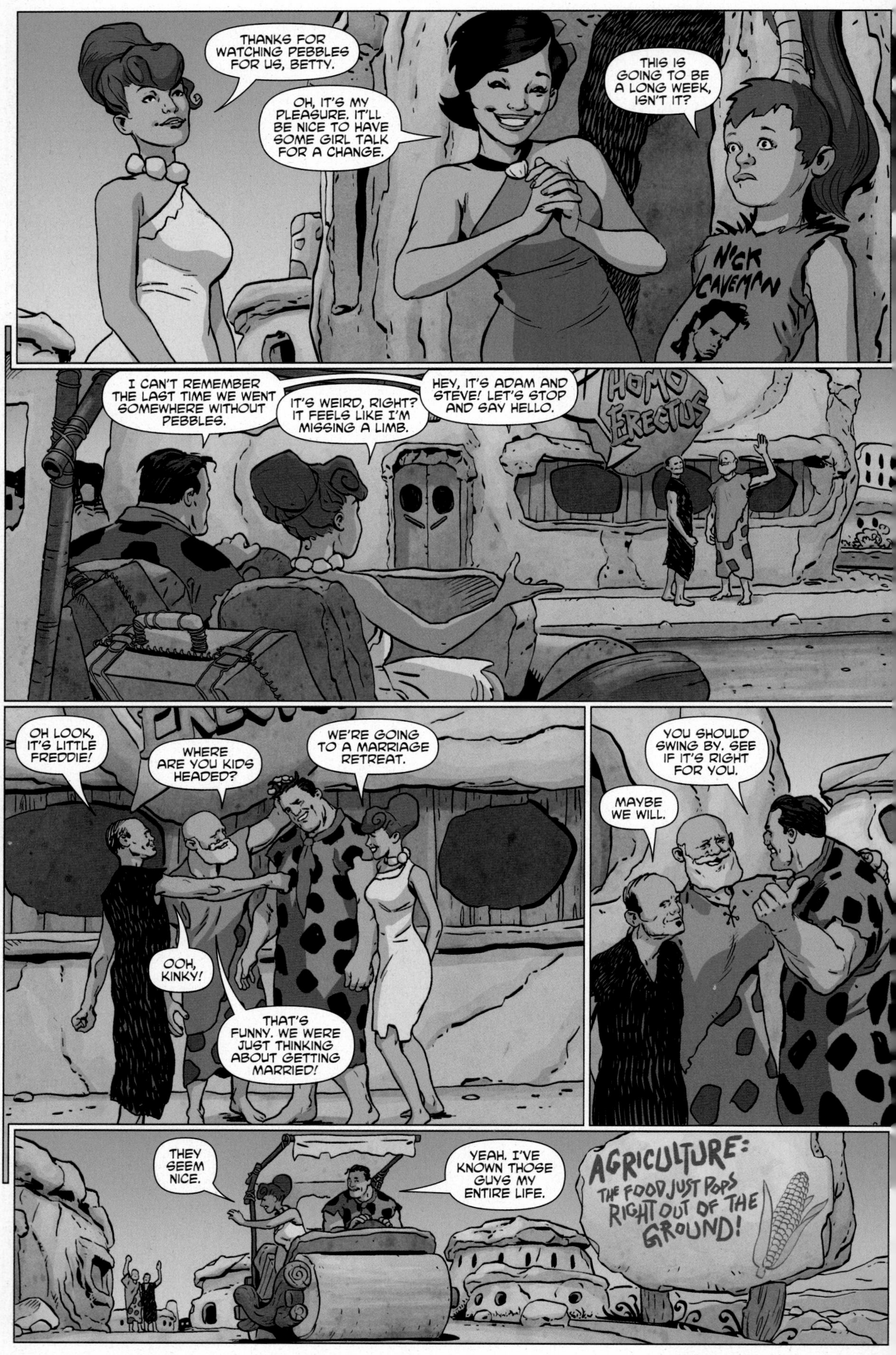
THANKS FOR WATCHING PEBBLES FOR US, BETTY.
OH, IT'S MY PLEASURE. IT'LL BE NICE TO HAVE SOME GIRL TALK FOR A CHANGE.
THIS IS GOING TO BE A LONG WEEK, ISN'T IT?
NICK CAVEMAN
I CAN'T REMEMBER THE LAST TIME WE WENT SOMEWHERE WITHOUT PEBBLES.
IT'S WEIRD, RIGHT? IT FEELS LIKE I'M MISSING A LIMB.
HEY, IT'S ADAM AND STEVE! LET'S STOP AND SAY HELLO.
HOMO ERECTUS
OH LOOK, IT'S LITTLE FREDDIE!
WHERE ARE YOU KIDS HEADED?
WE'RE GOING TO A MARRIAGE RETREAT.
OOH, KINKY!
THAT'S FUNNY. WE WERE JUST THINKING ABOUT GETTING MARRIED!
YOU SHOULD SWING BY. SEE IF IT'S RIGHT FOR YOU.
MAYBE WE WILL.
THEY SEEM NICE.
YEAH. I'VE KNOWN THOSE GUYS MY ENTIRE LIFE.
AGRICULTURE: THE FOOD JUST POPS RIGHT OUT OF THE GROUND!

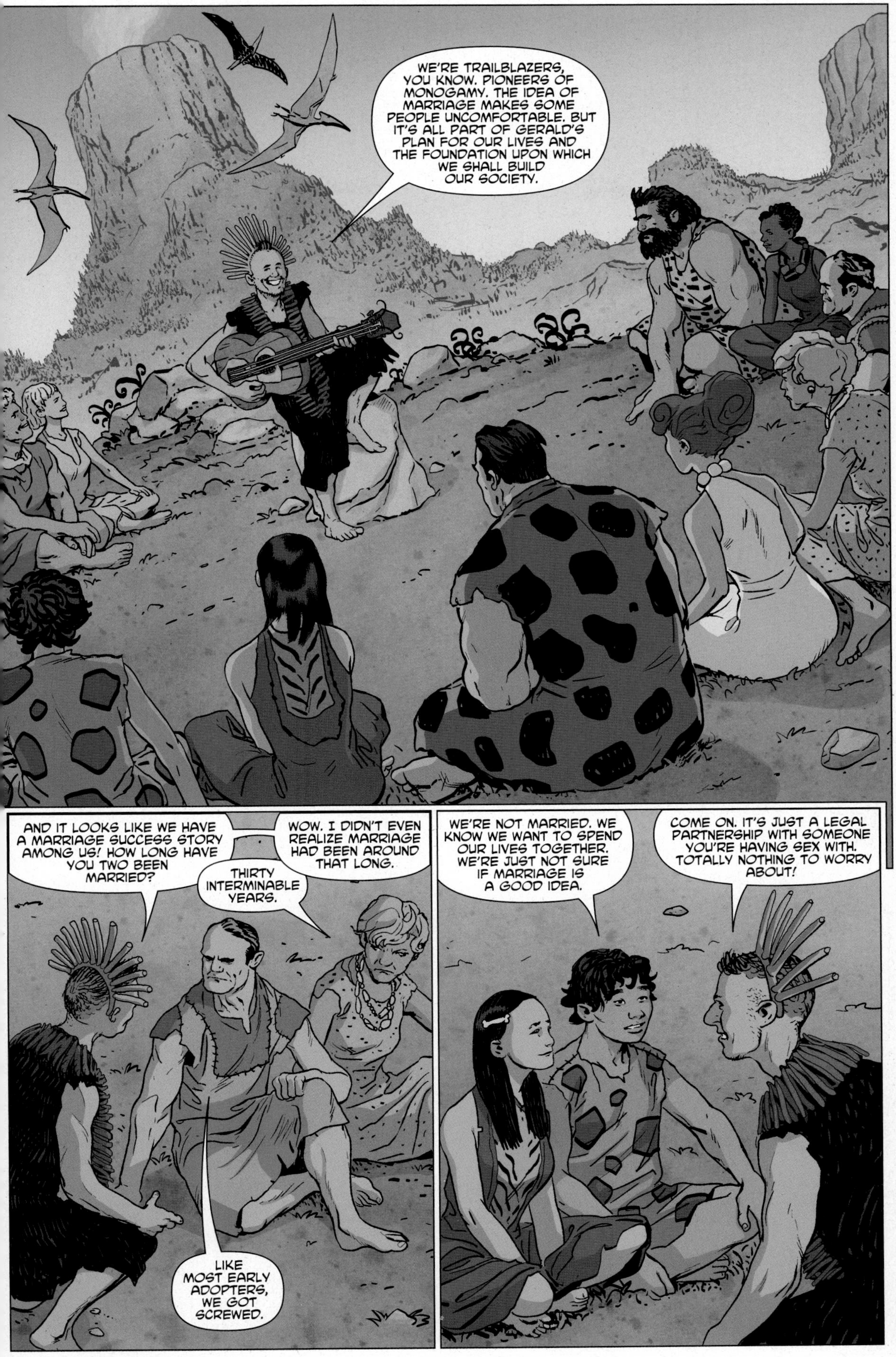
WE'RE TRAILBLAZERS, YOU KNOW. PIONEERS OF MONOGAMY. THE IDEA OF MARRIAGE MAKES SOME PEOPLE UNCOMFORTABLE. BUT IT'S ALL PART OF GERALD'S PLAN FOR OUR LIVES AND THE FOUNDATION UPON WHICH WE SHALL BUILD OUR SOCIETY.
AND IT LOOKS LIKE WE HAVE A MARRIAGE SUCCESS STORY AMONG US! HOW LONG HAVE YOU TWO BEEN MARRIED?
WOW. I DIDN'T EVEN REALIZE MARRIAGE HAD BEEN AROUND THAT LONG.
THIRTY INTERMINABLE YEARS.
LIKE MOST EARLY ADOPTERS, WE GOT SCREWED.
WE'RE NOT MARRIED. WE KNOW WE WANT TO SPEND OUR LIVES TOGETHER. WE'RE JUST NOT SURE IF MARRIAGE IS A GOOD IDEA.
COME ON. IT'S JUST A LEGAL PARTNERSHIP WITH SOMEONE YOU'RE HAVING SEX WITH. TOTALLY NOTHING TO WORRY ABOUT!

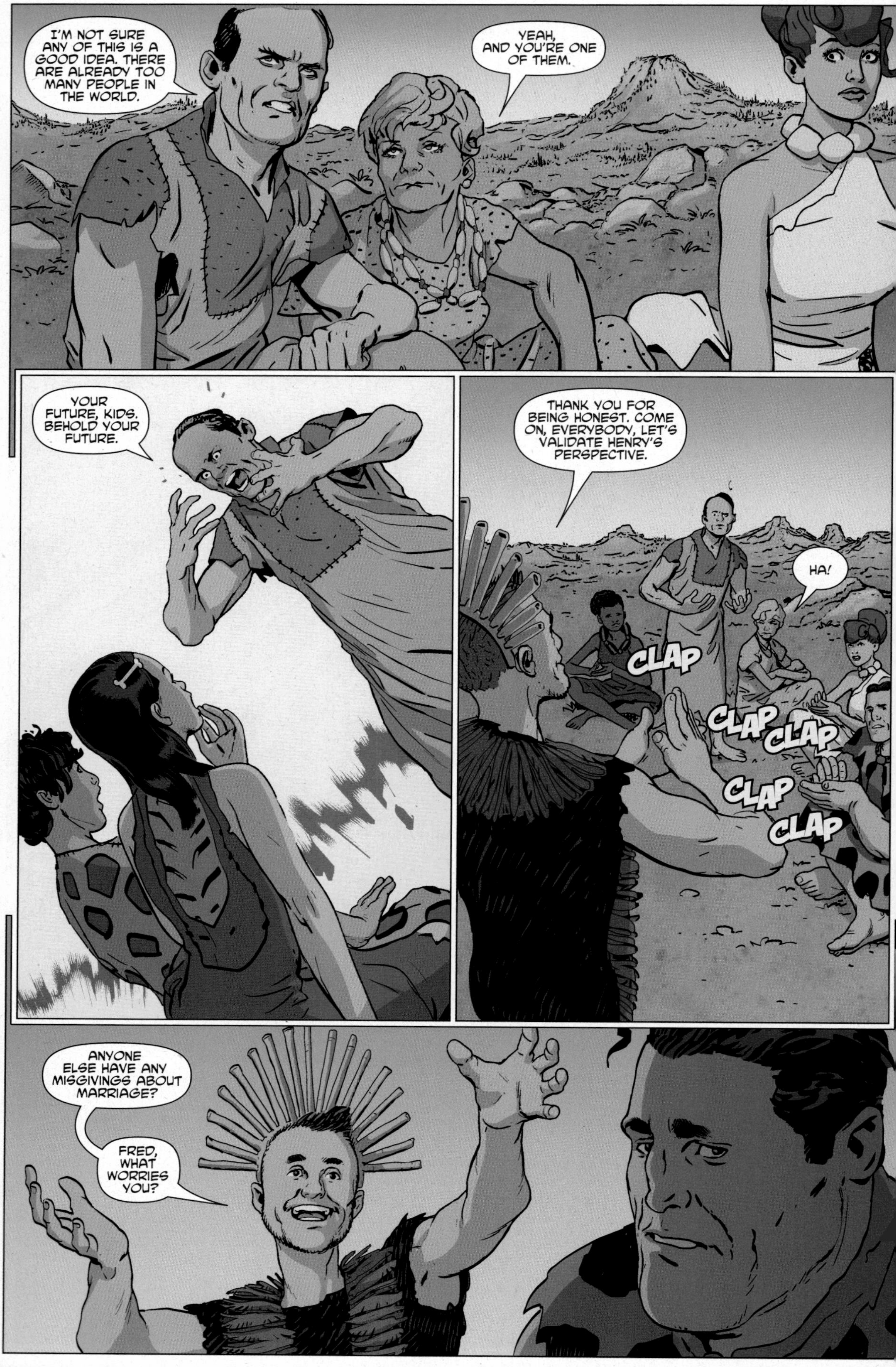
I'M NOT SURE ANY OF THIS IS A GOOD IDEA. THERE ARE ALREADY TOO MANY PEOPLE IN THE WORLD.
YEAH, AND YOU'RE ONE OF THEM.
YOUR FUTURE, KIDS. BEHOLD YOUR FUTURE.
THANK YOU FOR BEING HONEST. COME ON, EVERYBODY, LET'S VALIDATE HENRY'S PERSPECTIVE.
HA!
CLAP
CLAP
CLAP
CLAP
CLAP
ANYONE ELSE HAVE ANY MISGIVINGS ABOUT MARRIAGE?
FRED, WHAT WORRIES YOU?

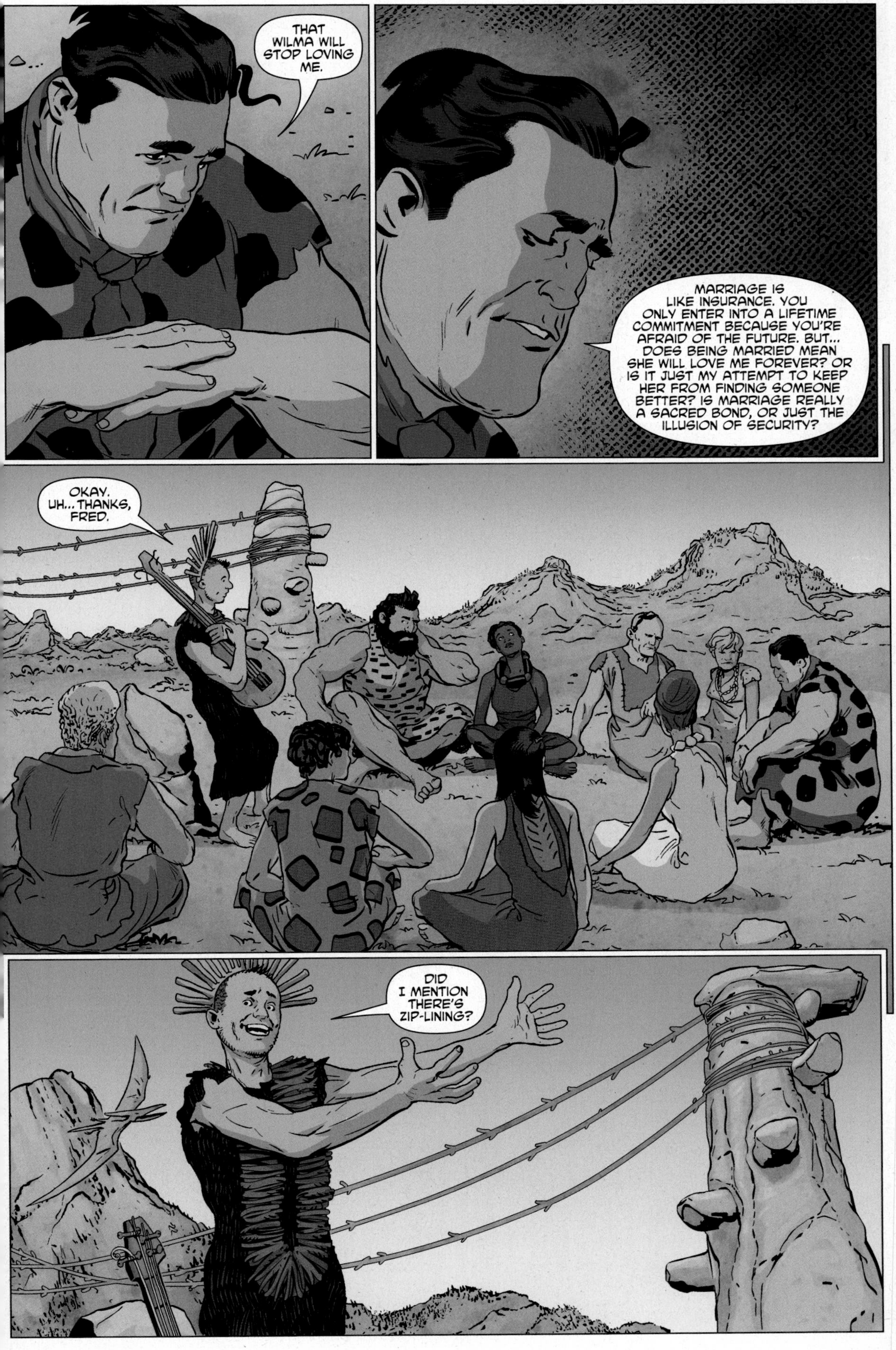
THAT WILMA WILL STOP LOVING ME.
MARRIAGE IS LIKE INSURANCE. YOU ONLY ENTER INTO A LIFETIME COMMITMENT BECAUSE YOU'RE AFRAID OF THE FUTURE. BUT... DOES BEING MARRIED MEAN SHE WILL LOVE ME FOREVER? OR IS IT JUST MY ATTEMPT TO KEEP HER FROM FINDING SOMEONE BETTER? IS MARRIAGE REALLY A SACRED BOND, OR JUST THE ILLUSION OF SECURITY?
OKAY. UH... THANKS, FRED.
DID I MENTION THERE'S ZIP-LINING?

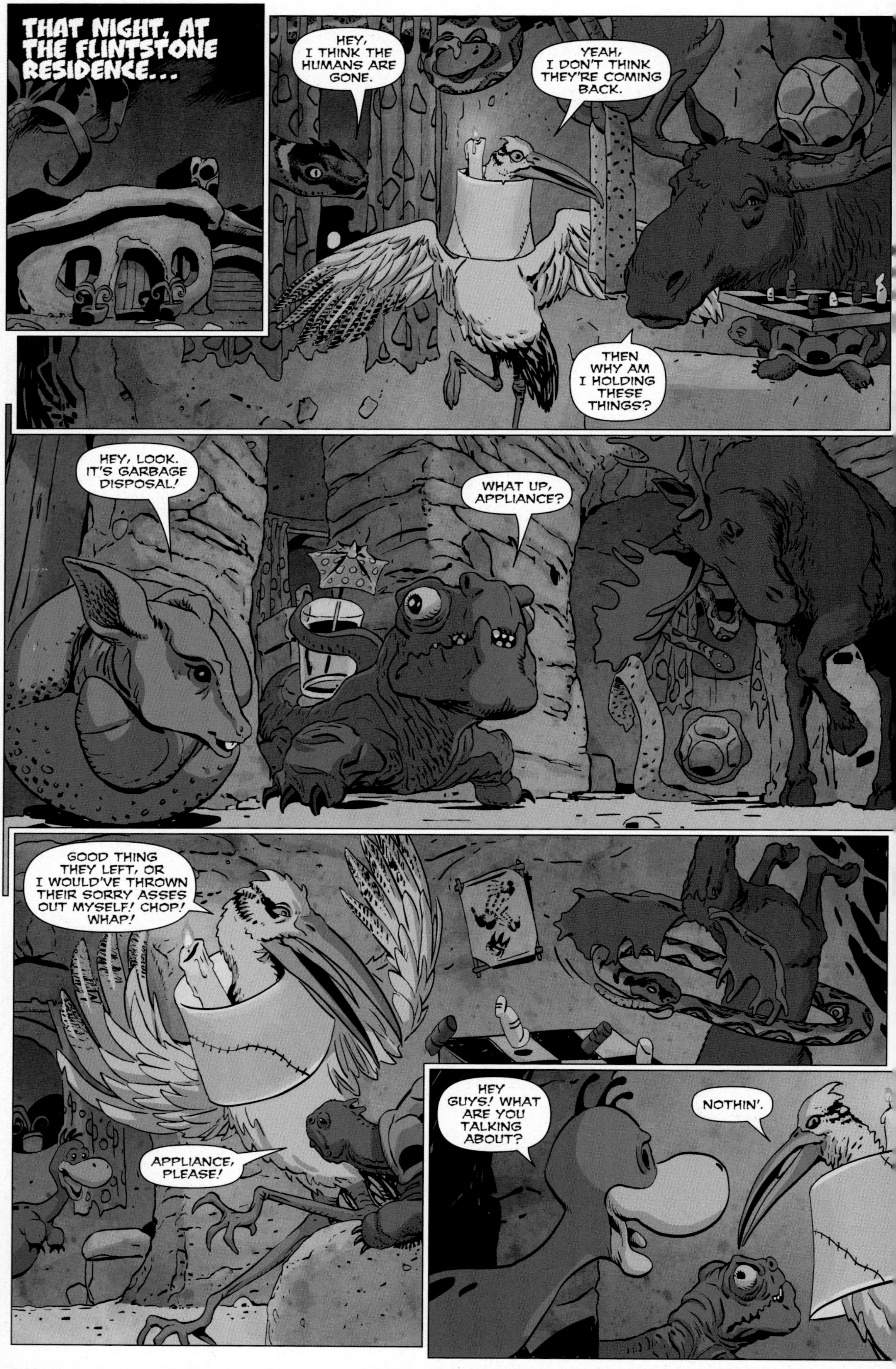

THAT NIGHT, AT THE FLINTSTONE RESIDENCE...
HEY, I THINK THE HUMANS ARE GONE.
YEAH, I DON'T THINK THEY'RE COMING BACK.
THEN WHY AM I HOLDING THESE THINGS?
HEY, LOOK. IT'S GARBAGE DISPOSAL!
WHAT UP, APPLIANCE?
GOOD THING THEY LEFT, OR I WOULD'VE THROWN THEIR SORRY ASSES OUT MYSELF! CHOP! WHAP!
APPLIANCE, PLEASE!
HEY GUYS! WHAT ARE YOU TALKING ABOUT?
NOTHIN'.

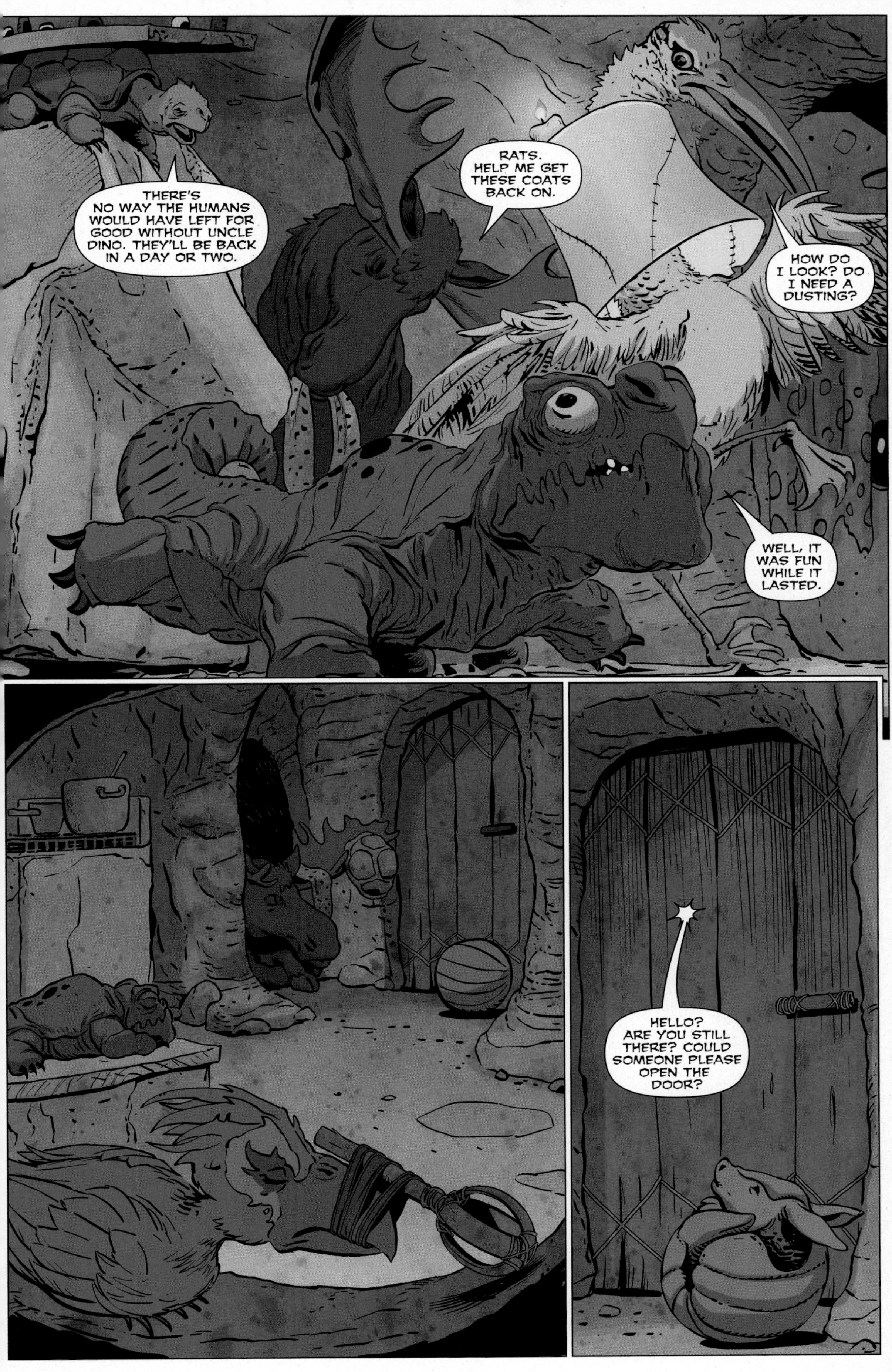

THERE'S NO WAY THE HUMANS WOULD HAVE LEFT FOR GOOD WITHOUT UNCLE DINO. THEY'LL BE BACK IN A DAY OR TWO.
RATS. HELP ME GET THESE COATS BACK ON.
HOW DO I LOOK? DO I NEED A DUSTING?
WELL, IT WAS FUN WHILE IT LASTED.
HELLO? ARE YOU STILL THERE? COULD SOMEONE PLEASE OPEN THE DOOR?

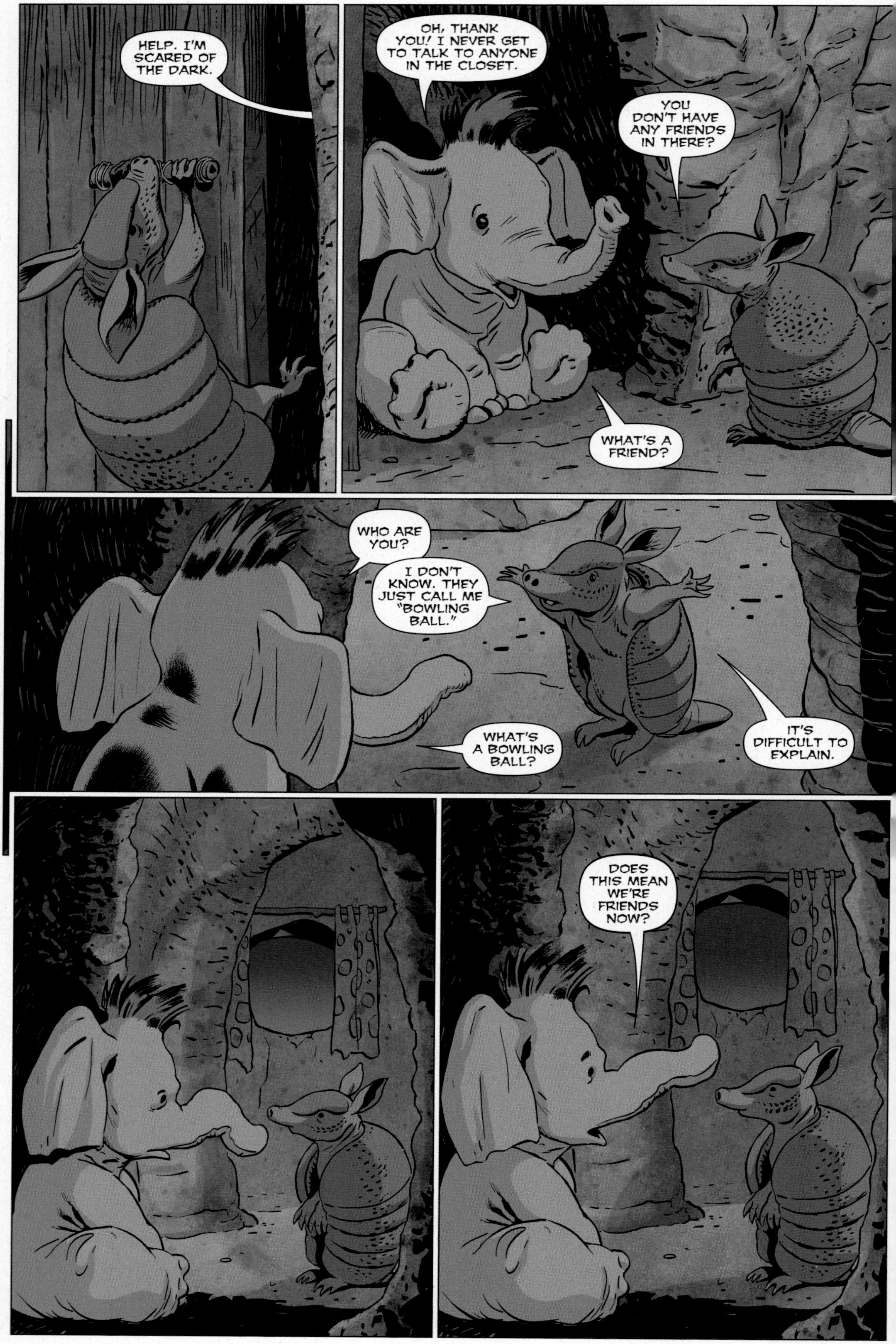
HELP. I'M SCARED OF THE DARK.
OH, THANK YOU! I NEVER GET TO TALK TO ANYONE IN THE CLOSET.
YOU DON'T HAVE ANY FRIENDS IN THERE?
WHAT'S A FRIEND?
WHO ARE YOU?
I DON'T KNOW. THEY JUST CALL ME "BOWLING BALL."
WHAT'S A BOWLING BALL?
IT'S DIFFICULT TO EXPLAIN.
DOES THIS MEAN WE'RE FRIENDS NOW?

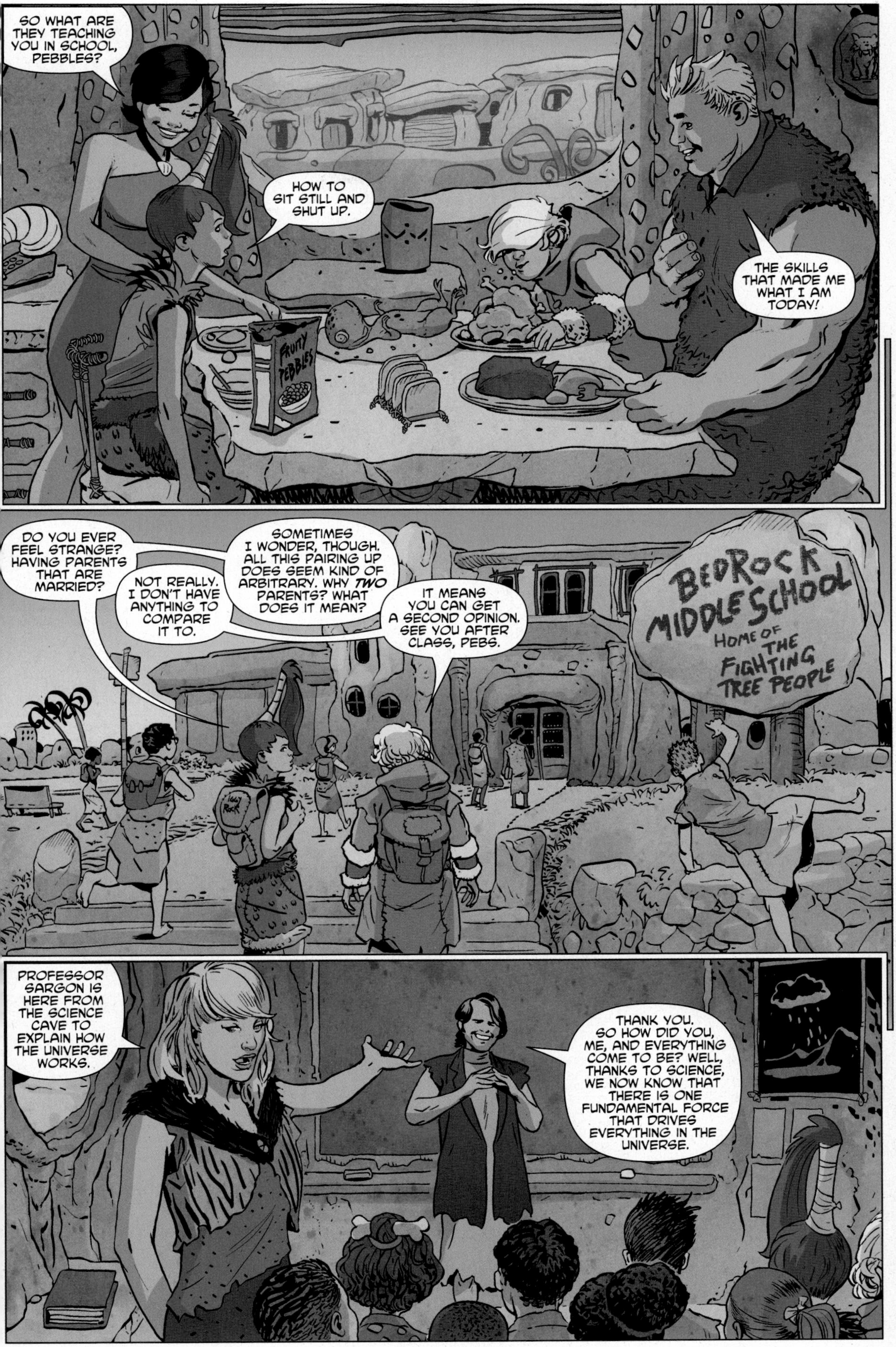
SO WHAT ARE THEY TEACHING YOU IN SCHOOL, PEBBLES?
HOW TO SIT STILL AND SHUT UP.
THE SKILLS THAT MADE ME WHAT I AM TODAY!
FRUITY PEBBLES
DO YOU EVER FEEL STRANGE? HAVING PARENTS THAT ARE MARRIED?
NOT REALLY. I DON'T HAVE ANYTHING TO COMPARE IT TO.
SOMETIMES I WONDER, THOUGH. ALL THIS PAIRING UP DOES SEEM KIND OF ARBITRARY. WHY *TWO* PARENTS? WHAT DOES IT MEAN?
IT MEANS YOU CAN GET A SECOND OPINION. SEE YOU AFTER CLASS, PEBS.
BEDROCK MIDDLE SCHOOL HOME OF THE FIGHTING TREE PEOPLE
PROFESSOR SARGON IS HERE FROM THE SCIENCE CAVE TO EXPLAIN HOW THE UNIVERSE WORKS.
THANK YOU. SO HOW DID YOU, ME, AND EVERYTHING COME TO BE? WELL, THANKS TO SCIENCE, WE NOW KNOW THAT THERE IS ONE FUNDAMENTAL FORCE THAT DRIVES EVERYTHING IN THE UNIVERSE.

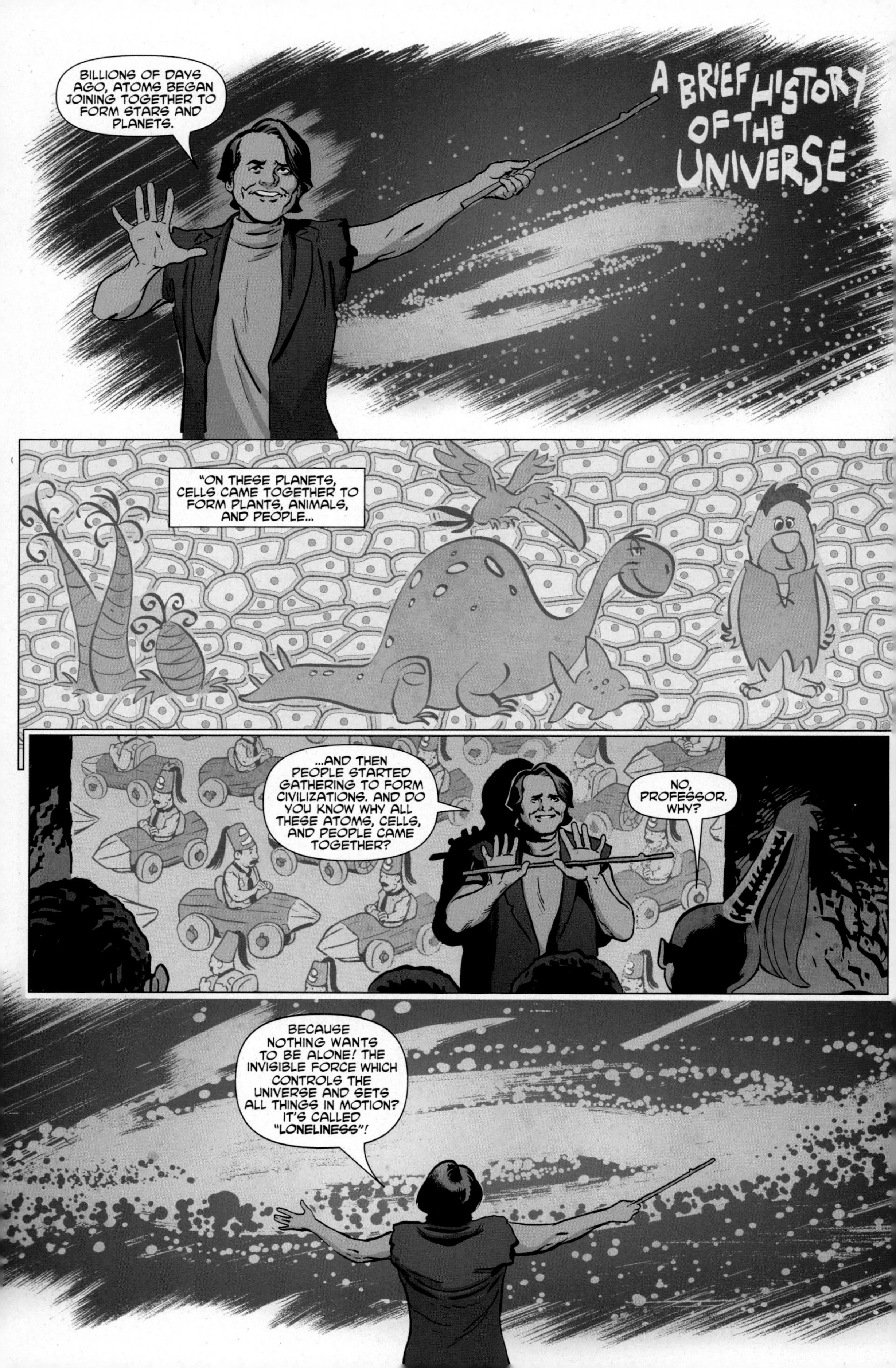
BILLIONS OF DAYS AGO, ATOMS BEGAN JOINING TOGETHER TO FORM STARS AND PLANETS.
A BRIEF HISTORY OF THE UNIVERSE
"ON THESE PLANETS, CELLS CAME TOGETHER TO FORM PLANTS, ANIMALS, AND PEOPLE...
...AND THEN PEOPLE STARTED GATHERING TO FORM CIVILIZATIONS. AND DO YOU KNOW WHY ALL THESE ATOMS, CELLS, AND PEOPLE CAME TOGETHER?
NO, PROFESSOR. WHY?
BECAUSE NOTHING WANTS TO BE ALONE! THE INVISIBLE FORCE WHICH CONTROLS THE UNIVERSE AND SETS ALL THINGS IN MOTION? IT'S CALLED "LONELINESS"!

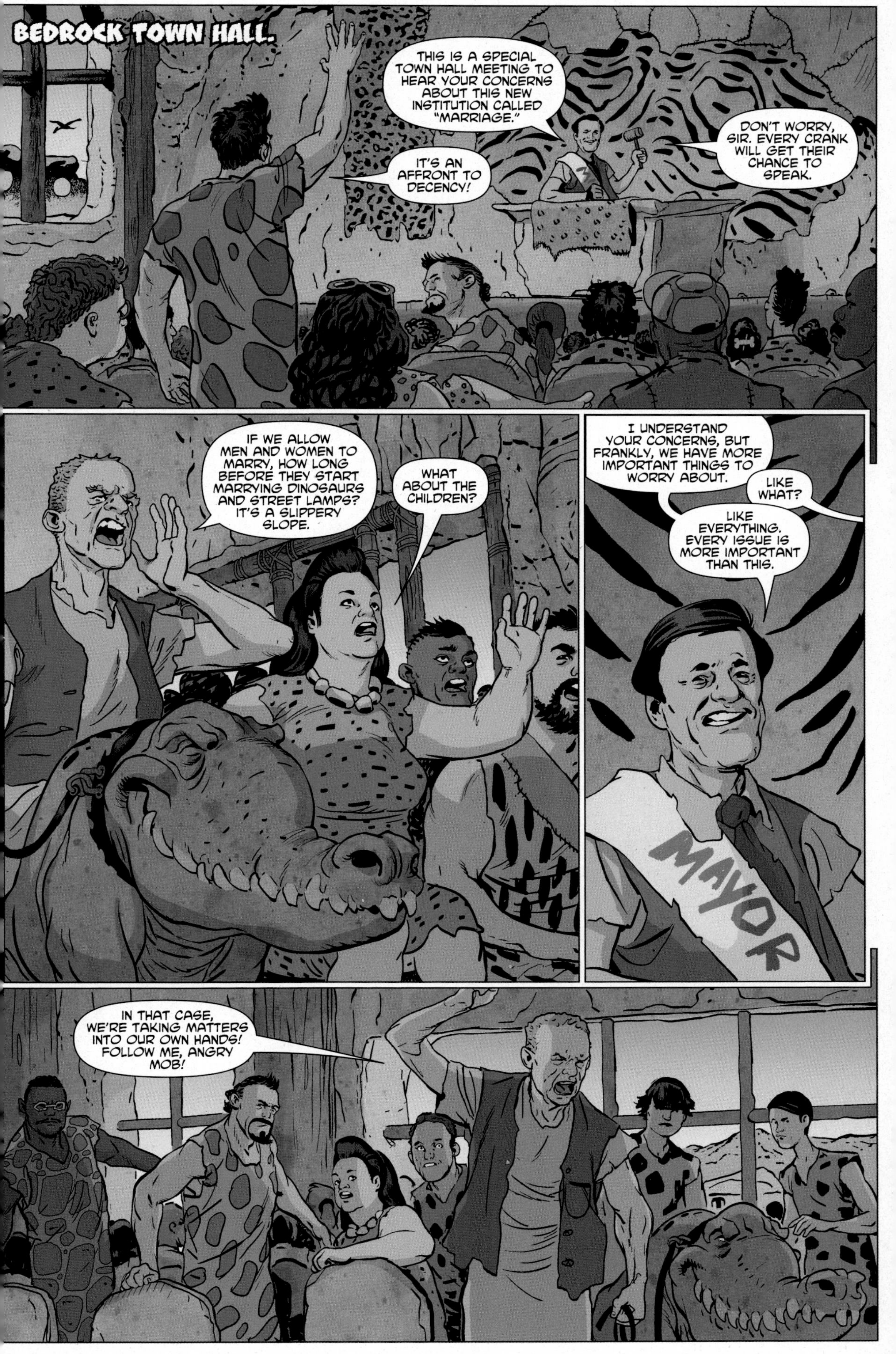
BEDROCK TOWN HALL.
THIS IS A SPECIAL TOWN HALL MEETING TO HEAR YOUR CONCERNS ABOUT THIS NEW INSTITUTION CALLED "MARRIAGE."
IT'S AN AFFRONT TO DECENCY!
DON'T WORRY, SIR. EVERY CRANK WILL GET THEIR CHANCE TO SPEAK.
IF WE ALLOW MEN AND WOMEN TO MARRY, HOW LONG BEFORE THEY START MARRYING DINOSAURS AND STREET LAMPS? IT'S A SLIPPERY SLOPE.
WHAT ABOUT THE CHILDREN?
I UNDERSTAND YOUR CONCERNS, BUT FRANKLY, WE HAVE MORE IMPORTANT THINGS TO WORRY ABOUT.
LIKE WHAT?
LIKE EVERYTHING. EVERY ISSUE IS MORE IMPORTANT THAN THIS.
MAYOR
IN THAT CASE, WE'RE TAKING MATTERS INTO OUR OWN HANDS! FOLLOW ME, ANGRY MOB!

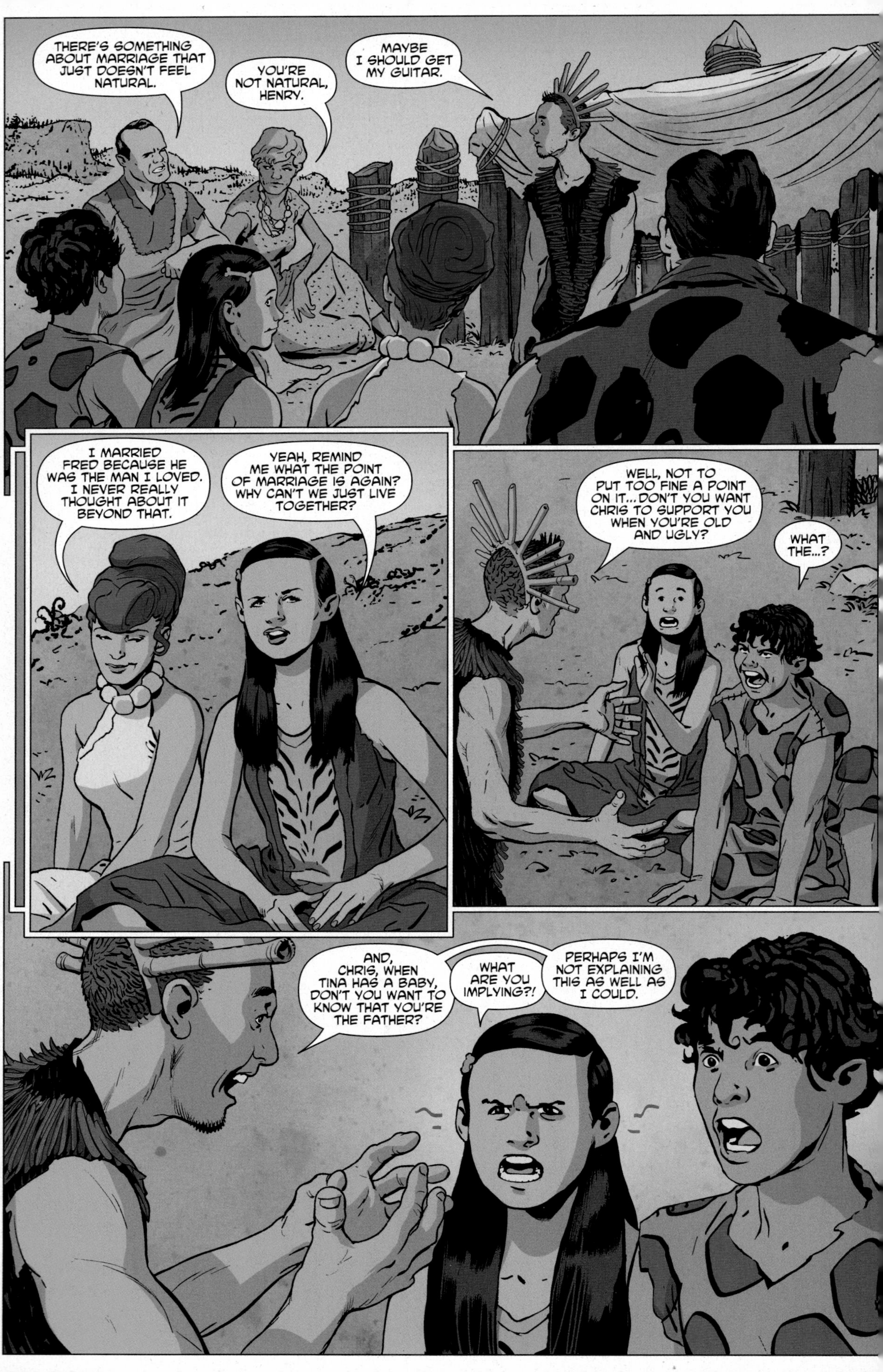
THERE'S SOMETHING ABOUT MARRIAGE THAT JUST DOESN'T FEEL NATURAL.
YOU'RE NOT NATURAL, HENRY.
MAYBE I SHOULD GET MY GUITAR.
I MARRIED FRED BECAUSE HE WAS THE MAN I LOVED. I NEVER REALLY THOUGHT ABOUT IT BEYOND THAT.
YEAH, REMIND ME WHAT THE POINT OF MARRIAGE IS AGAIN? WHY CAN'T WE JUST LIVE TOGETHER?
WELL, NOT TO PUT TOO FINE A POINT ON IT...DON'T YOU WANT CHRIS TO SUPPORT YOU WHEN YOU'RE OLD AND UGLY?
WHAT THE...?
AND, CHRIS, WHEN TINA HAS A BABY, DON'T YOU WANT TO KNOW THAT YOU'RE THE FATHER?
WHAT ARE YOU IMPLYING?!
PERHAPS I'M NOT EXPLAINING THIS AS WELL AS I COULD.

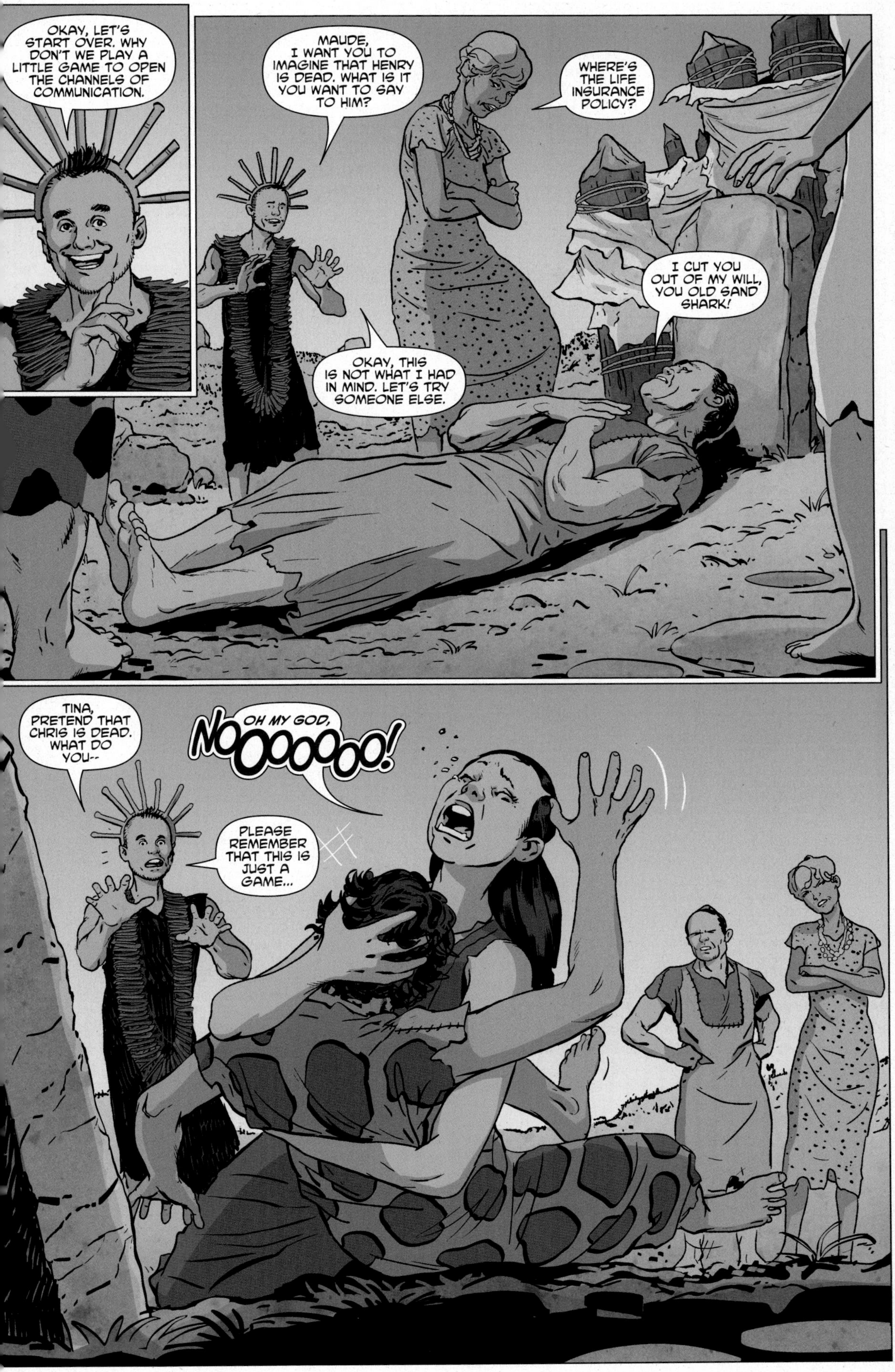
OKAY, LET'S START OVER. WHY DON'T WE PLAY A LITTLE GAME TO OPEN THE CHANNELS OF COMMUNICATION.
MAUDE, I WANT YOU TO IMAGINE THAT HENRY IS DEAD. WHAT IS IT YOU WANT TO SAY TO HIM?
WHERE'S THE LIFE INSURANCE POLICY?
I CUT YOU OUT OF MY WILL, YOU OLD SAND SHARK!
OKAY, THIS IS NOT WHAT I HAD IN MIND. LET'S TRY SOMEONE ELSE.
TINA, PRETEND THAT CHRIS IS DEAD. WHAT DO YOU--
OH MY GOD, NOOOOOOO!
PLEASE REMEMBER THAT THIS IS JUST A GAME...

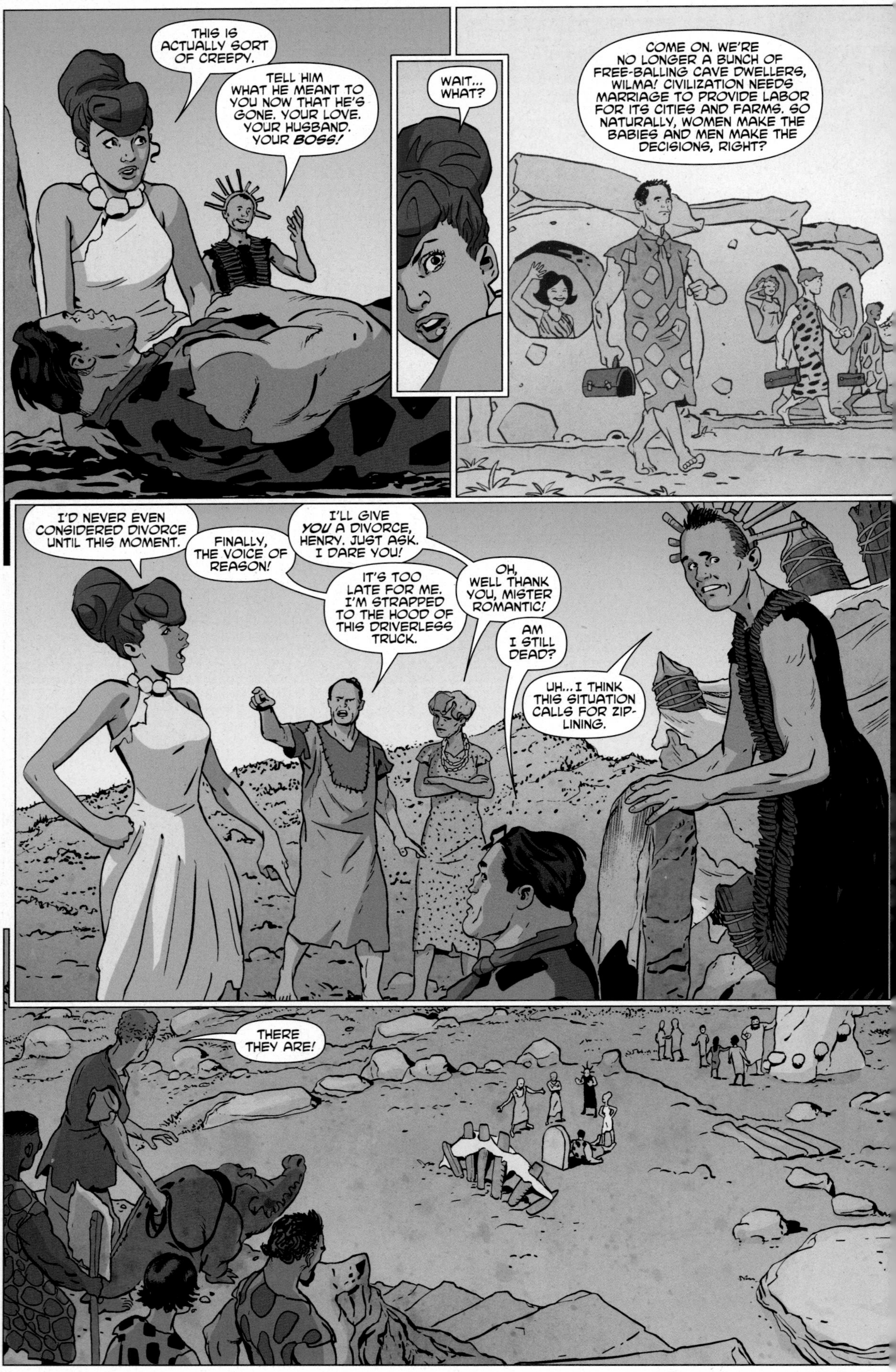
THIS IS ACTUALLY SORT OF CREEPY.
TELL HIM WHAT HE MEANT TO YOU NOW THAT HE'S GONE. YOUR LOVE. YOUR HUSBAND. YOUR *BOSS!*
WAIT... WHAT?
COME ON. WE'RE NO LONGER A BUNCH OF FREE-BALLING CAVE DWELLERS, WILMA! CIVILIZATION NEEDS MARRIAGE TO PROVIDE LABOR FOR ITS CITIES AND FARMS. SO NATURALLY, WOMEN MAKE THE BABIES AND MEN MAKE THE DECISIONS, RIGHT?
I'D NEVER EVEN CONSIDERED DIVORCE UNTIL THIS MOMENT.
FINALLY, THE VOICE OF REASON!
I'LL GIVE *YOU* A DIVORCE, HENRY. JUST ASK. I DARE YOU!
IT'S TOO LATE FOR ME. I'M STRAPPED TO THE HOOD OF THIS DRIVERLESS TRUCK.
OH, WELL THANK YOU, MISTER ROMANTIC!
AM I STILL DEAD?
UH... I THINK THIS SITUATION CALLS FOR ZIP-LINING.
THERE THEY ARE!

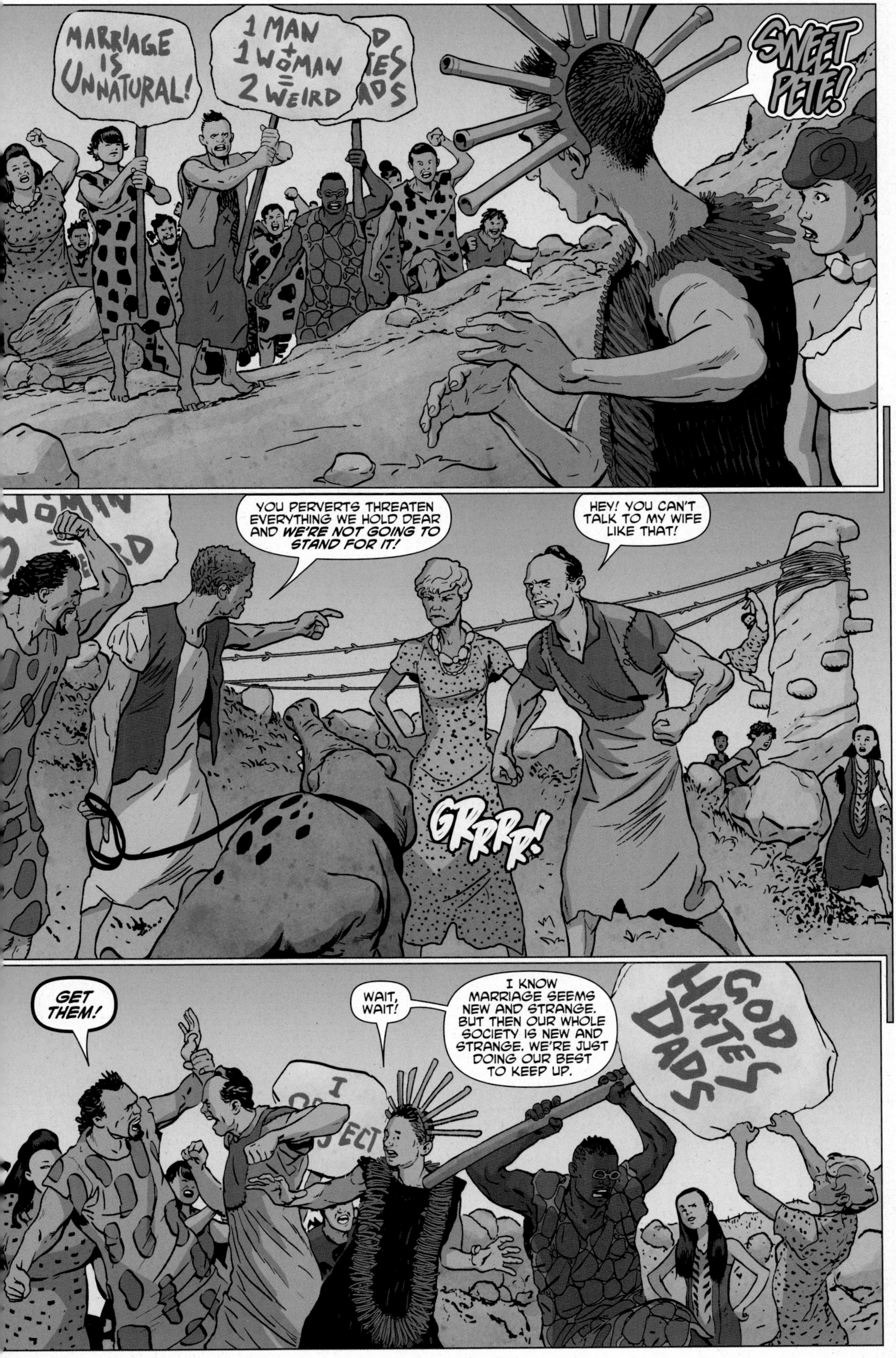
MARRIAGE IS UNNATURAL!
1 MAN + 1 WOMAN = 2 WEIRD
SWEET PETE!
YOU PERVERTS THREATEN EVERYTHING WE HOLD DEAR AND *WE'RE NOT GOING TO STAND FOR IT!*
HEY! YOU CAN'T TALK TO MY WIFE LIKE THAT!
GRRRR!
GET THEM!
WAIT, WAIT!
I KNOW MARRIAGE SEEMS NEW AND STRANGE. BUT THEN OUR WHOLE SOCIETY IS NEW AND STRANGE. WE'RE JUST DOING OUR BEST TO KEEP UP.
GOD HATES DADS

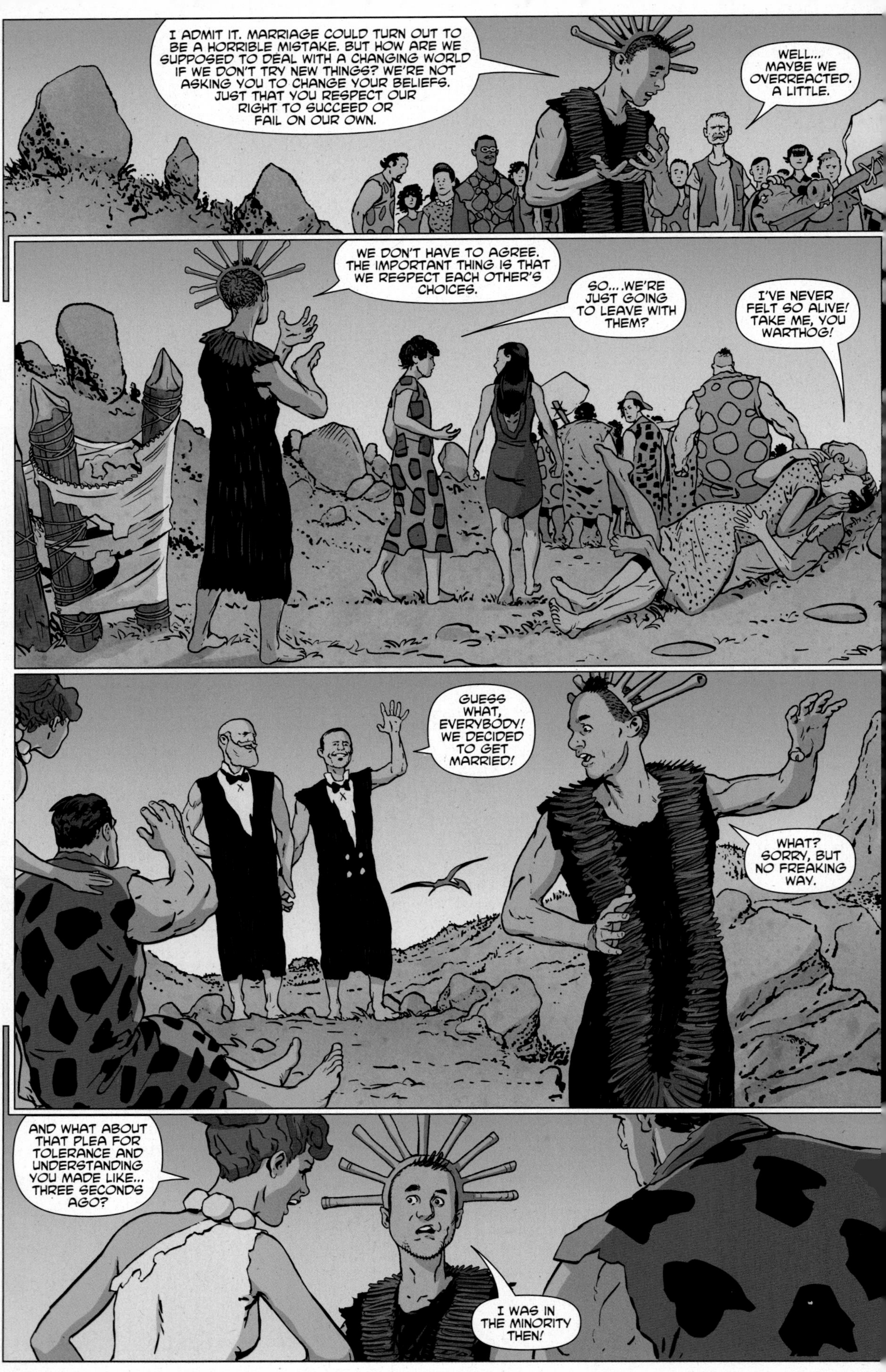
I ADMIT IT. MARRIAGE COULD TURN OUT TO BE A HORRIBLE MISTAKE. BUT HOW ARE WE SUPPOSED TO DEAL WITH A CHANGING WORLD IF WE DON'T TRY NEW THINGS? WE'RE NOT ASKING YOU TO CHANGE YOUR BELIEFS. JUST THAT YOU RESPECT OUR RIGHT TO SUCCEED OR FAIL ON OUR OWN.
WELL... MAYBE WE OVERREACTED. A LITTLE.
WE DON'T HAVE TO AGREE. THE IMPORTANT THING IS THAT WE RESPECT EACH OTHER'S CHOICES.
SO.... WE'RE JUST GOING TO LEAVE WITH THEM?
I'VE NEVER FELT SO ALIVE! TAKE ME, YOU WARTHOG!
GUESS WHAT, EVERYBODY! WE DECIDED TO GET MARRIED!
WHAT? SORRY, BUT NO FREAKING WAY.
AND WHAT ABOUT THAT PLEA FOR TOLERANCE AND UNDERSTANDING YOU MADE LIKE... THREE SECONDS AGO?
I WAS IN THE MINORITY THEN!

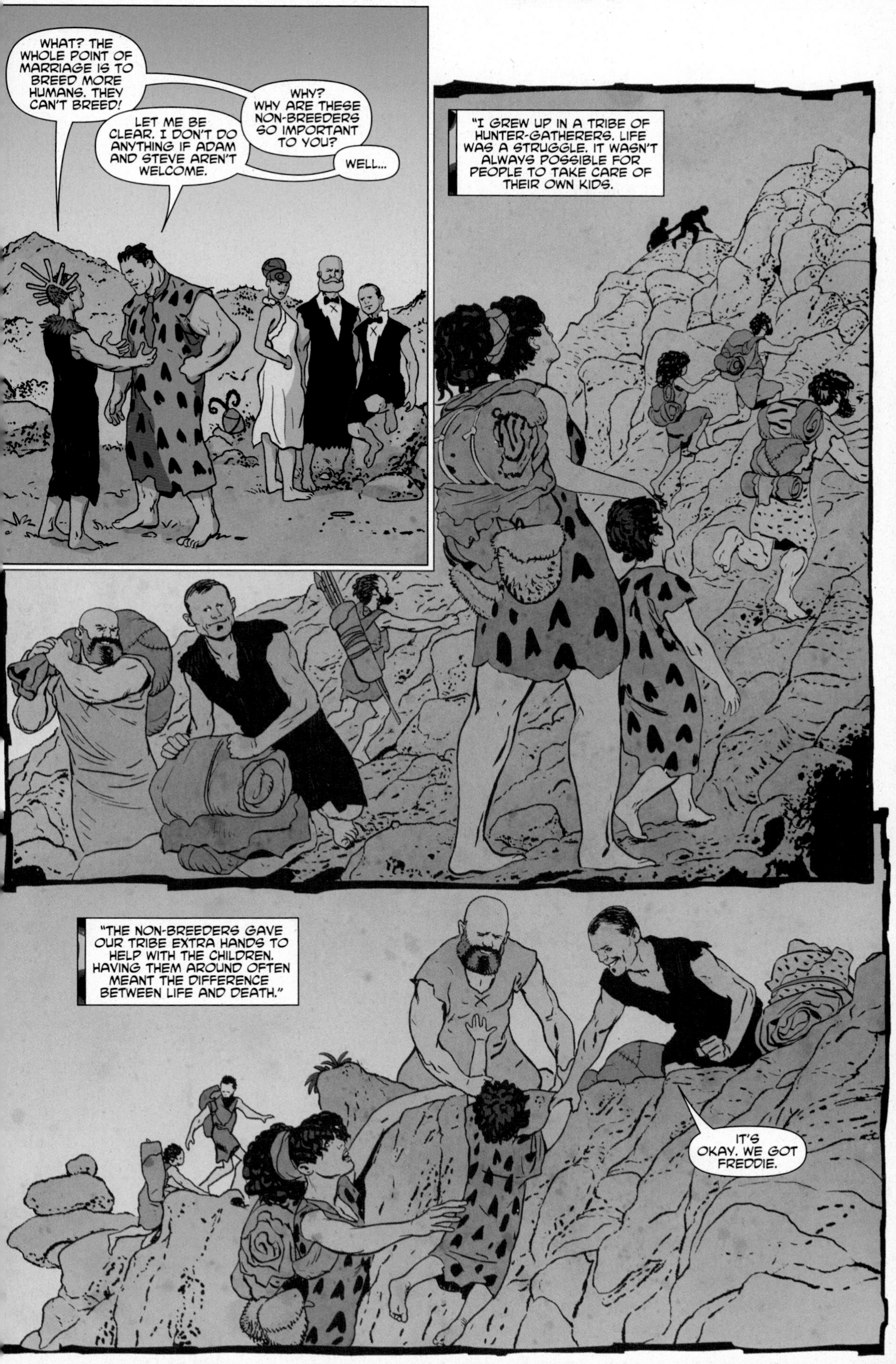
WHAT? THE WHOLE POINT OF MARRIAGE IS TO BREED MORE HUMANS. THEY CAN'T BREED!
LET ME BE CLEAR. I DON'T DO ANYTHING IF ADAM AND STEVE AREN'T WELCOME.
WHY? WHY ARE THESE NON-BREEDERS SO IMPORTANT TO YOU?
WELL...
"I GREW UP IN A TRIBE OF HUNTER-GATHERERS. LIFE WAS A STRUGGLE. IT WASN'T ALWAYS POSSIBLE FOR PEOPLE TO TAKE CARE OF THEIR OWN KIDS.
"THE NON-BREEDERS GAVE OUR TRIBE EXTRA HANDS TO HELP WITH THE CHILDREN. HAVING THEM AROUND OFTEN MEANT THE DIFFERENCE BETWEEN LIFE AND DEATH."
IT'S OKAY. WE GOT FREDDIE.

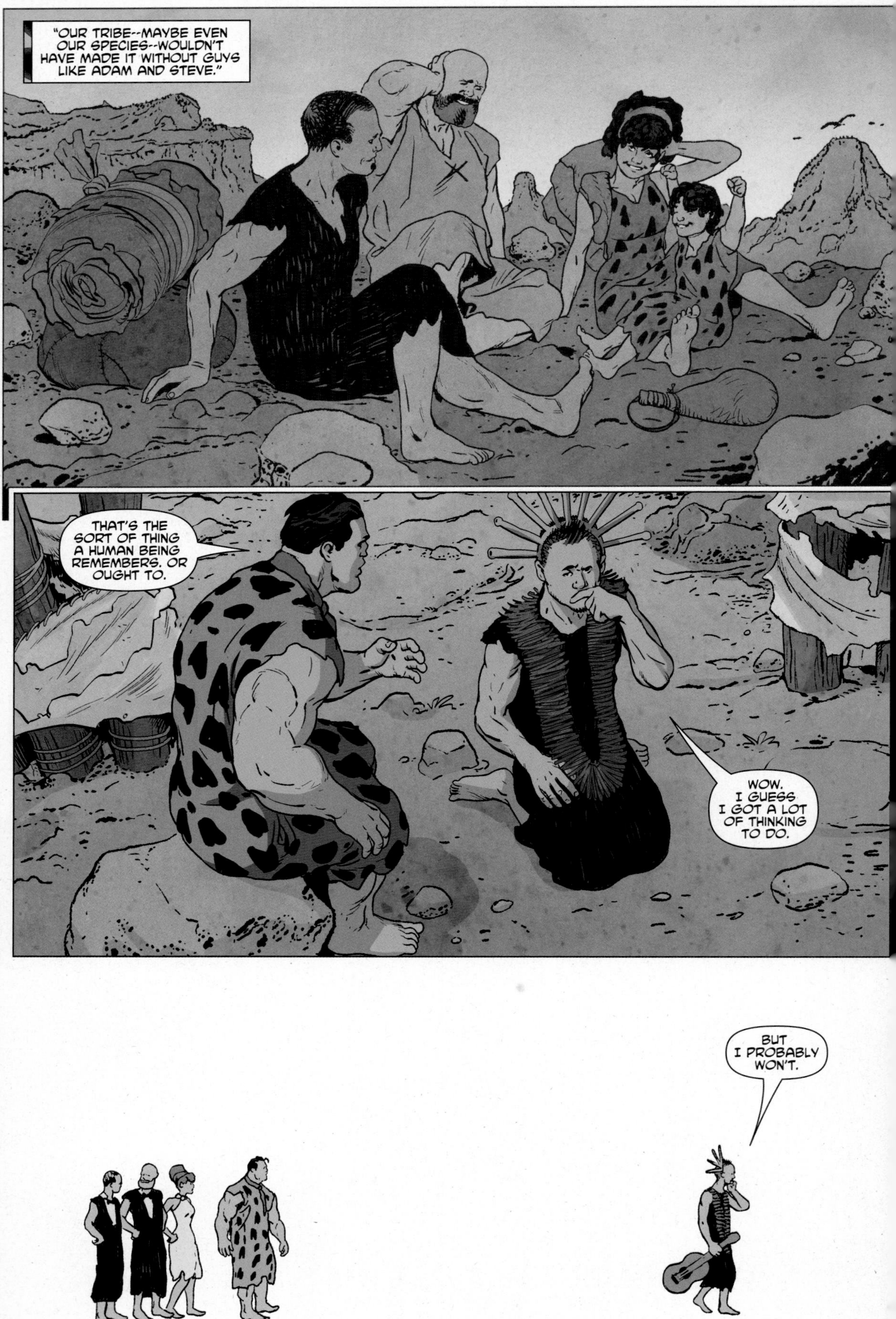
"OUR TRIBE--MAYBE EVEN OUR SPECIES--WOULDN'T HAVE MADE IT WITHOUT GUYS LIKE ADAM AND STEVE."
THAT'S THE SORT OF THING A HUMAN BEING REMEMBERS. OR OUGHT TO.
WOW. I GUESS I GOT A LOT OF THINKING TO DO.
BUT I PROBABLY WON'T.

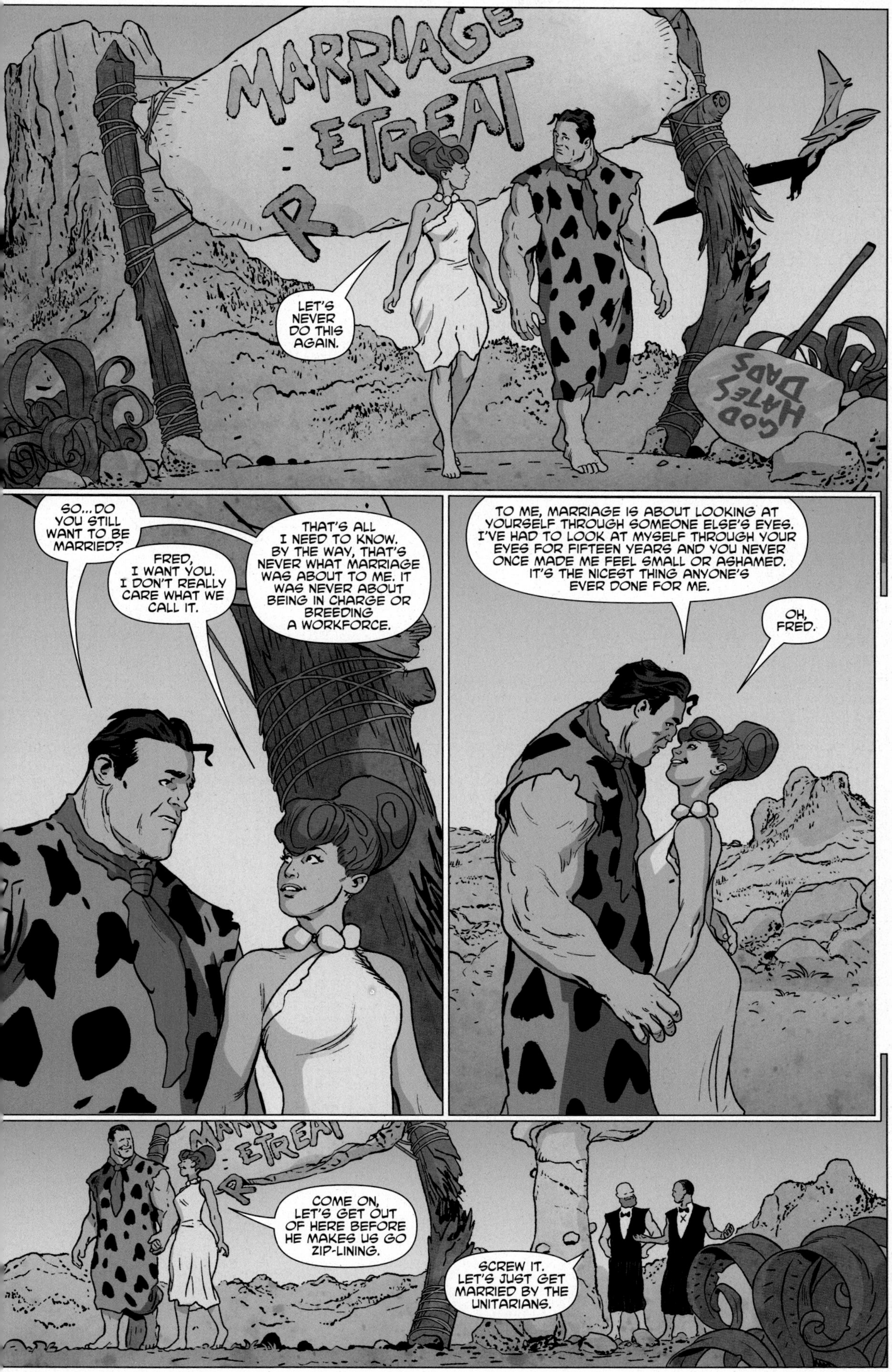

MARRIAGE RETREAT
LET'S NEVER DO THIS AGAIN.
GOD HATES DADS
SO...DO YOU STILL WANT TO BE MARRIED?
FRED, I WANT YOU. I DON'T REALLY CARE WHAT WE CALL IT.
THAT'S ALL I NEED TO KNOW. BY THE WAY, THAT'S NEVER WHAT MARRIAGE WAS ABOUT TO ME. IT WAS NEVER ABOUT BEING IN CHARGE OR BREEDING A WORKFORCE.
TO ME, MARRIAGE IS ABOUT LOOKING AT YOURSELF THROUGH SOMEONE ELSE'S EYES. I'VE HAD TO LOOK AT MYSELF THROUGH YOUR EYES FOR FIFTEEN YEARS AND YOU NEVER ONCE MADE ME FEEL SMALL OR ASHAMED. IT'S THE NICEST THING ANYONE'S EVER DONE FOR ME.
OH, FRED.
COME ON, LET'S GET OUT OF HERE BEFORE HE MAKES US GO ZIP-LINING.
SCREW IT. LET'S JUST GET MARRIED BY THE UNITARIANS.

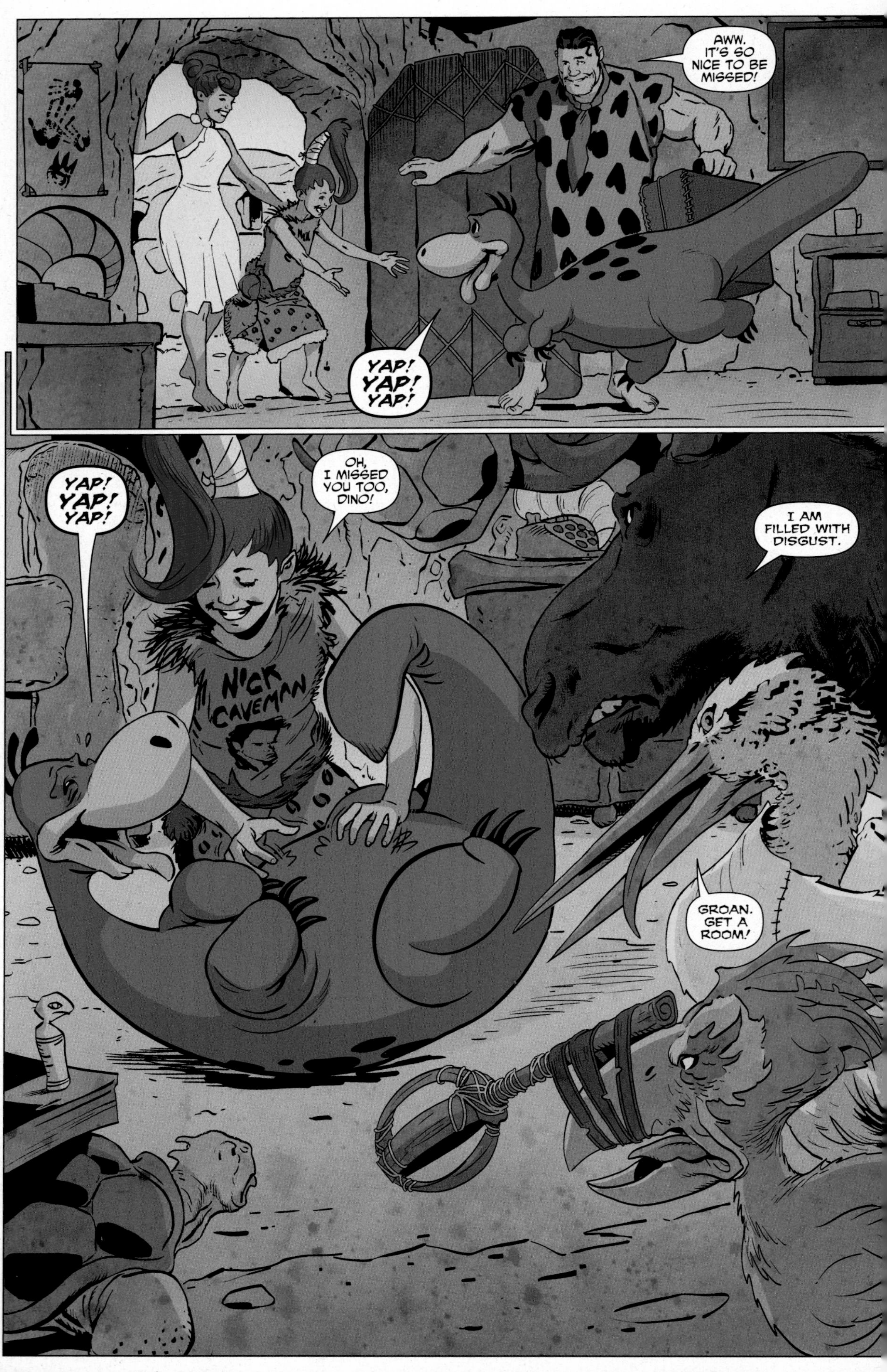
AWW. IT'S SO NICE TO BE MISSED!
YAP! YAP! YAP!
YAP! YAP! YAP!
OH, I MISSED YOU TOO, DINO!
I AM FILLED WITH DISGUST.
GROAN. GET A ROOM!
NICK CAVEMAN

THE FLINTSTONES #5 cover by LEE WEEKS and LAURA MARTIN

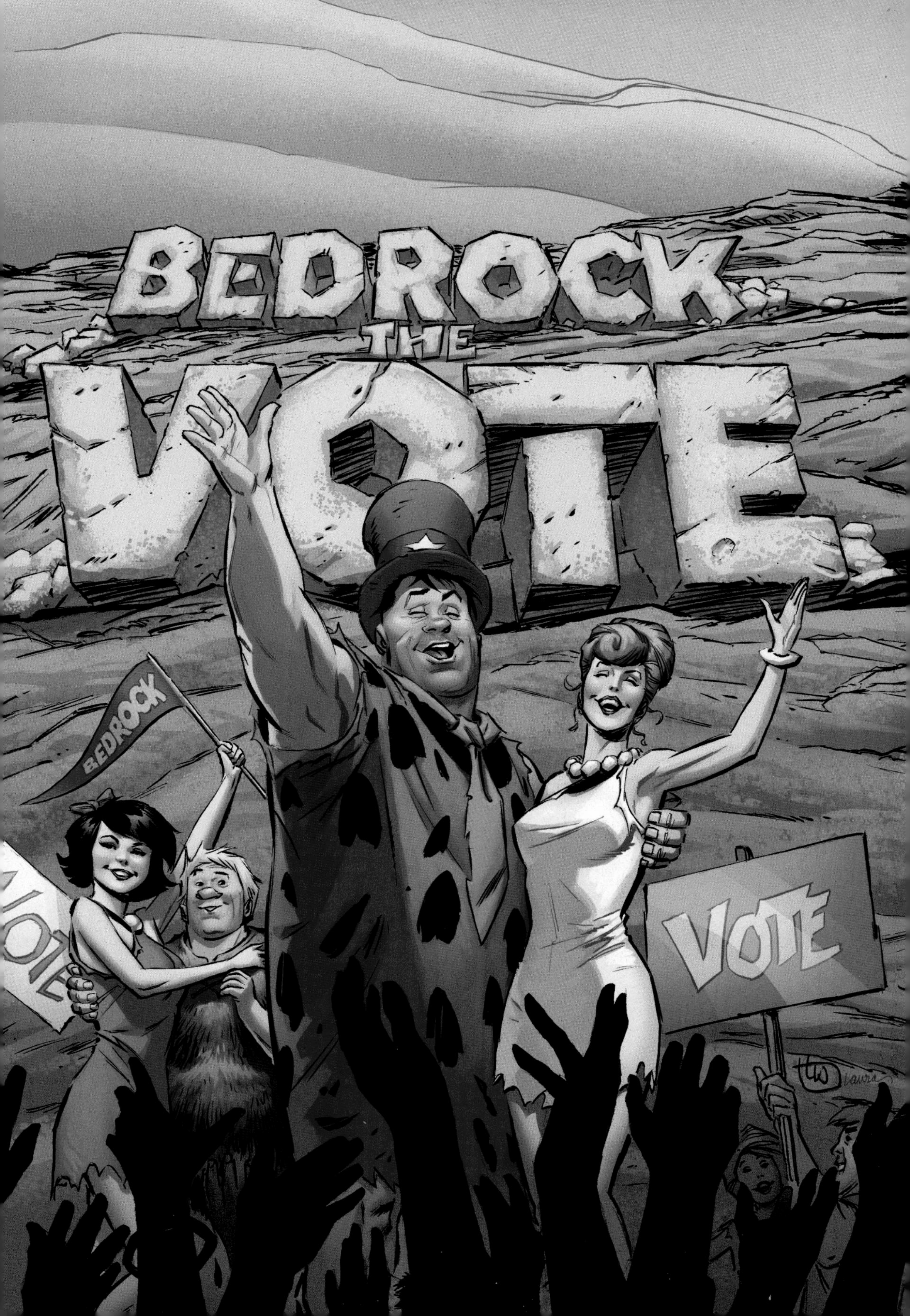

BEDROCK THE VOTE
BEDROCK
VOTE
VOTE

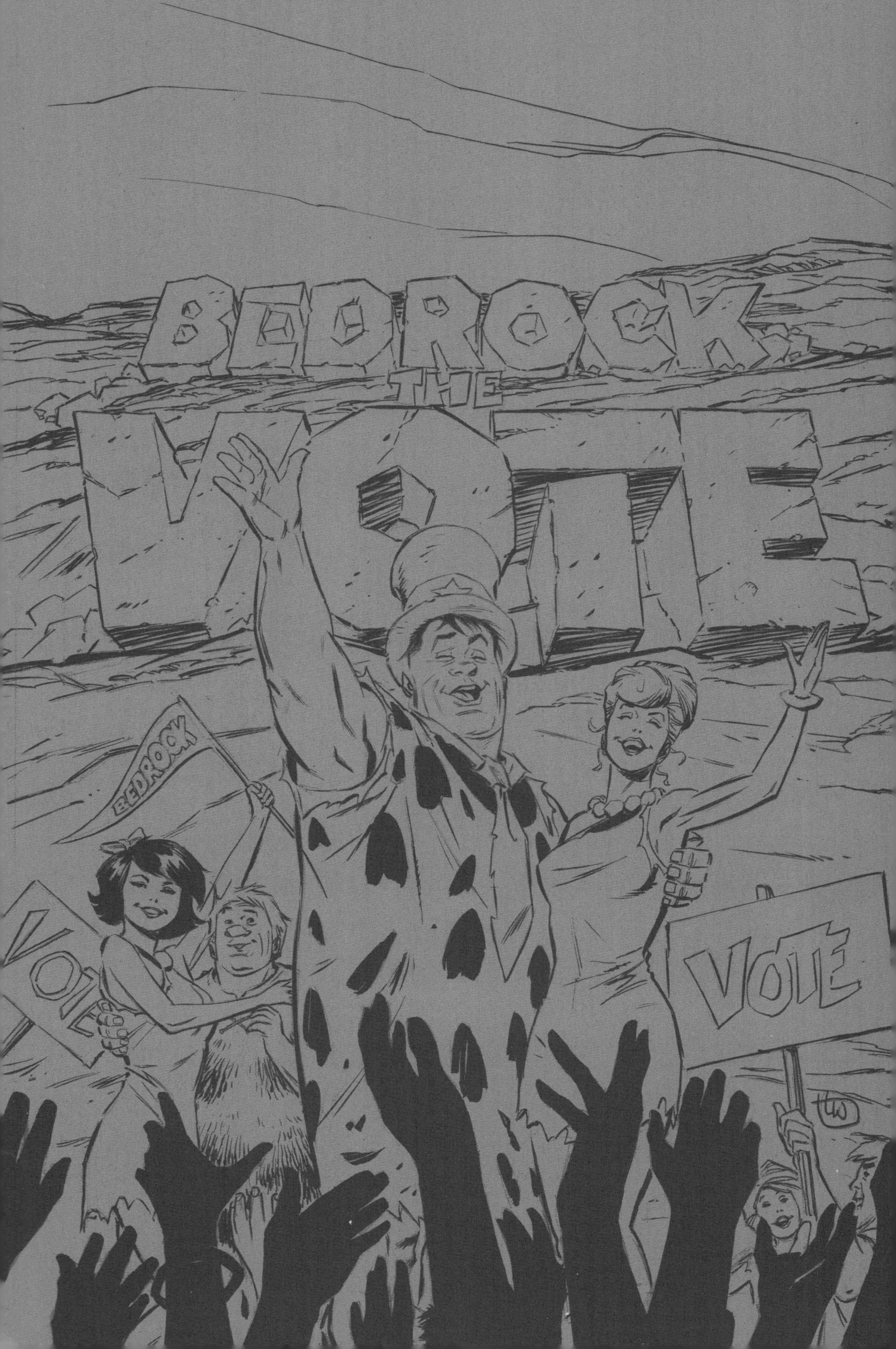
BEDROCK THE VOTE
BEDROCK
VOTE
VOTE

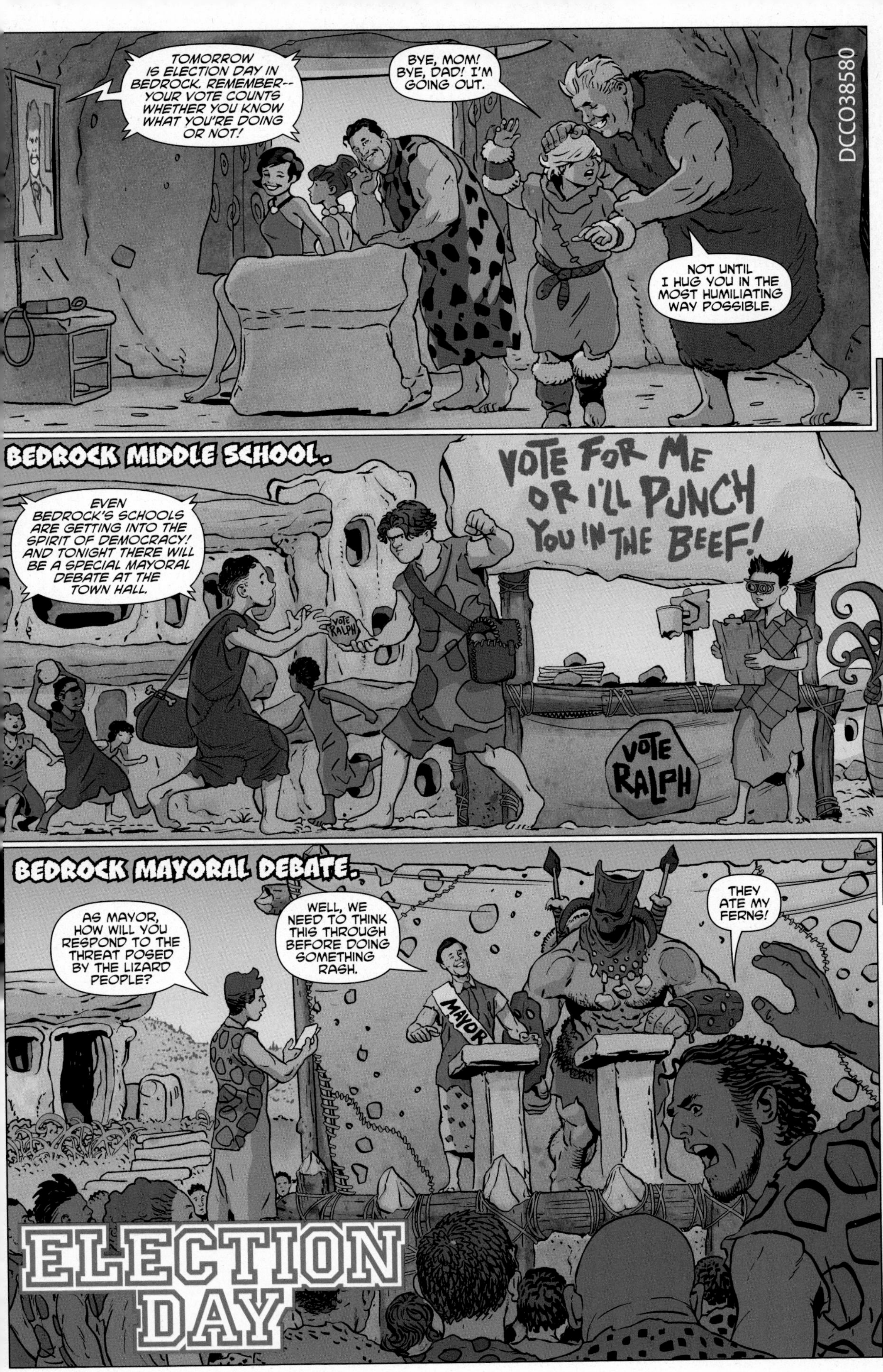
TOMORROW IS ELECTION DAY IN BEDROCK. REMEMBER-- YOUR VOTE COUNTS WHETHER YOU KNOW WHAT YOU'RE DOING OR NOT!
BYE, MOM! BYE, DAD! I'M GOING OUT.
NOT UNTIL I HUG YOU IN THE MOST HUMILIATING WAY POSSIBLE.
DCCO38580
BEDROCK MIDDLE SCHOOL.
EVEN BEDROCK'S SCHOOLS ARE GETTING INTO THE SPIRIT OF DEMOCRACY! AND TONIGHT THERE WILL BE A SPECIAL MAYORAL DEBATE AT THE TOWN HALL.
VOTE FOR ME OR I'LL PUNCH YOU IN THE BEEF!
VOTE RALPH
VOTE RALPH
BEDROCK MAYORAL DEBATE.
AS MAYOR, HOW WILL YOU RESPOND TO THE THREAT POSED BY THE LIZARD PEOPLE?
WELL, WE NEED TO THINK THIS THROUGH BEFORE DOING SOMETHING RASH.
THEY ATE MY FERNS!
MAYOR
ELECTION DAY

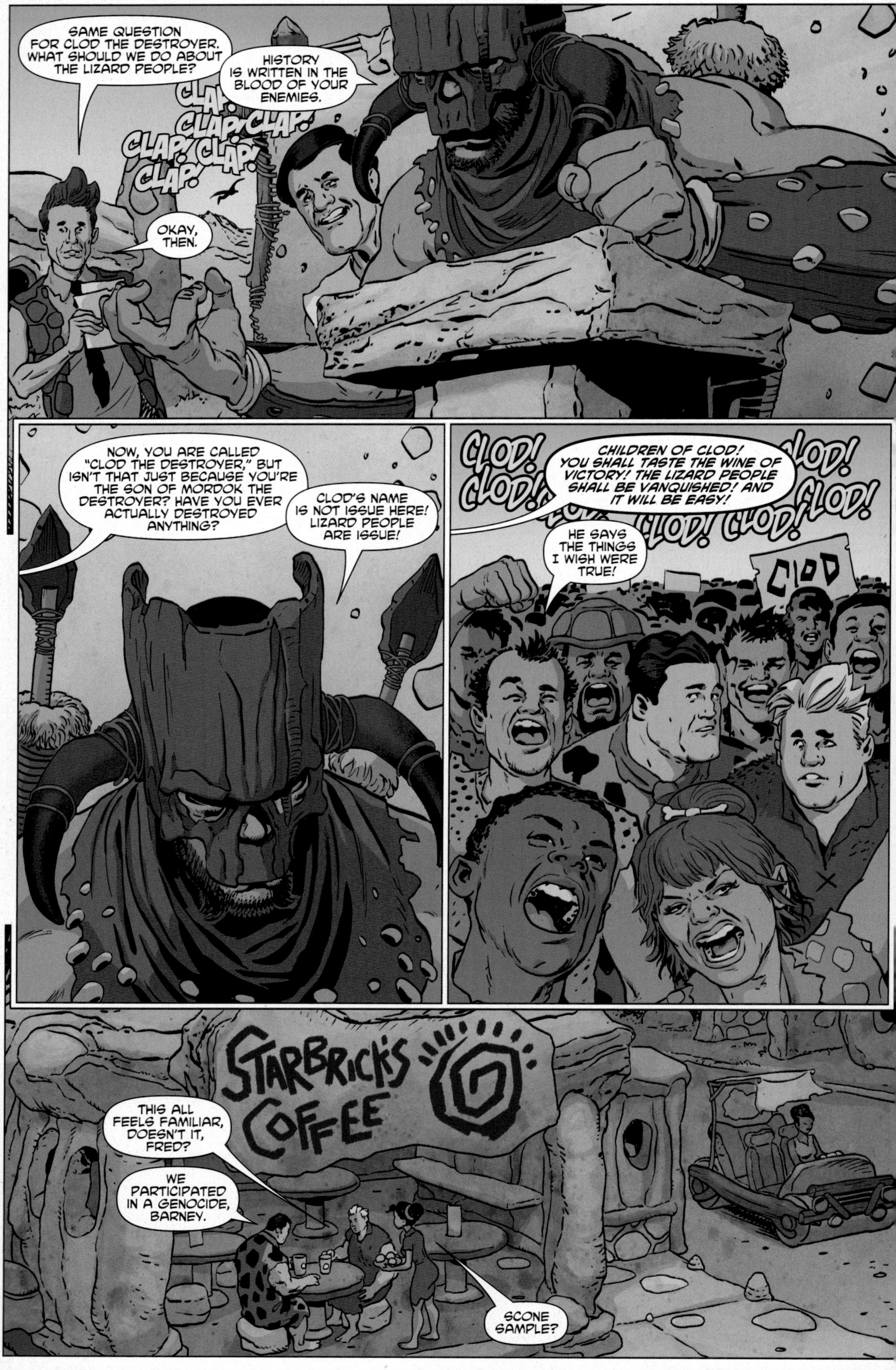
SAME QUESTION FOR CLOD THE DESTROYER. WHAT SHOULD WE DO ABOUT THE LIZARD PEOPLE?
HISTORY IS WRITTEN IN THE BLOOD OF YOUR ENEMIES.
CLAP! CLAP! CLAP! CLAP! CLAP! CLAP!
OKAY, THEN.
NOW, YOU ARE CALLED "CLOD THE DESTROYER," BUT ISN'T THAT JUST BECAUSE YOU'RE THE SON OF MORDOK THE DESTROYER? HAVE YOU EVER ACTUALLY DESTROYED ANYTHING?
CLOD'S NAME IS NOT ISSUE HERE! LIZARD PEOPLE ARE ISSUE!
CLOD! CLOD! CLOD! CLOD! CLOD! CLOD!
CHILDREN OF CLOD! YOU SHALL TASTE THE WINE OF VICTORY! THE LIZARD PEOPLE SHALL BE VANQUISHED! AND IT WILL BE EASY!
HE SAYS THE THINGS I WISH WERE TRUE!
CLOD
STARBRICK'S COFFEE
THIS ALL FEELS FAMILIAR, DOESN'T IT, FRED?
WE PARTICIPATED IN A GENOCIDE, BARNEY.
SCONE SAMPLE?

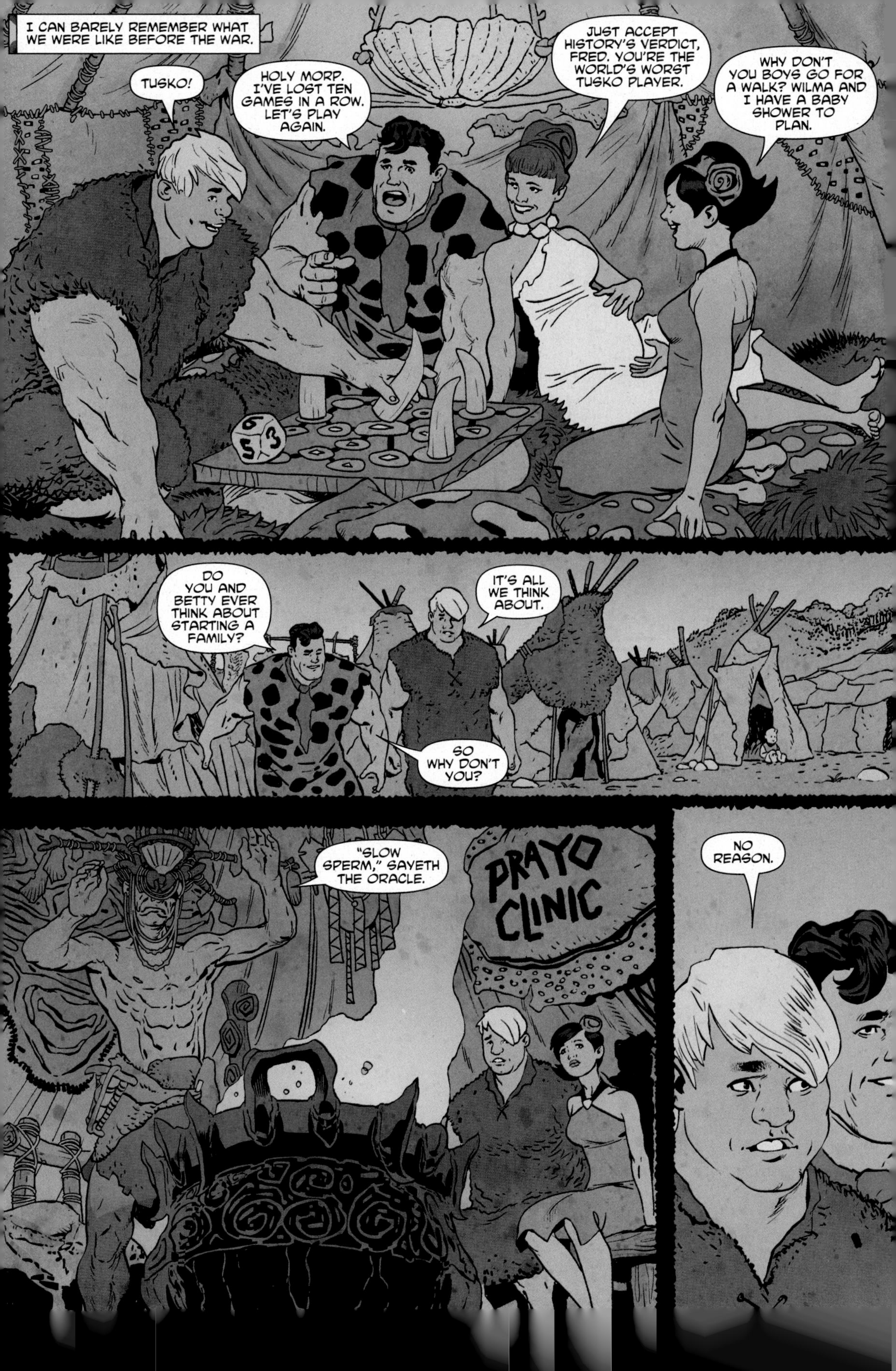
I CAN BARELY REMEMBER WHAT WE WERE LIKE BEFORE THE WAR.
TUSKO!
HOLY MORP. I'VE LOST TEN GAMES IN A ROW. LET'S PLAY AGAIN.
JUST ACCEPT HISTORY'S VERDICT, FRED. YOU'RE THE WORLD'S WORST TUSKO PLAYER.
WHY DON'T YOU BOYS GO FOR A WALK? WILMA AND I HAVE A BABY SHOWER TO PLAN.
DO YOU AND BETTY EVER THINK ABOUT STARTING A FAMILY?
IT'S ALL WE THINK ABOUT.
SO WHY DON'T YOU?
"SLOW SPERM," SAYETH THE ORACLE.
PRAYO CLINIC
NO REASON.

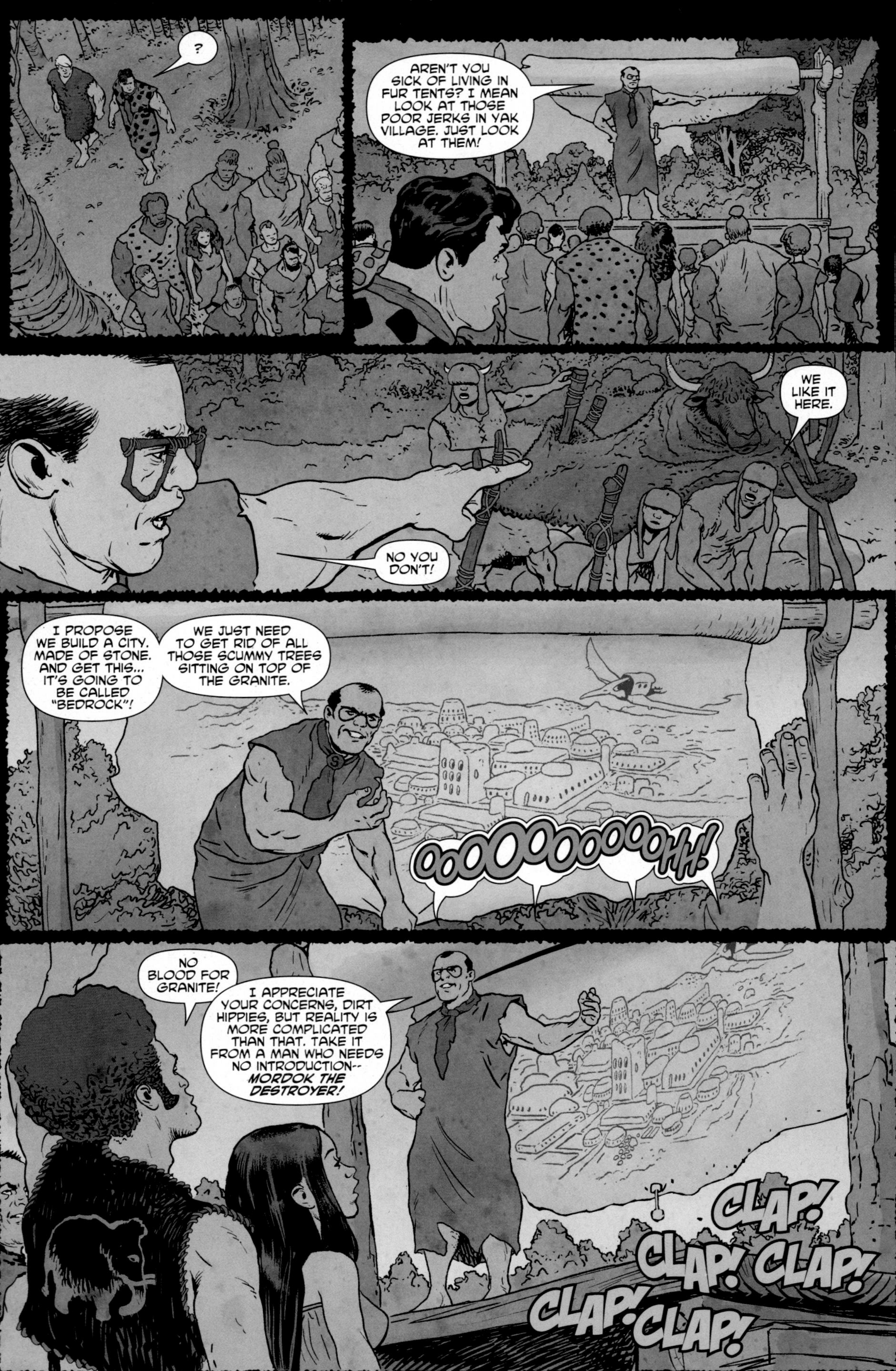
?
AREN'T YOU SICK OF LIVING IN FUR TENTS? I MEAN LOOK AT THOSE POOR JERKS IN YAK VILLAGE. JUST LOOK AT THEM!
WE LIKE IT HERE.
NO YOU DON'T!
I PROPOSE WE BUILD A CITY. MADE OF STONE. AND GET THIS... IT'S GOING TO BE CALLED "BEDROCK"!
WE JUST NEED TO GET RID OF ALL THOSE SCUMMY TREES SITTING ON TOP OF THE GRANITE.
OOOOOOOOOOOHH!
NO BLOOD FOR GRANITE!
I APPRECIATE YOUR CONCERNS, DIRT HIPPIES, BUT REALITY IS MORE COMPLICATED THAN THAT. TAKE IT FROM A MAN WHO NEEDS NO INTRODUCTION-- *MORDOK THE DESTROYER!*
CLAP!
CLAP! CLAP!
CLAP! CLAP!

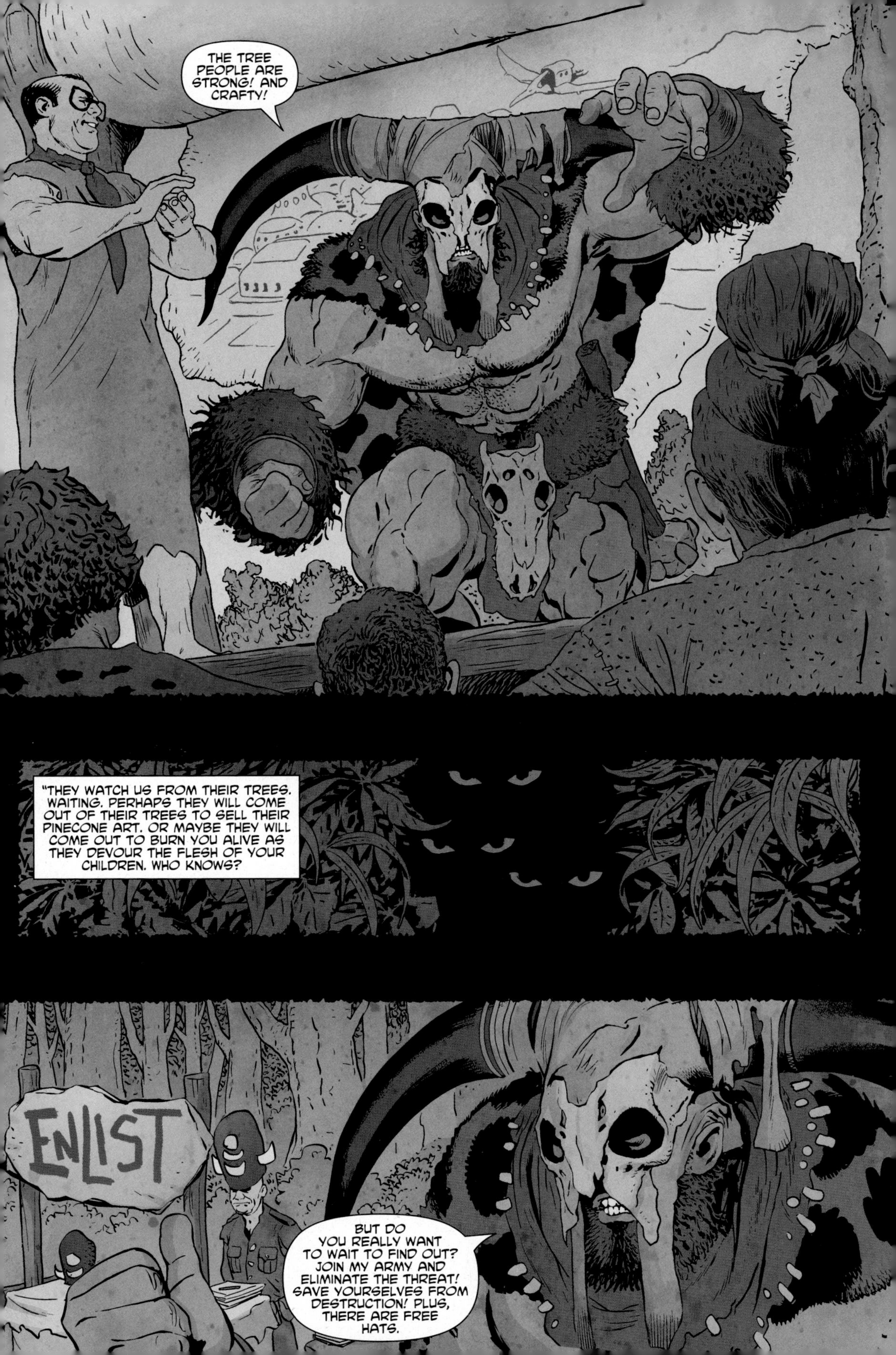
THE TREE PEOPLE ARE STRONG! AND CRAFTY!
"THEY WATCH US FROM THEIR TREES. WAITING. PERHAPS THEY WILL COME OUT OF THEIR TREES TO SELL THEIR PINECONE ART. OR MAYBE THEY WILL COME OUT TO BURN YOU ALIVE AS THEY DEVOUR THE FLESH OF YOUR CHILDREN. WHO KNOWS?
ENLIST
BUT DO YOU REALLY WANT TO WAIT TO FIND OUT? JOIN MY ARMY AND ELIMINATE THE THREAT! SAVE YOURSELVES FROM DESTRUCTION! PLUS, THERE ARE FREE HATS.

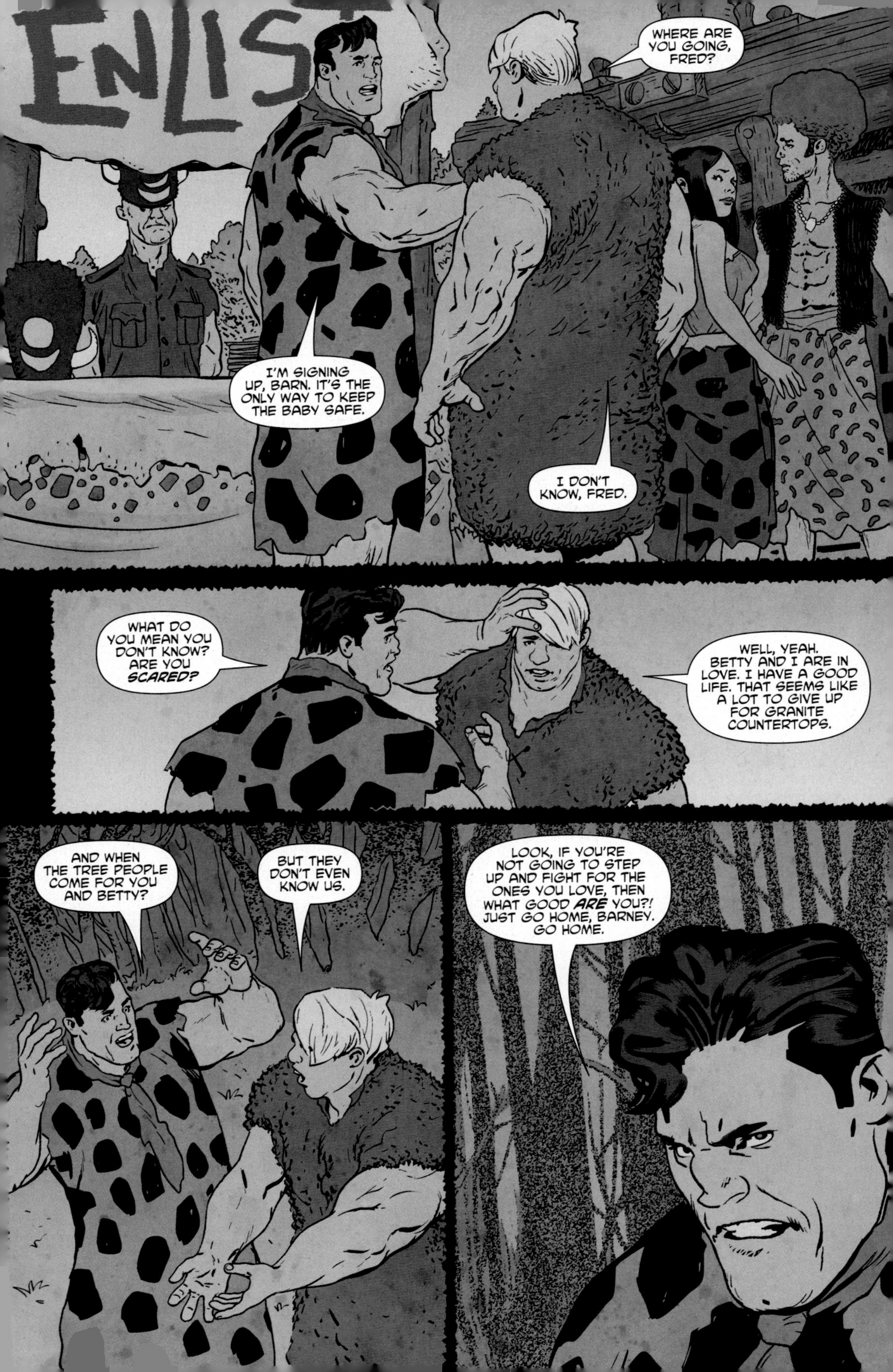
ENLIST
WHERE ARE YOU GOING, FRED?
I'M SIGNING UP, BARN. IT'S THE ONLY WAY TO KEEP THE BABY SAFE.
I DON'T KNOW, FRED.
WHAT DO YOU MEAN YOU DON'T KNOW? ARE YOU *SCARED?*
WELL, YEAH. BETTY AND I ARE IN LOVE. I HAVE A GOOD LIFE. THAT SEEMS LIKE A LOT TO GIVE UP FOR GRANITE COUNTERTOPS.
AND WHEN THE TREE PEOPLE COME FOR YOU AND BETTY?
BUT THEY DON'T EVEN KNOW US.
LOOK, IF YOU'RE NOT GOING TO STEP UP AND FIGHT FOR THE ONES YOU LOVE, THEN WHAT GOOD ***ARE*** YOU?! JUST GO HOME, BARNEY. GO HOME.

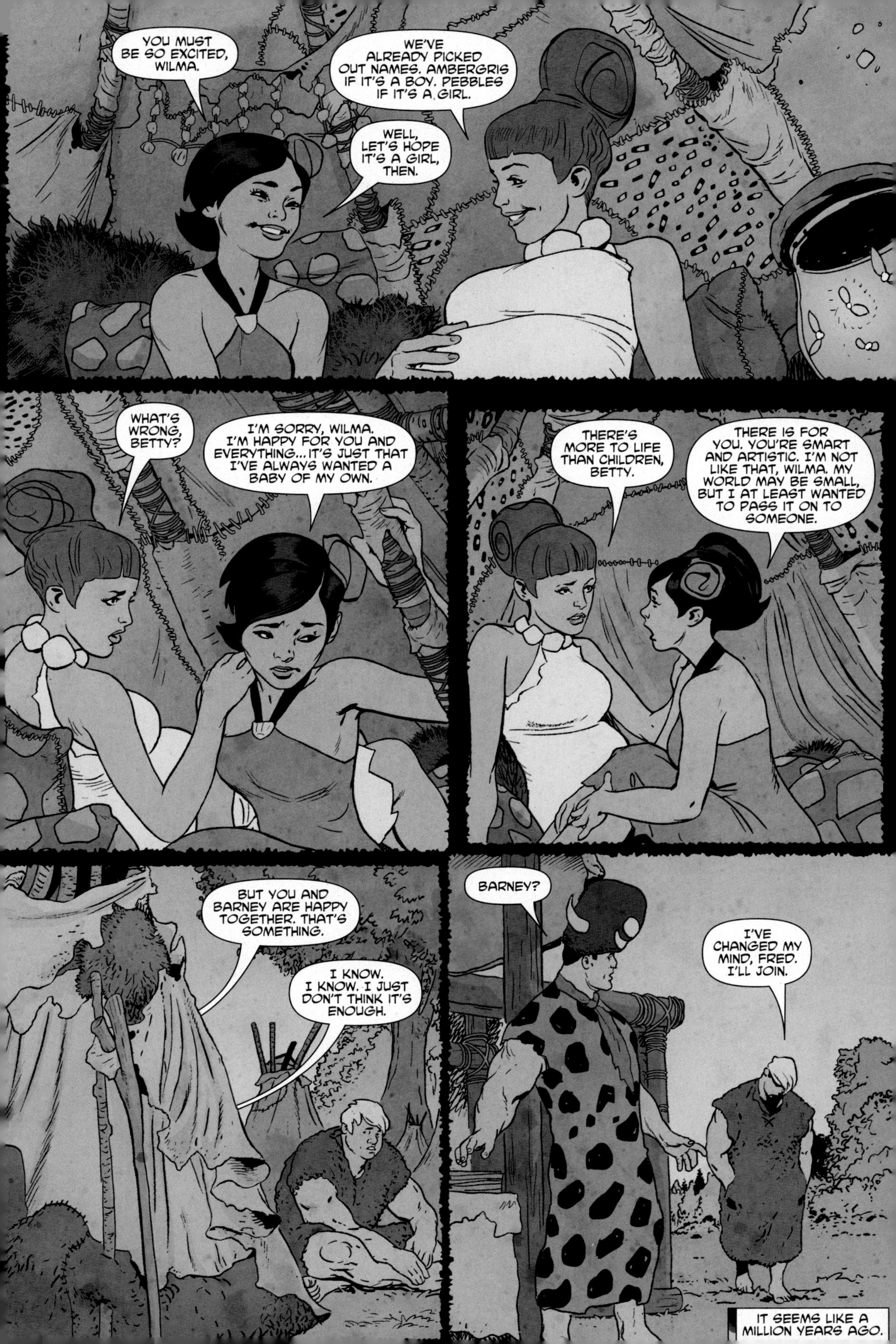
YOU MUST BE SO EXCITED, WILMA.
WE'VE ALREADY PICKED OUT NAMES. AMBERGRIS IF IT'S A BOY. PEBBLES IF IT'S A GIRL.
WELL, LET'S HOPE IT'S A GIRL, THEN.
WHAT'S WRONG, BETTY?
I'M SORRY, WILMA. I'M HAPPY FOR YOU AND EVERYTHING... IT'S JUST THAT I'VE ALWAYS WANTED A BABY OF MY OWN.
THERE'S MORE TO LIFE THAN CHILDREN, BETTY.
THERE IS FOR YOU. YOU'RE SMART AND ARTISTIC. I'M NOT LIKE THAT, WILMA. MY WORLD MAY BE SMALL, BUT I AT LEAST WANTED TO PASS IT ON TO SOMEONE.
BUT YOU AND BARNEY ARE HAPPY TOGETHER. THAT'S SOMETHING.
I KNOW. I KNOW. I JUST DON'T THINK IT'S ENOUGH.
BARNEY?
I'VE CHANGED MY MIND, FRED. I'LL JOIN.
IT SEEMS LIKE A MILLION YEARS AGO.

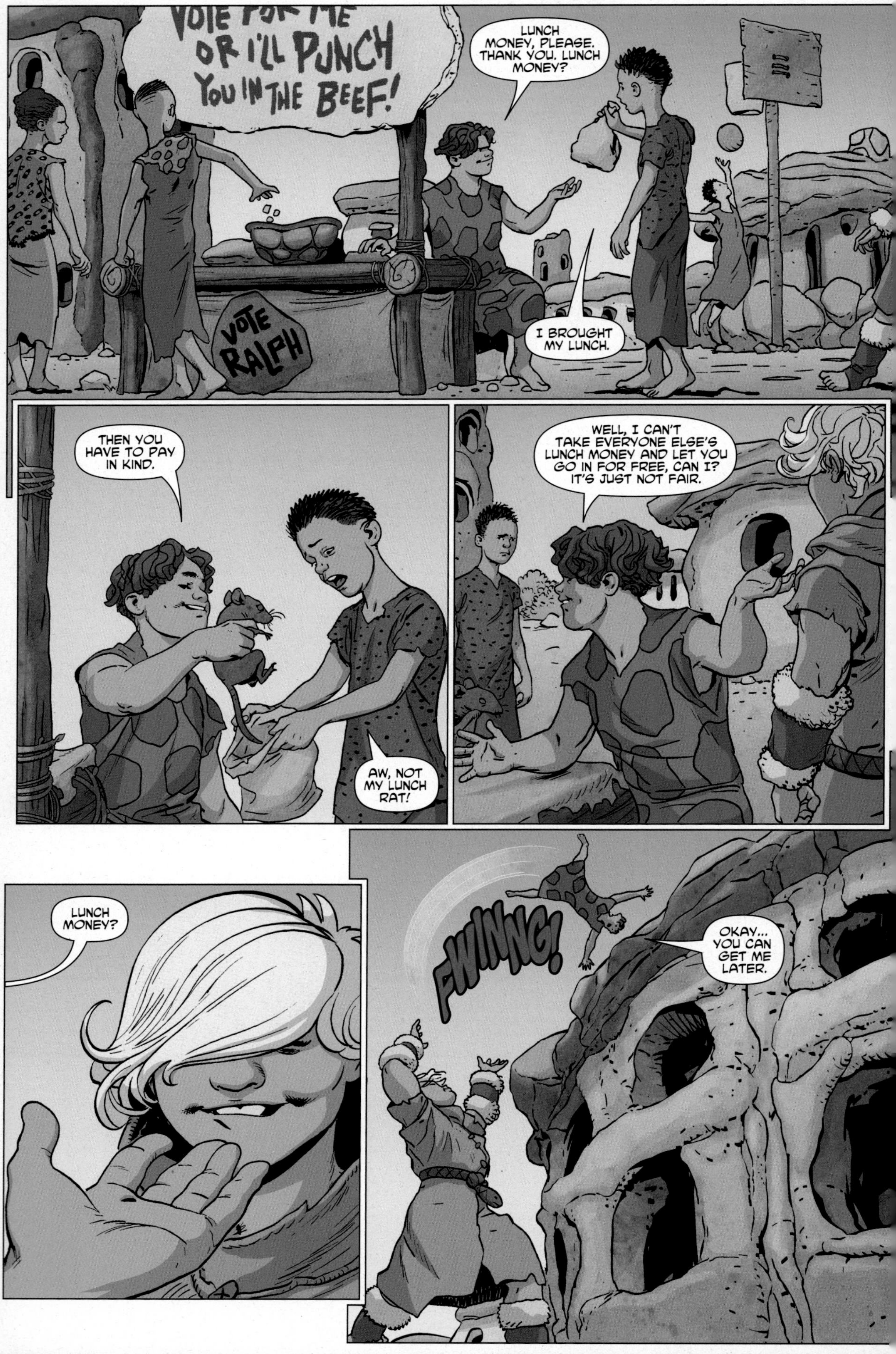
VOTE FOR ME OR I'LL PUNCH YOU IN THE BEEF!
LUNCH MONEY, PLEASE. THANK YOU. LUNCH MONEY?
VOTE RALPH
I BROUGHT MY LUNCH.
THEN YOU HAVE TO PAY IN KIND.
AW, NOT MY LUNCH RAT!
WELL, I CAN'T TAKE EVERYONE ELSE'S LUNCH MONEY AND LET YOU GO IN FOR FREE, CAN I? IT'S JUST NOT FAIR.
LUNCH MONEY?
FWINNG!
OKAY... YOU CAN GET ME LATER.

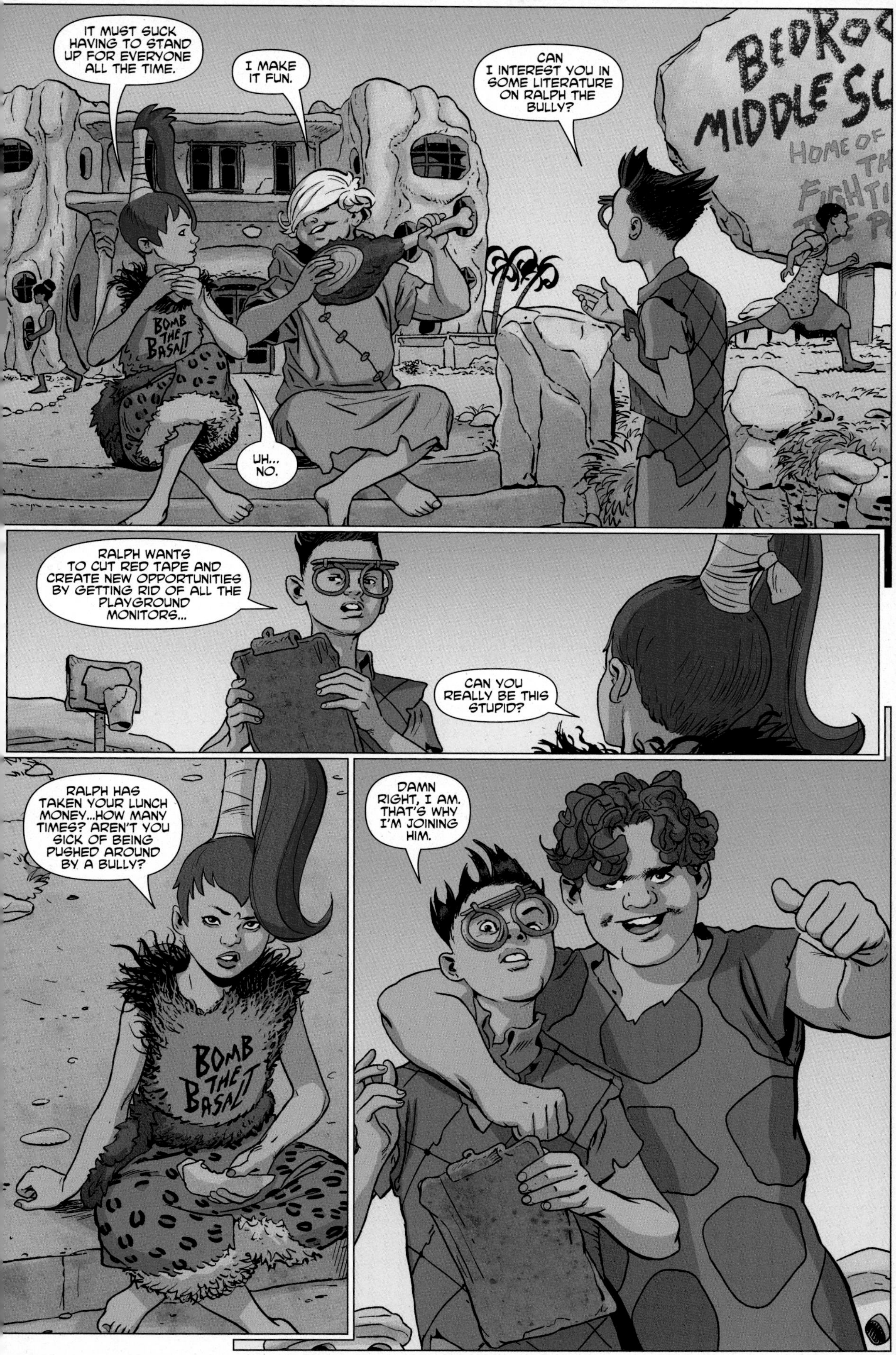
IT MUST SUCK HAVING TO STAND UP FOR EVERYONE ALL THE TIME.
I MAKE IT FUN.
CAN I INTEREST YOU IN SOME LITERATURE ON RALPH THE BULLY?
UH... NO.
BEDROC
MIDDLE SC
HOME OF
RALPH WANTS TO CUT RED TAPE AND CREATE NEW OPPORTUNITIES BY GETTING RID OF ALL THE PLAYGROUND MONITORS...
CAN YOU REALLY BE THIS STUPID?
RALPH HAS TAKEN YOUR LUNCH MONEY...HOW MANY TIMES? AREN'T YOU SICK OF BEING PUSHED AROUND BY A BULLY?
BOMB THE BASALT
DAMN RIGHT, I AM. THAT'S WHY I'M JOINING HIM.

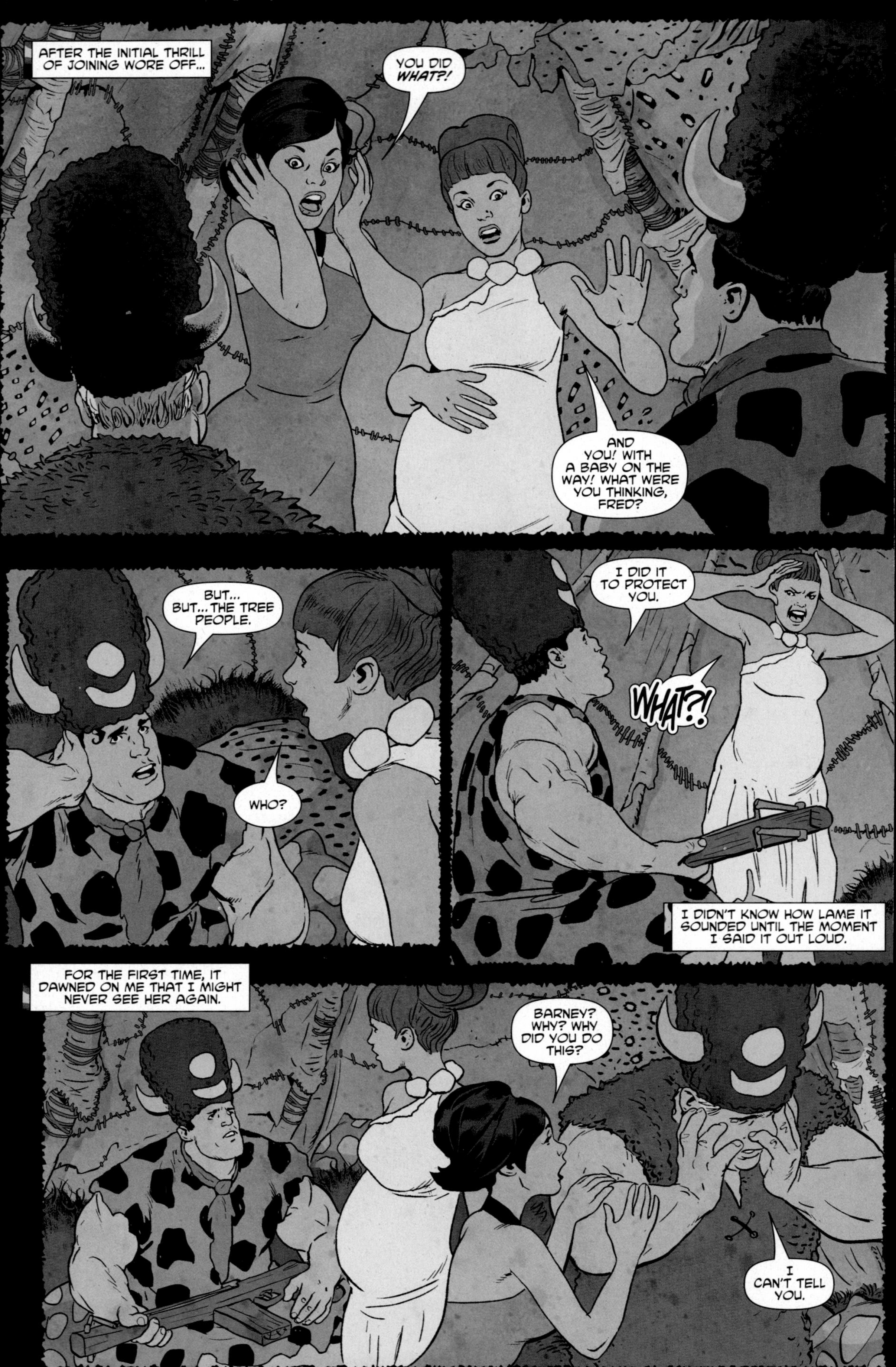

AFTER THE INITIAL THRILL OF JOINING WORE OFF...
YOU DID *WHAT?!*
AND YOU! WITH A BABY ON THE WAY! WHAT WERE YOU THINKING, FRED?
BUT... BUT... THE TREE PEOPLE.
WHO?
I DID IT TO PROTECT YOU.
WHAT?!
I DIDN'T KNOW HOW LAME IT SOUNDED UNTIL THE MOMENT I SAID IT OUT LOUD.
FOR THE FIRST TIME, IT DAWNED ON ME THAT I MIGHT NEVER SEE HER AGAIN.
BARNEY? WHY? WHY DID YOU DO THIS?
I CAN'T TELL YOU.

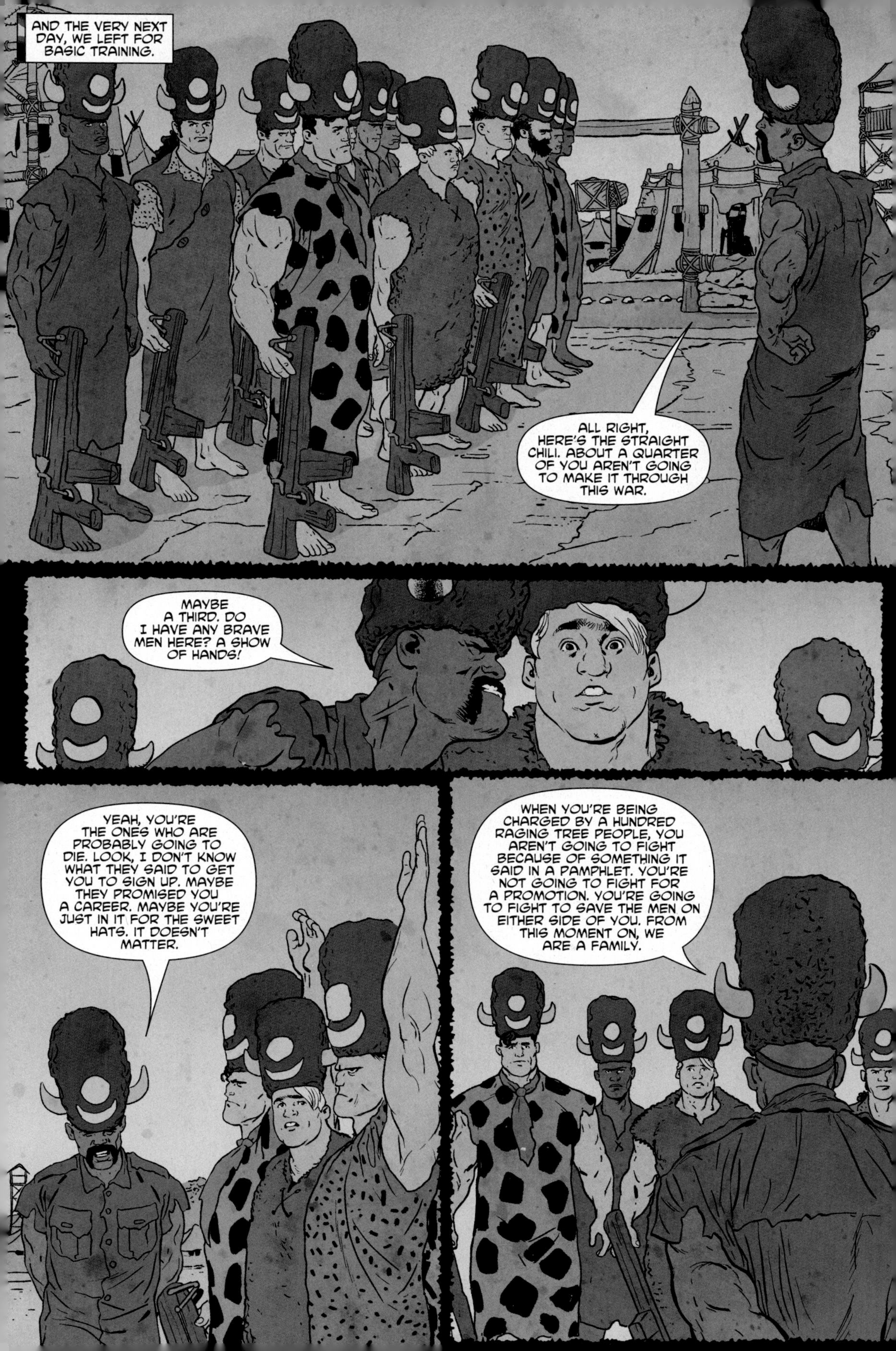
AND THE VERY NEXT DAY, WE LEFT FOR BASIC TRAINING.
ALL RIGHT, HERE'S THE STRAIGHT CHILI. ABOUT A QUARTER OF YOU AREN'T GOING TO MAKE IT THROUGH THIS WAR.
MAYBE A THIRD. DO I HAVE ANY BRAVE MEN HERE? A SHOW OF HANDS!
YEAH, YOU'RE THE ONES WHO ARE PROBABLY GOING TO DIE. LOOK, I DON'T KNOW WHAT THEY SAID TO GET YOU TO SIGN UP. MAYBE THEY PROMISED YOU A CAREER. MAYBE YOU'RE JUST IN IT FOR THE SWEET HATS. IT DOESN'T MATTER.
WHEN YOU'RE BEING CHARGED BY A HUNDRED RAGING TREE PEOPLE, YOU AREN'T GOING TO FIGHT BECAUSE OF SOMETHING IT SAID IN A PAMPHLET. YOU'RE NOT GOING TO FIGHT FOR A PROMOTION. YOU'RE GOING TO FIGHT TO SAVE THE MEN ON EITHER SIDE OF YOU. FROM THIS MOMENT ON, WE ARE A FAMILY.

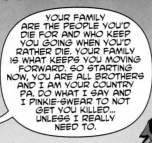

YOUR FAMILY ARE THE PEOPLE YOU'D DIE FOR AND WHO KEEP YOU GOING WHEN YOU'D RATHER DIE. YOUR FAMILY IS WHAT KEEPS YOU MOVING FORWARD. SO STARTING NOW, YOU ARE ALL BROTHERS AND I AM YOUR COUNTRY PA. DO WHAT I SAY AND I PINKIE-SWEAR TO NOT GET YOU KILLED... UNLESS I REALLY NEED TO.

THE TREE PEOPLE ARE KNOWN FOR THEIR PRODIGIOUS STRENGTH. SO YOU'LL BE TRAINING AGAINST MOCHA HERE.

YOU SMELL LIKE ROOT BEER AND FAILURE, RUBBLE! NEXT!

DO NOT GIVE UP ON THOSE MONKEY BARS! MONKEY BARS ARE VICTORY! MONKEY BARS ARE LIFE!

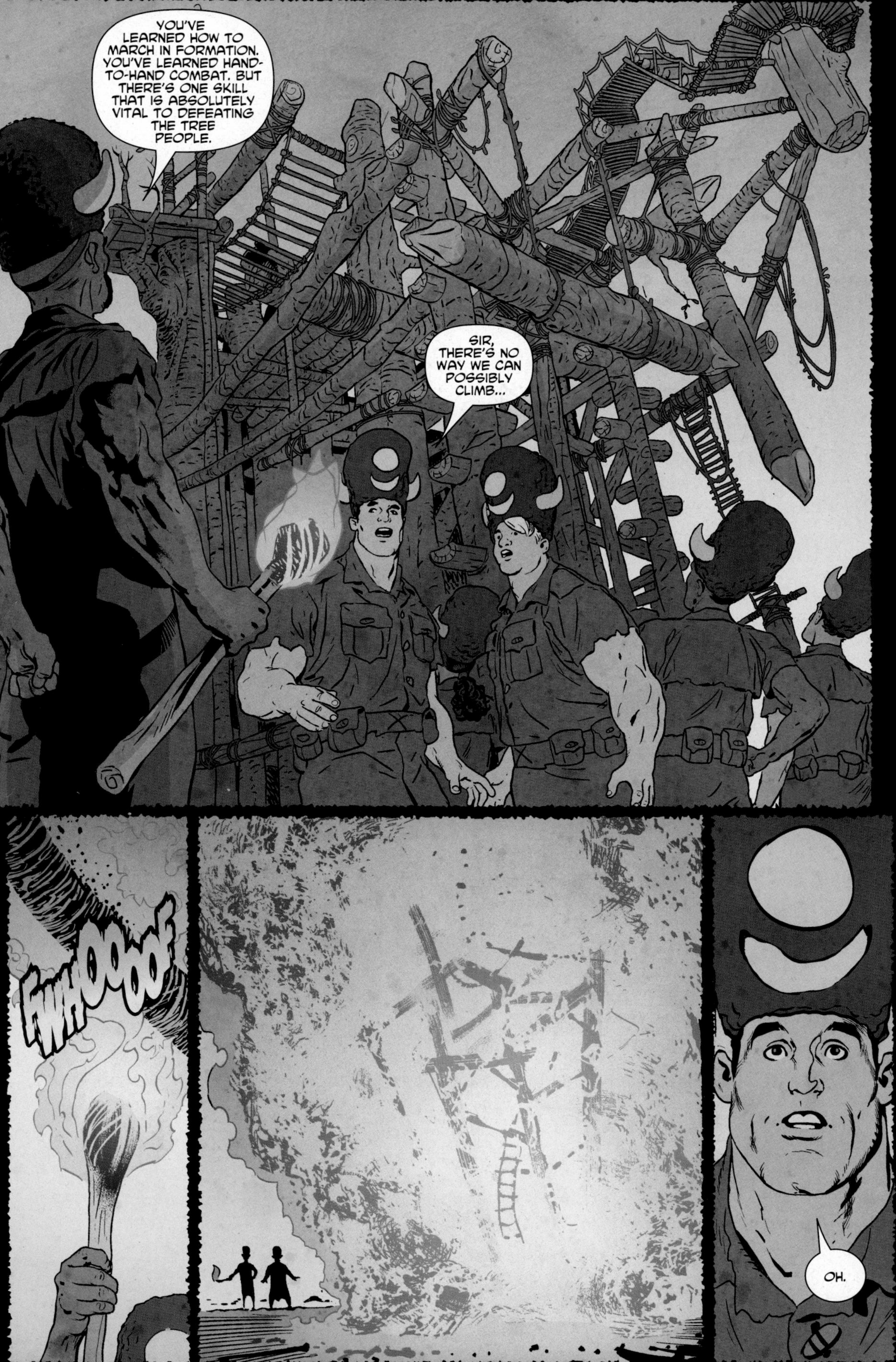
YOU'VE LEARNED HOW TO MARCH IN FORMATION. YOU'VE LEARNED HAND-TO-HAND COMBAT. BUT THERE'S ONE SKILL THAT IS ABSOLUTELY VITAL TO DEFEATING THE TREE PEOPLE.
SIR, THERE'S NO WAY WE CAN POSSIBLY CLIMB...
FWHOOOOF
OH.

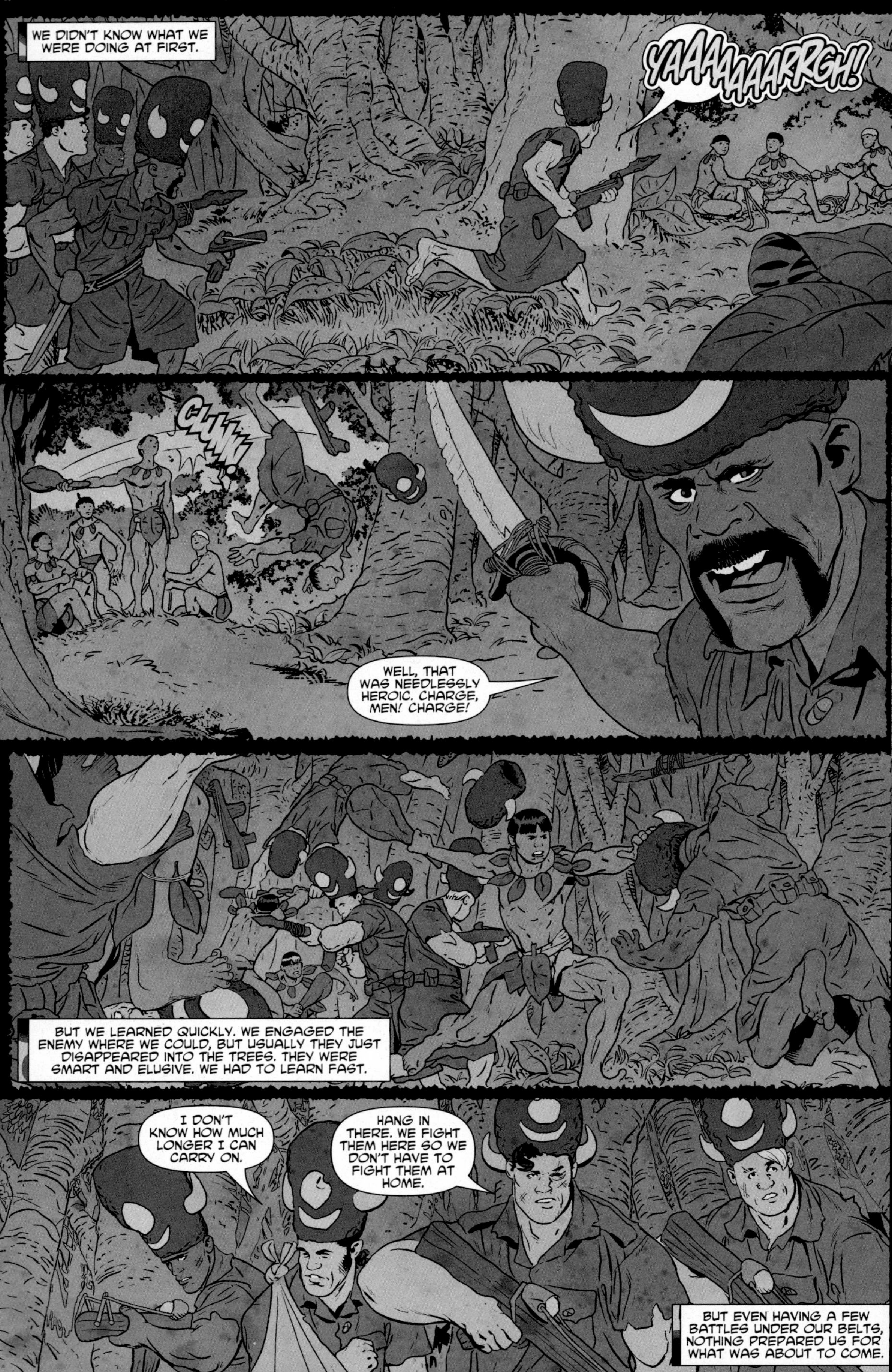
WE DIDN'T KNOW WHAT WE WERE DOING AT FIRST.
YAAAAAAARRGH!
CLUNK!
WELL, THAT WAS NEEDLESSLY HEROIC. CHARGE, MEN! CHARGE!
BUT WE LEARNED QUICKLY. WE ENGAGED THE ENEMY WHERE WE COULD, BUT USUALLY THEY JUST DISAPPEARED INTO THE TREES. THEY WERE SMART AND ELUSIVE. WE HAD TO LEARN FAST.
I DON'T KNOW HOW MUCH LONGER I CAN CARRY ON.
HANG IN THERE. WE FIGHT THEM HERE SO WE DON'T HAVE TO FIGHT THEM AT HOME.
BUT EVEN HAVING A FEW BATTLES UNDER OUR BELTS, NOTHING PREPARED US FOR WHAT WAS ABOUT TO COME.

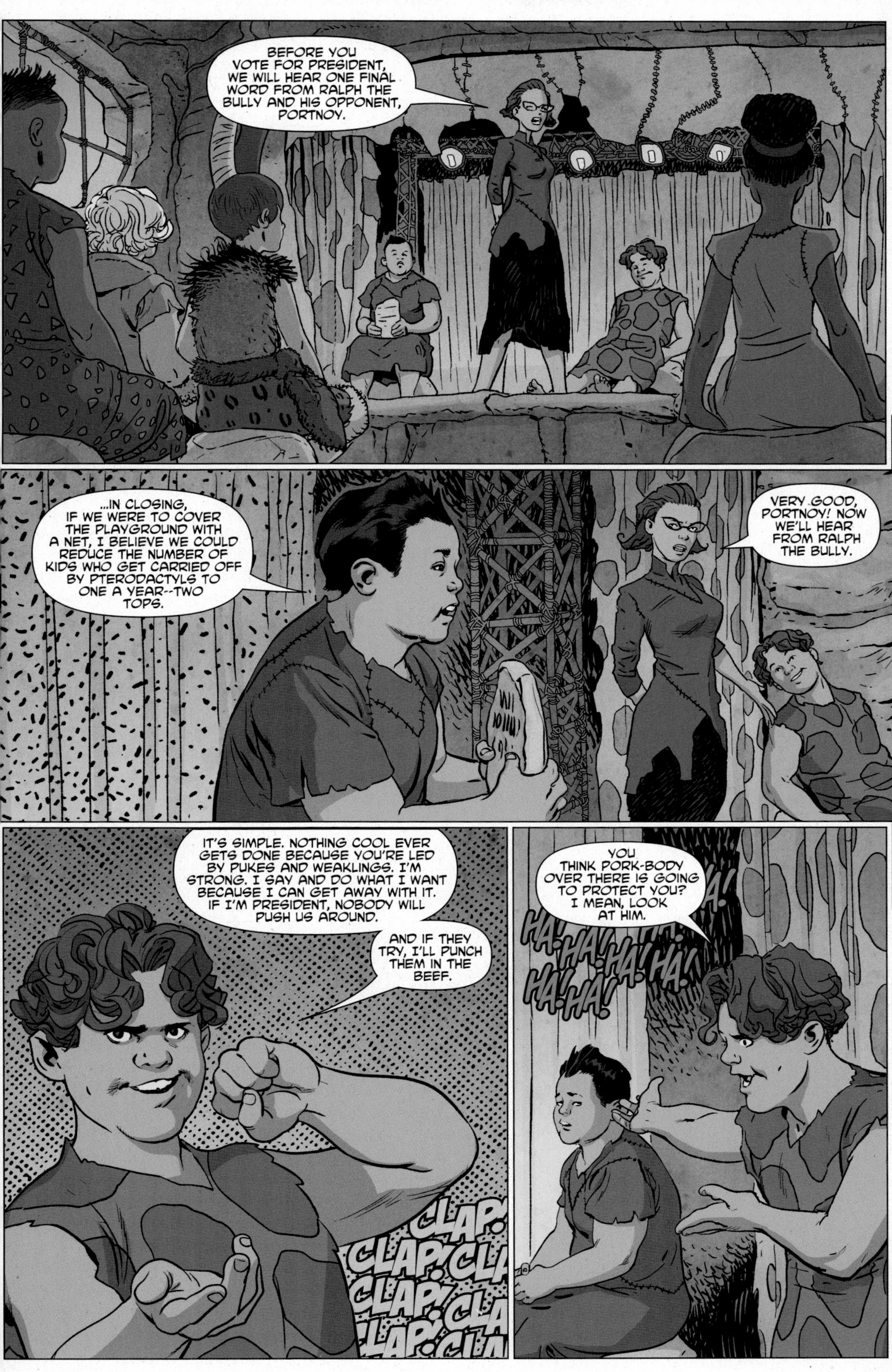
BEFORE YOU VOTE FOR PRESIDENT, WE WILL HEAR ONE FINAL WORD FROM RALPH THE BULLY AND HIS OPPONENT, PORTNOY.
...IN CLOSING, IF WE WERE TO COVER THE PLAYGROUND WITH A NET, I BELIEVE WE COULD REDUCE THE NUMBER OF KIDS WHO GET CARRIED OFF BY PTERODACTYLS TO ONE A YEAR--TWO TOPS.
VERY GOOD, PORTNOY! NOW WE'LL HEAR FROM RALPH THE BULLY.
IT'S SIMPLE. NOTHING COOL EVER GETS DONE BECAUSE YOU'RE LED BY PUKES AND WEAKLINGS. I'M STRONG. I SAY AND DO WHAT I WANT BECAUSE I CAN GET AWAY WITH IT. IF I'M PRESIDENT, NOBODY WILL PUSH US AROUND.
AND IF THEY TRY, I'LL PUNCH THEM IN THE BEEF.
CLAP! CLAP! CLAP! CLAP! CLAP!
YOU THINK PORK-BODY OVER THERE IS GOING TO PROTECT YOU? I MEAN, LOOK AT HIM.
HA-HA! HA-HA! HA-HA!

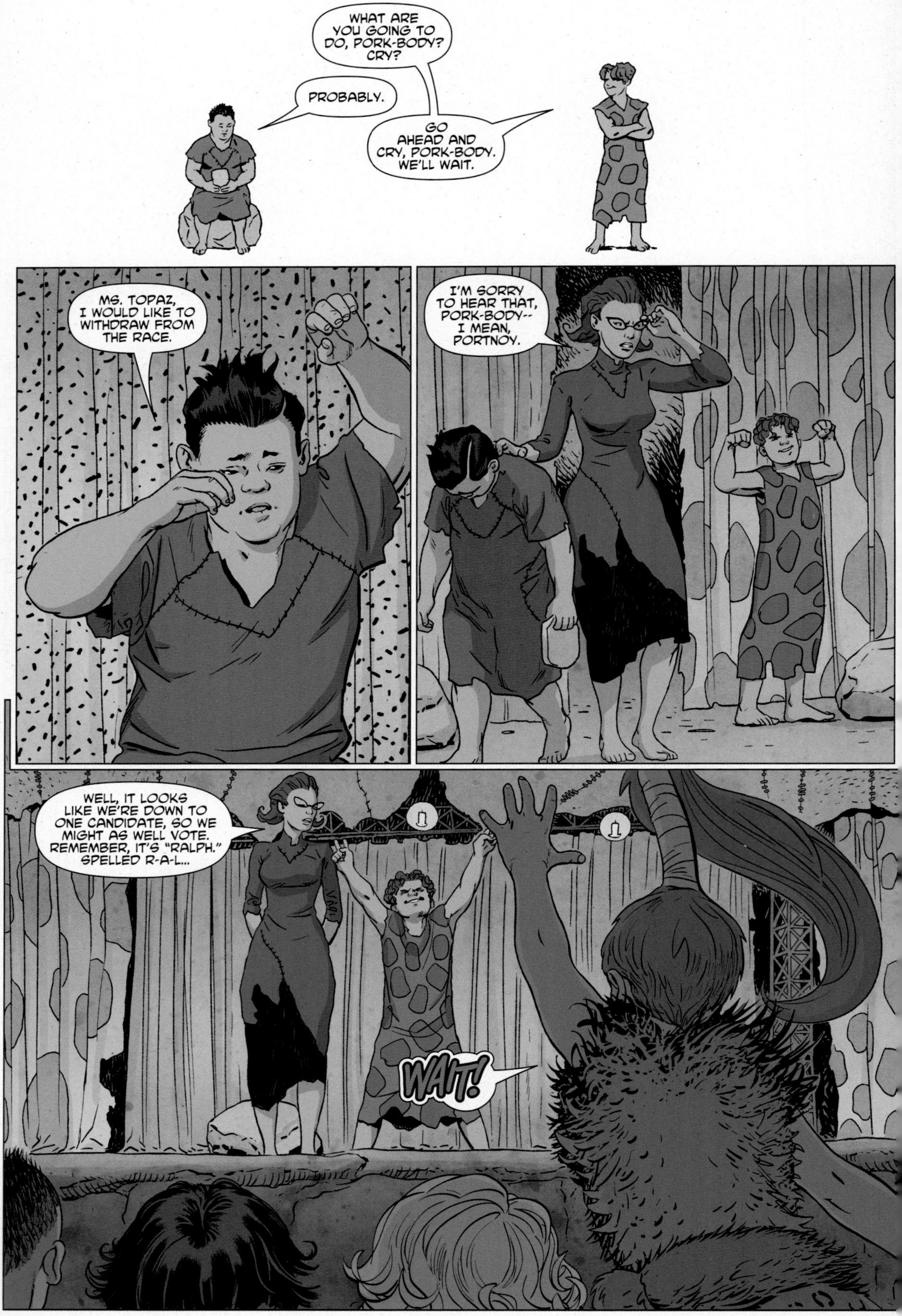
WHAT ARE YOU GOING TO DO, PORK-BODY? CRY?
PROBABLY.
GO AHEAD AND CRY, PORK-BODY. WE'LL WAIT.
MS. TOPAZ, I WOULD LIKE TO WITHDRAW FROM THE RACE.
I'M SORRY TO HEAR THAT, PORK-BODY-- I MEAN, PORTNOY.
WELL, IT LOOKS LIKE WE'RE DOWN TO ONE CANDIDATE, SO WE MIGHT AS WELL VOTE. REMEMBER, IT'S "RALPH." SPELLED R-A-L...
WAIT!

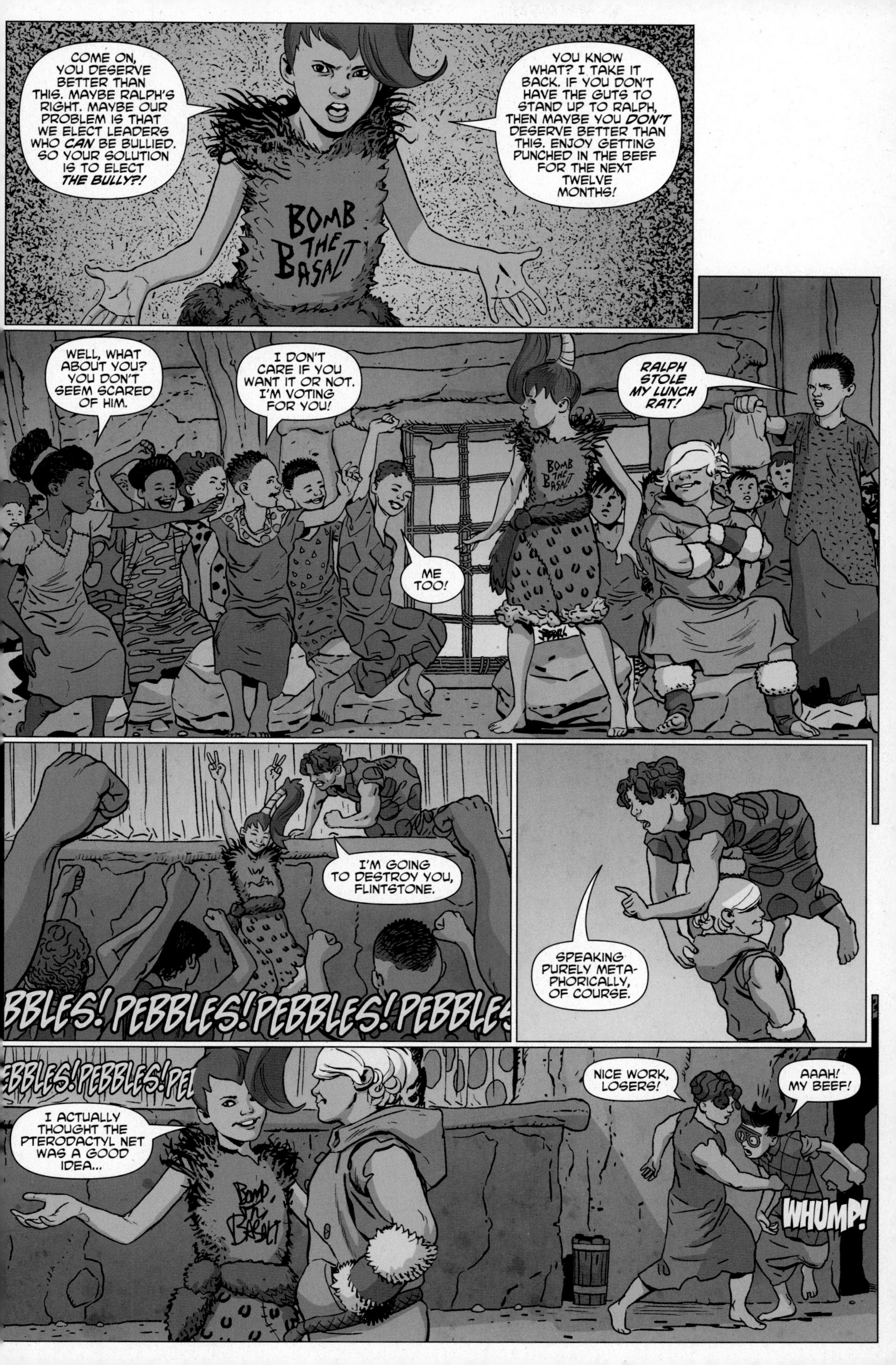
COME ON, YOU DESERVE BETTER THAN THIS. MAYBE RALPH'S RIGHT. MAYBE OUR PROBLEM IS THAT WE ELECT LEADERS WHO *CAN* BE BULLIED. SO YOUR SOLUTION IS TO ELECT *THE BULLY?!*
YOU KNOW WHAT? I TAKE IT BACK. IF YOU DON'T HAVE THE GUTS TO STAND UP TO RALPH, THEN MAYBE YOU *DON'T* DESERVE BETTER THAN THIS. ENJOY GETTING PUNCHED IN THE BEEF FOR THE NEXT TWELVE MONTHS!
BOMB THE BASALT
WELL, WHAT ABOUT YOU? YOU DON'T SEEM SCARED OF HIM.
I DON'T CARE IF YOU WANT IT OR NOT. I'M VOTING FOR YOU!
ME TOO!
BOMB THE BASALT
RALPH STOLE MY LUNCH RAT!
I'M GOING TO DESTROY YOU, FLINTSTONE.
PEBBLES! PEBBLES! PEBBLES! PEBBLES!
SPEAKING PURELY META-PHORICALLY, OF COURSE.
PEBBLES! PEBBLES! PEB
I ACTUALLY THOUGHT THE PTERODACTYL NET WAS A GOOD IDEA...
NICE WORK, LOSERS!
AAAH! MY BEEF!
WHUMP!

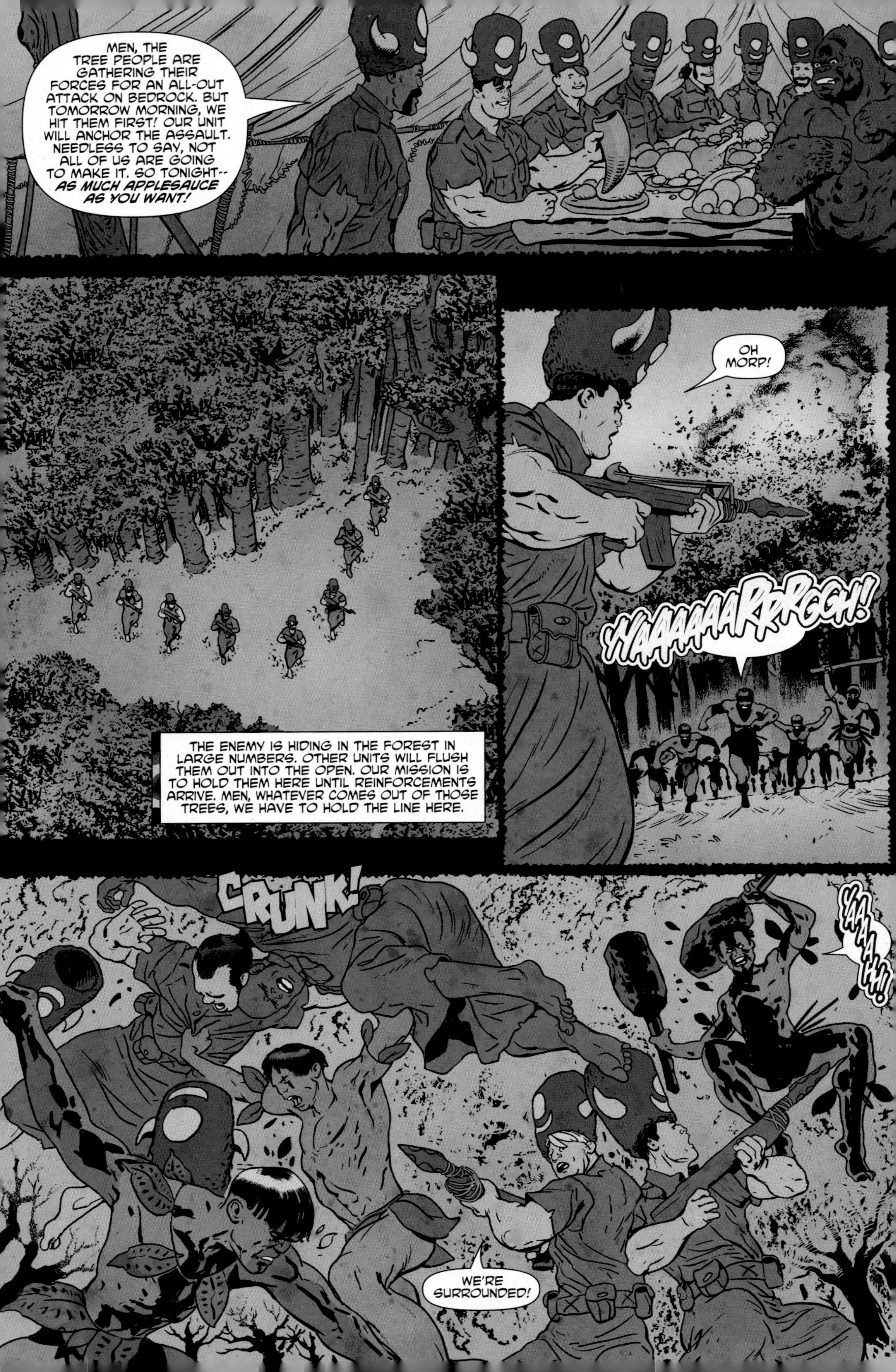
MEN, THE TREE PEOPLE ARE GATHERING THEIR FORCES FOR AN ALL-OUT ATTACK ON BEDROCK. BUT TOMORROW MORNING, WE HIT THEM FIRST! OUR UNIT WILL ANCHOR THE ASSAULT. NEEDLESS TO SAY, NOT ALL OF US ARE GOING TO MAKE IT. SO TONIGHT-- AS MUCH APPLESAUCE AS YOU WANT!
THE ENEMY IS HIDING IN THE FOREST IN LARGE NUMBERS. OTHER UNITS WILL FLUSH THEM OUT INTO THE OPEN. OUR MISSION IS TO HOLD THEM HERE UNTIL REINFORCEMENTS ARRIVE. MEN, WHATEVER COMES OUT OF THOSE TREES, WE HAVE TO HOLD THE LINE HERE.
OH MORP!
YAAAAAAARRRGGH!
CRUNK!
YAAAAH!!
WE'RE SURROUNDED!

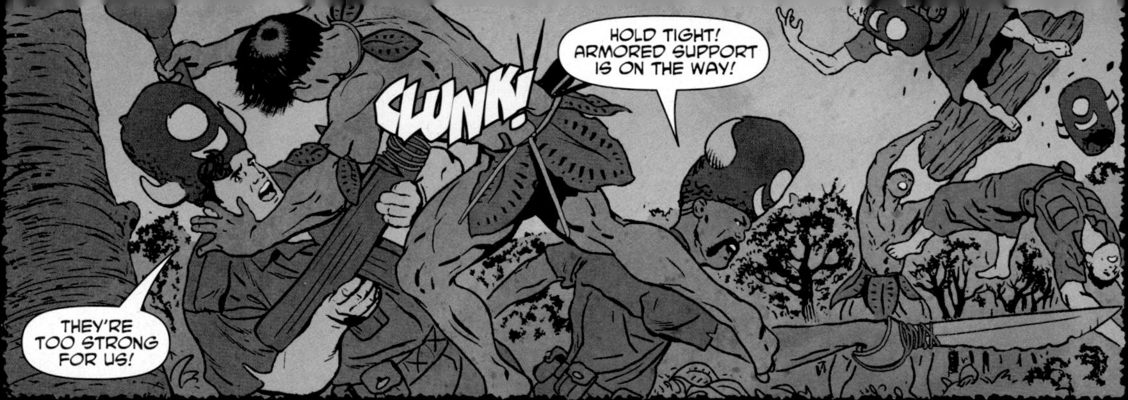
CLUNK!
HOLD TIGHT! ARMORED SUPPORT IS ON THE WAY!
THEY'RE TOO STRONG FOR US!

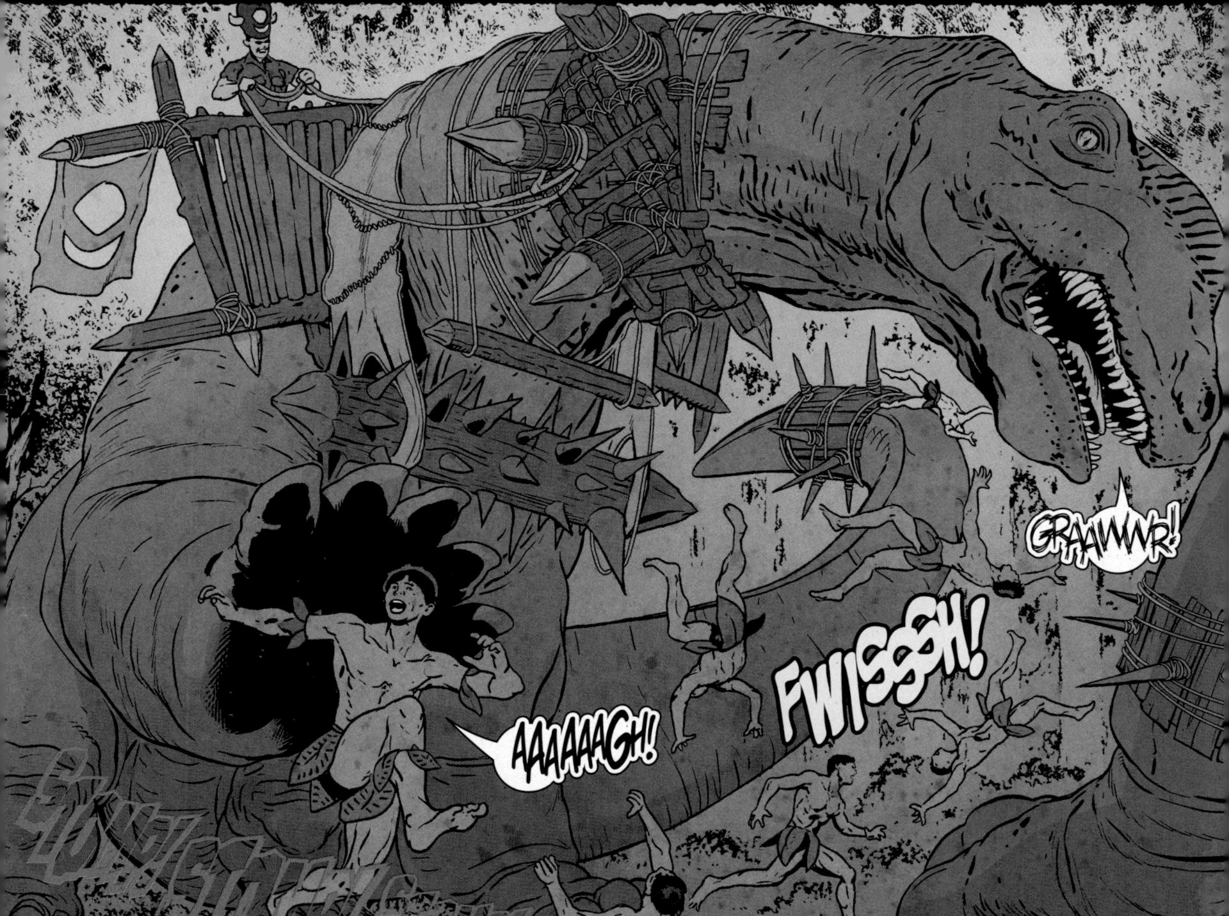
GRAAWWR!
FWISSSH!
AAAAAAGH!

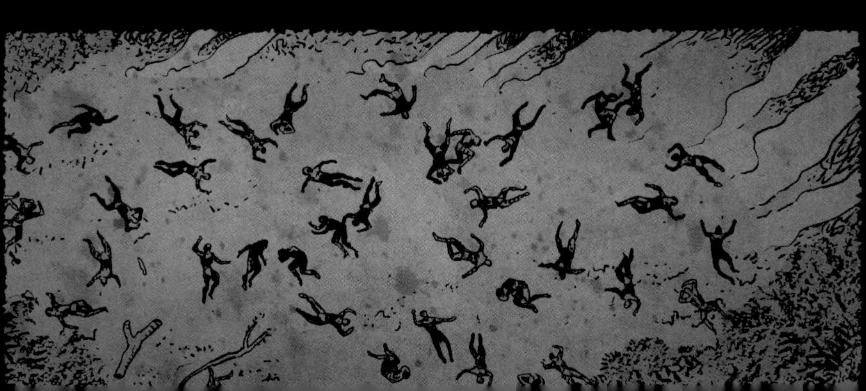

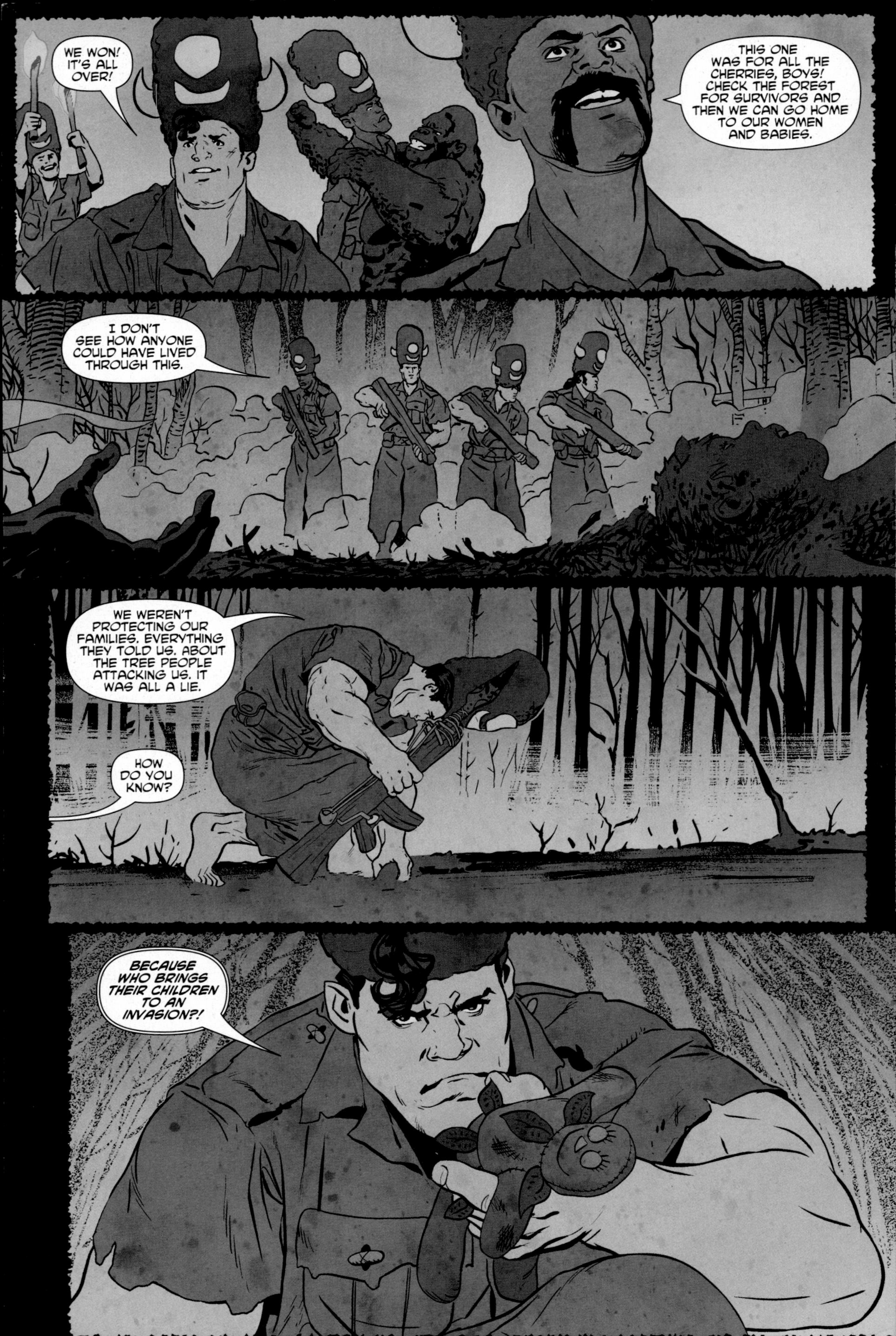
WE WON! IT'S ALL OVER!
THIS ONE WAS FOR ALL THE CHERRIES, BOYS! CHECK THE FOREST FOR SURVIVORS AND THEN WE CAN GO HOME TO OUR WOMEN AND BABIES.
I DON'T SEE HOW ANYONE COULD HAVE LIVED THROUGH THIS.
WE WEREN'T PROTECTING OUR FAMILIES. EVERYTHING THEY TOLD US. ABOUT THE TREE PEOPLE ATTACKING US. IT WAS ALL A LIE.
HOW DO YOU KNOW?
BECAUSE WHO BRINGS THEIR CHILDREN TO AN INVASION?!

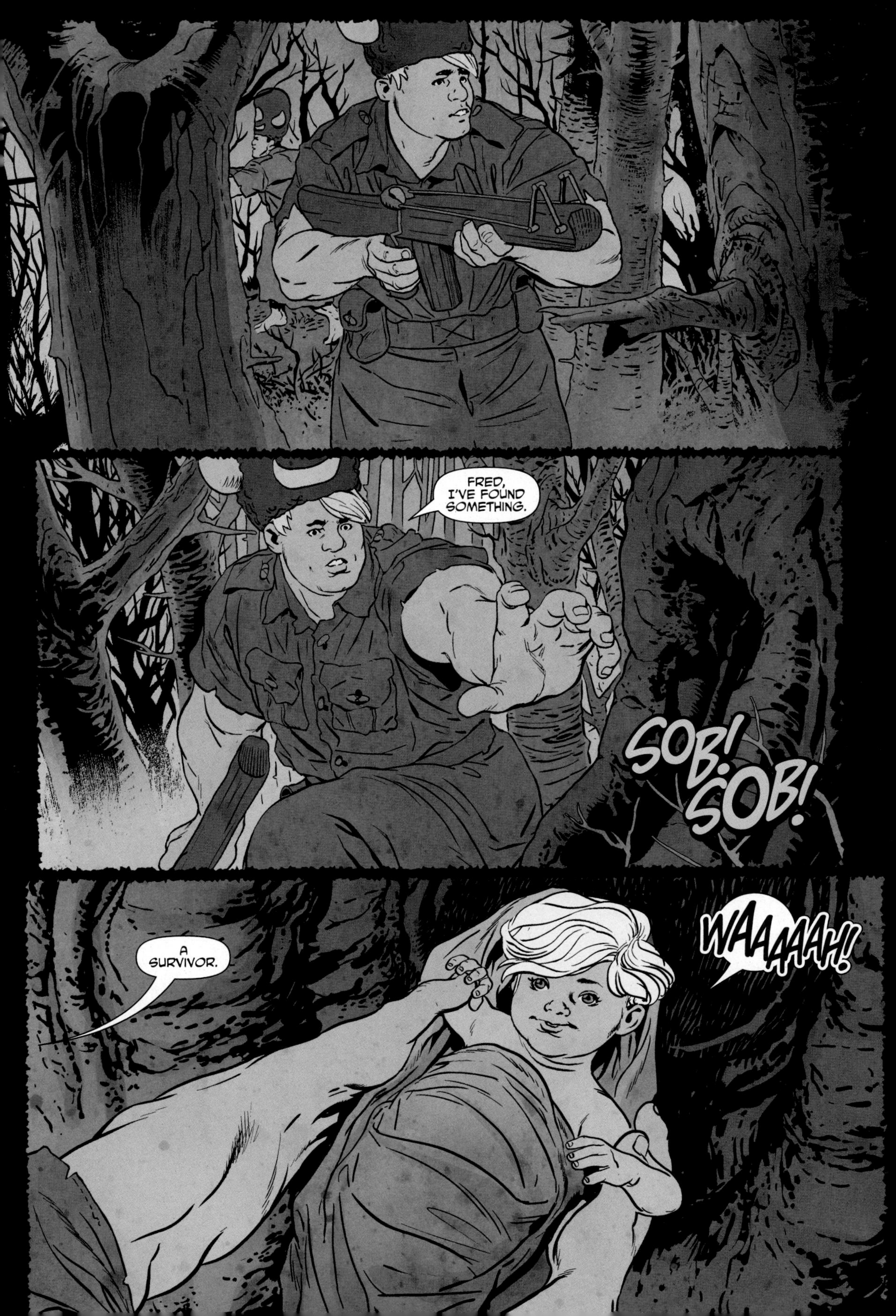
FRED, I'VE FOUND SOMETHING.
SOB! SOB!
A SURVIVOR.
WAAAAAH!

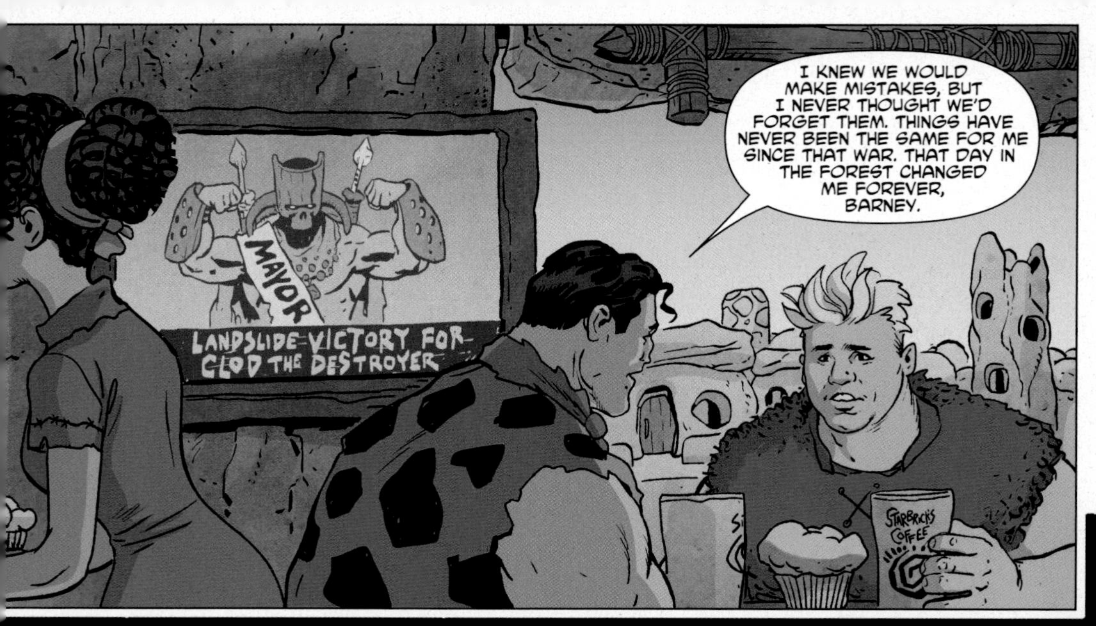
MAYOR
LANDSLIDE VICTORY FOR CLOD THE DESTROYER
I KNEW WE WOULD MAKE MISTAKES, BUT I NEVER THOUGHT WE'D FORGET THEM. THINGS HAVE NEVER BEEN THE SAME FOR ME SINCE THAT WAR. THAT DAY IN THE FOREST CHANGED ME FOREVER, BARNEY.

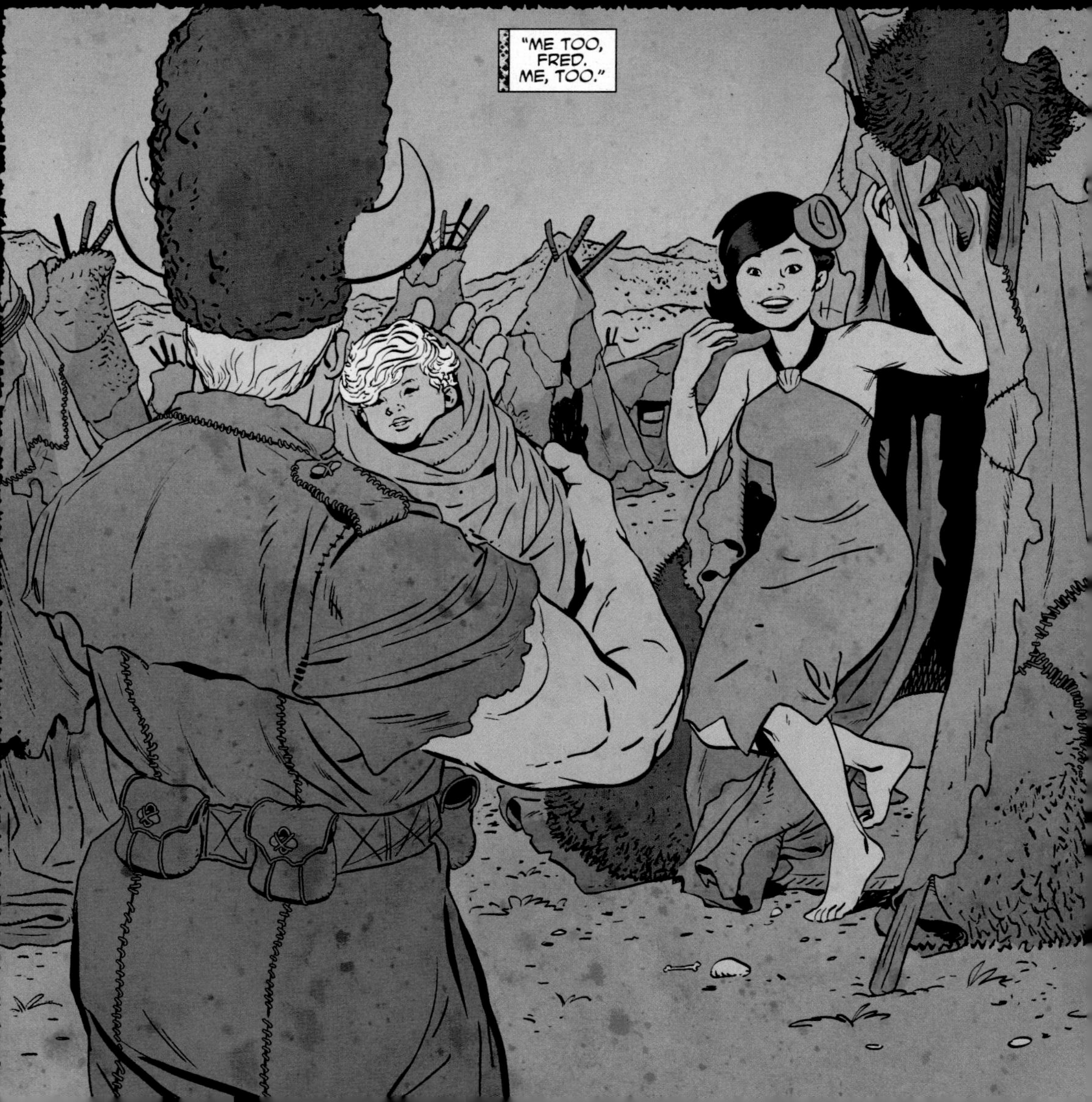
"ME TOO, FRED. ME, TOO."

THE FLINTSTONES #6 cover by BILL SIENKIEWICZ

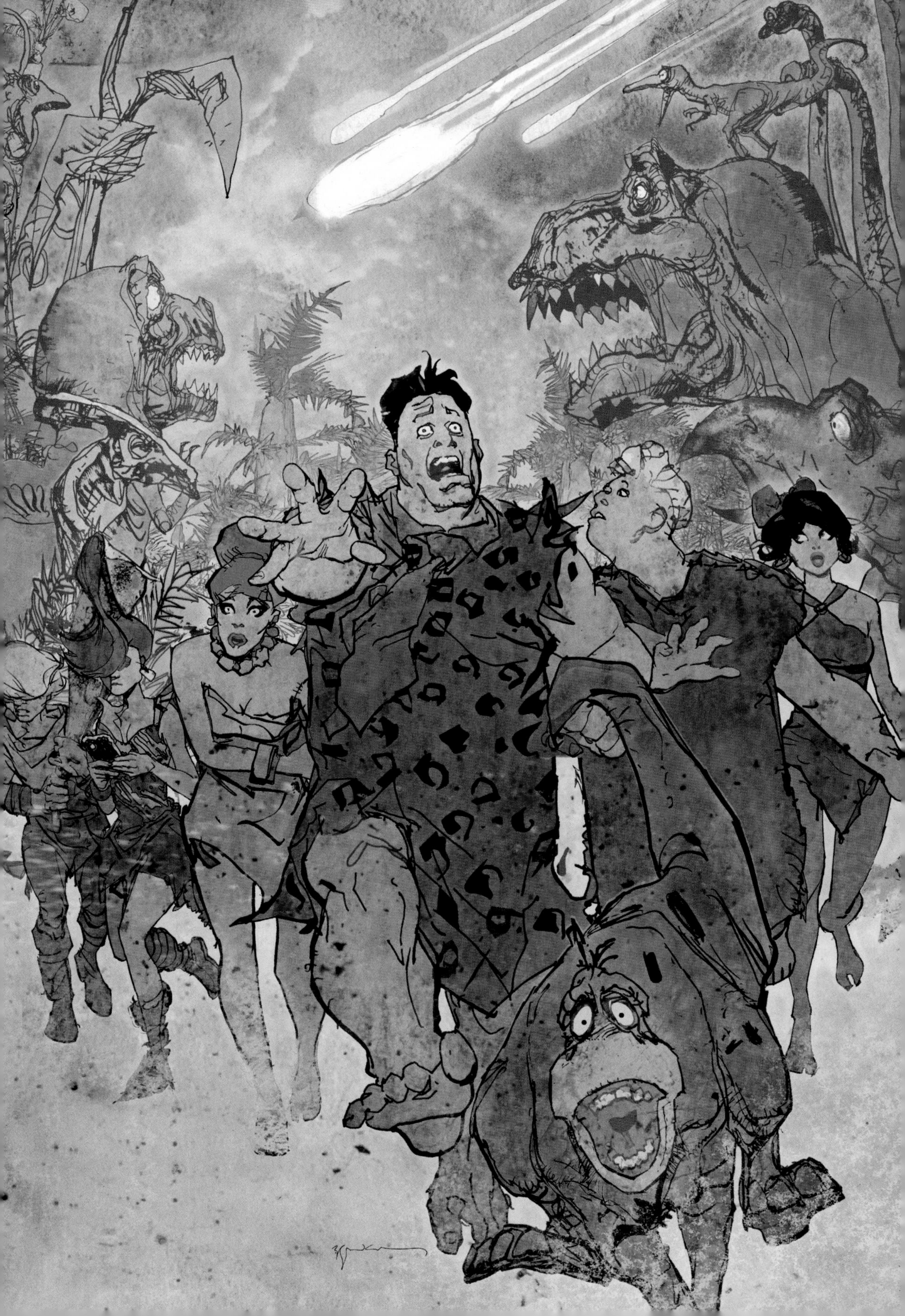

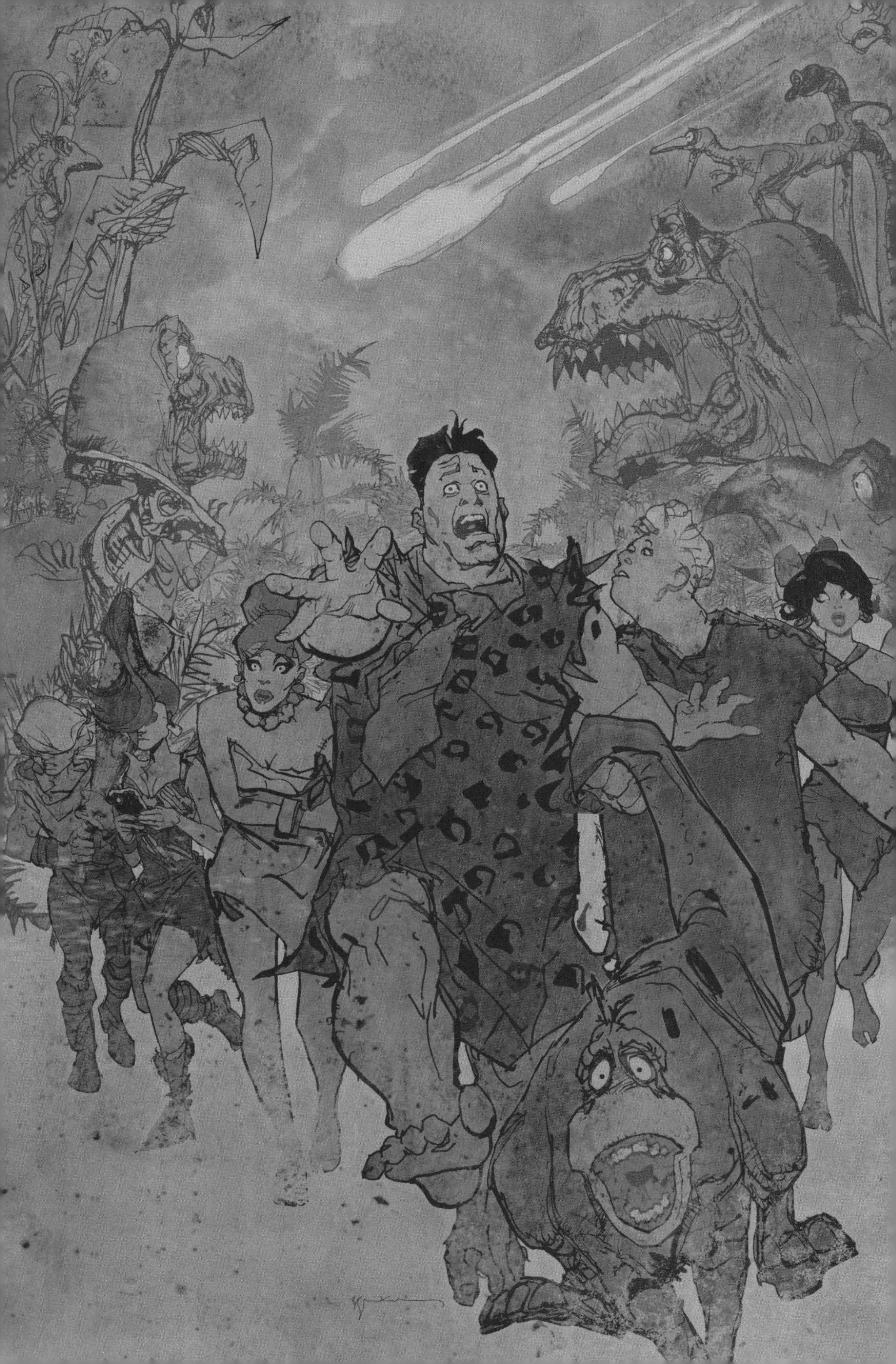

DCCO38774

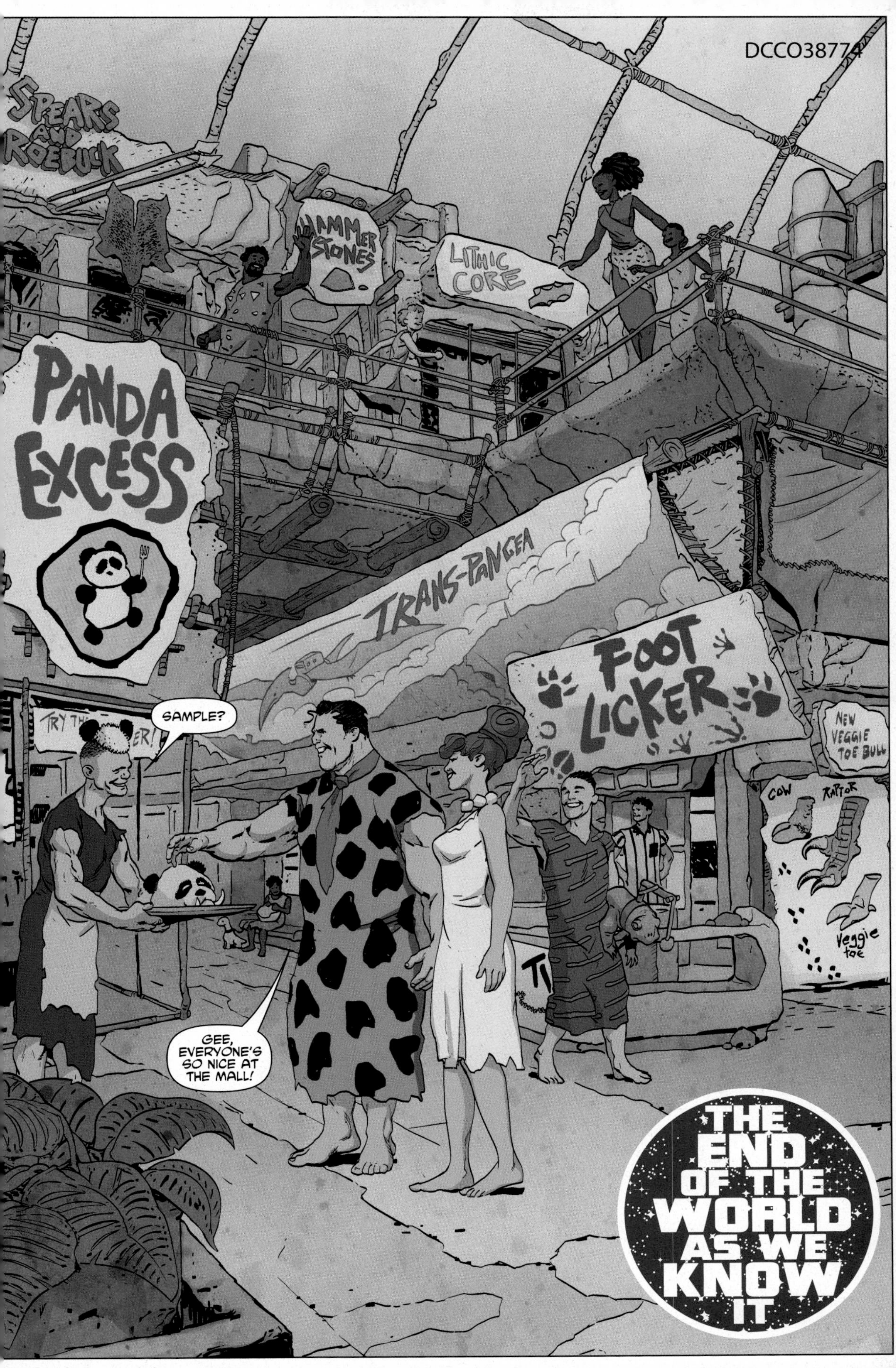
SPEARS AND ROEBUCK
HAMMER STONES
LITHIC CORE
PANDA EXCESS
TRANS-PANGEA
FOOT LICKER
NEW VEGGIE TOE BULL
COW
RAPTOR
Veggie toe
SAMPLE?
GEE, EVERYONE'S SO NICE AT THE MALL!
THE END OF THE WORLD AS WE KNOW IT

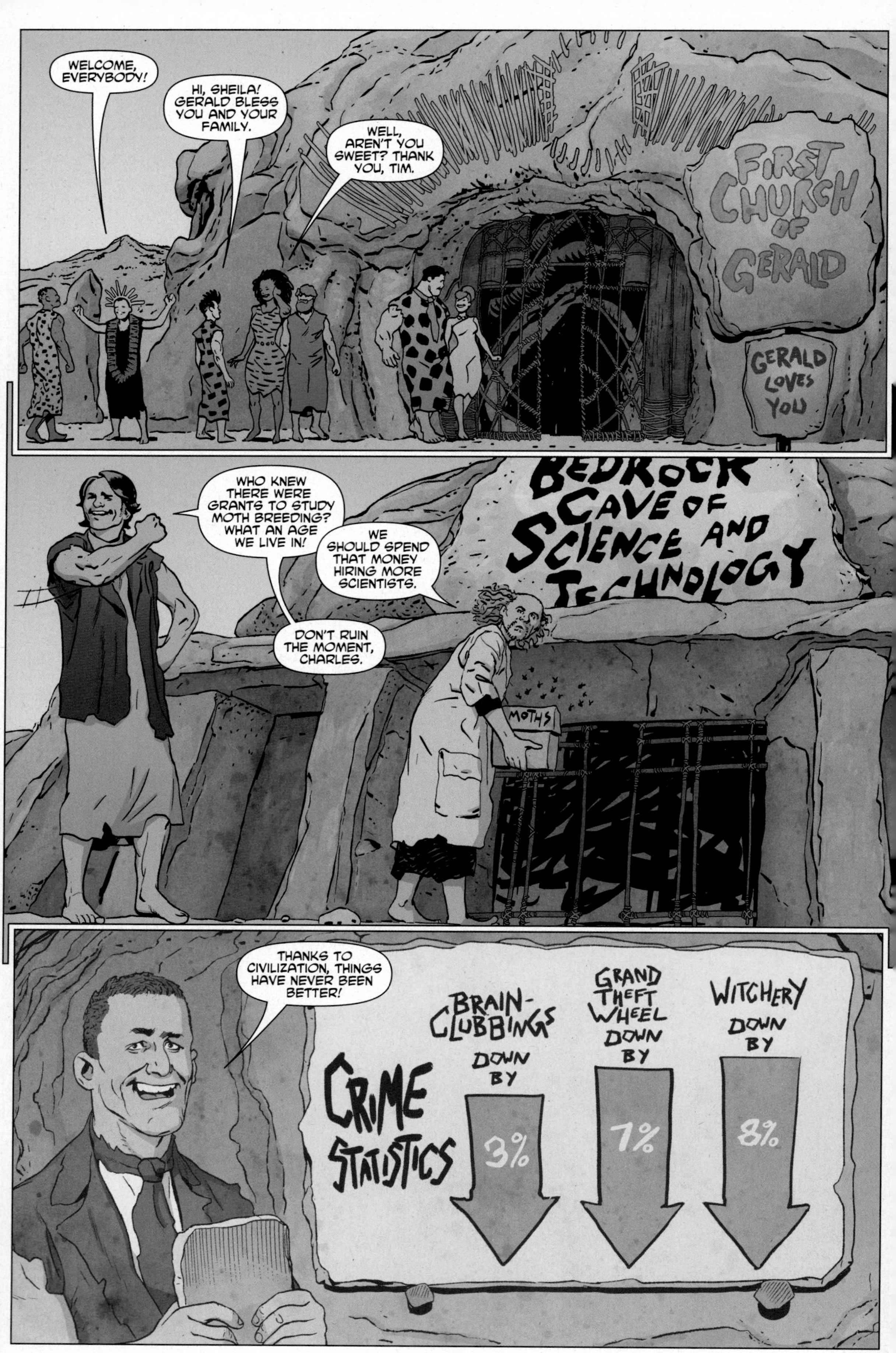
WELCOME, EVERYBODY!
HI, SHEILA! GERALD BLESS YOU AND YOUR FAMILY.
WELL, AREN'T YOU SWEET? THANK YOU, TIM.
FIRST CHURCH OF GERALD
GERALD LOVES YOU
BEDROCK CAVE OF SCIENCE AND TECHNOLOGY
WHO KNEW THERE WERE GRANTS TO STUDY MOTH BREEDING? WHAT AN AGE WE LIVE IN!
WE SHOULD SPEND THAT MONEY HIRING MORE SCIENTISTS.
DON'T RUIN THE MOMENT, CHARLES.
MOTHS
THANKS TO CIVILIZATION, THINGS HAVE NEVER BEEN BETTER!
CRIME STATISTICS
BRAIN-CLUBBINGS DOWN BY 3%
GRAND THEFT WHEEL DOWN BY 7%
WITCHERY DOWN BY 8%

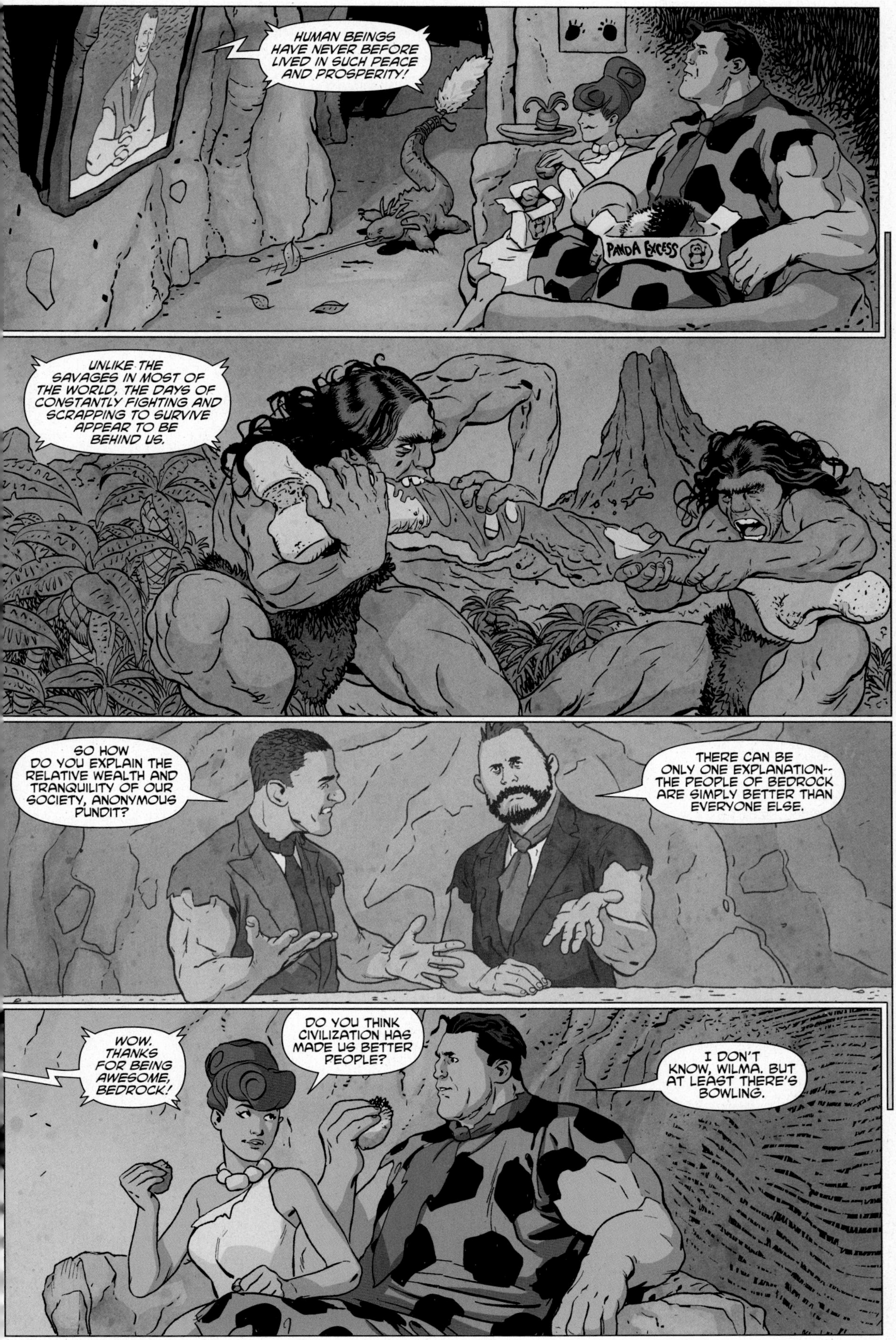
HUMAN BEINGS HAVE NEVER BEFORE LIVED IN SUCH PEACE AND PROSPERITY!
PANDA EXCESS
UNLIKE THE SAVAGES IN MOST OF THE WORLD, THE DAYS OF CONSTANTLY FIGHTING AND SCRAPPING TO SURVIVE APPEAR TO BE BEHIND US.
SO HOW DO YOU EXPLAIN THE RELATIVE WEALTH AND TRANQUILITY OF OUR SOCIETY, ANONYMOUS PUNDIT?
THERE CAN BE ONLY ONE EXPLANATION-- THE PEOPLE OF BEDROCK ARE SIMPLY BETTER THAN EVERYONE ELSE.
WOW. THANKS FOR BEING AWESOME, BEDROCK!
DO YOU THINK CIVILIZATION HAS MADE US BETTER PEOPLE?
I DON'T KNOW, WILMA. BUT AT LEAST THERE'S BOWLING.

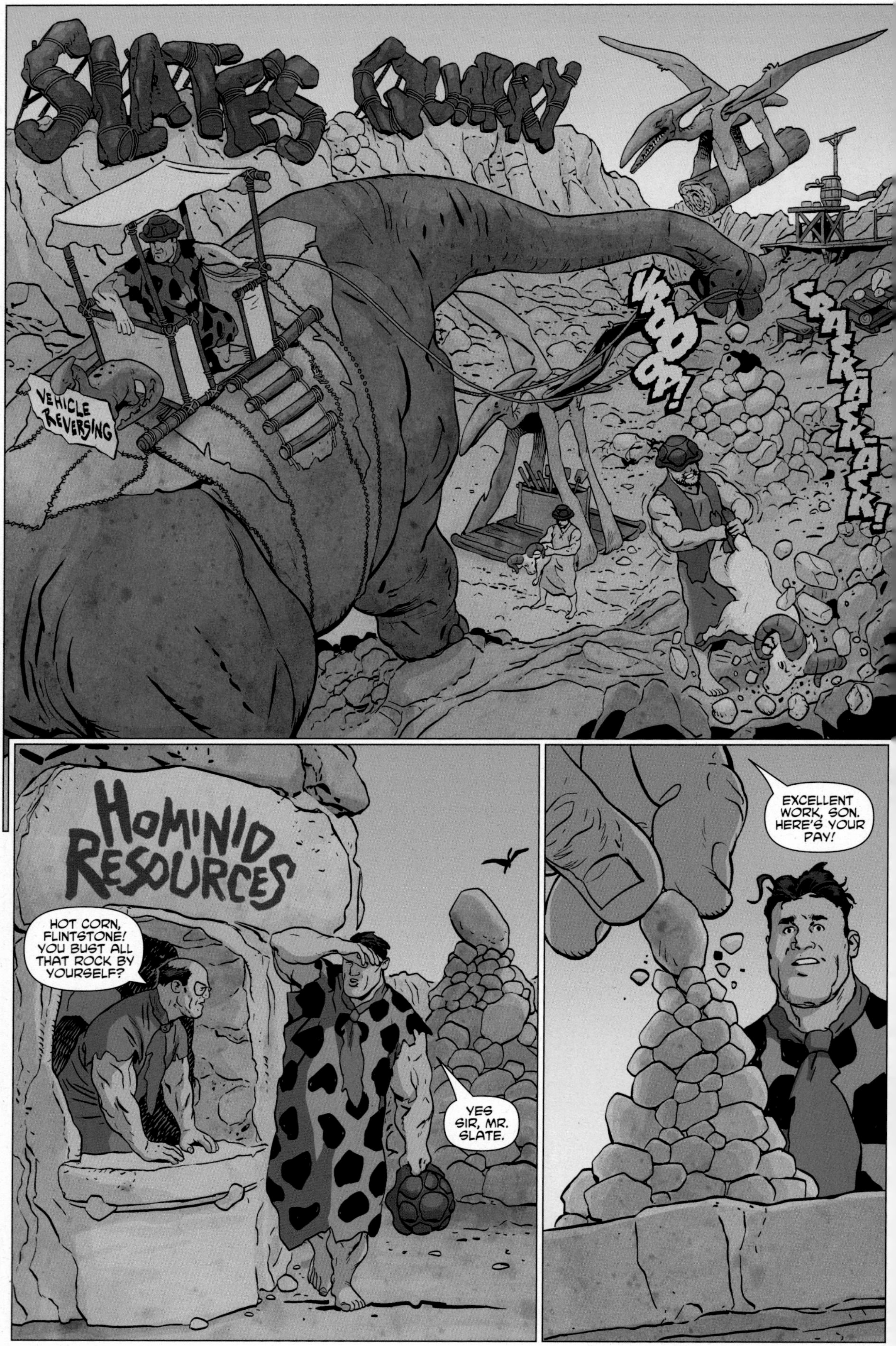
SLATE'S QUARRY
VEHICLE REVERSING
VROOOP!
CRAKAKAKAK!
HOMINID RESOURCES
HOT CORN, FLINTSTONE! YOU BUST ALL THAT ROCK BY YOURSELF?
YES SIR, MR. SLATE.
EXCELLENT WORK, SON. HERE'S YOUR PAY!

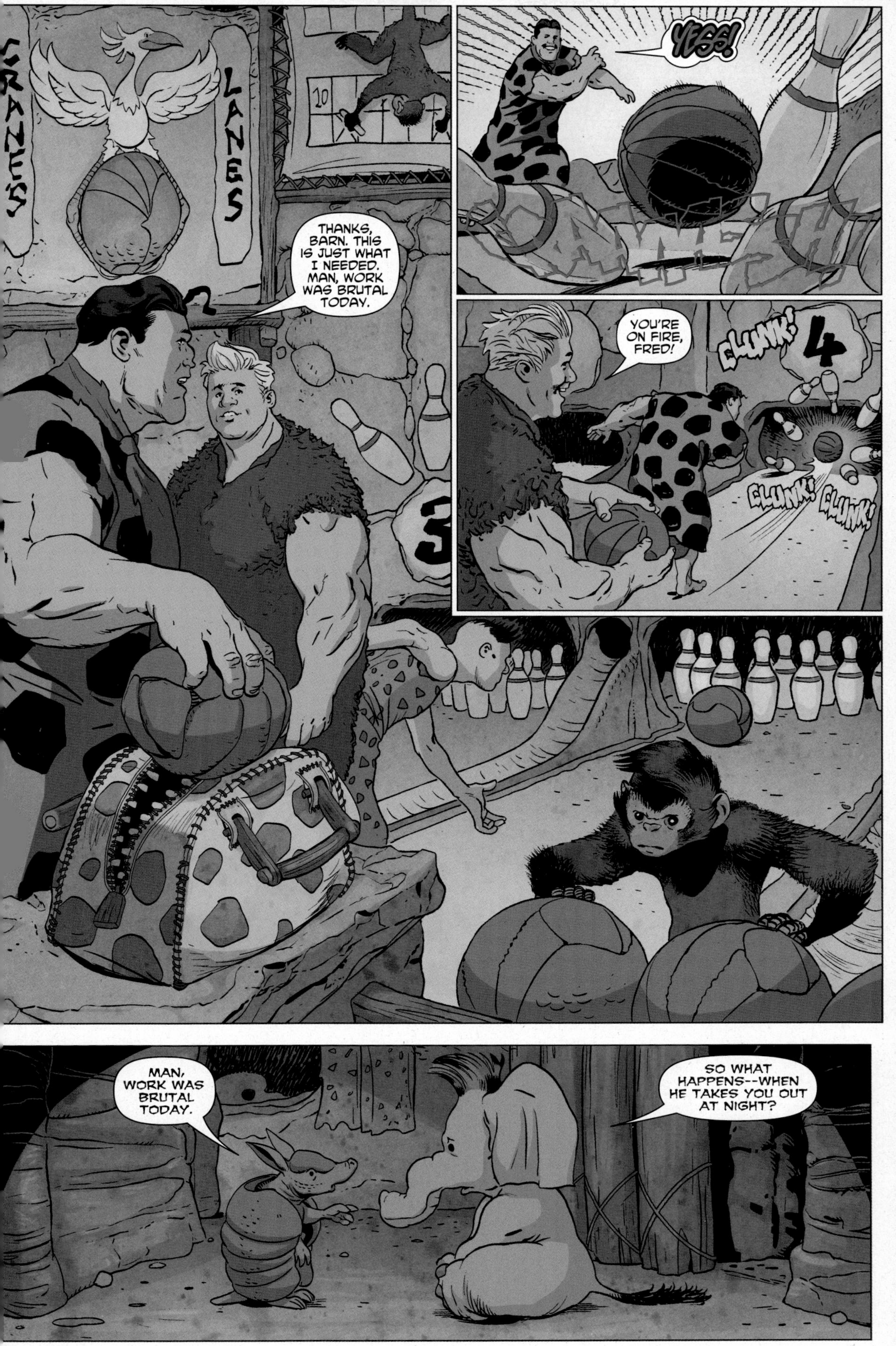
CRANES
LANES
THANKS, BARN. THIS IS JUST WHAT I NEEDED. MAN, WORK WAS BRUTAL TODAY.
YESS!
YOU'RE ON FIRE, FRED!
CLUNK!
CLUNK!
CLUNK!
MAN, WORK WAS BRUTAL TODAY.
SO WHAT HAPPENS--WHEN HE TAKES YOU OUT AT NIGHT?

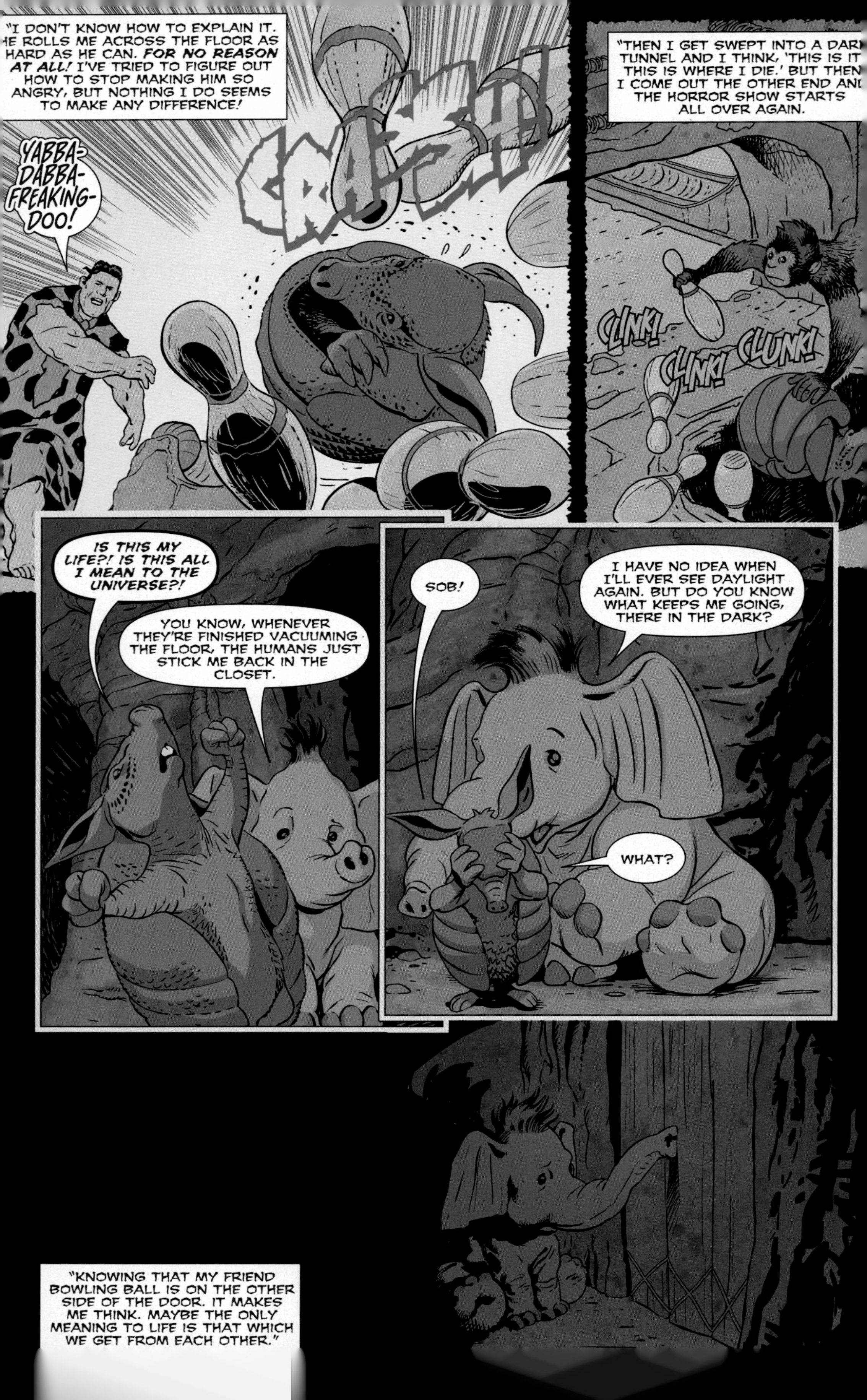

"I DON'T KNOW HOW TO EXPLAIN IT. HE ROLLS ME ACROSS THE FLOOR AS HARD AS HE CAN. *FOR NO REASON AT ALL!* I'VE TRIED TO FIGURE OUT HOW TO STOP MAKING HIM SO ANGRY, BUT NOTHING I DO SEEMS TO MAKE ANY DIFFERENCE!
YABBA-DABBA-FREAKING-DOO!
CRASSH!
"THEN I GET SWEPT INTO A DARK TUNNEL AND I THINK, 'THIS IS IT. THIS IS WHERE I DIE.' BUT THEN I COME OUT THE OTHER END AND THE HORROR SHOW STARTS ALL OVER AGAIN.
CLINK!
CLINK!
CLUNK!
IS THIS MY LIFE?! IS THIS ALL I MEAN TO THE UNIVERSE?!
YOU KNOW, WHENEVER THEY'RE FINISHED VACUUMING THE FLOOR, THE HUMANS JUST STICK ME BACK IN THE CLOSET.
SOB!
I HAVE NO IDEA WHEN I'LL EVER SEE DAYLIGHT AGAIN. BUT DO YOU KNOW WHAT KEEPS ME GOING, THERE IN THE DARK?
WHAT?
"KNOWING THAT MY FRIEND BOWLING BALL IS ON THE OTHER SIDE OF THE DOOR. IT MAKES ME THINK. MAYBE THE ONLY MEANING TO LIFE IS THAT WHICH WE GET FROM EACH OTHER."

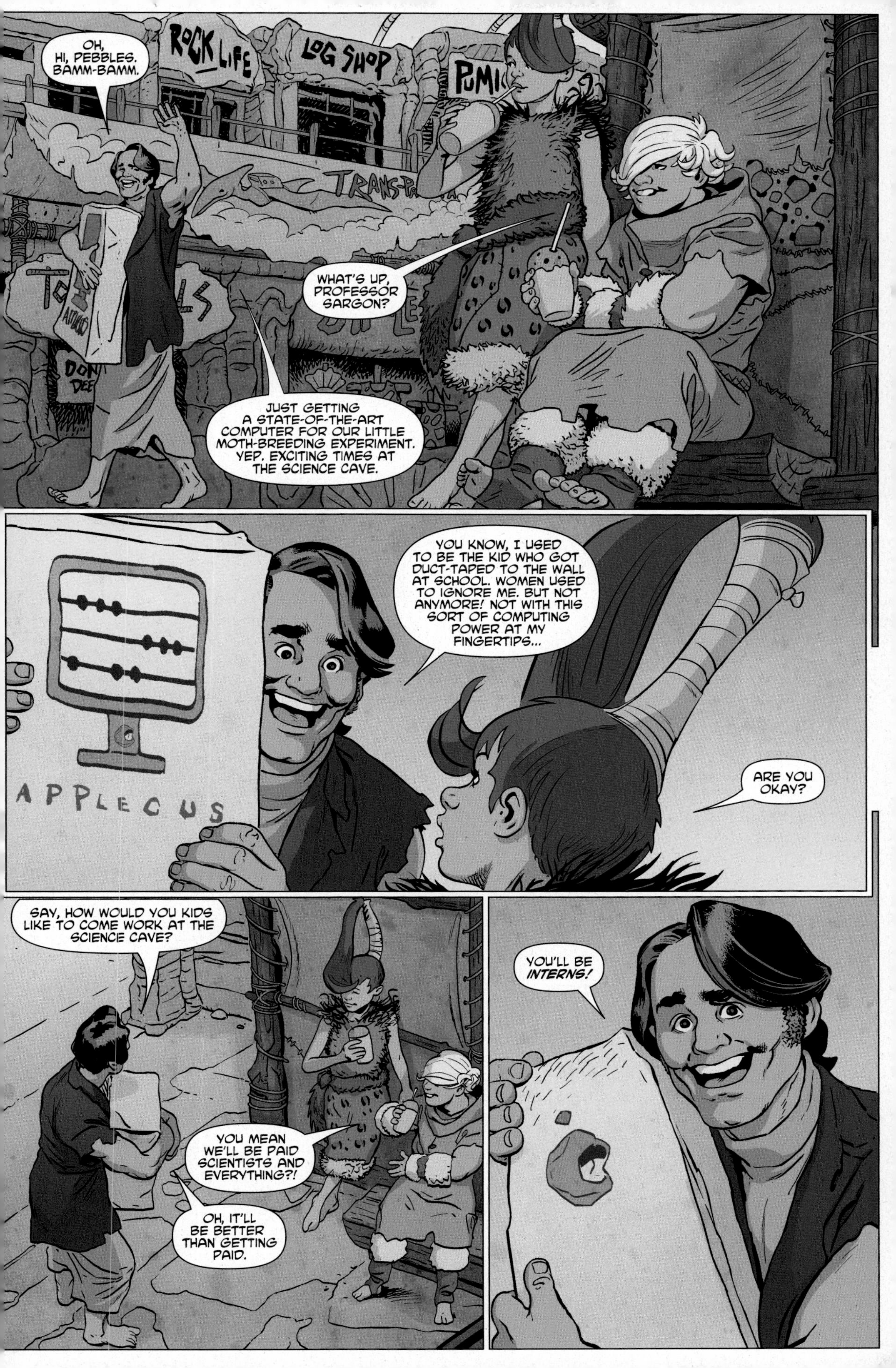

ROCK LIFE
LOG SHOP
OH, HI, PEBBLES. BAMM-BAMM.
WHAT'S UP, PROFESSOR SARGON?
JUST GETTING A STATE-OF-THE-ART COMPUTER FOR OUR LITTLE MOTH-BREEDING EXPERIMENT. YEP. EXCITING TIMES AT THE SCIENCE CAVE.
APPLECUS
YOU KNOW, I USED TO BE THE KID WHO GOT DUCT-TAPED TO THE WALL AT SCHOOL. WOMEN USED TO IGNORE ME. BUT NOT ANYMORE! NOT WITH THIS SORT OF COMPUTING POWER AT MY FINGERTIPS...
ARE YOU OKAY?
SAY, HOW WOULD YOU KIDS LIKE TO COME WORK AT THE SCIENCE CAVE?
YOU MEAN WE'LL BE PAID SCIENTISTS AND EVERYTHING?!
OH, IT'LL BE BETTER THAN GETTING PAID.
YOU'LL BE *INTERNS!*

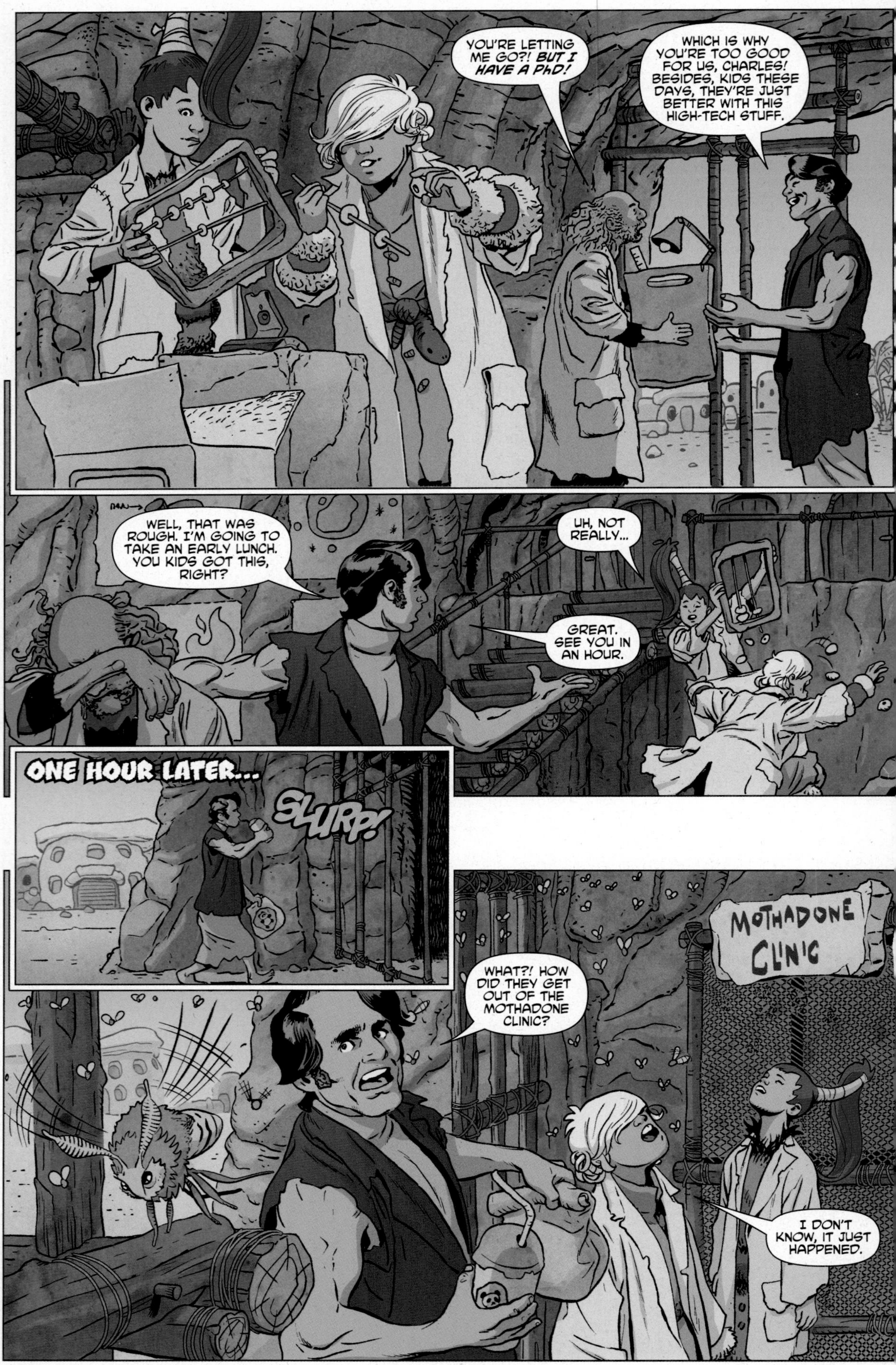
YOU'RE LETTING ME GO?! BUT I HAVE A PhD!
WHICH IS WHY YOU'RE TOO GOOD FOR US, CHARLES! BESIDES, KIDS THESE DAYS, THEY'RE JUST BETTER WITH THIS HIGH-TECH STUFF.
WELL, THAT WAS ROUGH. I'M GOING TO TAKE AN EARLY LUNCH. YOU KIDS GOT THIS, RIGHT?
UH, NOT REALLY...
GREAT. SEE YOU IN AN HOUR.
ONE HOUR LATER...
SLURP!
MOTHADONE CLINIC
WHAT?! HOW DID THEY GET OUT OF THE MOTHADONE CLINIC?
I DON'T KNOW, IT JUST HAPPENED.

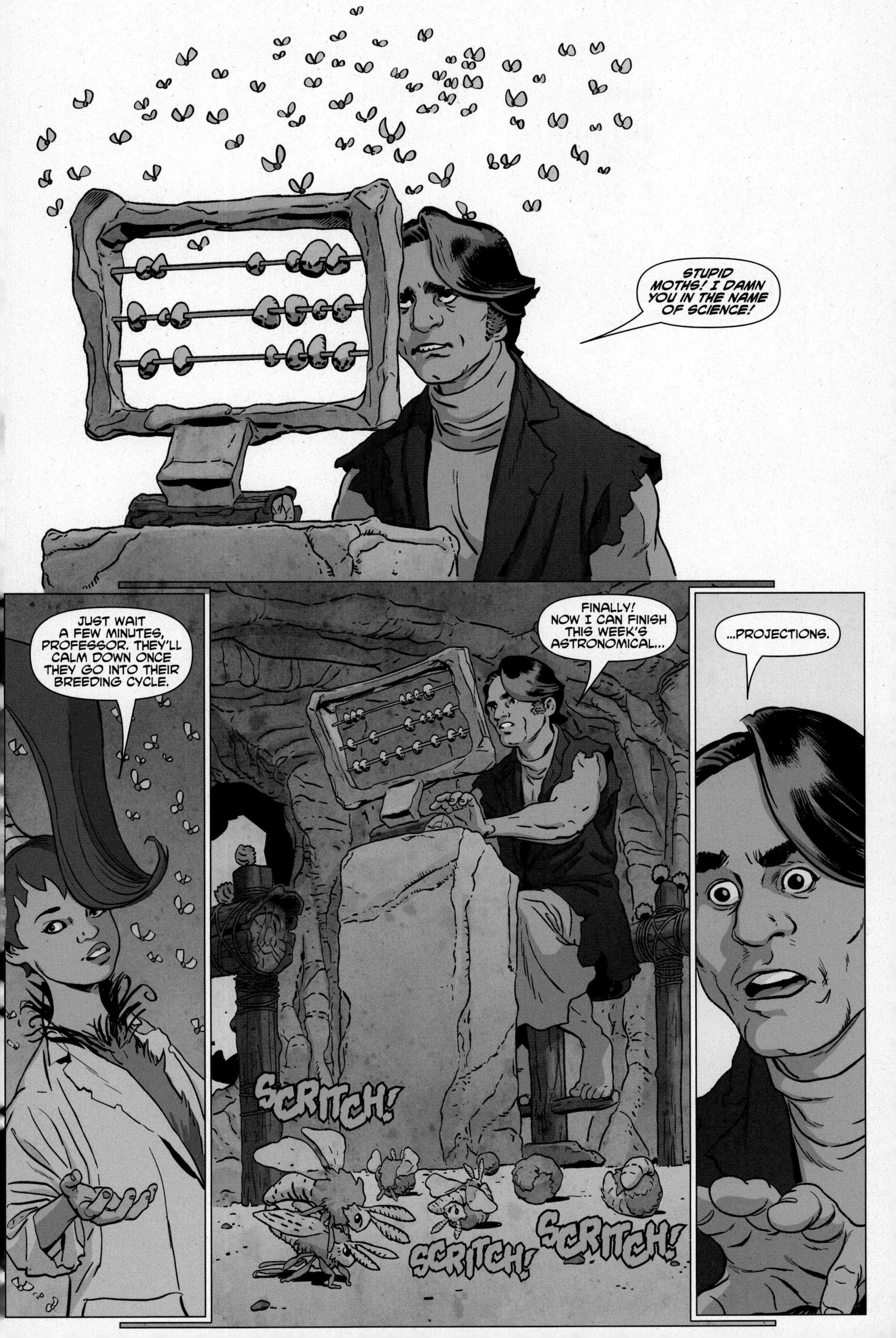

STUPID MOTHS! I DAMN YOU IN THE NAME OF SCIENCE!
JUST WAIT A FEW MINUTES, PROFESSOR. THEY'LL CALM DOWN ONCE THEY GO INTO THEIR BREEDING CYCLE.
FINALLY! NOW I CAN FINISH THIS WEEK'S ASTRONOMICAL...
SCRITCH!
SCRITCH!
SCRITCH!
...PROJECTIONS.

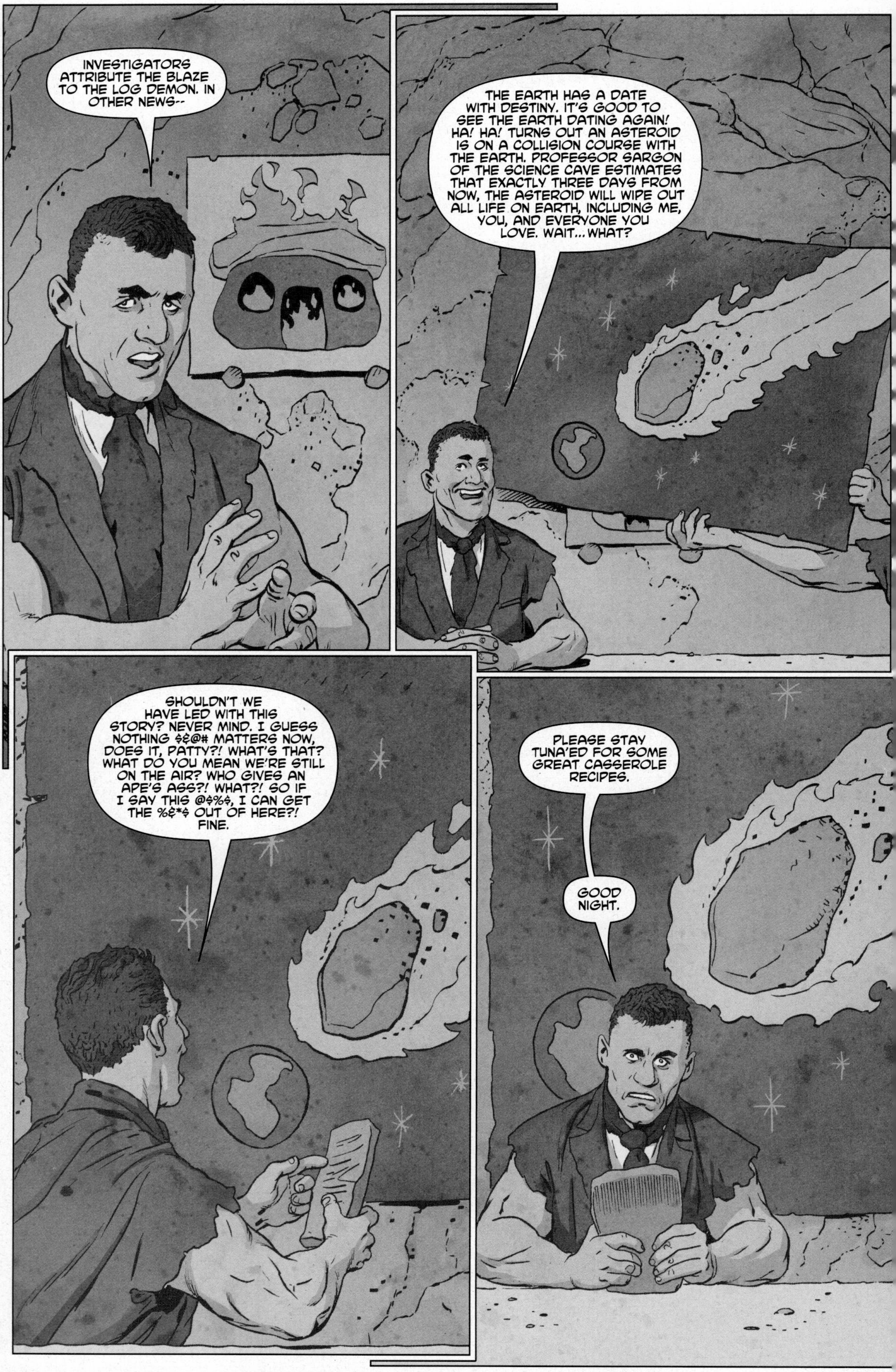
INVESTIGATORS ATTRIBUTE THE BLAZE TO THE LOG DEMON. IN OTHER NEWS--
THE EARTH HAS A DATE WITH DESTINY. IT'S GOOD TO SEE THE EARTH DATING AGAIN! HA! HA! TURNS OUT AN ASTEROID IS ON A COLLISION COURSE WITH THE EARTH. PROFESSOR SARGON OF THE SCIENCE CAVE ESTIMATES THAT EXACTLY THREE DAYS FROM NOW, THE ASTEROID WILL WIPE OUT ALL LIFE ON EARTH, INCLUDING ME, YOU, AND EVERYONE YOU LOVE. WAIT... WHAT?
SHOULDN'T WE HAVE LED WITH THIS STORY? NEVER MIND. I GUESS NOTHING $&@# MATTERS NOW, DOES IT, PATTY?! WHAT'S THAT? WHAT DO YOU MEAN WE'RE STILL ON THE AIR? WHO GIVES AN APE'S ASS?! WHAT?! SO IF I SAY THIS @$%$, I CAN GET THE %&*$ OUT OF HERE?! FINE.
PLEASE STAY TUNA'ED FOR SOME GREAT CASSEROLE RECIPES.
GOOD NIGHT.

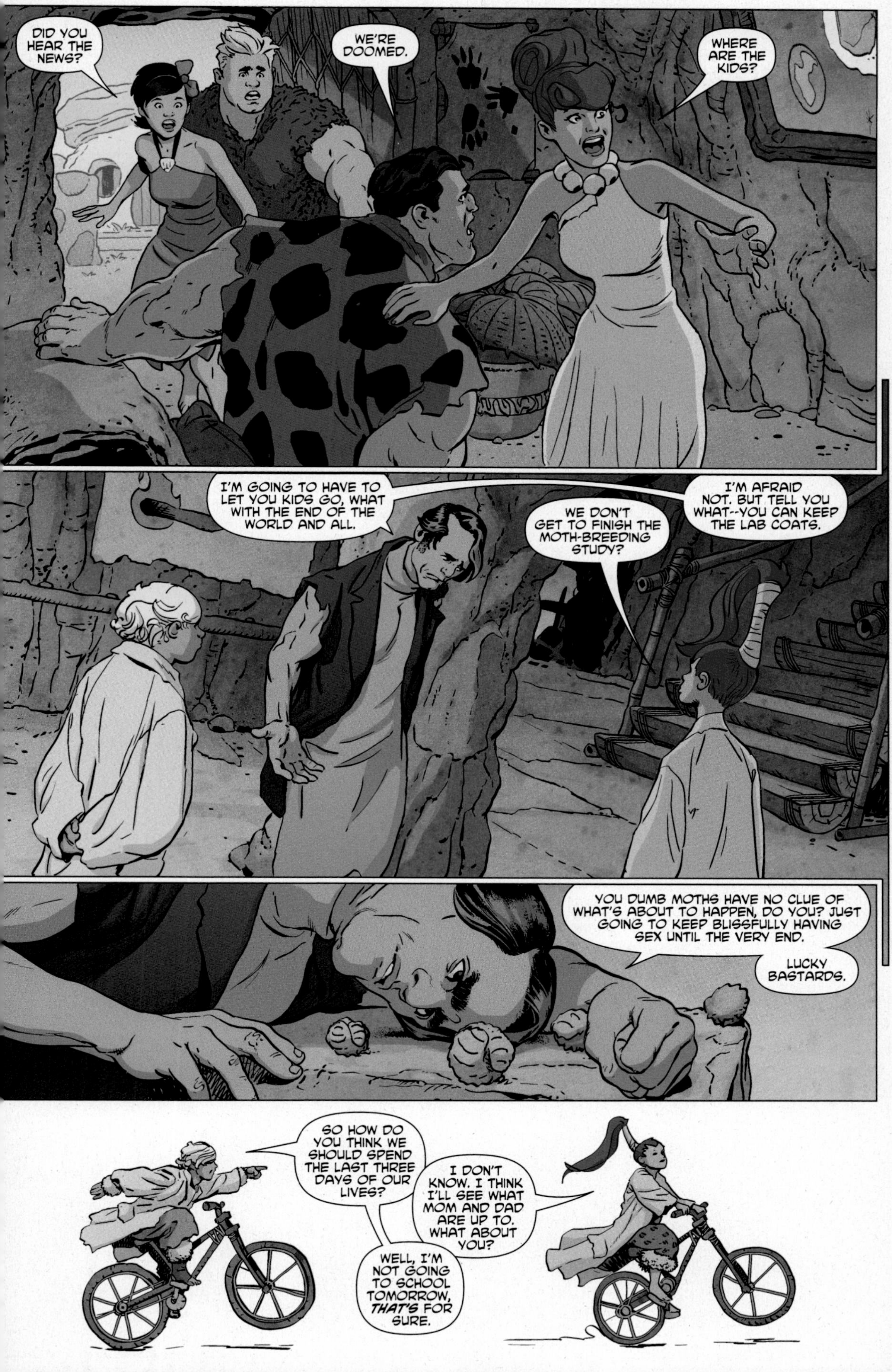
DID YOU HEAR THE NEWS?
WE'RE DOOMED.
WHERE ARE THE KIDS?
I'M GOING TO HAVE TO LET YOU KIDS GO, WHAT WITH THE END OF THE WORLD AND ALL.
WE DON'T GET TO FINISH THE MOTH-BREEDING STUDY?
I'M AFRAID NOT. BUT TELL YOU WHAT--YOU CAN KEEP THE LAB COATS.
YOU DUMB MOTHS HAVE NO CLUE OF WHAT'S ABOUT TO HAPPEN, DO YOU? JUST GOING TO KEEP BLISSFULLY HAVING SEX UNTIL THE VERY END.
LUCKY BASTARDS.
SO HOW DO YOU THINK WE SHOULD SPEND THE LAST THREE DAYS OF OUR LIVES?
I DON'T KNOW. I THINK I'LL SEE WHAT MOM AND DAD ARE UP TO. WHAT ABOUT YOU?
WELL, I'M NOT GOING TO SCHOOL TOMORROW, *THAT'S* FOR SURE.

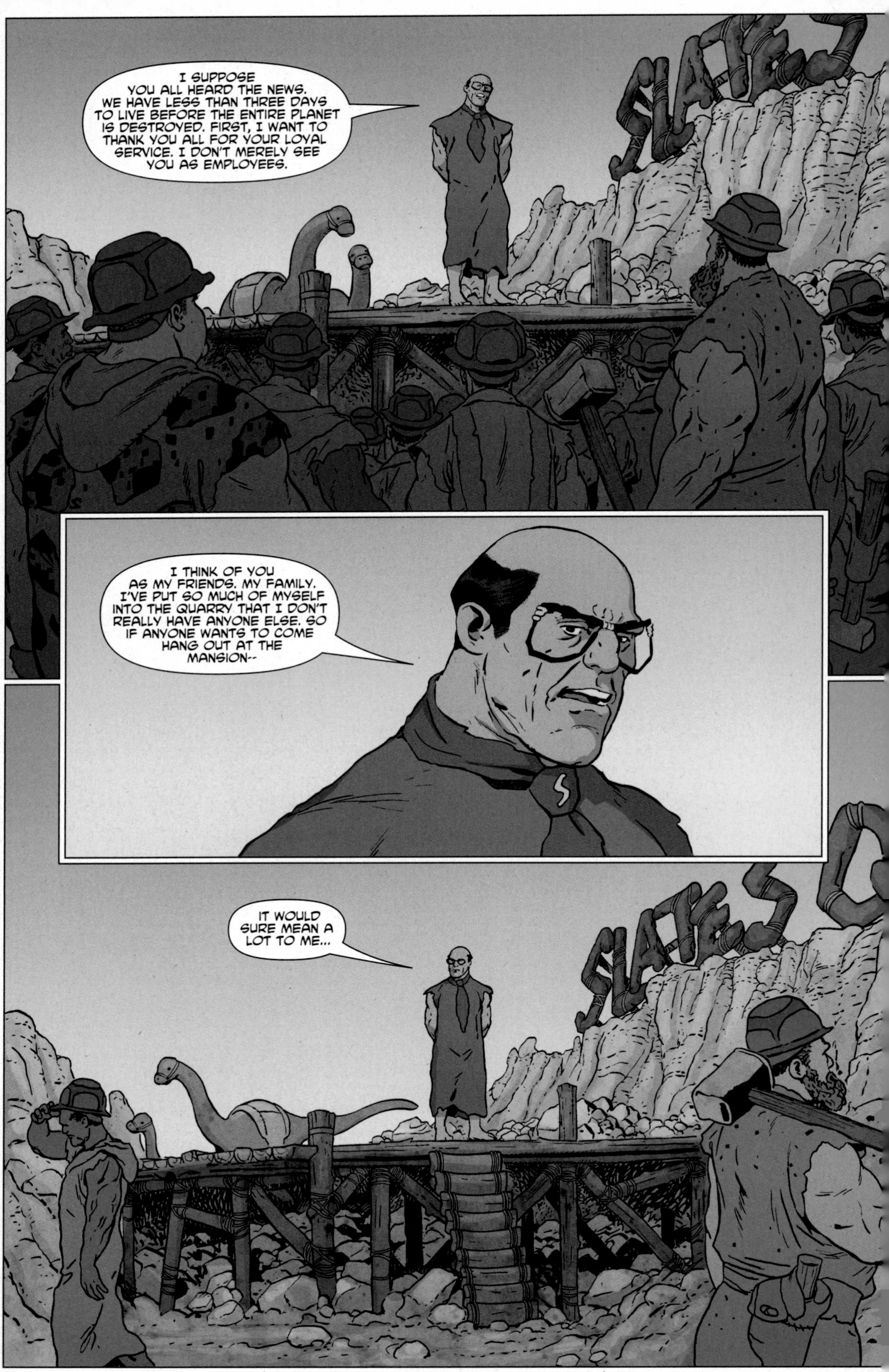
I SUPPOSE YOU ALL HEARD THE NEWS. WE HAVE LESS THAN THREE DAYS TO LIVE BEFORE THE ENTIRE PLANET IS DESTROYED. FIRST, I WANT TO THANK YOU ALL FOR YOUR LOYAL SERVICE. I DON'T MERELY SEE YOU AS EMPLOYEES.
I THINK OF YOU AS MY FRIENDS. MY FAMILY. I'VE PUT SO MUCH OF MYSELF INTO THE QUARRY THAT I DON'T REALLY HAVE ANYONE ELSE. SO IF ANYONE WANTS TO COME HANG OUT AT THE MANSION--
IT WOULD SURE MEAN A LOT TO ME...

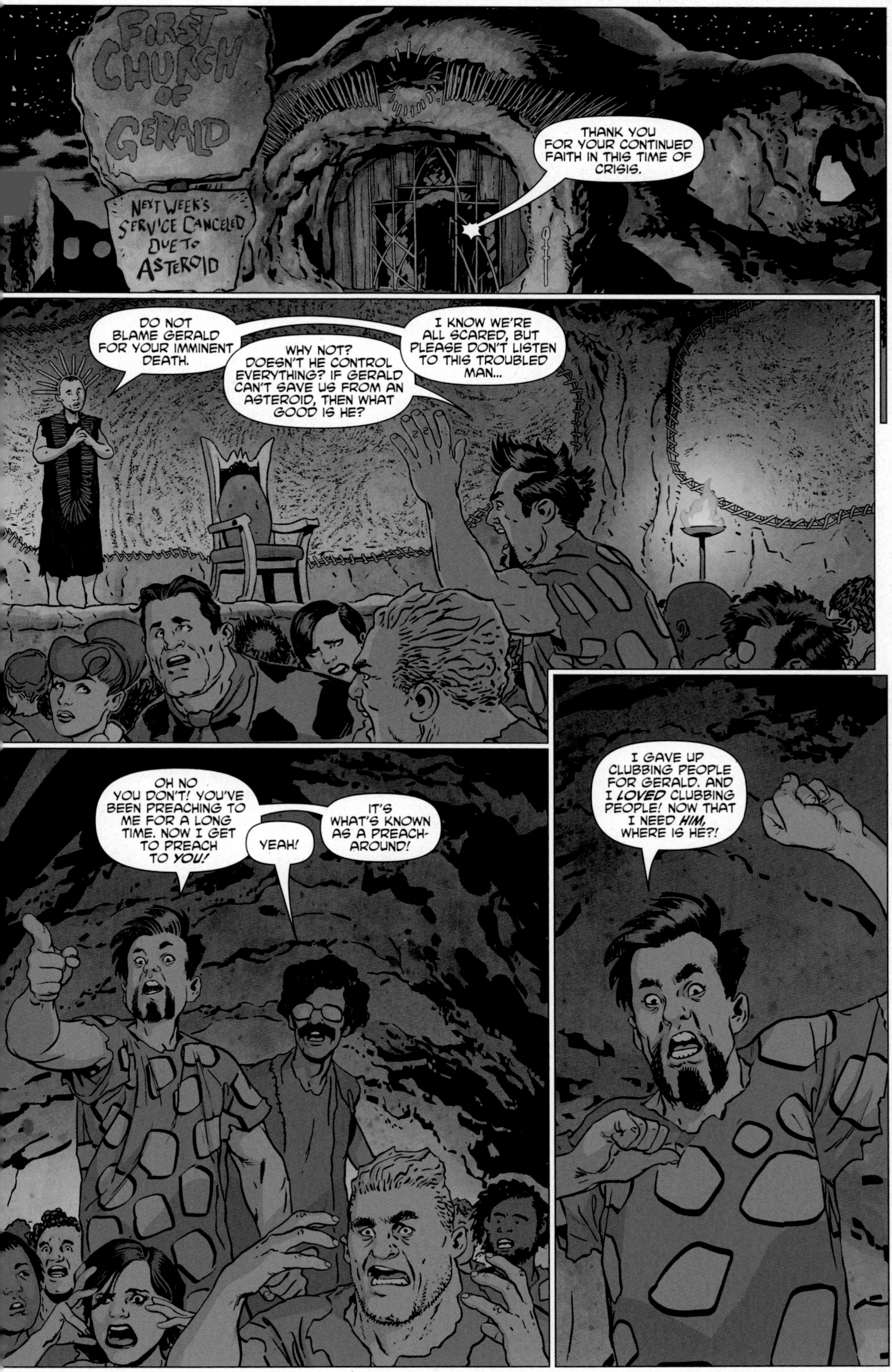
FIRST CHURCH OF GERALD
NEXT WEEK'S SERVICE CANCELED DUE TO ASTEROID
THANK YOU FOR YOUR CONTINUED FAITH IN THIS TIME OF CRISIS.
DO NOT BLAME GERALD FOR YOUR IMMINENT DEATH.
WHY NOT? DOESN'T HE CONTROL EVERYTHING? IF GERALD CAN'T SAVE US FROM AN ASTEROID, THEN WHAT GOOD IS HE?
I KNOW WE'RE ALL SCARED, BUT PLEASE DON'T LISTEN TO THIS TROUBLED MAN...
OH NO YOU DON'T! YOU'VE BEEN PREACHING TO ME FOR A LONG TIME. NOW I GET TO PREACH TO *YOU!*
YEAH!
IT'S WHAT'S KNOWN AS A PREACH-AROUND!
I GAVE UP CLUBBING PEOPLE FOR GERALD. AND I *LOVED* CLUBBING PEOPLE! NOW THAT I NEED *HIM,* WHERE IS HE?!

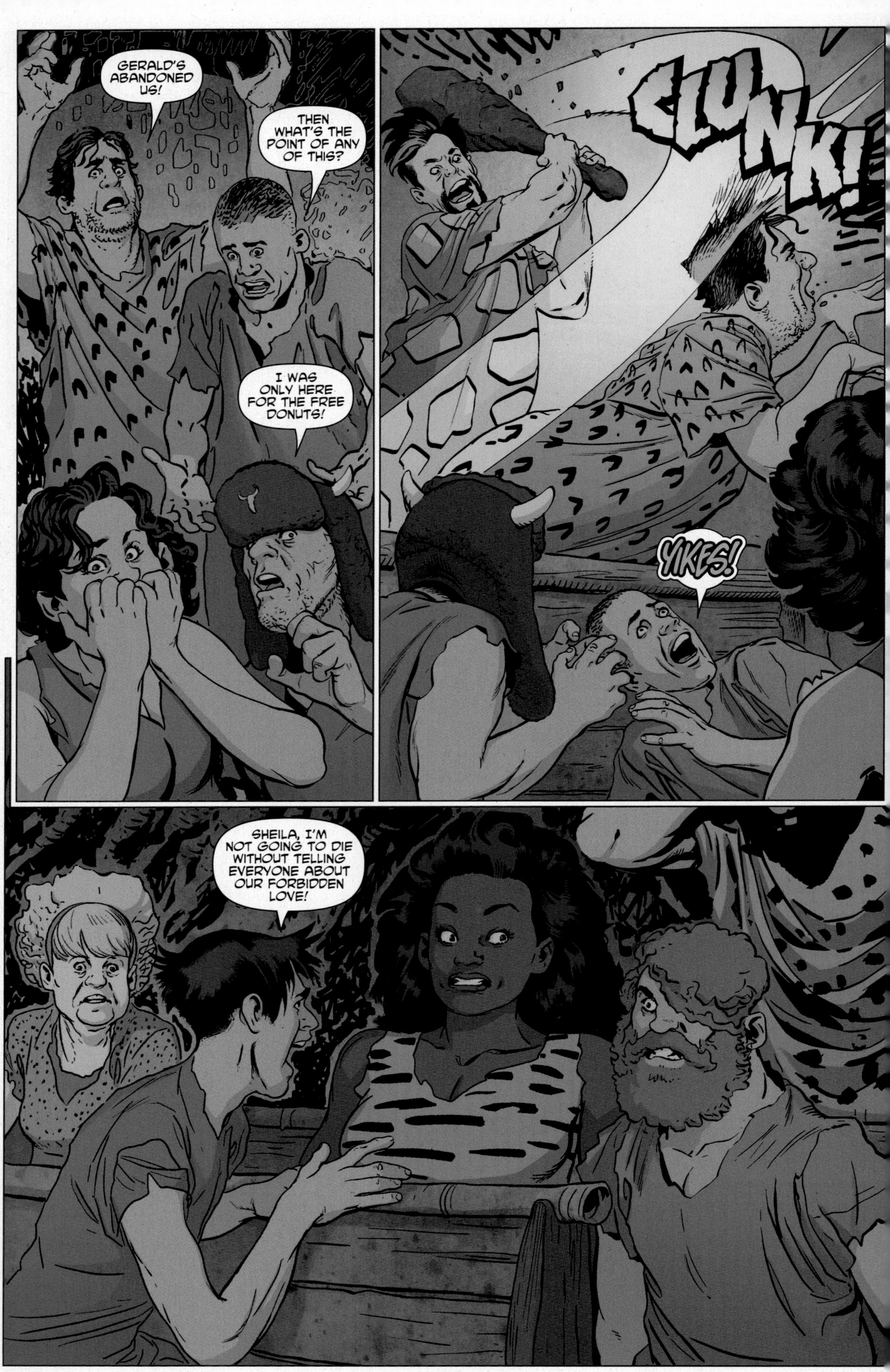
GERALD'S ABANDONED US!
THEN WHAT'S THE POINT OF ANY OF THIS?
I WAS ONLY HERE FOR THE FREE DONUTS!
CLUNK!
YIKES!
SHEILA, I'M NOT GOING TO DIE WITHOUT TELLING EVERYONE ABOUT OUR FORBIDDEN LOVE!

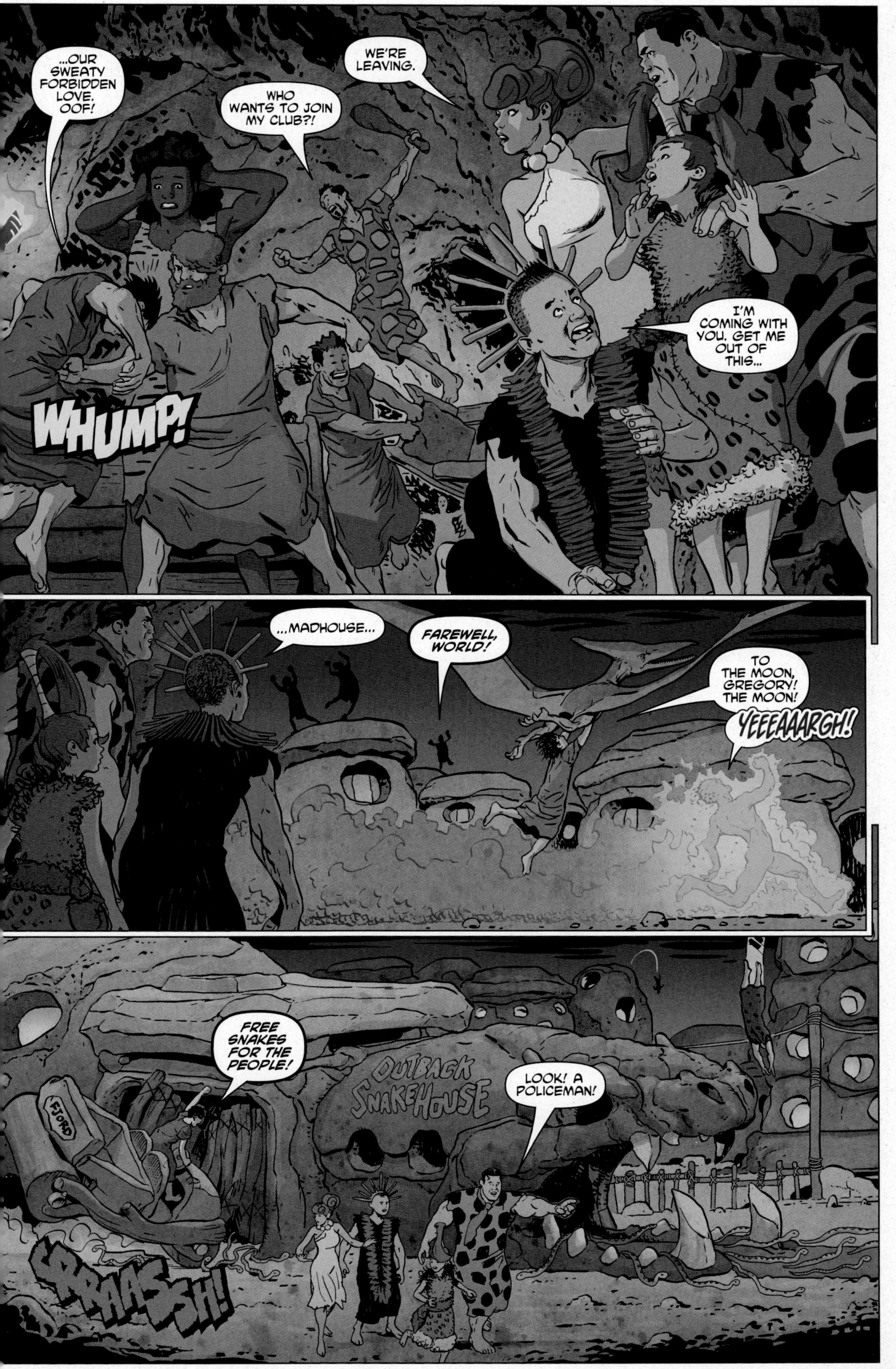
...OUR SWEATY FORBIDDEN LOVE. OOF!
WHO WANTS TO JOIN MY CLUB?!
WE'RE LEAVING.
WHUMP!
I'M COMING WITH YOU. GET ME OUT OF THIS...
...MADHOUSE...
FAREWELL, WORLD!
TO THE MOON, GREGORY! THE MOON!
YEEEAAARGH!
FREE SNAKES FOR THE PEOPLE!
OUTBACK SNAKEHOUSE
LOOK! A POLICEMAN!
FJORD
SPRAASSH!

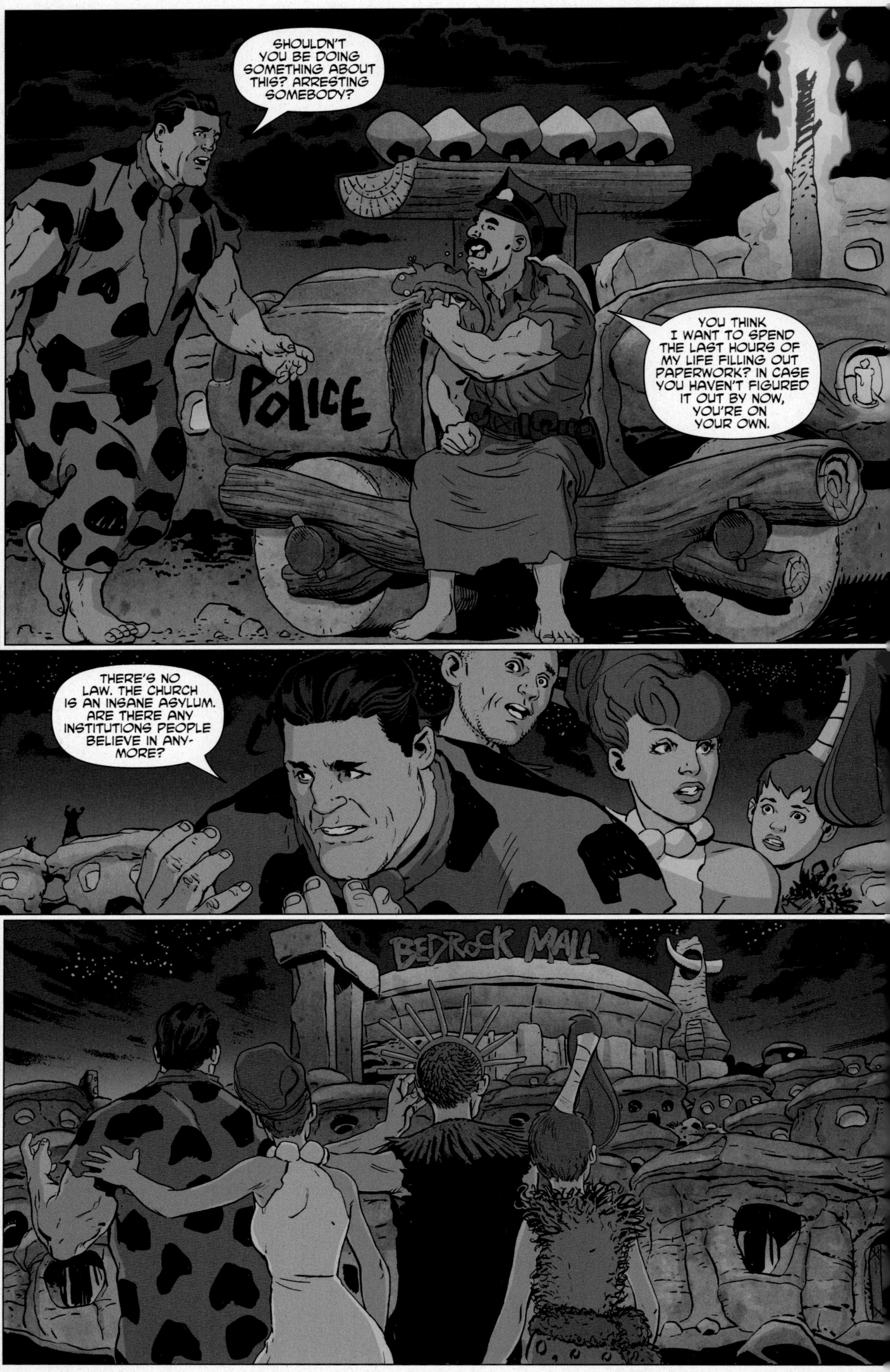
SHOULDN'T YOU BE DOING SOMETHING ABOUT THIS? ARRESTING SOMEBODY?
YOU THINK I WANT TO SPEND THE LAST HOURS OF MY LIFE FILLING OUT PAPERWORK? IN CASE YOU HAVEN'T FIGURED IT OUT BY NOW, YOU'RE ON YOUR OWN.
POLICE
THERE'S NO LAW. THE CHURCH IS AN INSANE ASYLUM. ARE THERE ANY INSTITUTIONS PEOPLE BELIEVE IN ANY-MORE?
BEDROCK MALL

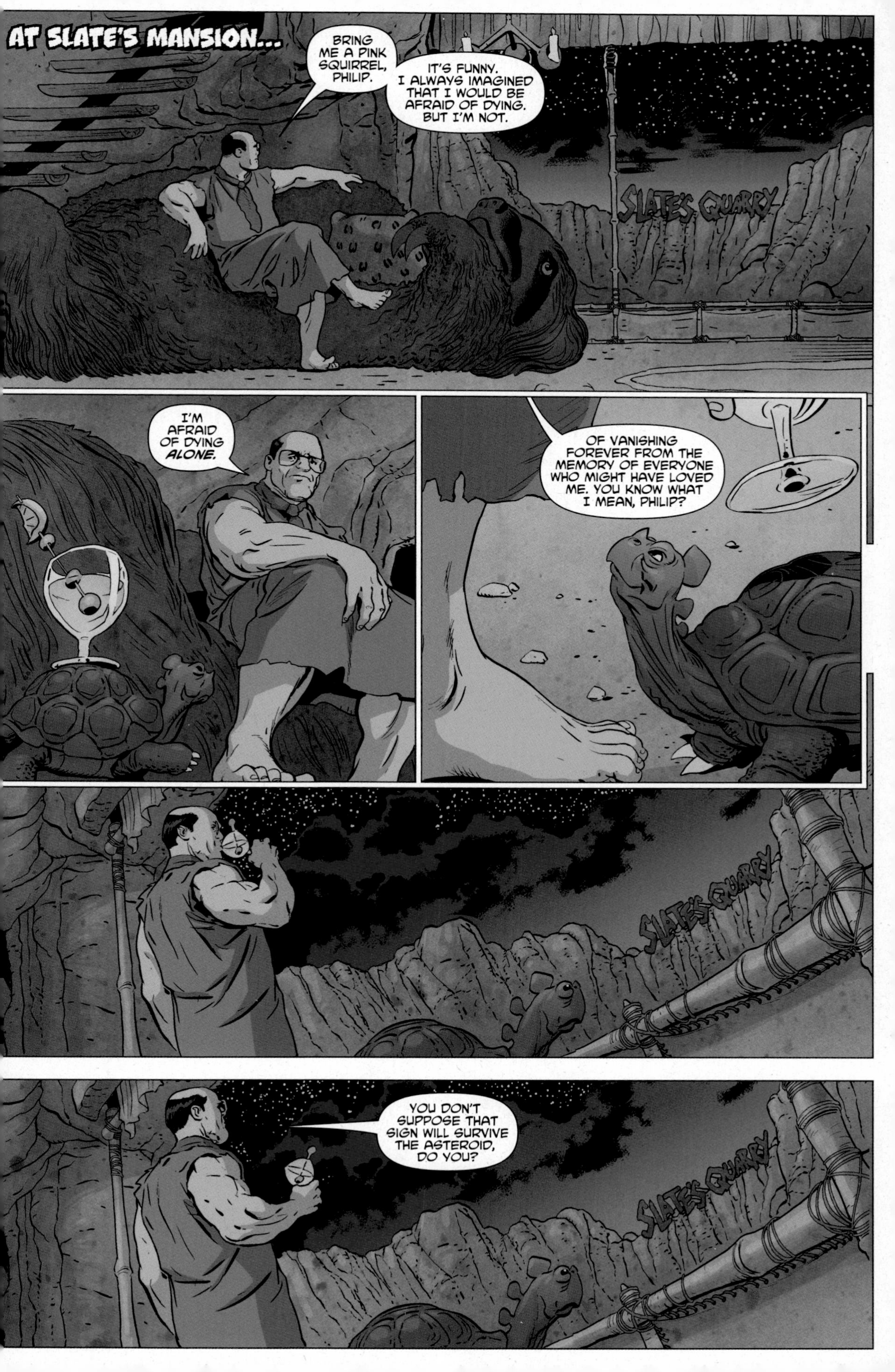
AT SLATE'S MANSION...
BRING ME A PINK SQUIRREL, PHILIP.
IT'S FUNNY. I ALWAYS IMAGINED THAT I WOULD BE AFRAID OF DYING. BUT I'M NOT.
SLATE'S QUARRY
I'M AFRAID OF DYING *ALONE.*
OF VANISHING FOREVER FROM THE MEMORY OF EVERYONE WHO MIGHT HAVE LOVED ME. YOU KNOW WHAT I MEAN, PHILIP?
SLATE'S QUARRY
YOU DON'T SUPPOSE THAT SIGN WILL SURVIVE THE ASTEROID, DO YOU?
SLATE'S QUARRY

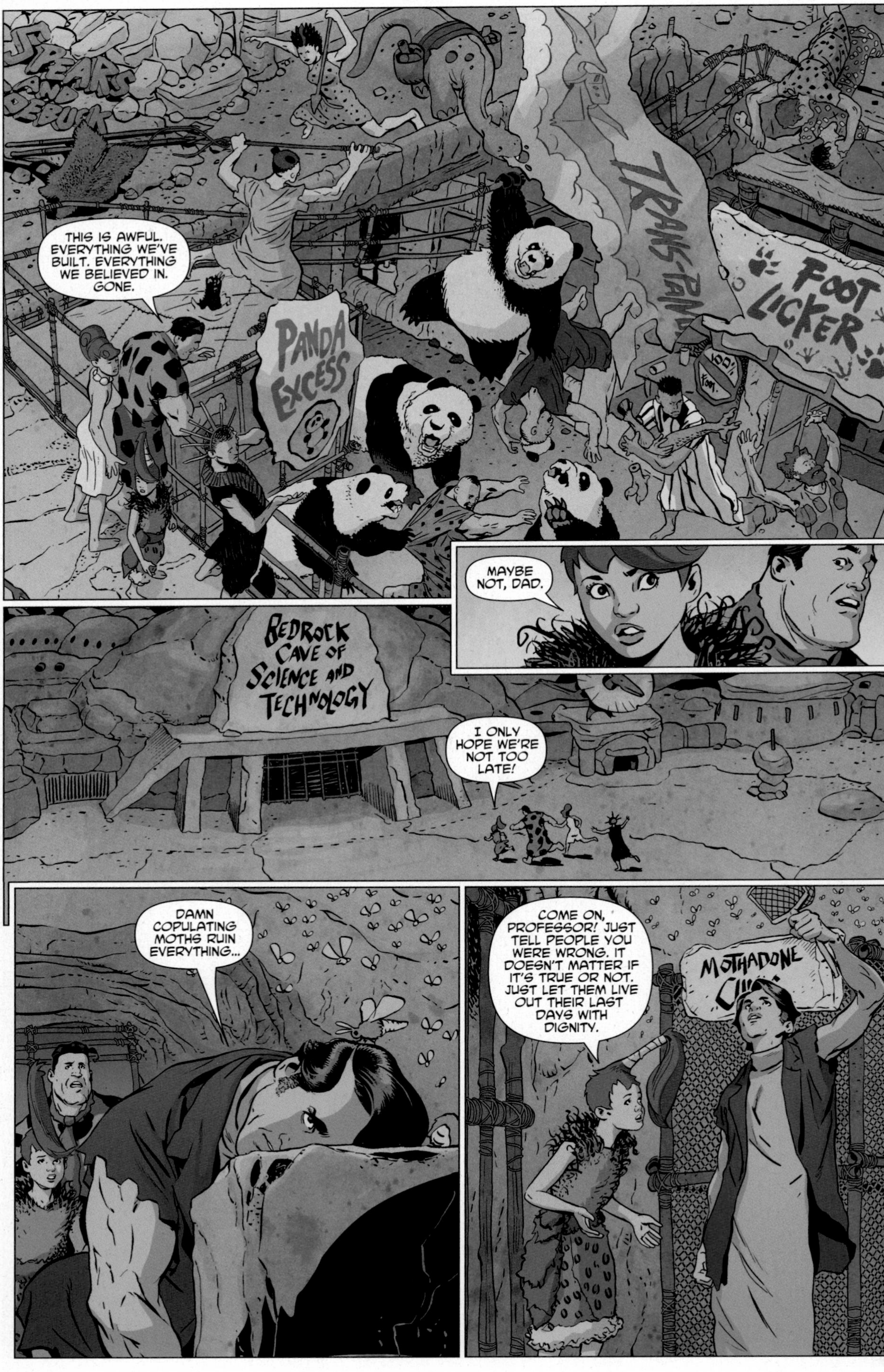
SPEARS AND DEBUCK
THIS IS AWFUL. EVERYTHING WE'VE BUILT. EVERYTHING WE BELIEVED IN. GONE.
PANDA EXCESS
FOOT LICKER
MAYBE NOT, DAD.
BEDROCK CAVE OF SCIENCE AND TECHNOLOGY
I ONLY HOPE WE'RE NOT TOO LATE!
DAMN COPULATING MOTHS RUIN EVERYTHING...
COME ON, PROFESSOR! JUST TELL PEOPLE YOU WERE WRONG. IT DOESN'T MATTER IF IT'S TRUE OR NOT. JUST LET THEM LIVE OUT THEIR LAST DAYS WITH DIGNITY.

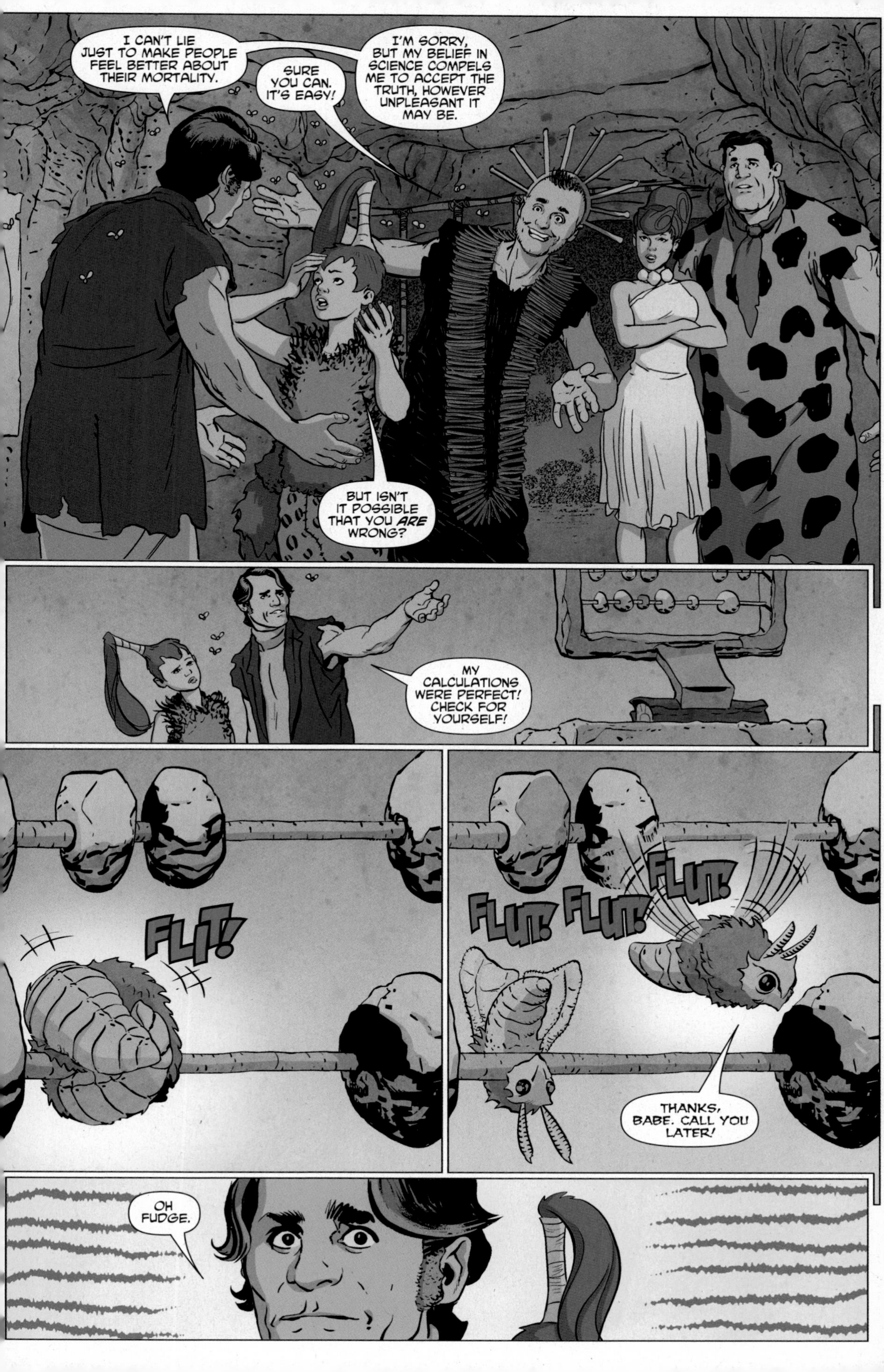
I CAN'T LIE JUST TO MAKE PEOPLE FEEL BETTER ABOUT THEIR MORTALITY.
SURE YOU CAN. IT'S EASY!
I'M SORRY, BUT MY BELIEF IN SCIENCE COMPELS ME TO ACCEPT THE TRUTH, HOWEVER UNPLEASANT IT MAY BE.
BUT ISN'T IT POSSIBLE THAT YOU *ARE* WRONG?
MY CALCULATIONS WERE PERFECT! CHECK FOR YOURSELF!
FLIT!
FLUT! FLUT! FLUT!
THANKS, BABE. CALL YOU LATER!
OH FUDGE.

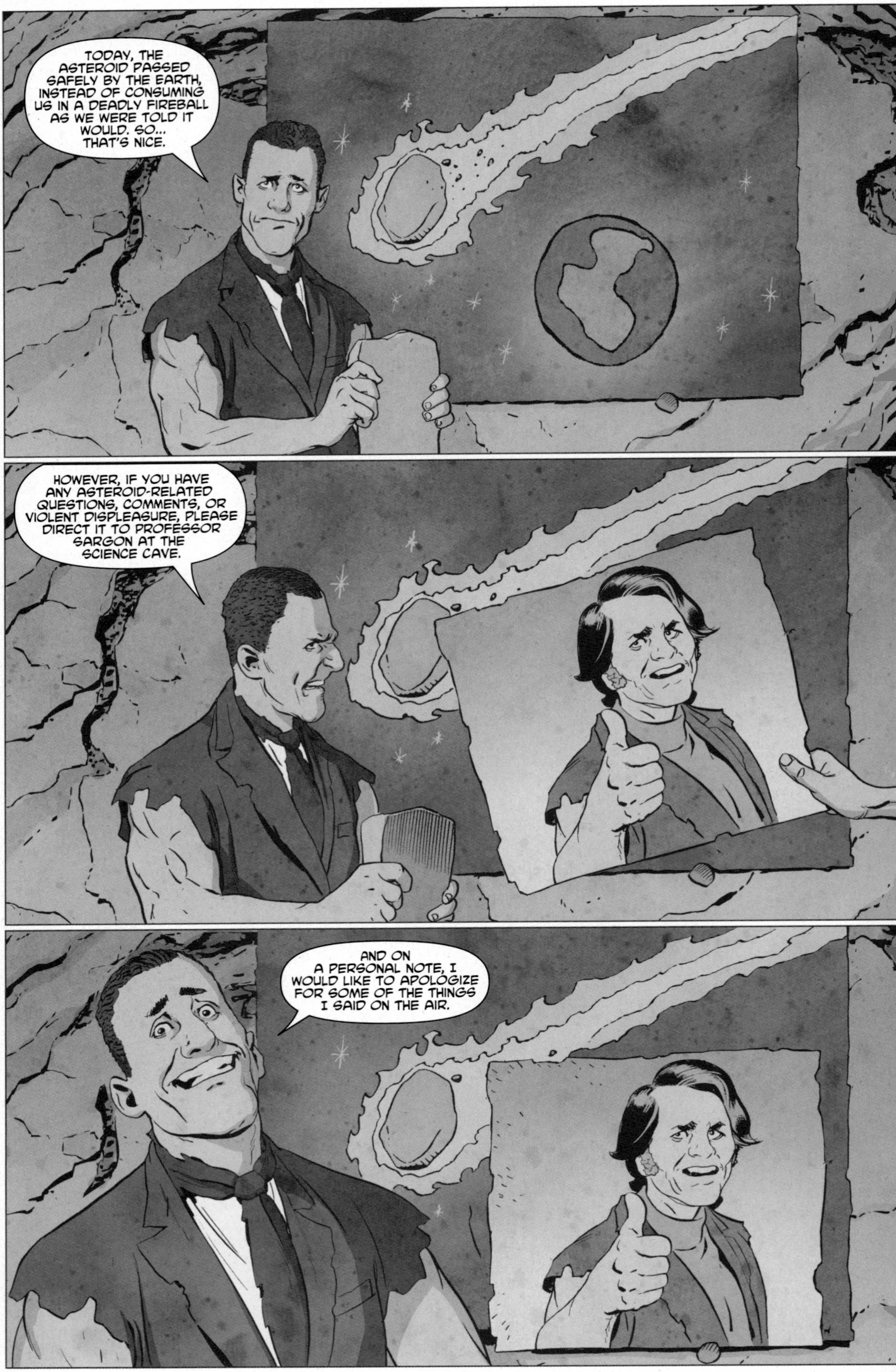
TODAY, THE ASTEROID PASSED SAFELY BY THE EARTH, INSTEAD OF CONSUMING US IN A DEADLY FIREBALL AS WE WERE TOLD IT WOULD. SO... THAT'S NICE.
HOWEVER, IF YOU HAVE ANY ASTEROID-RELATED QUESTIONS, COMMENTS, OR VIOLENT DISPLEASURE, PLEASE DIRECT IT TO PROFESSOR SARGON AT THE SCIENCE CAVE.
AND ON A PERSONAL NOTE, I WOULD LIKE TO APOLOGIZE FOR SOME OF THE THINGS I SAID ON THE AIR.

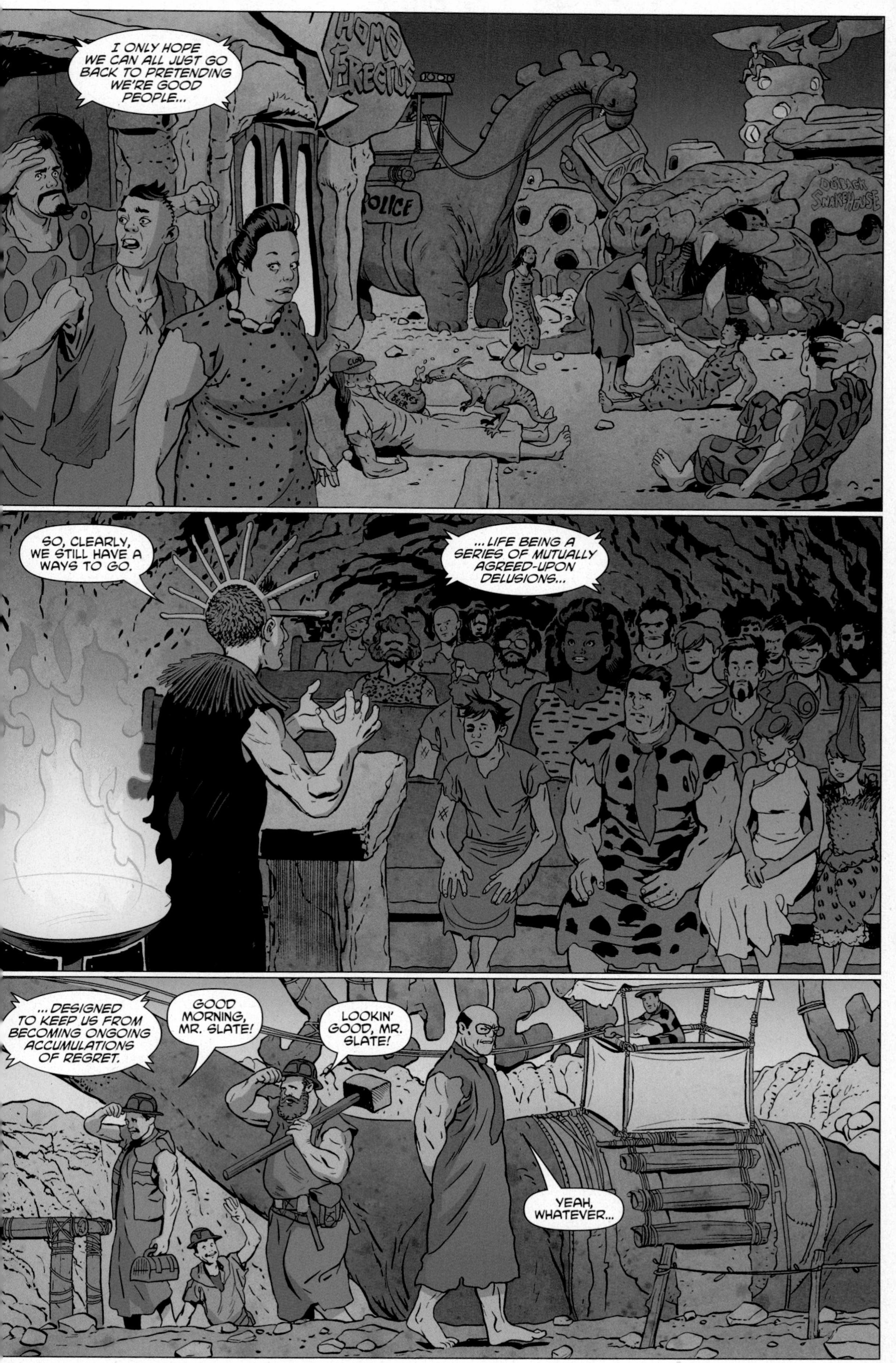
HOMO ERECTUS
POLICE
I ONLY HOPE WE CAN ALL JUST GO BACK TO PRETENDING WE'RE GOOD PEOPLE...
SO, CLEARLY, WE STILL HAVE A WAYS TO GO.
...LIFE BEING A SERIES OF MUTUALLY AGREED-UPON DELUSIONS...
...DESIGNED TO KEEP US FROM BECOMING ONGOING ACCUMULATIONS OF REGRET.
GOOD MORNING, MR. SLATE!
LOOKIN' GOOD, MR. SLATE!
YEAH, WHATEVER...

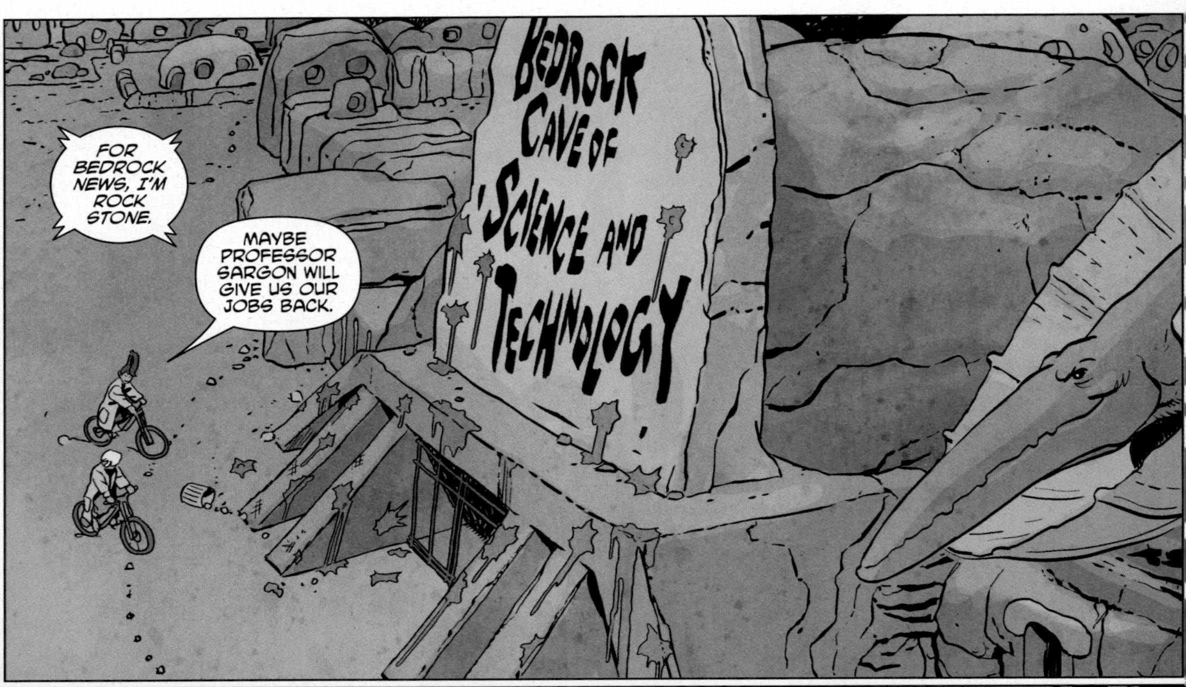
BEDROCK CAVE OF SCIENCE AND TECHNOLOGY
FOR BEDROCK NEWS, I'M ROCK STONE.
MAYBE PROFESSOR SARGON WILL GIVE US OUR JOBS BACK.

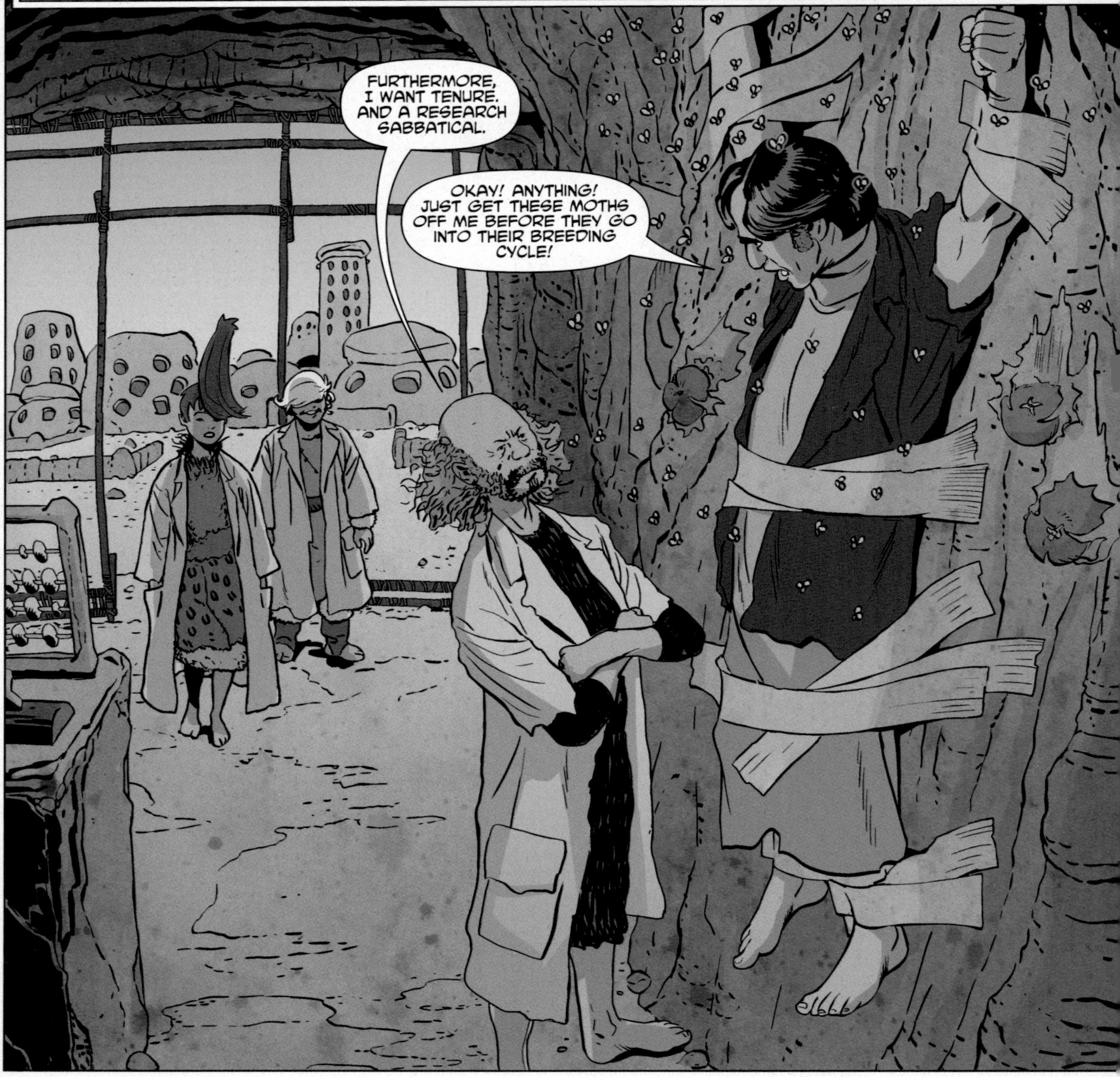
FURTHERMORE, I WANT TENURE. AND A RESEARCH SABBATICAL.
OKAY! ANYTHING! JUST GET THESE MOTHS OFF ME BEFORE THEY GO INTO THEIR BREEDING CYCLE!

THE FLINTSTONES #1 variant cover by IVAN REIS and MARCELO MAIOLO

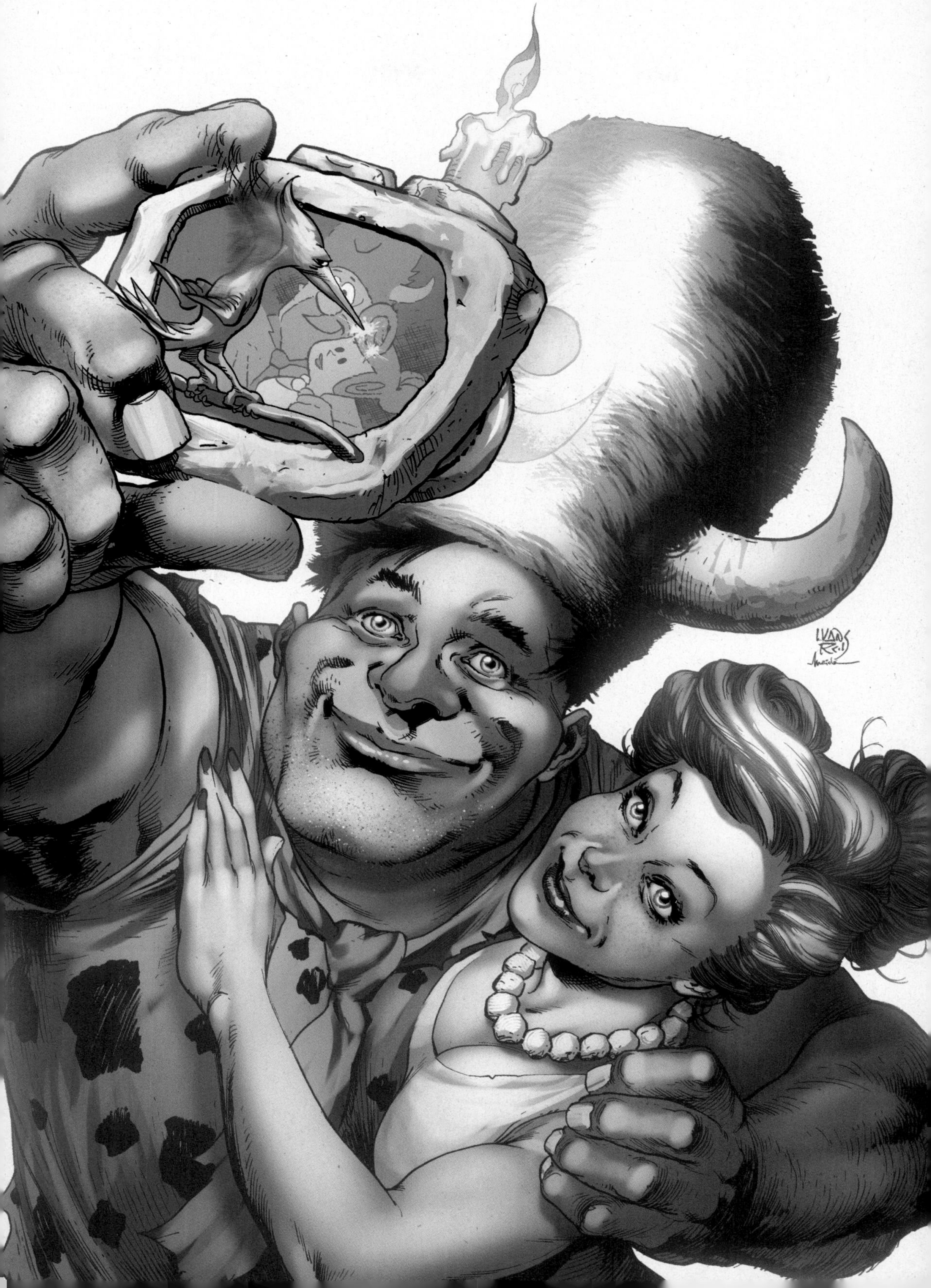

THE FLINTSTONES #1 variant cover by WALTER SIMONSON and STEVE BUCCELLATO

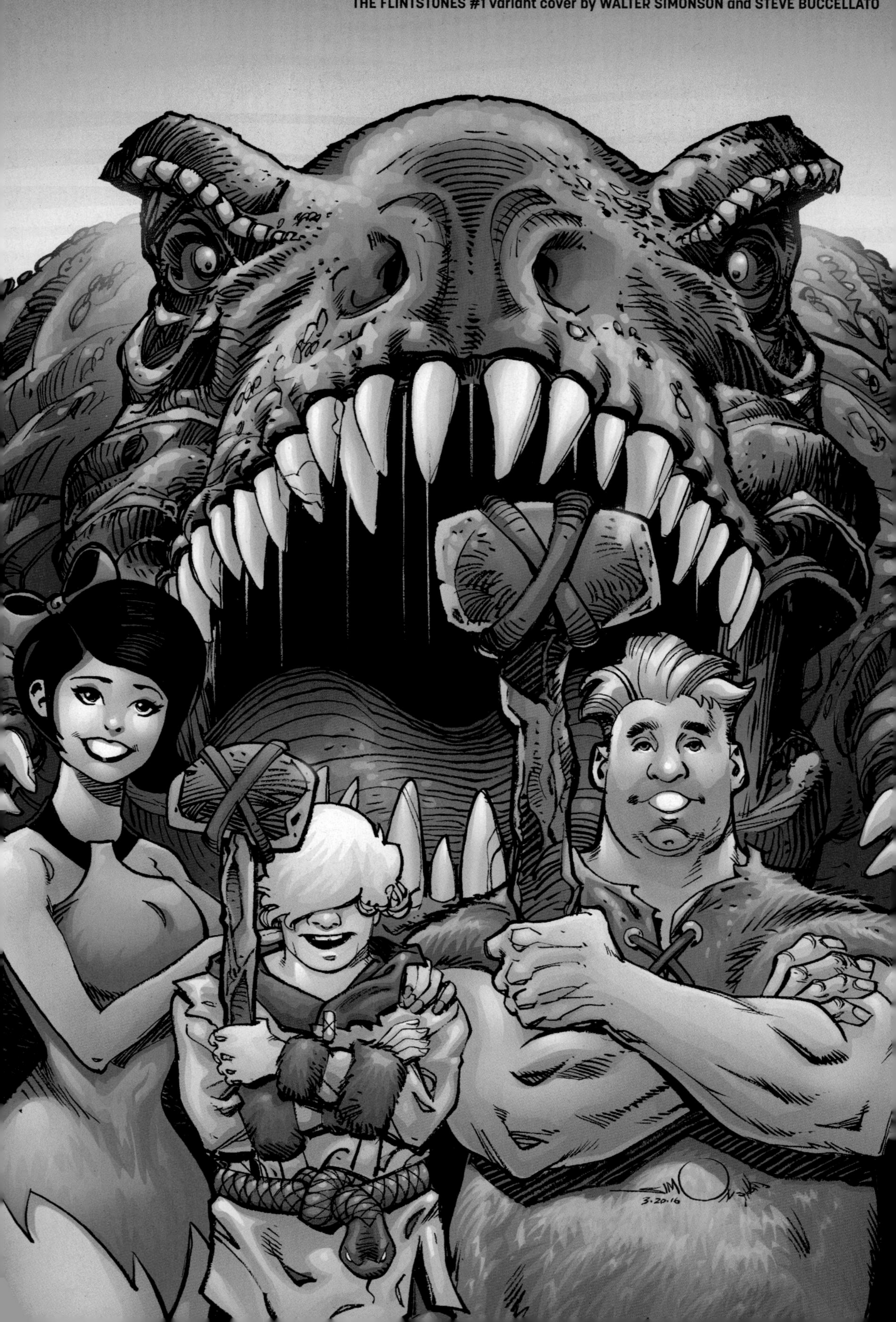

THE FLINTSTONES #1 variant cover by DUSTIN NGUYEN

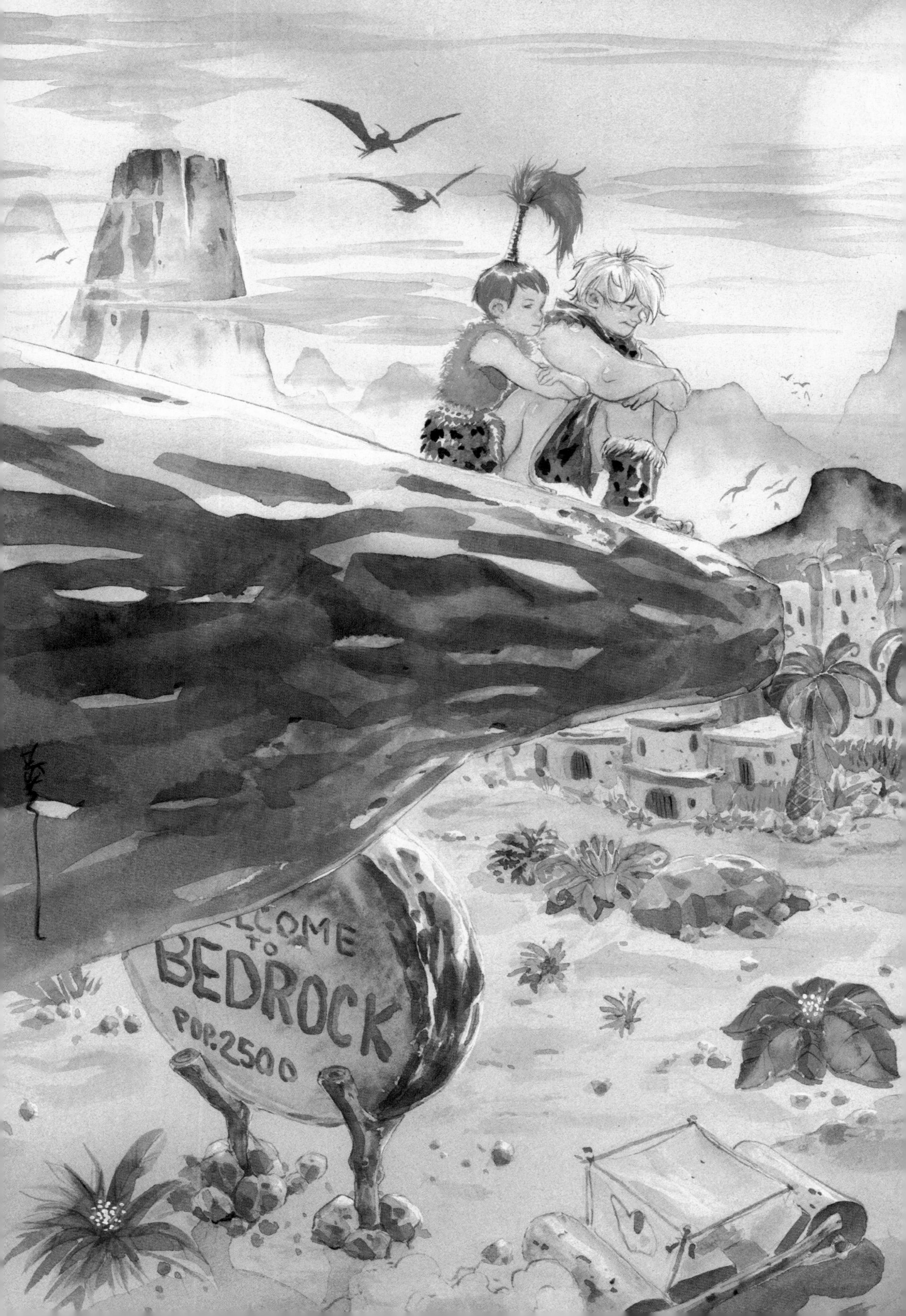
LCOME
TO
BEDROCK
POP.2500

THE FLINTSTONES #1 variant cover by DAN HIPP

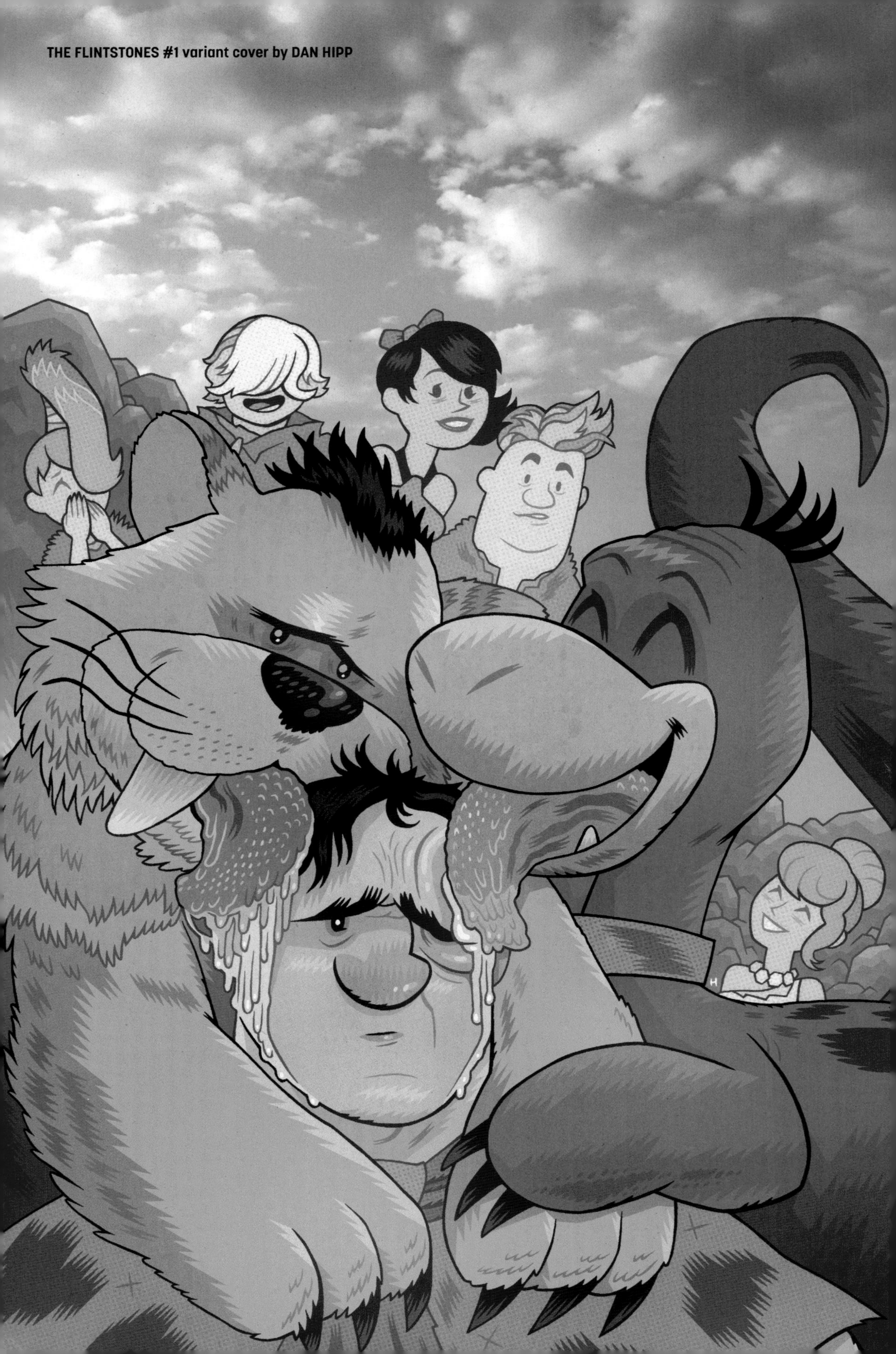
H

THE FLINTSTONES #1 adult coloring book variant cover by IVAN REIS

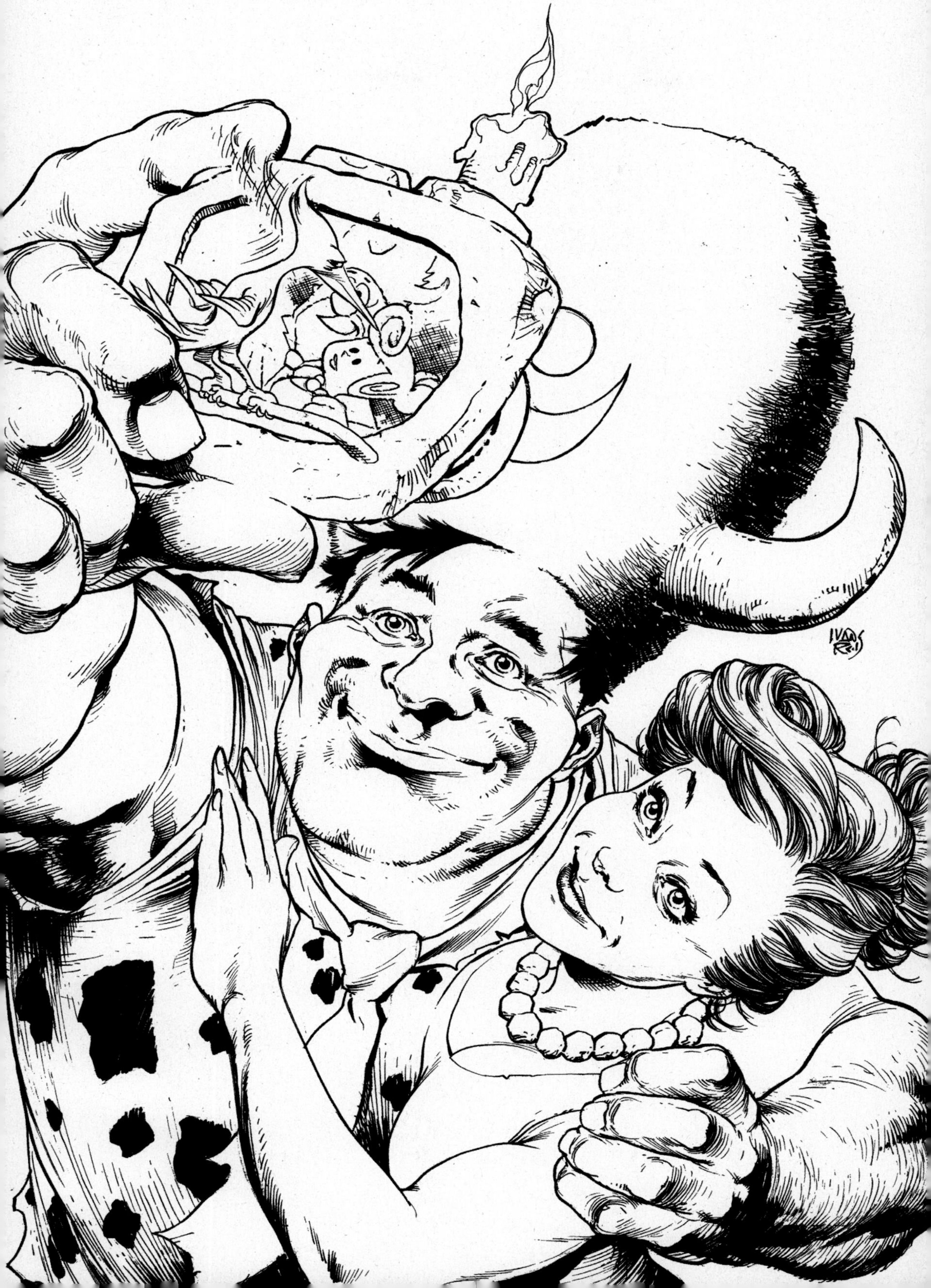

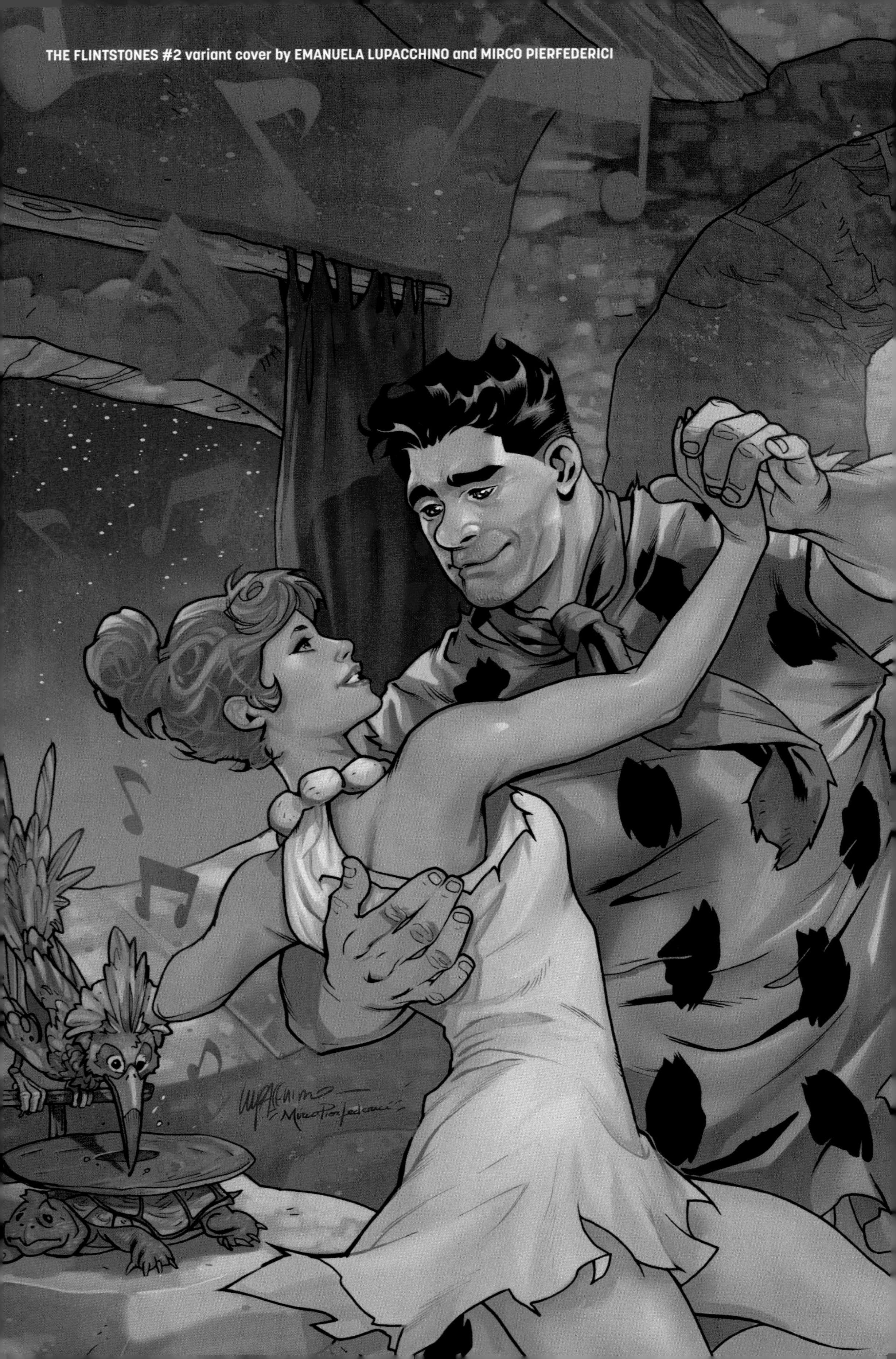

THE FLINTSTONES #2 variant cover by EMANUELA LUPACCHINO and MIRCO PIERFEDERICI

THE FLINTSTONES #3 variant cover by BILQUIS EVELY

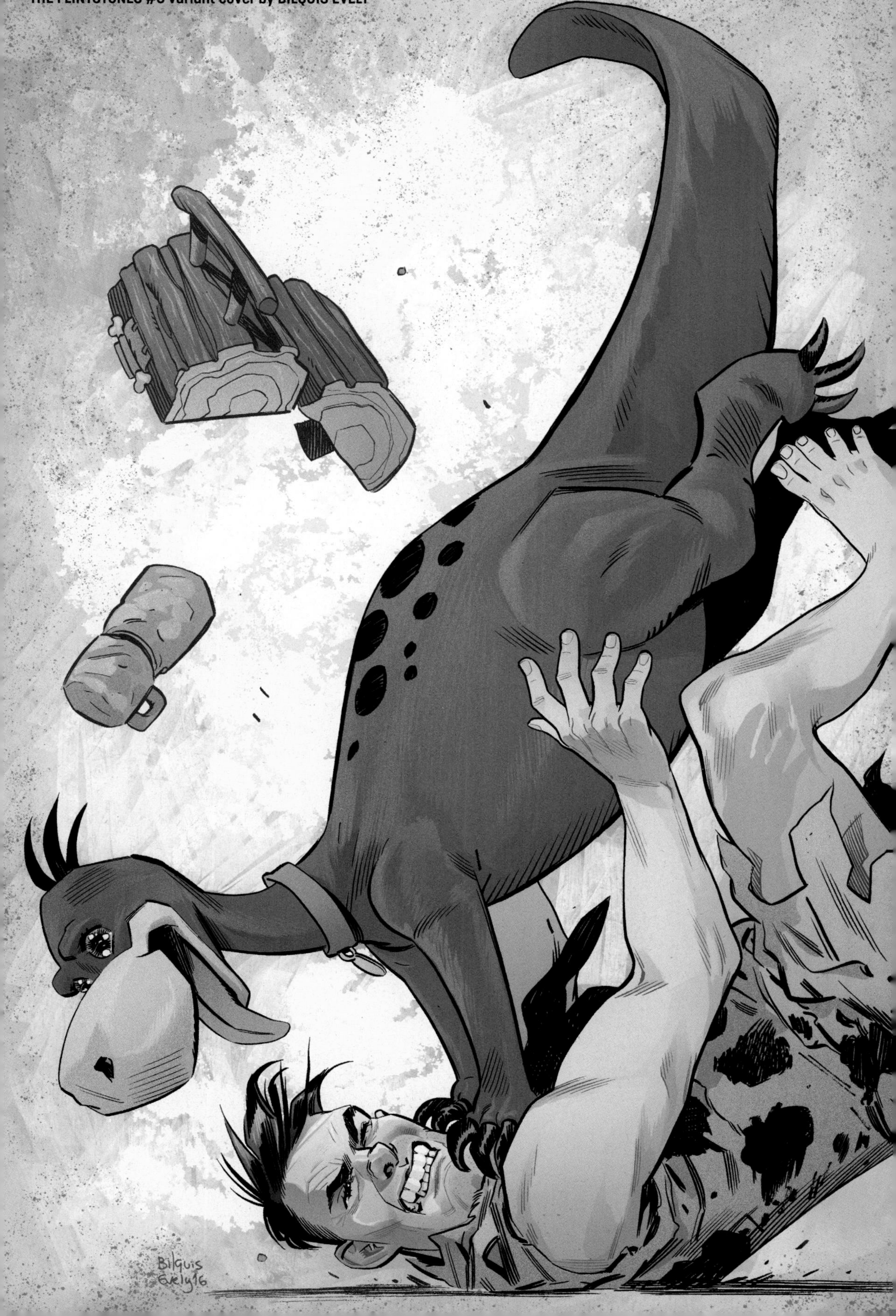
Bilquis
Evely16

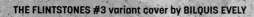

THE FLINTSTONES #4 variant cover by DAN PARENT

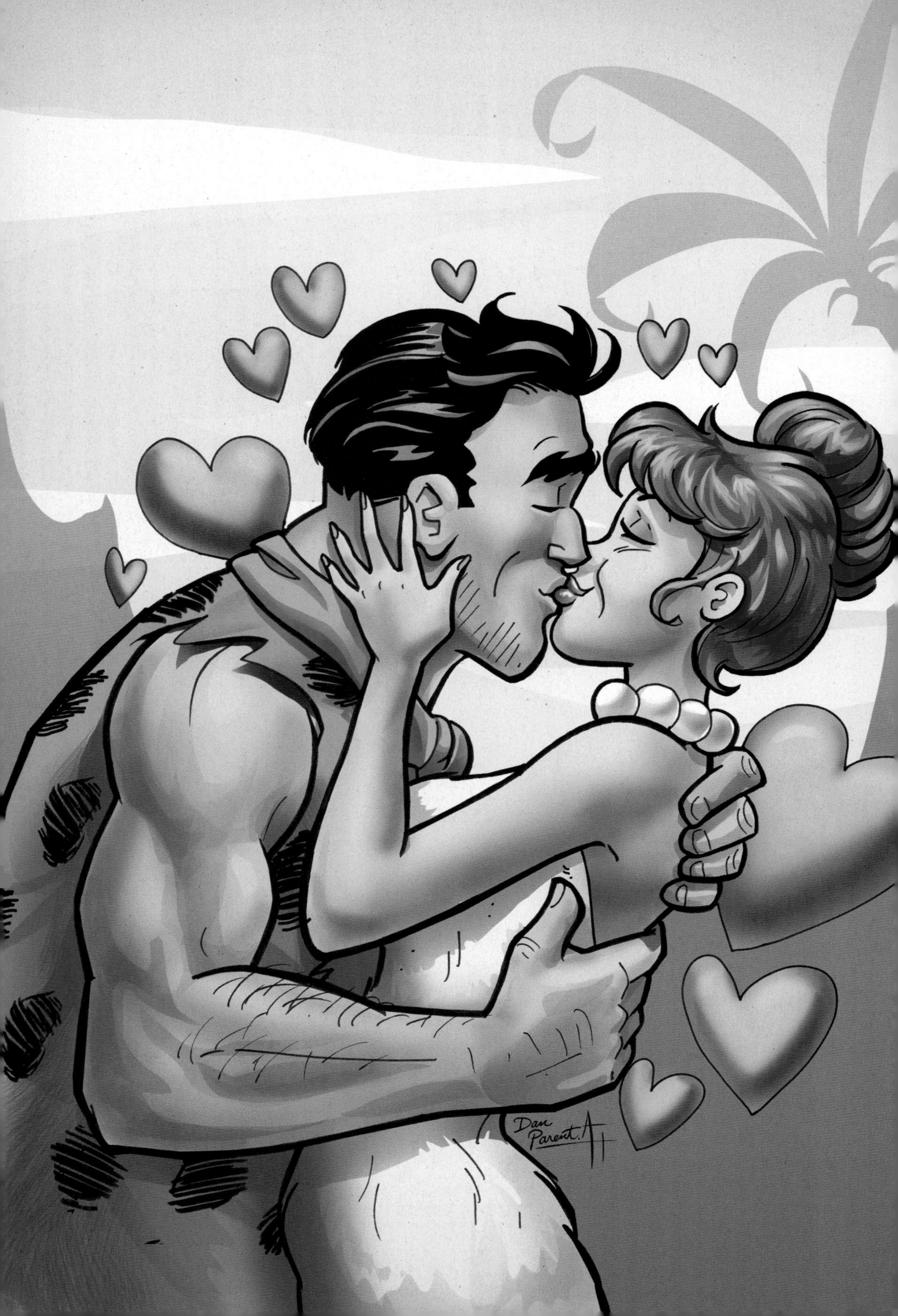

Dan Parent

THE FLINTSTONES #5 variant cover by BENGAL

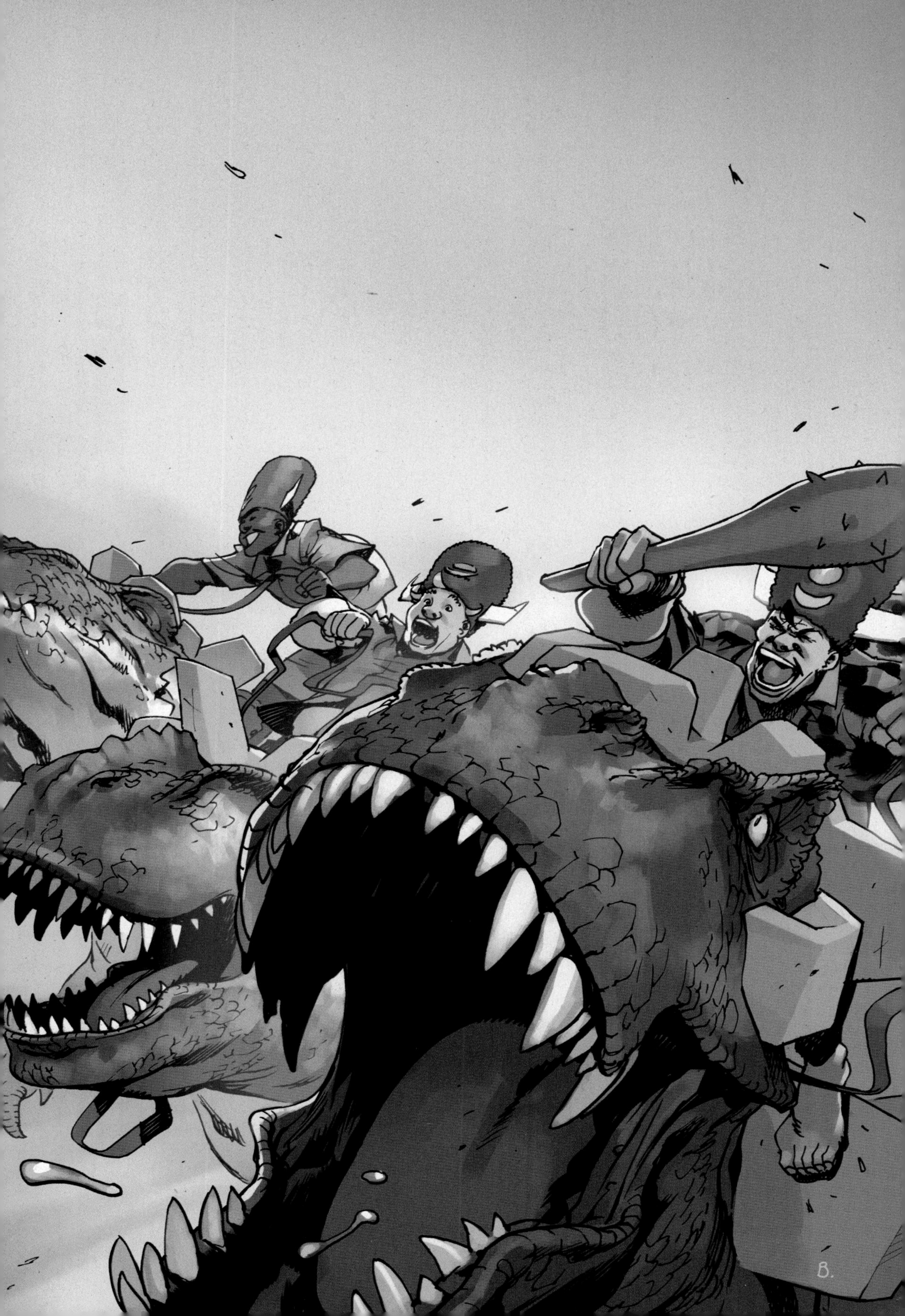
B.

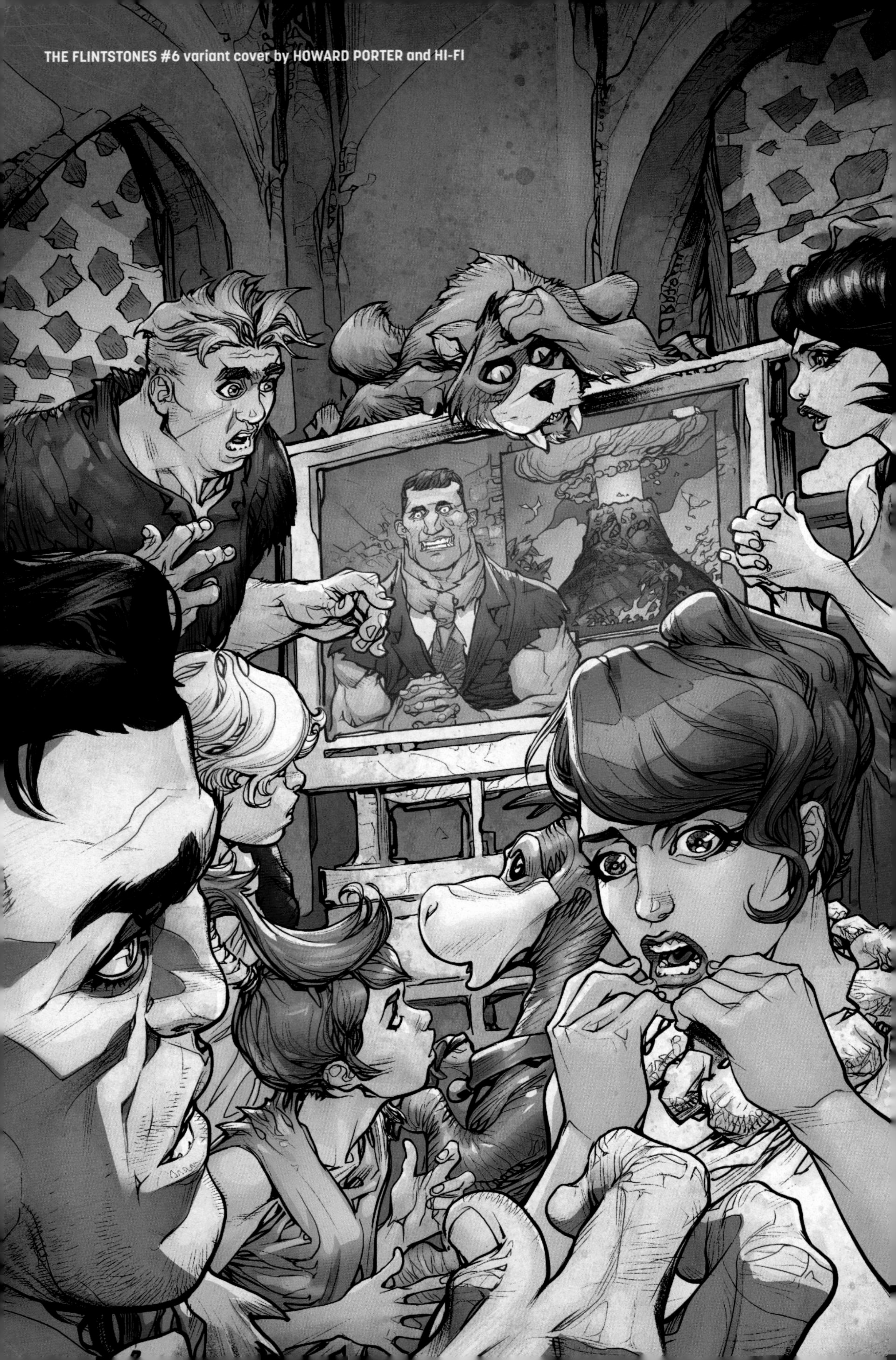

THE FLINTSTONES #6 variant cover by HOWARD PORTER and HI-FI

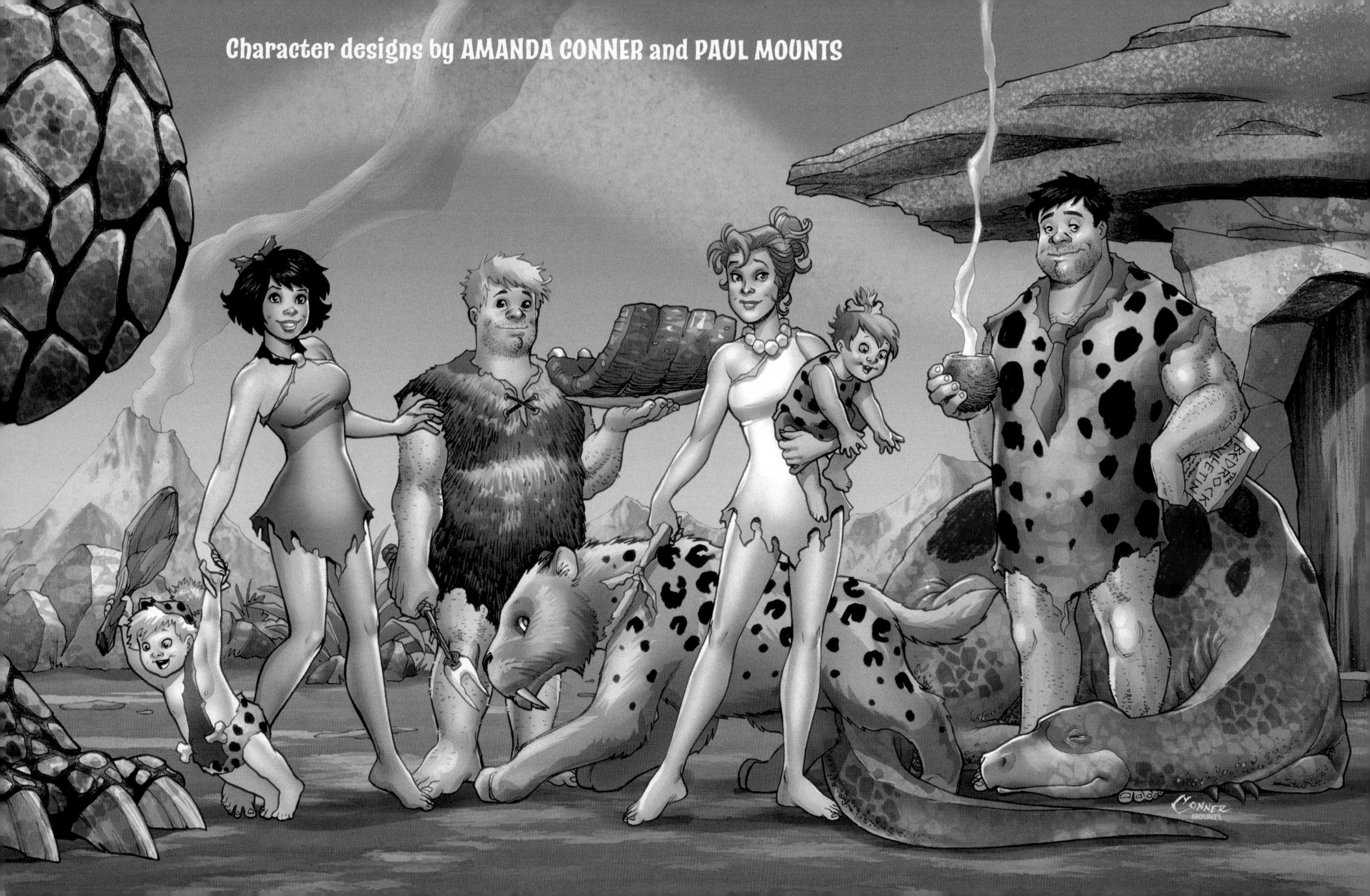
THE BEDROCK BULLETIN
CONNER
MOUNTS
Character designs by AMANDA CONNER and PAUL MOUNTS

Character designs by STEVE PUGH

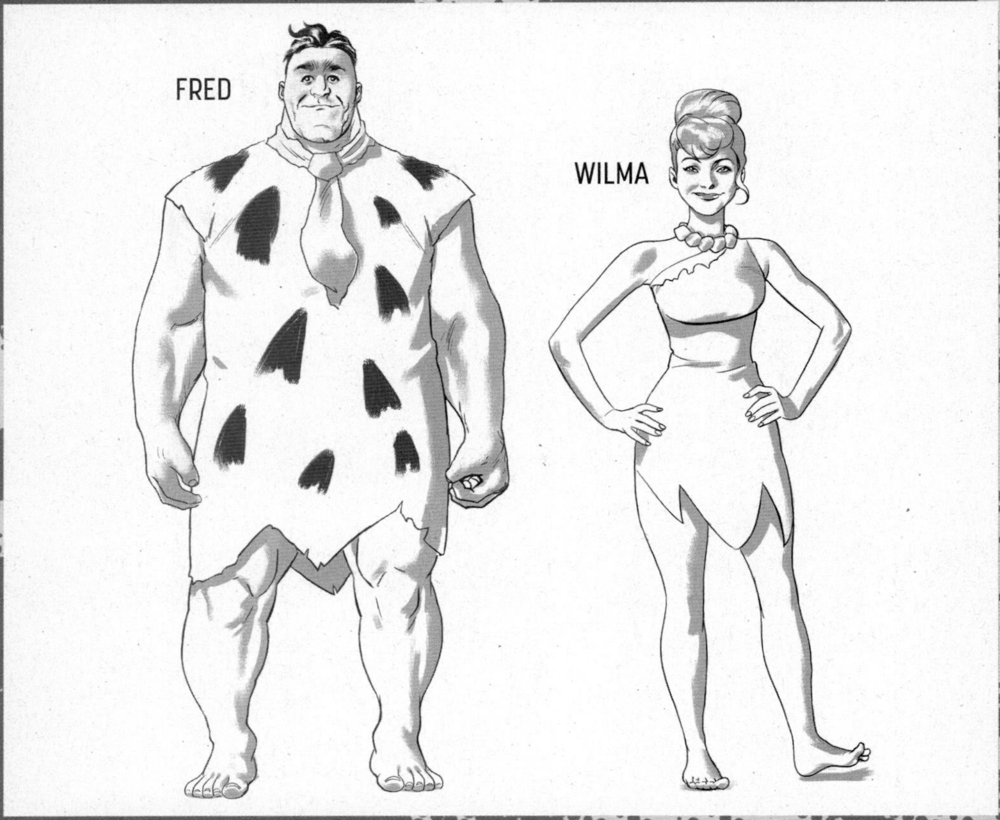
FRED
WILMA

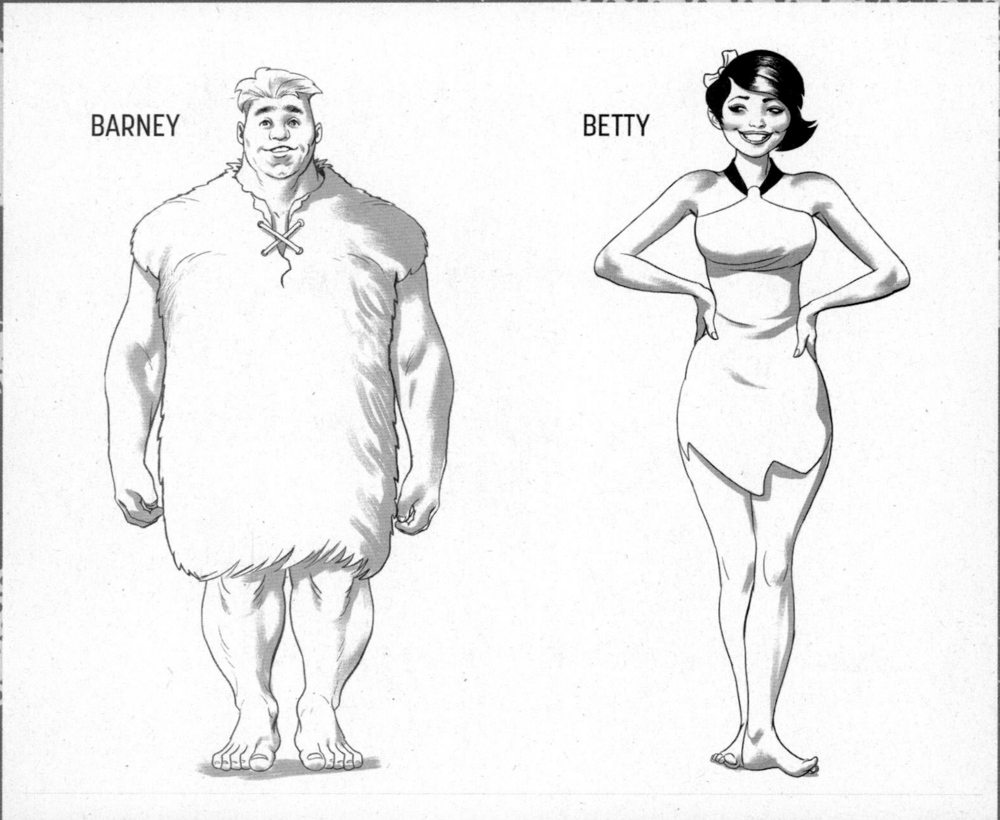
BARNEY
BETTY

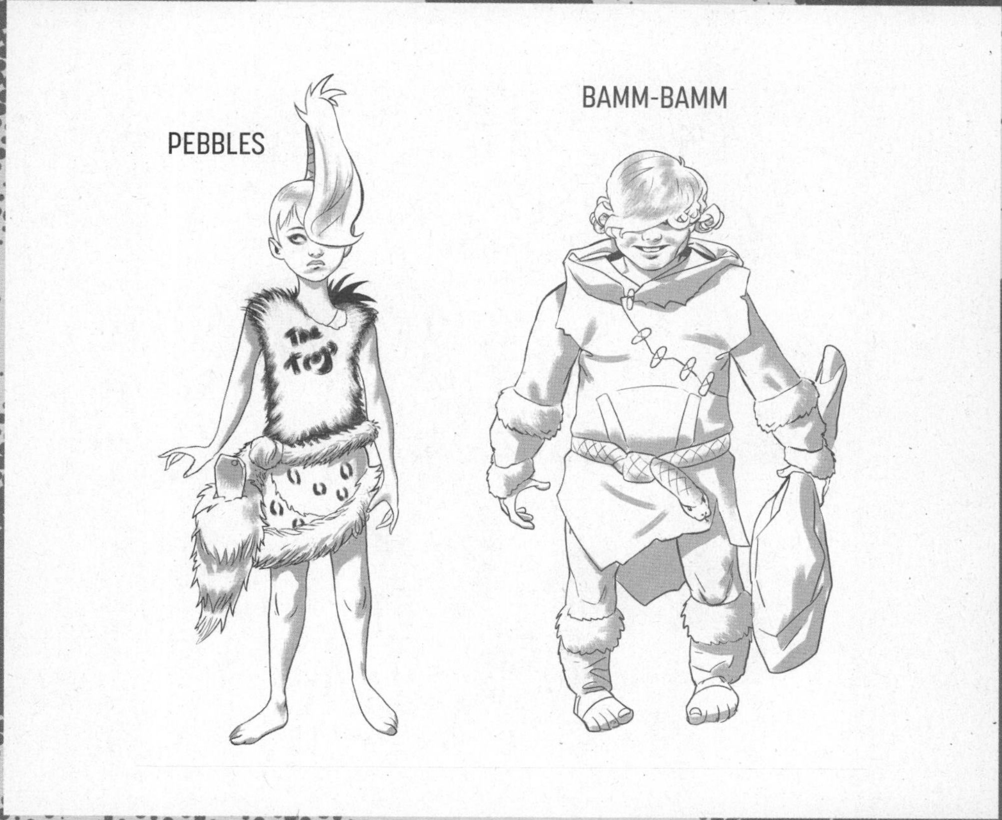
PEBBLES
BAMM-BAMM

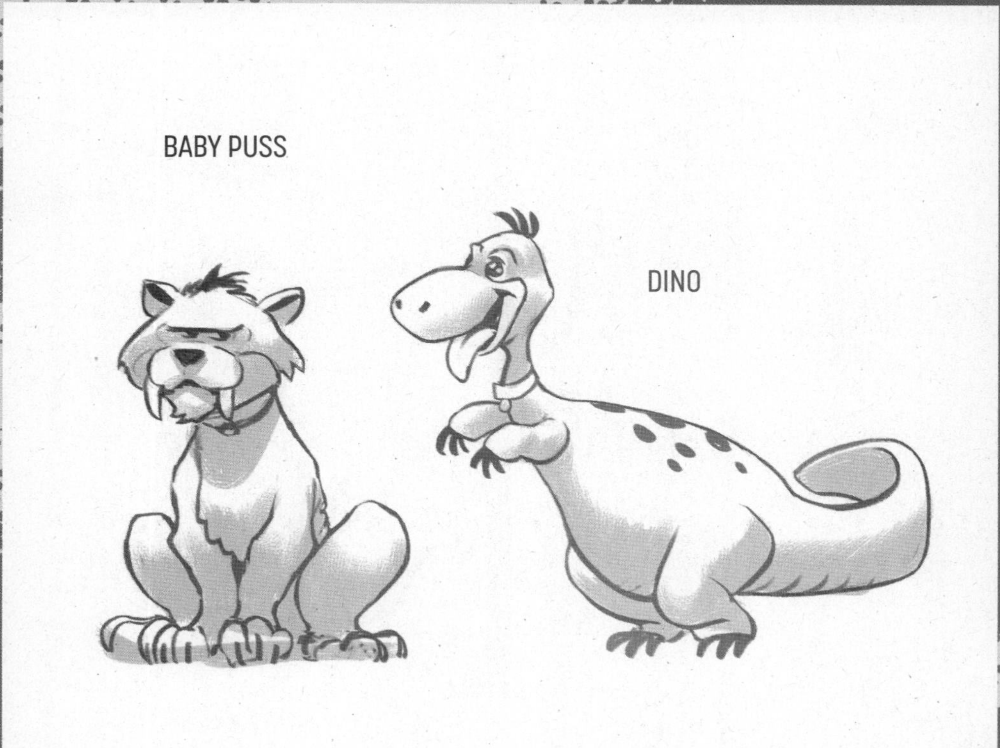
BABY PUSS
DINO

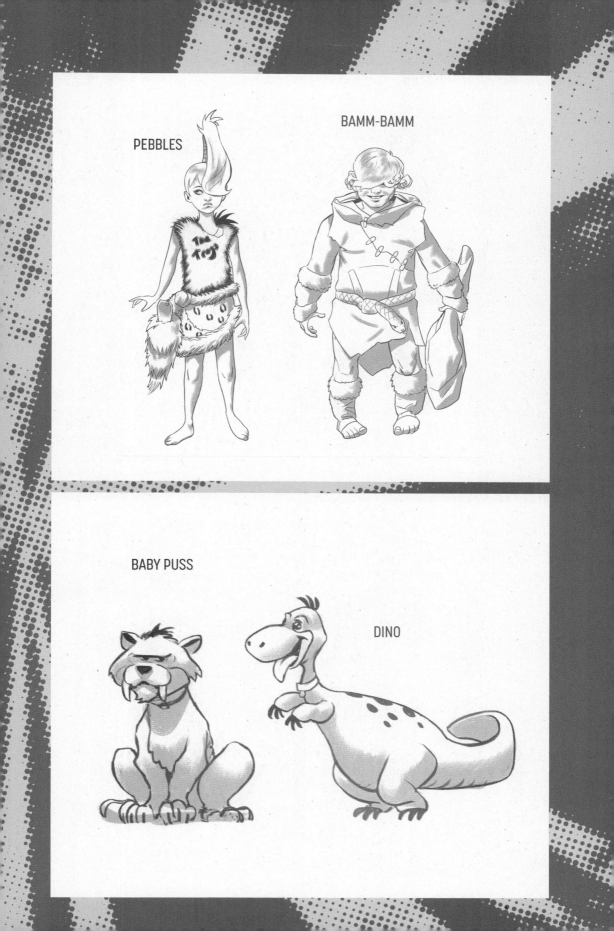

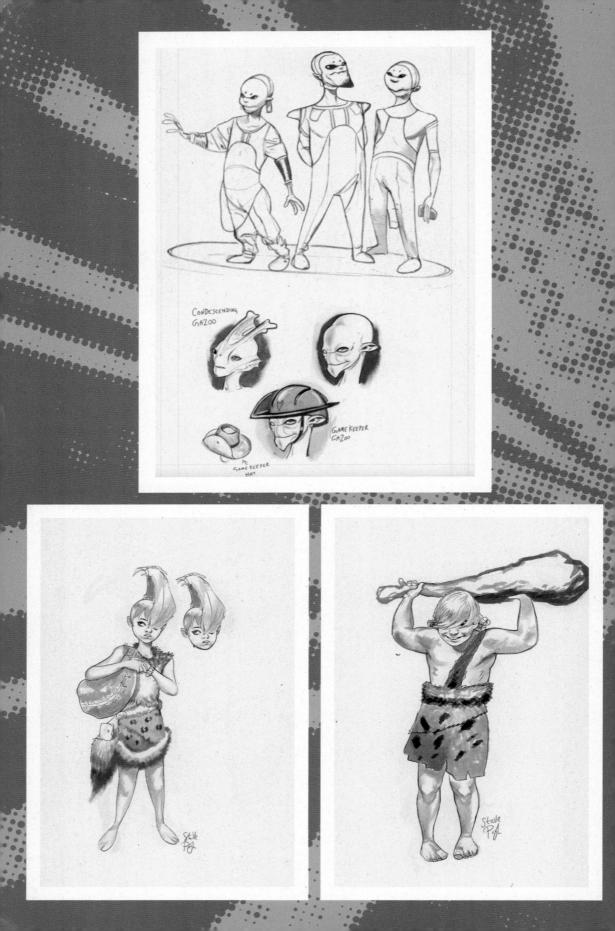

CONDESCENDING GAZOO

GAME KEEPER GAZOO

GAME KEEPER HAT